From Birth to Five

*A Study of the Health and Behaviour
of Britain's 5-year-olds*

From Birth to Five

A Study of the Health and Behaviour of Britain's 5-year-olds

Edited by

N. R. BUTLER and JEAN GOLDING

Data Editor
BRIAN HOWLETT

with the assistance of
SUE DOWLING
A. OSBORN
MARY HASLUM
A. C. MORRIS
T. J. PETERS
MARY PATERSON

PERGAMON PRESS

OXFORD · NEW YORK · TORONTO · SYDNEY · FRANKFURT

U.K.	Pergamon Press Ltd., Headington Hill Hall, Oxford OX3 0BW, England
U.S.A.	Pergamon Press Inc., Maxwell House, Fairview Park, Elmsford, New York 10523, U.S.A.
CANADA	Pergamon Press Canada Ltd., Suite 104, 150 Consumers Road, Willowdale, Ontario M2J 1P9, Canada
AUSTRALIA	Pergamon Press (Aust.) Pty. Ltd., P.O. Box 544, Potts Point, N.S.W. 2011, Australia
FEDERAL REPUBLIC OF GERMANY	Pergamon Press GmbH, Hammerweg 6, D-6242 Kronberg, Federal Republic of Germany
JAPAN	Pergamon Press Ltd., 8th Floor, Matsuoka Central Building, 1–7–1 Nishishinjuku, Shinjuku-ku, Tokyo 160, Japan
BRAZIL	Pergamon Editora Ltda., Rua Eça de Queiros, 346, CEP 04011, São Paulo, Brazil
PEOPLE'S REPUBLIC OF CHINA	Pergamon Press, Qianmen Hotel, Beijing, People's Republic of China

First edition 1986

Library of Congress Cataloging in Publication Data
From birth to five.
Includes bibliographical references.
1. Children—Diseases—Great Britain—Longitudinal studies.
2. Children—Mental health—Great Britain—Longitudinal studies.
3. Child health services—Great Britain—Utilization.
4. Preventive health services—Great Britain—Utilization.
5. Health surveys—Great Britain.
I. Butler, Neville R.   II. Golding, Jean.
RJ103.G7F76   1985   362.1'9892'000941   85–19212

British Library Cataloguing in Publication Data
From birth to five: a study of the health and behaviour of Britain's five-year-olds.
1. Child development—Great Britain
2. Children—Care and hygiene—Great Britain
I. Butler, N. R.   II. Golding, Jean   III. Howlett, Brian
155.4'22   BF721

ISBN 0-08-032692-7 (Hardcover)
ISBN 0-08-033372-9 (Flexicover)

Printed in Great Britain by A. Wheaton & Co. Ltd., Exeter

Acknowledgements

The work involved in mounting and carrying out a sweep of a cohort study such as this one involves a considerable number of people, not only in tracing and interviewing the parents, and examining the children, but also in coding the results, putting the coded data onto computer and analysing the final edited information. None of the present work would have been possible, were it not for the generous financial support received from the Medical Research Council, the Social Science Research Council, the National Birthday Trust Fund, Action for the Crippled Child, the Rowntree Trust and many other independent trusts.

We are particularly grateful to the Area Nurses (Child Health) of the Area Health Authorities of England and Wales, together with the Nursing Officers in the Scottish Health Boards. It was their administration and the cooperation of their Health Visitors who helped to trace the study children and carry out the survey. We are also extremely grateful for the collaboration of the Health Visitors Association who were co-sponsors of the study. In addition, the National Health Service Central Register and the Family Practitioner Committees of England and Wales together with the Administrators of Primary Care in Scotland and their colleagues in the Health Authorities/Boards assisted in locating the whereabouts of the children.

The huge amount of clerical work involved in the administration of the survey and the coding of questionnaire data called for enormous patience and fortitude. We were fortunate in finding these qualities in Sylvia Zair who supervised the coding process and our principal clerical workers Pam Lyons, James Parsons, Britta Pendry, Mary Probert and Sheila Taylor. The principal scientific officers who designed and organised the 5 year sweep were Professor N. R. Butler, Dr. Sue Dowling, Mr. B. Howlett and Mr. A. Osborn.

The actual preparation of the present volume would have been impossible without the willing and enthusiastic assistance of personnel currently working on the project including: Yasmin Iles, Penny Hicks, Tim Sladden, Mary Paterson, Michael Mack, Valerie Duffield, Michael Johns, Jean Lawrie, Andrew Bernard and Ian Collier.

To all, we offer our sincere thanks, but especially to the mothers and children of the cohort.

Contents

4   The first months   46

JEAN GOLDING & N. R. BUTLER

5   Soiling and wetting   64

JEAN GOLDING & G. TISSIER

6   Feeding and sleeping problems   80

JEAN GOLDING

7   Temper tantrums and other behaviour problems   98

JEAN GOLDING & D. RUSH

8   Disorder of speech and language   113

MARY PATERSON & JEAN GOLDING

13   Squints and vision defects   187

JEAN GOLDING & N. R. BUTLER

14   Bronchitis and pneumonia   201

JEAN GOLDING

15   Sore throats, ear discharge and mouth breathing   215

JEAN GOLDING & N. R. BUTLER

16   Hearing disorders   230

JEAN GOLDING & N. R. BUTLER

List of Tables

List of Figures

Child Health and Education Study

This was a national longitudinal study of children born during the week 5–11 April 1970 in England, Scotland and Wales.

The children in this survey were originally subjects of the British Births survey carried out in 1970 under the auspices of the National Birthday Trust Fund and the Royal College of Obstetricians and Gynaecologists.

The 1975 follow-up survey was carried out by the Department of Child Health, University of Bristol, under the directorship of Professor Neville Butler and with the collaboration of the Health Visitors Association.

The Director

Professor Neville Butler, MD, FRCP, FRCOG, DCH was Professor of Child Health at the University of Bristol, consultant to the World Health Organisation and to the Pan-American Health Organisation. His work with British child development studies began in 1958 when he was Director of the Perinatal Mortality Survey.

Principal Research Officers in 1975

Medical — Dr. Sue Dowling, MB, BS, MSc (Soc Med), MFCM
Social — Albert Osborn, BA, PhD
Computing — Brian Howlett, BSc, BA, FSS, MBCS

Research Associate

Statistics — Anthony Morris, BA, MSc

Dr. Sue Dowling is currently lecturer in Epidemiology and Community Medicine at the University of Bristol.

CHAPTER 1

Introduction

by JEAN GOLDING and N. R. BUTLER

Life progresses forward in time, but, as Kierkegaard said, we only understand in retrospect. Thus in individual persons we wait for an abnormal facet of health or behaviour to occur and then search back through time for factors on which we may pin responsibility. In any one life, there are a multitude of interwoven events and influences, but those that we choose to consider as causative are likely to conform to the received wisdom of our generation. Thus, we are now likely to associate our neurotic behaviour with an authoritarian upbringing, our child's asthma with our own stress. Search for explanations in individual cases is natural. Determination of an acceptable cause is consoling, but rarely capable of rigorous proof. Nevertheless, it is important that we have a firm foundation on which to link events together. Belief is not enough. After all, whole populations in the Middle Ages were convinced that women who gave birth to severely malformed infants were guilty of witchcraft. Can we be certain that the associations that we tend to accept now are any more valid?

Studies of single individuals can rarely help answer this question, but a long-term study of a larger population can aid considerably. Nevertheless, it must always be remembered that an epidemiological study can only rarely provide positive proof of the 'cause' of an event—rather it will suggest guilt by association. Such studies can, however, point the way to fruitful areas for more detailed investigation—and occasionally they may provide clues for primary prevention of a disorder even though the understanding of the mechanism of the genesis of that disorder may be years away (the association between smoking and cancer of the lung is an obvious example).

Historical Background

Since 1946 there has been a unique tradition of national longitudinal cohort studies in Britain. The first study was mounted in the immediate postwar period because it was felt that little sound knowledge was available concerning the social and economic aspects of pregnancy and childbirth. The then College of Obstetricians and Gynaecologists and the Population Investigation Committee initiated a survey designed to assess: (a) the availability of the maternity services to different social classes and in different parts of Great Britain; (b) the use made of these services; (c) their effectiveness in educating mothers and in reducing mortality and morbidity among mothers and infants; (d) the need for domestic help during pregnancy and after delivery; (e) the nature and extent of parental expenditure on childbirth.

To obtain data on sufficient numbers for valid analysis, a survey was carried out of all births in England, Scotland and Wales in 1 week. For administrative rather than scientific reasons the week chosen was that of 3–9 March 1946. The mothers were interviewed by their health visitor some 8 weeks after delivery. The conclusions and recommendations of this study were far-reaching in their implications and, interestingly, are still largely pertinent today (*Maternity in Great Britain 1948*). They emphasise the need for the maternity services to cater for the physical and psychological well-being of the mother, as well as for the medical requirements of both mother and infant. The last of thirty-four recommendations suggested that childbirth should not be regarded solely as an event relevant to mother and baby for only a short period of time, but rather as an occasion with potential effects which might not become apparent until much later in the child's or mother's life. It was for this reason that it was decided to follow up the cohort first at the age of 2 years and subsequently a sample has been contacted at frequent periods ever since (*The National Survey of Health and Development*). The results of the study of this cohort have been of importance in the educational, sociological and psychological fields (Douglas and Blomfield, 1958; Douglas, 1964; Douglas *et al.*, 1968). Among other findings, it has been responsible for showing an association between prolonged or repeated hospital admission in early childhood and later behavioural and learning problems (Douglas, 1975), that disruptions of early family life were strongly associated with delinquent behaviour in adolescence (Wadsworth, 1979), that children who had pneumonia or bronchitis in the first 2 years of life were more likely to have a chronic cough at the age of 25 (Kiernan *et al.*, 1976) and that serum cholesterol of 32-year-old males was lower in those that had been breast fed (Marmot *et al.*, 1980).

The first survey has now started to collect information on the offspring of the children in the original sample, and the study of intergenerational differences is uniquely fascinating. For example, Kiernan (1980) has shown that the girls in this cohort who became pregnant in their teens had parents who had themselves married early, and who had relatively low levels of education.

The second cohort, like the first, devolved from a study of the perinatal period (*The Perinatal Mortality Survey*). The initial 1958 birth survey had somewhat different ends in view from those of Douglas in 1946. Undertaken by the National Birthday Trust Fund, it was initiated in 1958 because, in the postwar period the perinatal mortality rate had remained fairly static (3.85% in 1948, 3.51% in 1958), although the maternal and childhood mortality rates had fallen dramatically. For this reason, the survey was designed specifically to examine the individual causes of perinatal deaths.

It was designed in two overlapping parts: the first was concerned with all deliveries in the United Kingdom in the week of 3–9 March 1958. For each birth a questionnaire was filled in by the midwife shortly after delivery. Information was obtained on social background, history of pregnancy, delivery and the neonatal period partly from obstetric notes and partly by interviewing the mother. The second part of the survey was concerned with all stillbirths and neonatal deaths in the 3 month period of March, April and May 1958. For the majority of these, detailed post-mortems were carried out. The questionnaire on the maternal background, pregnancy and delivery was also completed for all these deaths. Details of 7117 still births and neonatal deaths were compared with 17,204 total births occurring in the 1 week (Butler and Bonham, 1963; Butler and Alberman, 1969).

The results of this survey were used widely by obstetricians, paediatricians, midwives, general practitioners and others. The survey showed that it was possible to predict which women were at highest risk of having a stillbirth or neonatal death. A comparison of the ways in which the obstetric services varied throughout the country resulted in the rethinking of many obstetric procedures, the reorganisation of obstetric practice and the stimulation of further research (Peel, 1969). Whether or not this survey was directly responsible, the perinatal mortality rate fell dramatically from 1958 onwards.

Again, it was something of an afterthought that this survey of obstetric practice was expanded into a follow-up to embrace child development (*The National Child Development Study*). Those children born in that 1 week in March who had survived were traced when they were 7 years old: medical and social histories were taken; medical examinations were performed; and the children underwent a number of educational tests. They have been contacted also at the ages of 11, 16 and 21, and much valuable information has accrued. An important fact to emerge is that children from disadvantaged backgrounds differ not only in reduced physical stature and increased prevalence of medical problems, but also in difficult behaviour and poor educational attainment (Davie, Butler and Goldstein, 1972). On a more optimistic note, there was little to suggest that traumatic events of pregnancy and delivery had any long-term effects provided the child survived the perinatal period.

Several studies from this data-base have found associations between smoking during pregnancy and reduction in birthweight, increased perinatal mortality rate, and some reduction in the child's subsequent height and educational attainment (Butler *et al.*, 1972; Butler and Goldstein, 1973; Fogelman, 1980). A further hypothesis was generated from the finding that children of women who had reported having 'flu in pregnancy were at increased risk of developing cancer (Fedrick and Alberman, 1972). This has prompted a large number of prospective studies in various parts of the world on the possible effects of infection in pregnancy. Other interesting points have been found in the comparison of the two cohorts: for example, the children born in 1958 were far less likely to undergo tonsillectomy or circumcision than those born in 1946 (Calnan *et al.*, 1978), though the later cohort was much more likely to develop diabetes (Calnan and Peckham, 1977).

The 1970 Cohort

The third national cohort study and the survey on which the present report is based again began primarily as a study of the perinatal period. It was carried out by the National Birthday Trust Fund in association with the Royal College of Obstetricians and Gynaecologists and is known as the *British Births Survey*. Its aims were to look at the obstetric services and the social and biological characteristics of the mother in regard to neonatal morbidity, and to compare the results with those of the 1958 study. As in the two previous surveys, a week of deliveries was studied, that chosen being the period 5–11 April 1970. A questionnaire was filled in by the midwife, after interviewing the mother and having access to the clinical notes. This survey provides a valuable glimpse into the patterns of obstetric and neonatal care in the United Kingdom in 1970 (R. Chamberlain *et al.*, 1975; G. Chamberlain *et al.*, 1978).

The first follow-up of survivors from this survey occurred at the age of 22 months and comprised (a) the twins, (b) the small-for-dates and postmature and (c) a 10% random sample of all legitimate births. A medical and developmental history was completed by the health visitor, and the child was not only examined medically and measured, but also completed some simple developmental tests. The same subsamples were seen at 3 years and subjected to medical examination and developmental tests appropriate for their chronological age. The data thus obtained have shown the prevalence of illness in early infancy (Chamberlain and Simpson, 1979), the development of children aged 22 months (Chamberlain and Davey, 1976) and the differential growth of the subsamples (Chamberlain and Davey, 1975).

The disadvantage in using relatively small samples is that in any analysis of a particular type of illness or behaviour problem the numbers are often too small for valid conclusions to be reached. For this reason it was decided early in 1973 to attempt to contact the whole population of children born in this 1 week of 1970 at around their 5th birthday. The Medical Research Council provided the funding for the central organisation and administration of the study, but all the field-work relied on the voluntary co-operation and enthusiasm of the local health visitors.

Tracing the children

The population we wished to study was defined solely by date of birth. In this way we hoped to identify the estimated 2% of children whose births had not been recorded in the original birth survey, as well as those children who had been born outside Great Britain but were resident in Britain by the age of 5 years. The original birth survey had included births in Northern Ireland, but by 1975 it was felt to be too sensitive an area to be included. Therefore, only those eleven children born in Northern Ireland, but subsequently resident in England, Scotland and Wales, were included in the 5-year cohort.

In order to trace the whereabouts of the population, the Office of Population Censuses and Surveys (OPCS) generated a computer-listing of all children registered as having their date of birth in the sample week. This list was sent to the National Health Service Central Register (NHSCR) at Southport, who were able to identify either the Area Health Authority in which the child was registered with a general practitioner, or whether the child had gone abroad or died. From the details given, a list of children believed to be living in each Area Health Authority was sent to the appropriate Family Practitioner Committee who was able to identify the child's current address. This information was passed by the Family Practitioner Committee to the Area Health Visiting Service, which then contacted the parents of the child and invited them to participate in the study.

A similar procedure was adopted in Scotland, although the Scottish records were unable to yield information on those children born in the survey week who had not been included in the original birth survey. Children of servicemen who were registered with a Service Medical Officer were traced with the help of the Service Children's Education Authority.

A further method of ascertaining the study population was also attempted as a fail-safe mechanism, by asking all health visitors throughout Britain to go through their files to identify children born in the study week but not yet traced.

Administering the questionnaires

Once the child had been traced, and the parents agreed to participate, a health visitor arranged to call. She interviewed one or both of the parents (usually the mother alone) by means of a structured questionnaire (the Home Interview Questionnaire, reproduced on pages 379–398). This included detailed information on the child's medical history as well as the social and family background.

A second questionnaire (the Maternal Self-Completion Questionnaire, reproduced on pages 399–406) had been designed for the mother to fill in on her own, so that any biases introduced by the interviewer could be minimised. The information was concerned largely with the mother's perception of her child's behaviour, as well as of her own well-being. On the same occasion, measures of the child's general development were obtained using a specially designed Test Booklet, and the health visitor measured the child's height and head circumference.

Lastly, a questionnaire entitled the Developmental History Schedule was completed on the study child by the health visitor herself with the help of her own child health clinic records. Information was sought on all attendances at child health clinics and visits by the health visitors in the first 5 years, on perinatal and subsequent risk factors and inclusions on registers, as well as results of all screening and assessment procedures.

Case ascertainment

In all, 13,961 children were traced: i.e. an estimated 85.8% of the population at risk (Table 1.1). Of these, 631 parents refused permission for their child to take part and 195 were not included either because, in spite of repeated efforts, the health visitor was unable to arrange an interview, or because the information obtained was incomplete. A total

TABLE 1.1   Results of attempt to trace and interview the population of children born 5–11 April at age 5

All children born in England, Scotland and Wales and included in British Births Survey (BBS)	16,567	
No. of those stillborn or known to have died before follow up was possible	563	
No. thus assumed alive at 5	16,004	
No. of the above surveyed at 5		12,732 (79.6%)
Surveyed at 5 in BBS, but born in Northern Ireland		11
Surveyed at 5, but not in BBS		392
Total surveyed at 5		13,135

of 13,135 sets of completed forms (i.e. Home Interview Questionnaire, Maternal Self-Completion and Test Booklet) were received. The total yield of Developmental History Schedules was less, since often the clinic and health visitor notes were absent or incomplete. Nevertheless, by the end of the 5-year study, over 10,000 completed schedules had been received.

In order to establish the extent to which the sample of 5-year-olds was biased, we have compared the proportion of children surveyed at 5 years of age according to various items of information collected at their birth (Table 1.2). The children for whom questionnaires were *not* filled in at 5 years were slightly more likely to be of low gestation and/or birthweight, and to have mothers who smoked heavily. The major difference, however, was in the marital status of the mothers: only 59% of those children with unmarried mothers at the time of birth were included in the survey at 5 years of age, compared with 81% of those whose mothers were married.

A further exercise, undertaken when the children were 7, attempted to trace those children not included in the 5-year cohort. By this time, of course, all the children were at school and the tracing of the birth cohort was a relatively easy exercise, facilitated by the education record system. For the 1917 new children contacted, a simple questionnaire on parental circumstances and certain aspects of medical history was filled in. Comparison of the events of the first 5 years of these children's lives (Osborn *et al.*, 1984) revealed that those who had not been traced at 5 years were far more likely to be living apart from their natural father, to have either Asian parents or parents of mixed race, to have moved house at least twice and to have been 'in care'.

In spite of these differences, and notwithstanding their statistical significance, the bias caused by omission of these children is unlikely to have a profound effect on the overall results we are presenting here. Where potential bias may exist, it will be fully discussed.

The Present Report

In this volume we shall describe the health and behaviour of the study children in the first 5 years of their lives. The first chapters present a description of the social and environmental background of the families, and subsequent chapters analyse those factors which may influence the prevalence of the various behaviour traits, signs or symptoms in the child. In later sections we shall indicate the environmental and social characteristics of families who appear not to use the health services to their full advantage.

In order to define clearly the remit of our study, we have examined the epidemiological associations between various health outcomes in the

TABLE 1.2   Proportion of the surviving children born in Great Britain and appearing in the British Birth Survey who were surveyed at 5 (singletons only)

Factor at birth	Proportion surveyed	
		%
Social class:		
I and II	2012/2502	(80.4)
III M and III NM	7150/8673	(82.4)
IV and V	2547/3216	(79.2)
Mother's age:		
< 20	1105/1536	(71.9)
20–34	10,266/12,703	(80.8)
35+	982/1258	(78.1)
Parity:		
0	4648/5886	(79.0)
1	4169/5100	(81.7)
2–3	2891/3655	(79.1)
4+	757/1026	(73.8)
Maternal smoking:		
non-smoker	5214/6562	(79.5)
stopped pre-pregnancy	1571/1894	(82.9)
stopped during pregnancy	596/747	(79.8)
< 15 per day	3487/4368	(79.8)
15+ per day	1574/2061	(76.4)
Marital status:		
married	11,788/14,528	(81.1)
single	493/869	(56.7)
separated, widowed, divorced	181/271	(66.8)
Sex of child:		
male	6457/8091	(79.8)
female	6019/7593	(79.3)
Time to regular respirations:		
< 3 min	11,905/14,944	(79.7)
3 min+	498/647	(77.0)
Birthweight:		
< 5 lb 8 oz	580/767	(75.6)
5 lb 8 oz+	11,885/14,902	(79.8)
Gestation:		
< 37	404/529	(76.4)
37+	9678/11,949	(81.0)
unbelievable/unknown	2394/3207	(74.6)

child and fourteen variables: sex of the child; birthweight; duration of breast feeding; maternal age; social class; parental situation when the child was 5; ethnic group of parents; maternal and paternal smoking habits; maternal employment history during the child's life; number of other children in the household; number of times the child moved house; the type of neighbourhood and region in which the child lived.

Obviously, there is a massive body of statistical data which, for reasons of space and price, must be excluded from this volume. All the many hundreds of tables used in compiling this report have therefore been deposited with the British Lending Library, Boston Spa, Wetherby, West Yorks LS23 7BQ, UK. To obtain a copy, write to the British Lending Library requesting Supplementary Publication No. 90, 119 (958 pages). Identification of particular tables may be made using the index to this volume. In general, all significant results will be referred to fully in the text and illustrated with the aid of simple diagrams.

With such a large amount of information trivial differences are often statistically significant at the 5% level. We have, therefore, only considered associations to be statistically significant if the probability that they might have arisen by chance was less than 0.01 (i.e. 1%). Nevertheless, it is important to recognise that on average one in a hundred of our results will be significant by chance—i.e. they will indicate an association that is not really present. How can one detect such misleading findings? In examining the validity of any association, evidence that it is not spurious can only be obtained if confirmatory evidence is available from reports in the literature. In all other cases care must be taken to verify the results in other studies before associations are accepted as real.

There are other ways in which associations may be misleading initally, but from which statistical analysis can assist in interpretation. Consider, for example, a disease X. Suppose that the prevalence of this disease varies with social class, such that children in the upper social classes are at only half the risk of the disorder compared with those in the lower social classes (Fig. 1.1a).

Imagine then that prevalence by maternal age was also statistically significant: the younger the mother, the more likely the child to have had the disorder (Fig. 1.1b)

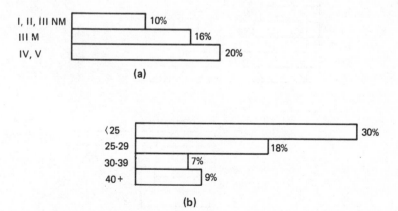

FIG. 1.1 Hypothetical prevalence of disease X by (a) social class, (b) maternal age

Within Britain, mothers from the lower social classes are, in general, younger than those from upper social classes. The findings illustrated in Figs. 1.1a,b could be the result of three possible eventualities: (a) the disease X is strongly associated with a lower social class and because the lower social classes are younger, the pattern in Fig. 1.1b was bound to result; (b) the disease X is strongly associated with youthful mothers, and since very young mothers are mostly from the lower social classes, the pattern of Fig. 1.1a was bound to result; (c) disease X is strongly and independently associated with both youthful maternal age and low social class.

In order to distinguish between these three possibilities, various statistical methods are possible. We have actually used indirect standardisation, a method which is described more fully in the Appendix (pages 356–7). The results of such standardisation are given in terms of observed and expected numbers, and published in the microfiched Appendix tables. Associations that are still statistically significant are given as Relative Risks. These are easy to interpret: a Relative Risk of 1.0 means that the chance of the outcome in that particular group is equal to the risk of the whole study population; a risk of 2.0 is twice that of the whole population; but 0.6 is only 60% of the population risk.

Relative Risks computed in this way can be extremely useful in estimating the prevalence of a disorder in a closely defined sub-population. Suppose, for example, that standardisation on the data depicted in Figs. 1.1a and 1.1b revealed that both social class and maternal age were independently associated with disease X in the way depicted in Fig. 1.2. This shows that children of social class I have only

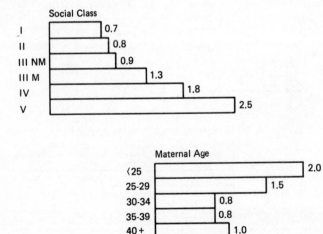

Fig. 1.2 Hypothetical independent Relative Risks of disease X

70% of the risk of the population as a whole, whereas social class V has two-and-a-half times the risk. Suppose the health profession wished to ascertain the risk to a population of mothers aged under 25 of social class IV. The estimate takes the relative risk to the child in social class IV (i.e. 1.8), and that to the child of the young mother (2.0) and multiplies the risks together. The risk to children in this sub-population will be approximately 3.6 times the population average.

Obviously, with so much information, and the complex inter-relationships between the child's health and behaviour, his parents and his geographical environment, we have been able to do little more than skim the surface. The data presented form a fascinating glimpse into the factors which do and do not appear to influence the child's health and behaviour. We hope that some of our results may prompt in depth studies to help unravel or confirm our findings. Child health is not static, and the most exciting projects await our research team as we watch the children in the cohort grow and develop. As they navigate problems, some will flounder, and others will toss off the difficulties.

CHAPTER 2

The children and their families

by JEAN GOLDING and JANE HENRIQUES

Introduction

'Parentage is a very important profession: but no test of fitness for it is ever imposed in the interest of children' (Shaw, 1944). This telling quotation begs the question of *what* test should be undertaken apart from the one that is currently operational—the ability to conceive.

This chapter will present details of some of the basic characteristics of the parents of children in the survey population. Subsequent chapters will show the ways in which certain of these characteristics are associated with adverse health or behaviour of the child.

Osborn *et al.* (1984) have compared the homes and families of our pre-school study children with those of the 1946 national birth cohort studied a quarter of a century earlier by Douglas and Blomfield (1958). The children of the 1970 cohort were less likely to have grown up with a large number of siblings; substantial improvements had occurred in their housing circumstances and in the educational qualifications of their parents, but the children were far more likely to be living with a single parent.

In this chapter we will be describing the children and their families as they were in 1975. In Chapter 3 we shall be looking in more detail at their physical environment, and the ways in which this varied with the different characteristics of the families, and in Chapter 4 we will describe the characteristics of the baby and his early feeding history.

Children in one-parent families are a cause for concern since their health can be affected, often indirectly, by the circumstances that are unfortunately common to the majority of such families. One of the primary factors is poverty, which, of course, gives rise to a complex of problems. Others, often contingent on the first, are poor and unsuitable housing, and feelings of depression and isolation.

At least one in seven families in Great Britain is now thought to be headed by a lone parent (Segal, 1983). In general, the average disposable income of a one-parent family is just over half that of a two-parent family (National Council for One Parent Families, 1982). Children in one-parent families currently represent 65% of all children in families dependent on supplementary benefit (Popay, Rimmer and Rossiter, 1983).

Poverty compounds the stresses that are likely to affect one-parent families. It places them in the worst position for housing (a large proportion are at one time homeless), results in poor diets, insufficiently heated homes, inadequate clothing, and restricted social life (Burghes, 1980) and the lack of amenities such as a phone, which could relieve the isolation from which many suffer. Travel to visit friends or relatives is restricted by low income—a severe disadvantage for one-parent families housed, as is often the case, at a distance from their families—and a factor that also restricts their ability to visit clinics and dentists. Anxiety and depression, exacerbated by poverty, can lead to the 'downward spiral' that may destroy a one-parent family.

Mother and Father Figures

When the study child was 5, the health visitor obtained a number of facts concerning the person(s) resident in the household and currently acting as mother and father to the child.

At the time of the interview, 1.9% of the children were no longer living with their *natural* mother and one-fifth of these had no mother figure at all (Table 2.1). A much higher proportion of the children (9.2%) were living apart from their natural father and in more than half of these families (655) there was no father figure in the household.

For many of the 13,135 children, the parental situation had changed quite markedly since their birth. Of the 692 5-year-olds who had been born to unmarried mothers, over a third (263) were living with both the natural mother and the natural father. Other children had started life

TABLE 2.1 Relationship of the mother and father figure to the child

Relationship of Parent figure	Mothers of Children		Fathers of Children	
Natural (biological)	12,880	(98.1%)	11,937	(90.8%)
Parent by legal adoption	97	(0.7%)	155	(1.2%)
Step-parent	13	(0.1%)	191	(1.5%)
Foster parent	26	(0.2%)	23	(0.2%)
Grandparent	45	(0.3%)	85	(0.6%)
Cohabitee of parent	14	(0.1%)	79	(0.6%)
Other relationship	8	(0.1%)	10	(0.1%)
No such figure	52	(0.4%)	655	(5.0%)
All	13,135	(100.0%)	13,135	(100.0%)

with both parents and had, presumably, been through a phase of life with a single parent before becoming part of a two-parent family again. The effect of these changes on the child is currently being studied in more depth.

For the purpose of the present description of the cohort we will be concentrating on the family status when the child was 5 years old. The analyses will distinguish between five different parental situations, depending on the persons who were then residing in the same household as the child. This classification does not distinguish between married and unmarried partnerships.

Both natural parents: when both natural parents are living with the child.

One natural + one substitute parent: where the non-natural parent may be an adoptive parent, a step-parent or the cohabitee of the natural parent.

Single supported parent: One natural parent with at least one other adult living in the same household, who may or may not be cited as a parent figure (e.g. grandparent, elder sibling, lodger, etc.).

Unsupported single parent: One natural parent but no other adult resident in the household.

Neither parent natural: This includes all situations where the child was living in a family situation but where neither parent figure was the child's natural parent. This will include both adoptive and fostering parents.

The numbers of 5-year-old children in each parental situation are shown in Table 2.2.

The Age of the Mother

Study of the 1946 birth cohort, as they reached child-bearing age,

TABLE 2.2   Number of study children in each type of parental situation at age 5

Parental situation	Number of children	
Two natural parents	11,851	(90.2%)
One natural parent + substitute parent	357	(2.7%)
One natural parent + other adult	250	(1.9%)
Single natural parent, no other adult	505	(3.9%)
Neither parent natural		
(a) Adopted	96	(0.7%)
(b) Other (fostered, living with grandparents, etc.)	62	(0.5%)
No parent figure (i.e. in residential care)	14	(0.1%)
All	13,135	(100.0%)

showed that girls who became pregnant whilst in their teens tended to have scored poorly on educational tests throughout their school life, and to have had parents of relatively low levels of education, who had themselves married young (Kiernan, 1980). It is well known that children of teenage mothers have higher than average risks of perinatal death (Butler and Bonham, 1963; Chamberlain et al., 1978) and sudden unexpected infant death (Chamberlain and Simpson, 1979). Even among apparently normal babies there is evidence that those of adolescent mothers are less alert, less able to control their behaviour, and less capable of responding to social stimuli (Thompson et al., 1979). The association of various aspects of the health and behaviour of the children throughout the first 5 years, as related to the age of the mother or mother figure, is important and one that will recur throughout this volume.

In all analyses, by *mother* we shall be referring to the *mother figure*. Thus, maternal age will indicate the age of the mother figure at the time of the child's 5th birthday.

When the child was 5, the youngest mother was 18 and the oldest 70. In all, 8.6% of mothers were young (i.e. they had been teenagers at the time of the birth and were under 25 when the child was 5); another 8.4% could be considered relatively elderly (i.e. aged 40 or more when the child was 5); the great majority (67.4%) of the mothers were, however, in the age range 25–34.

Not surprisingly, the age distribution varied with the parental situation (Fig. 2.1): the children from homes with only one natural

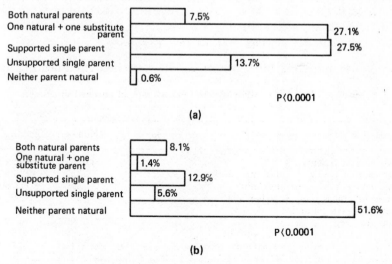

Both natural parents — 7.5%
One natural + one substitute parent — 27.1%
Supported single parent — 27.5%
Unsupported single parent — 13.7%
Neither parent natural — 0.6%

P⟨0.0001

(a)

Both natural parents — 8.1%
One natural + one substitute parent — 1.4%
Supported single parent — 12.9%
Unsupported single parent — 5.6%
Neither parent natural — 51.6%

P⟨0.0001

(b)

FIG. 2.1 Proportion of (a) young mothers (< 25), (b) elderly mothers (40+) in each parental situation when child was 5

parent were far more likely to have mothers who had been teenagers at the time of their birth, whereas over half the children in the group with neither parent natural, had mothers who were 'elderly'.

Social Class

The concept of 'social class', based on the classification of the occupation of the male head of the household, has been used in Britain for 100 years (Eyler, 1979). It is a useful parameter in the study of mortality and morbidity, but has never been assumed to be other than a crude indicator of social differences.

Our classification has been based on the employment status, occupation and type of industry of the child's father figure at the time of the 5-year survey, using the published classification (Office of Population Censuses, and Surveys, 1970). This is described in more detail in the Glossary (page 361). In brief, the *non-manual* classes comprise the higher professional (I), the managerial and other professional (II) and the clerical and other skilled non-manual occupations (III NM). The *manual* classes include the skilled (III M), the partially skilled (IV) and the unskilled (V). Instances where the mother was living with no male support are considered as a separate group, NFF (no father figure).

In all, of the 12,268 children with derivable social class, the majority (47%) were of social class III M, and the smallest group was that of social class V (Table 2.3).

The proportion of children living with both natural parents was very high in each social class group, varying from 96.8% in social class I to 93.5% in social class V. Nevertheless, there was a marked trend among children with step-parents, being 3 times more prevalent in social class V (4.3%) than in social class I (1.4%).

TABLE 2.3   Distribution of social class when children were 5 years old

Social class	Number of children	Percentage
I	843	6.9
II	2,405	19.6
III NM	1,069	8.7
III M	5,726	46.7
IV	1,620	13.2
V	605	4.9
All I–V	12,268	100.0

Not classified were 655 with no father figure (NFF), 191 where the father's occupation was not stated, 4 where it was unknown and 17 which were unclassifiable.

The maternal age distribution within each social class showed the expected pattern. Mothers under 25 were six times more prevalent in social class V as in social class I (Fig. 2.2). In contrast, there was no significant variation in the distribution of older mothers with social class.

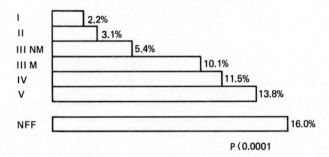

FIG. 2.2 Proportion of young mothers (under 25) in each social class

Ethnic Group of the Parents

The health visitor was asked to assess to which broad ethnic categories each of the current parents of the child belonged. The options used were (a) European (UK), (b) European (other), (c) West Indian, (d) Indian/Pakistani, (e) African, (f) Other. From the replies we were able to identify 12,007 children with both parents from the United Kingdom, 179 with both parents from elsewhere in Europe (including the Republic of Ireland), 174 from the West Indies, 257 from Asia, and 386 with other or mixed parentage. Although the size of each group is relatively small, the ethnic minority groups are important in that, as we shall show, their children were reported as having certain distinct behaviour patterns, differing morbidity patterns and health behaviour.

Where only one parent figure was present, the ethnic group of that parent was used since the child's environment, attitudes and choices are likely to have been dominated by that parent. It must be remembered that the grouping is not necessarily a genetic one, as it refers only to the parent figure(s) present at 5 years.

The significant differences between the ethnic groups are shown in Fig. 2.3. Although West Indian and Asian households were almost equally likely to be of social classes IV and V, the former were at high risk of living with only one parent, whereas almost all Asian children were living with both natural parents.

There was no variation among these ethnic groups in the proportion of young mothers (i.e. under 25 when child was 5), but in both the 'other European' and West Indian groups the mother figures were three times

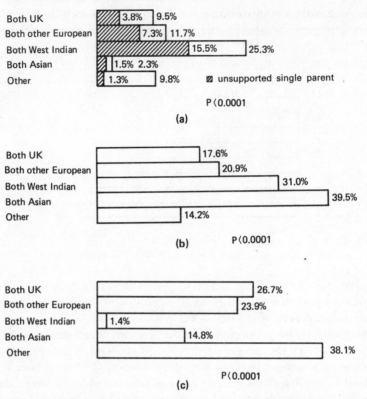

FIG. 2.3 Ethnic group of current parents: proportion of children (a) living in situations other than with two natural parents, (b) of social classes IV and V, (c) of social classes I and II

as likely to have been 45 or over, compared with the overall rate (6.9% and 9.5% compared with 2.3%).

Numbers of Children in the Family

By the time they were 5 only 10% of the cohort (1338) were 'only' children (i.e. not living with other children), 49% had one sibling and a further 25% had two siblings. The maximum number of siblings was thirteen. (Here 'sibling' is defined as another child living with the same parent figures as the study child.) The study children included 3664 who were the eldest, and 5932 who were the youngest in the family (Table 2.4).

Although a relatively small proportion (16%) of the children came from households where there were three or more other children, there were substantial variations in this proportion within different categories of the population. The variation with ethnic group, for example, was

TABLE 2.4 Other children in same household as study child

Number older	Number younger						In care	All
	0	1	2	3	4	5		
0	1338	3136	483	41	3	1	—	5002
1	3242	1121	165	18	1	0	—	4547
2	1637	427	83	8	1	0	—	2156
3	702	170	31	7	0	0	—	910
4	221	72	10	6	1	0	—	310
5	85	29	6	3	1	0	—	124
6	33	17	2	0	0	0	—	52
7	11	3	3	1	0	0	—	18
8	1	0	0	0	0	0	—	1
10	0	0	0	1	0	0	—	1
In care	—	—	—	—	—	—	14	14
All	7270	4975	783	85	7	1	14	13,135

dramatic (Fig. 2.4): only one-sixth of 5-year-olds from households with UK parents had three or more siblings, compared with roughly half of those study children who came from West Indian or Asian households.

Interestingly, the proportion of children with three or more siblings was increased in the single parent situations, and the manual social classes were also more likely to have large families. Not surprisingly, the probability of the child having at least three siblings varied almost linearly with maternal age: 30% of study children whose mothers were 35 or over had at least three siblings, compared with 9% of children with mothers under 30.

The proportion of 'only' children varied markedly with parental situation (Fig. 2.5), being lowest in families with both natural parents, and highest among the group of supported single parents.

There were no social class variations in the proportion who were 'only' children, but the proportion varied substantially with the age of the mother, being highest at each extremity of the age range (under 25 or over 40).

Maternal Employment During the Child's Life

Some 54% of the mothers of the children in the survey had been in paid employment since the child was born. Nevertheless, the jobs had been mostly part-time and of fairly short duration (Table 2.5). Only 1% of mothers said they had worked full-time continuously throughout the child's first 5 years.

The proportion of women who had been employed during the child's life did vary quite markedly with maternal age: the younger the mother,

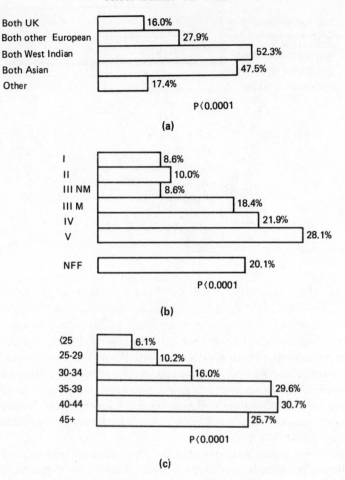

FIG. 2.4 Proportion of study children with three or more siblings by (a) ethnic group of parents, (b) social class and (c) maternal age

the more likely was she to have had a job (Fig. 2.6). At the same time, not surprisingly, the more children in the household, the less likely was the mother to have worked; some 86% of mothers of 'only' children had had a job compared with only 30% of mothers who had at least seven other children.

The differences between social classes, however, were less dramatic, though still statistically significant; women of social class I were the least likely to have worked in the previous 5 years, and those of social class III NM, III M and IV were more likely to have done so. The mothers most likely to have worked were in the group where there was no father figure in the household.

In addition to social class variation, the probability of the mother

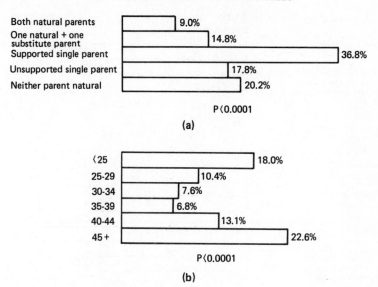

FIG. 2.5 Proportion of study children who were 'only' children by (a) parental situation, (b) maternal age

having worked during the child's life was related to the parental situation. More of those mothers from the categories 'one natural + one step parent' (68%) and 'supported single parent' (67%) had worked compared with unsupported single mothers (59%) and 'both natural parents' (55%). Children living with neither natural parent (i.e. adopted, fostered, etc.), were least likely to have had a mother who had worked during the child's life.

There was considerable variation in the history of maternal employment within ethnic groups. Women from the West Indies were significantly more likely to have worked (78%) than mothers from the United Kingdom (55%). Conversely, only 35% of the Asian mothers had taken a job during the child's life.

Discussion

In this chapter we have outlined the ways in which the basic characteristics of the parents of the study children differ and interact with one another. As well as these aspects, the child is affected intellectually and physically by his environment. This will be described in some detail in the next chapter.

Conclusions

1. Children of young mothers (under 25 when the child was 5) are

TABLE 2.5   Patterns of work of the mother figure since the birth of the child

Pattern of work	Number of children	Percentage
Full-time housewife throughout	5841	44.5
Worked full-time away from home:		
< 1 year	251	1.9
1 year	154	1.2
2 years	167	1.3
3 years	139	1.1
4 years	89	0.7
throughout	134	1.0
duration N.S.	17	0.1
Worked part-time away from home:		
< 1 year	1911	14.5
1 year	991	7.5
2 years	809	6.2
3 years	357	2.7
4 years	270	2.1
throughout	332	2.5
duration N.S.	99	0.8
Worked away from home, a mixture of full- and part-time (or unstated)		
< 1 year	104	0.8
1 year	107	0.8
2 years	109	0.8
3 years	77	0.6
4 years	52	0.4
throughout	41	0.3
duration N.S.	10	0.1
Worked away from home occasionally	283	2.2
Worked regularly at home:		
full-time	84	0.6
part-time	297	2.3
hours not stated	95	0.7
occasionally	122	0.9
Other situation	38	0.3
Student, voluntary work, etc.	56	0.4
Not stated	47	0.3
No mother figure	52	0.4
All	13,135	100.0

less likely to be living with both natural parents, more likely to be of manual social classes and to be 'only' children.

2. Children with elderly mothers (40+) are more likely to be living with neither natural parent, to have West Indian parent(s), to be 'only' children or one of a large family.

3. Children from West Indian backgrounds are more likely to be from social classes IV or V, to have working mothers, to be living

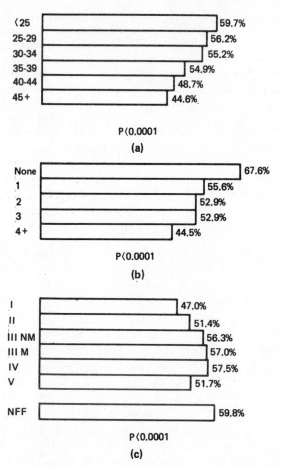

FIG. 2.6 Proportion of mothers who had been employed since the child's birth by (a) maternal age, (b) number of other children in the household, (c) social class

with a single unsupported parent, and to have a large number of siblings.

4. Children from Asian backgrounds were more likely to be living with both natural parents, more likely to be of social classes IV and V, and to have a large number of siblings. Their mothers were less likely to work.

5. Mothers who had worked during the child's life tended to be younger, and to have relatively few children.

CHAPTER 3

The children and their physical environment

by JEAN GOLDING

Introduction

It has been well-documented in many countries that there are strong differences in patterns of childhood disease and disorder between urban and rural areas. For example, Kastrup (1976), in Finland, showed that children from urban areas were more likely to suffer from stomach ache, whereas those from rural areas had significantly more speech disorders. In Britain, mortality figures are published so that urban–rural differences can be detected, but little information is available on morbidity. Unfortunately, neither of the previous cohorts examined their data in regard to urban–rural variation. We shall therefore be providing unique information on the way in which the child's disorders vary with the type of neighbourhood in which he lives.

Type of housing and crowding has, however, been analysed by previous authors. For example, the 1958 cohort data has shown that, once social class had been taken into account, housing *per se* had little effect on the health of the children (Essen *et al.*, 1978a,b) but that there were marked associations with scholastic attainment, the children from over-crowded homes being at a disadvantage. Richman (1974) has attempted to assess the psychological effects of housing on both pre-school children and their mothers. She too found no association between housing conditions and either maternal psychiatric illness or behaviour problems in the child.

Housing

In classical terms, crowding is measured by taking the number of people resident in the household and dividing by the number of rooms (including the kitchen if it is over 6 ft 6 in wide). A ratio of 1.5:1 is technically considered to indicate over-crowding. Measured in this way the housing conditions of Britain's young children has improved

24

radically in the past 24 years. Among under 5s in the 1946 cohort, 23% lived in over-crowded conditions, whereas only 3½% of the 1970 cohort came from such a background.

Among 5-year-olds in the first cohort, 44% had no bath or shower and 50% had no hot water supply (Osborn *et al.*, 1984). Corresponding figures for the children born in 1970 were 3% and 2%. This improvement in housing over time is reflected in the fact that in the latest cohort 88% of children were living in houses (19% detached, 41% semi-detached and 28% terraced). Only one family in ten lived in a self-contained flat or maisonette and less then 1% lived in 'rooms'. Much has been published on the problems, both physical and psychological, of looking after young children in high rise flats, but numerically in this cohort the problem was small. Only 3% of our 5-year-olds were living above the first floor level.

Type of Neighbourhood

At the end of the Home Interview Questionnaire the health visitor was asked to indicate which of a number of general descriptions best fitted the district in which the child lived. A neighbourhood classification was developed from this (further details are provided in the Glossary). It comprises four distinct categories: 'urban poor'; 'urban average'; 'urban well-to-do'; 'rural'. A validation study showed this to be relatively consistent between interviewers and to correlate well with census material (Osborn and Carpenter, 1980).

A fifth of the children were described as living in a rural area, and the remainder in one of the three types of urban area: 23% well-to-do, 50% average and 8% poor. Although the children from the urban poor areas form a comparatively small group, they do tend to have high rates of various disorders.

The data will be presented in two ways: (i) to contrast urban with rural areas; (ii) to look for trends within the urban population by contrasting rates in the poor, the average and the well-to-do areas.

(i) *Urban–rural differences*

There was some difference in the social class distribution, with slightly more social class I and II children living in the rural rather than urban areas, and correspondingly fewer children of either social class V or with no father figure (Fig. 3.1).

In contrast, children from homes with neither natural parent were much more likely to live in rural areas. There were only slight differences in maternal age distribution, and mothers living in rural areas were just as likely to have had a job during the child's life as those

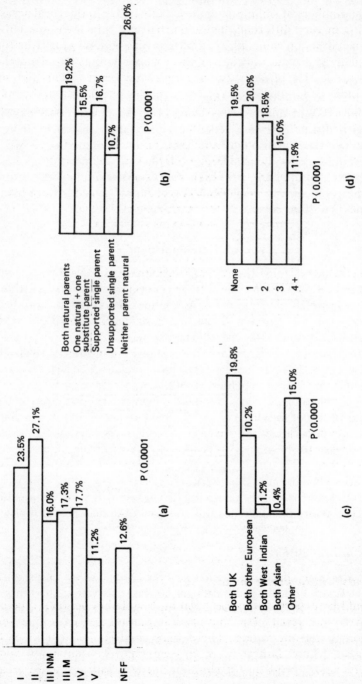

FIG. 3.1 Proportion of children resident in rural areas by (a) social class, (b) parental situation, (c) ethnic group of parents, (d) number of other children in the household

in urban areas. There were slight differences in family size, the children with large numbers of siblings being less likely to live in the rural areas.

The most marked difference between urban and rural areas was in the ethnic mix. Although some 20% of children with both parents from the U.K. lived in rural areas, only 10% of those whose parents were from the rest of Europe, 1% of West Indians and even fewer Asians did so.

Using indirect standardisation on these results, one finds that the only independent significant associations with residence in rural areas consist of ethnic group and social class (Fig. 3.2).

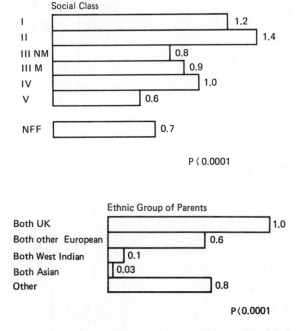

FIG. 3.2 Ways in which the children living in rural areas differ significantly from the rest of the population (independent Relative Risks)

(ii) *Trends within urban areas*

As would be expected, there is a strong correlation between type of urban area and social class, but it is important to stress that the correlation is not one-to-one. There were children resident in poor urban areas whose fathers were in non-manual occupations and, conversely, nearly two-fifths of children in the urban well-to-do areas had fathers in manual occupations (Fig. 3.3).

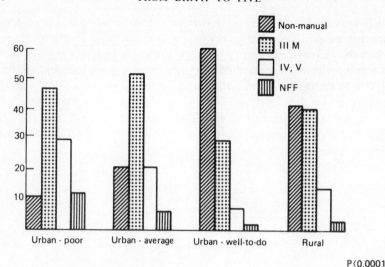

Fig. 3.3 Social class distribution in each neighbourhood

There was little difference in maternal age distribution apart from the proportion of young mothers in each area, such young mothers being relatively uncommon in the 'well-to-do' urban areas (3.4%) compared with the 'average' (10.7%) and 'poor' urban areas (13.0%).

There were slight differences in the numbers of mothers who had worked in each area, women in the 'poor' and the 'well-to-do' areas being less likely to have worked (53%, 51%) than those in the average urban areas (58%). There was a substantial variation with parental situation though (Fig. 3.4), with a great increase in the proportion of children from single parent and step-parent situations living in the urban poor areas.

There were also highly significant ethnic differences. Some 28% of children in poor urban areas had an immigrant parent, compared with 7% of children in average and 5% of children in well-to-do areas. The contrast was most dramatic for children of West Indian and Asian parents (Fig. 3.9). Approximately half of these children lived in poor urban areas.

The proportion of children from large families also varied dramatically with type of neighbourhood: 34% of those in 'poor' urban areas had three or more siblings, compared with 19% of those from 'average' urban areas and only 9% of those from 'well-to-do' areas.

The factors that we have discussed are obviously complex and interact to some extent. By indirect standardisation, however, it is possible to quantify the independent associations. In Fig. 3.5a it can be seen that the risk of living in poor urban areas is nearly twice the average among

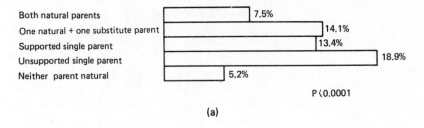

P ⟨0.0001

(a)

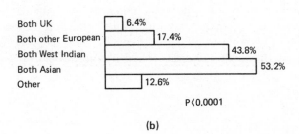

P ⟨0.0001

(b)

FIG. 3.4 Proportion of children resident in poor urban areas by (a) parental situation, (b) ethnic group of parents

children from social class V, or those with no father figure or who live with a step-parent. Very young mothers (i.e. under 25) are more likely to live in these areas and immigrant groups of all types are over-represented. In addition, families with four or more children are more likely to be found there.

Average urban areas were also more likely to include families from the manual social classes or with no father figure. Young mothers (under 30) and families with several children (Fig. 3.5b) were also somewhat more likely to be found there. In contrast with the poor urban areas, however, there were less likely to be immigrant families. Mothers in these areas were significantly more likely to have had a paid job since the child's birth, but the difference in Relative Risks was small (0.95 and 1.04).

In well-to-do urban areas (Fig. 3.5c), however, there was the expected excess of upper social class families, of mothers in the age range 30–44, and one- or two-child households. Mothers in this area were less likely to have worked. There were also fewer children than expected living with a step-parent. Interestingly, the numbers of parents in each ethnic group did not differ significantly from the rest of the population after standardisation. In other words, an immigrant family of given social class, maternal age, and family size was as likely to live in well-to-do urban areas as any indigenous U.K. family with the same social class and other characteristics.

Household Moves

The mother was asked how often the family had moved house since the birth of the study child. Less than half of the families (43%) were still living in the same place, 35% had moved once, 11% had moved twice and 11% had moved at least three times. There were no consistent trends in the frequency of moves within social class, the most likely to have moved house were social classes I, IV and V. Residents of rural areas were slightly less likely to have moved (54%), than those of urban areas (58%).

The children who had moved frequently (i.e. on at least three occasions) were interesting. They were twice as likely to be living in poor as opposed to well-to-do urban areas, their mothers tended to be younger, and they were likely to have immigrant parents (Fig. 3.6).

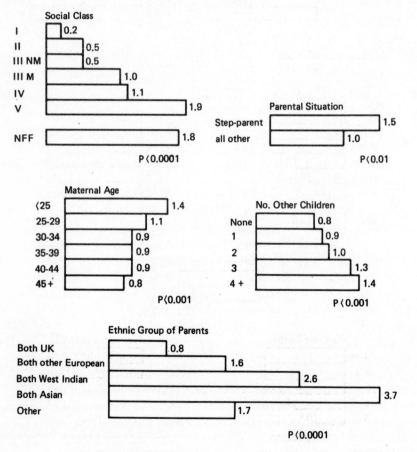

FIG. 3.5a Ways in which children resident in poor urban areas differ from the rest of the population (independent Relative Risks)

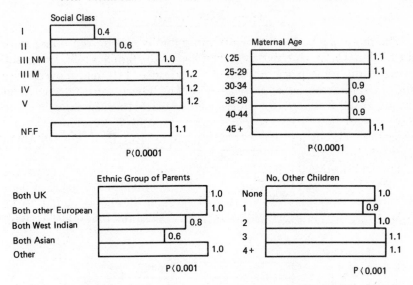

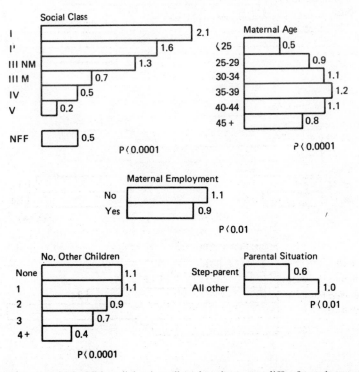

FIG. 3.5b Ways in which children resident in average urban areas differ from the rest of the population (independent Relative Risks)

FIG. 3.5c Ways in which children living in well-to-do urban areas differ from the rest of the population (independent Relative Risks)

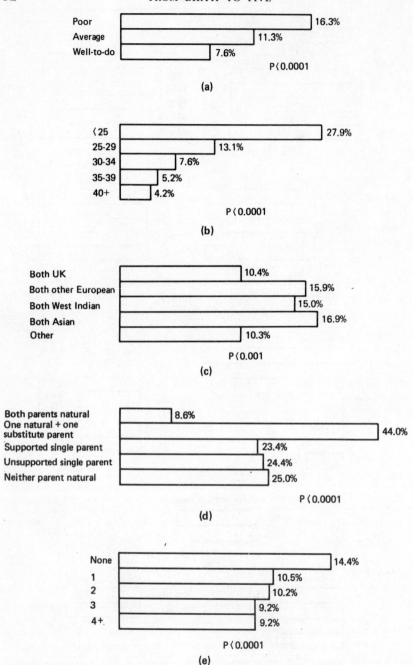

FIG. 3.6 Proportion of children to have moved at least three times by (a) type of urban neighbourhood, (b) maternal age, (c) ethnic group of parents, (d) parental situation, (e) number of other children in the household

Compared with children with both natural parents, those who lived with a step-parent were over five times as likely to have moved house frequently, and other groups were some three times more likely to have done so.

That there should be a difference was not surprising—the mere changing of parental situation will often result in a move of house. That there should be quite as many moves as shown here is distressing though—the child who has already suffered through lack of parental stability is likely to be compromised further by having instability in his home environment.

Although we have shown that, in general, the children living in the more disadvantaged circumstances were the more likely to have moved frequently, there is a negative association with number of siblings: the more siblings the child had, the less likely was he to have moved frequently.

Clearly, the factors which are associated with frequent household moves are largely inter-related: for example, residence in a poor urban area is correlated with frequent household moves and with immigrant population groups, and the immigrant population moves frequently; can one of these factors take account of the others? Indirect standardisation showed that (Fig. 3.7) the characteristics which independently appear to distinguish the child who had moved frequently from the rest of the population are: maternal youth and single or step-parent situation. Over and above this, there was an excess of a history of frequent moves if the child lived in a poor urban area. There were no

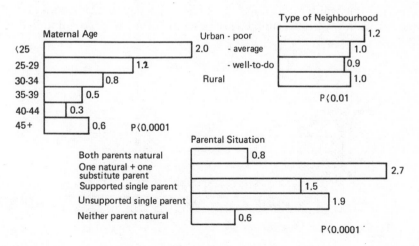

FIG. 3.7 Factors independently associated with three or more household moves (Relative Risks)

independent significant associations with maternal employment, ethnic group of parents, or number of siblings in the household.

Parental Smoking

The average adult must now be well aware of the risks to his own health if he smokes. The pregnant mother is becoming more aware that her unborn child is at risk of growth retardation or even of miscarriage or perinatal death. Relatively little emphasis, however, has been put on the potential dangers of passive smoking, although a recent study has suggested an increased risk of adult lung cancer if the patient's mother smoked (Correa *et al.*, 1983). As we shall confirm, a child in his early sensitive stages of development certainly appears to suffer more from respiratory disorders such as bronchitis and pneumonia if he is in a smoky environment. We shall, throughout this book, enquire of the information we have collected to assess whether there are other adverse effects of passive smoking, previously unidentified.

The health visitor collected information in the home interview on the smoking habits of both parent figures at that time. She also acquired details of the smoking history over the previous 5 years. In all, at the time of the interview, 41.5% of mothers and 54.4% of fathers were reported as currently smoking. Heavy smoking, defined as twenty or more cigarettes per day, was found in 17.3% of mothers and 26.6% of fathers.

There was a clear relationship between the mother's smoking habit and that of the father of the child. Figure 3.8 shows clearly that the more cigarettes he smokes, the more she is likely to smoke. There is a clear message for health education here—it seems likely that persuading one parent to stop without similar advice to the other would be doomed to failure.

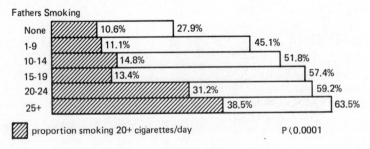

Fig. 3.8 Proportion of mothers who smoke according to the amount smoked by the father of the child

Profiles of the factors associated with smoking parents are shown in Fig. 3.9 and 3.10. The smoking habit of the mother was strongly related to the number of times the child had moved house: the more times this happened, the more likely was the mother to be a smoker, especially a heavy smoker. Though not as strong, a similar association was seen for fathers.

There were significant urban–rural differences: of the mothers in urban areas, 43% were smoking, 19% were smoking heavily, whereas

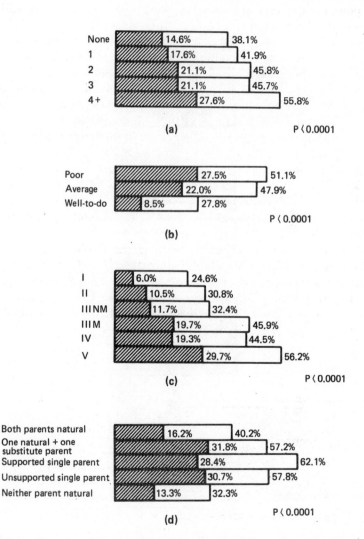

FIG. 3.9 Proportion of mothers currently smoking by (a) number of household moves, (b) type of urban area, (c) social class, (d) parental situation (*continued on next page*)

36% of mothers in rural areas smoked and only 13% were smoking twenty or more a day. For fathers, the urban–rural differences were 56%–50% for smoking overall, and 28%–23% for heavy smokers.

As might have been anticipated, there was a trend in prevalence of smoking with type of urban area: the poorer the area, the more likely either parent to be a smoker. Nevertheless, the differences between the poor and average areas are small compared with those between the average and well-to-do.

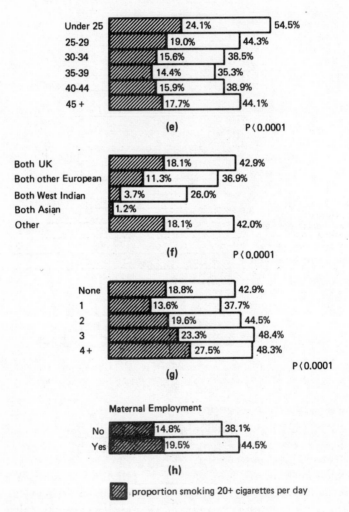

FIG. 3.9 *continued* (e) maternal age, (f) ethnic group of parents, (g) number of other children in the household, (h) whether the mother had been employed during the child's life

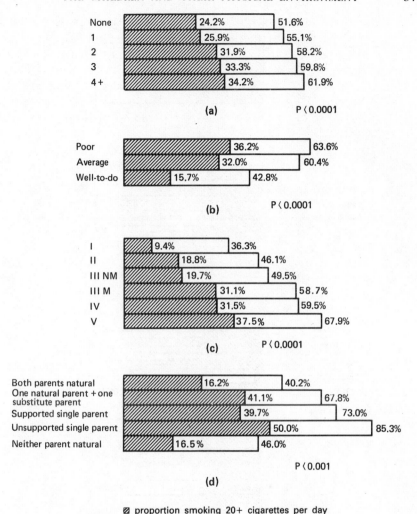

Ø proportion smoking 20+ cigarettes per day

FIG. 3.10 Proportion of fathers currently smoking by (a) number of household moves, (b) type of urban area, (c) social class, (d) parental situation (*continued on next page*)

There is a strong variation in smoking habit with social class, with mothers in social class V being over twice as likely to smoke as those in social class I. Among the heavy smokers, the differences between social class I and V is over four-fold for both mothers and fathers. The financial implication for a family with a low income where one or other parent is a heavy smoker can be disastrous. It seems likely that the diet, clothing and toys provided by such a family can only be less than optimal.

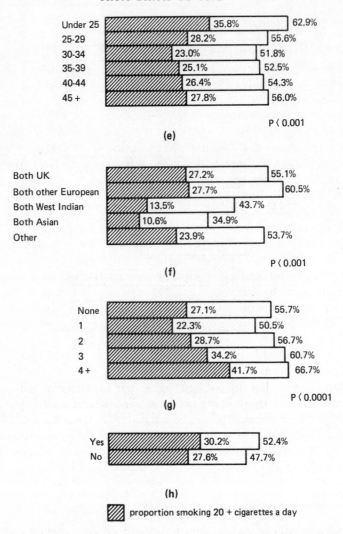

FIG. 3.10 *continued* (e) maternal age, (f) ethnic group of parents, (g) number of other children in the household, (h) whether the mother had been employed during the child's life

Even more distressing is the fact that parents in other potentially deprived and low-income situations (such as single parent families) tend to be both more likely to smoke and to smoke heavily than parents in situations where both parent figures are the natural parents. The group most likely to smoke, and to smoke heavily, are the single unsupported fathers.

There was a U-shaped variation in smoking habit with maternal age. Both young mothers and older mothers were more likely to smoke themselves and to be living with a man who smoked, and smoked heavily.

So far, we have shown that the parents most likely to smoke are those living in relatively reduced or disadvantaged circumstances. There is, however, an important exception to this generalisation. Only 3 of the 257 Asian mothers and comparatively few of the West Indian mothers in our study were cigarette smokers, findings similar to those found for smoking during pregnancy by Cardozo *et al.*, (1982). In contrast, the Asian fathers were fast catching the habits of their European peers, and the West Indian fathers had almost achieved par. Nevertheless, the proportion of *heavy* cigarette smokers among West Indian or Asian fathers was still much less than among the rest of the community.

In the population in general the tendency to smoke was associated with the number of children in the household. Parents with a two-child family were least likely to smoke and those with five or more children the most likely to do so. The pattern is most marked for heavy smokers.

Clearly, with all the factors strongly associated with maternal smoking, it is important to see which factors are independent of the others. Indirect standardisation showed that the maternal age association with heavy smoking disappeared after taking account of social class, the type of neighbourhood, the number of children in the household and the number of household moves. All other associations remained highly significant, as can be seen in Fig. 3.11.

It can be seen that the women most likely to smoke heavily, given all other factors, are those living on their own without male support (NFF group) and those who are living with a man who is not the child's natural father (the step-parent group). As we shall show in the next section, however, there was an even stronger association with the region in which the mother lived.

Region

At the time of the survey, sixty-four children were abroad with fathers who were in the Armed Services. They have been included in our population, since their absence is only temporary and questionnaires were filled in on all of them. For obvious reasons, however, they have been omitted from any regional analysis.

The regions used are the standard regions as defined by the Office of Population Censuses and Surveys. They are described in detail in the Glossary and are shown diagrammatically in Fig. 3.12.

Although relatively small geographical areas, the different parts of Great Britain vary in many aspects. The warm Gulf Stream bathes the West coast of the islands, as does the rain brought on the prevailing South-Westerly winds. The eastern areas are drier, but colder in the

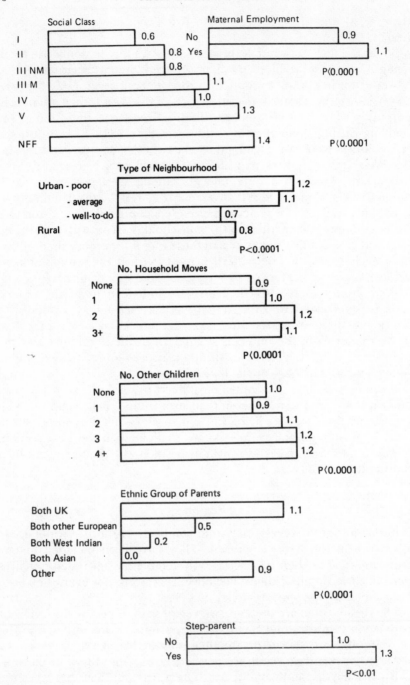

Fig. 3.11 Ways in which mothers who smoke heavily differ from the rest of the population
(independent Relative Risks)

FIG. 3.12 Percentage distribution of survey children by region

winter. Geologically there are major differences—with the South-East of England in general consisting of chalky downs with consequent hard water supplies and the Western parts of the island consisting of granite bed-rock with relatively soft water.

Genetically too, there is considerable variation—the inhabitants of Scotland, Wales and the extreme South-West are largely Celtic in origin, inhabitants of the East coast of England, notably East Anglia and Yorkshire, had an excess of immigrants many decades ago of Scandinavian and Flemish origin. The remainder of the country is a mixture of white racial groups with Anglo-Saxon predominating.

Overall, in our study there were statistically significant differences between the ten regions in the following: frequent household moves; immigrant families; maternal smoking habit; number of other children in the household and maternal employment. There was no significant variation with type of parental situation. The ways in which each region differed from the overall pattern are shown in Table 3.1 and described below.

The population of the *North of England* is largely clustered along the East coast around Newcastle-upon-Tyne. In comparison with the rest of the nation, there were 30% more mothers who were heavy cigarette smokers (20+ cigarettes per day) but substantially fewer immigrant families or large families. There were also proportionally less fathers in social classess I and II and fewer families lived in rural areas.

Yorkshire and Humberside, in contrast, varied little in comparison with the rest of Britain. There were slightly more large families and slightly fewer homes in rural areas, but these results were barely significant.

The *North-West* of England includes the Merseyside areas as well as the Lancashire textile areas which had their prosperous hey-day at the turn of the century. The largest cities in the region are Liverpool and Manchester. As a whole, the members of the cohort who lived here were markedly different from the rest of the children in the study: they were more likely to have mothers who were heavy cigarette smokers, or who had worked during the child's life (RR 1.1), and more likely to have fathers of social classes IV and V. They were substantially less likely to have immigrant parents or to live in rural areas, and slightly less likely to move frequently or be in social classes I and II (RR 0.9).

The *West Midlands* includes the conurbation of Birmingham with much industrial development. Not surprisingly, therefore, in comparison with the rest of Britain there were fewer study children living in rural areas. There were 70% more children with immigrant parents living in this area, and more children from large families (i.e. three or more siblings). Fewer study children than expected had mothers who were heavy cigarette smokers.

East Midlands is a region which includes no large cities or conurbations. The children in this region were 45% more likely to live in rural areas. Their mothers were also less likely to smoke heavily.

East Anglia is largely rural: proportionately over twice as many of the study children in this region lived in rural areas compared with the rest of the country. At the same time, there were substantially fewer children resident in poor urban areas, or whose mothers were heavy smokers, or whose parents were immigrants.

The *South-East* of England includes London and her conurbations as well as the salubrious rural areas in the surrounding counties. In comparison with the rest of the country, there were substantially more children with immigrant parents, more from social classes I and II and slightly more residing in poor urban areas (RR 1.1). Mothers were significantly less likely to be heavy smokers, to have had the child when they were a teenager, to be in social classes IV and V (RR 0.9) or to live in rural areas.

Region	Significantly more	Significantly less
North	Heavy cigarette smokers (1.3)***	Immigrant families (0.4)**** Rural households (0.7)**** Social classes I and II (0.7)*** 3+ other children (0.8)*
Yorkshire and Humberside	3+ other children (1.1)*	Rural households (0.8)*
North-West	Heavy cigarette smokers (1.3)***** Social classes IV and V (1.3)****	Rural households (0.6)**** Immigrant families (0.7)*** 3+ household moves (0.8)*
East Midlands	Rural households (1.5)****	Urban poor areas (0.8)* Heavy cigarette smokers (0.8)*
West Midlands	Immigrant parents (1.7)**** 3+ other children (1.2)*	Rural households (0.8)* Heavy cigarette smokers (0.8)**
East Anglia	Rural household (2.3)****	Poor urban areas (0.4)**** Immigrant families (0.6)* Heavy smokers (0.6)***
South-East	Immigrant parents (1.6)**** Social classes I and II (1.3)****	Very young mothers (0.8)*** Rural households (0.8)*** Heavy smoker (0.9) 3+ other children (0.8)
South-West	Rural households (1.8)***** 3+ household moves (1.3)*** Social classes I and II (1.2)**	Poor urban areas (0.4)**** Immigrant parents (0.5)***** 3+ other children (0.7)** Heavy cigarette smokers (0.7)** Social classes IV and V (0.8)*
Wales	Rural households (1.4)****	Immigrant parents (0.5)***
Scotland	Heavy cigarette smokers (1.3)**** 3+ other children (1.3)*** Social classes IV and V (1.2)** Poor urban areas (1.2)*	Immigrant parents (0.5)**** Social classes I and II (0.8)**

*P < 0.05; **P < 0.01; ***P < 0.001; ****P < 0.0001.

The *South-West* is mainly rural with much farming and some light industry. In comparison with the rest of the country, the children in this region were more likely to have moved frequently and to be from social classes I and II. They only rarely lived in poor urban areas or had immigrant parents. Their mothers were less likely to be heavy cigarette smokers or have large families.

Wales also had more children living in rural areas and fewer immigrant parents. The mothers were slightly less likely to have been employed during the child's life (RR 0.9).

Scotland differed in many ways. Although, like Wales, there were very few immigrants and mothers were less likely to have had a job (RR 0.9). In comparison with Britain as a whole the mothers were 33% more likely to be heavy smokers; the families were larger; there were more fathers in social classes IV and V; and more children lived in poor urban areas.

Having shown the ways in which the regions differ from one another in the basic structure of the population, it is hardly surprising that attitudes and habits vary—as indeed does the health of the population. Such variation will be described in later chapters.

Conclusions

In addition to the associations with region depicted in Table 3.1, the other independent significant findings are shown in Table 3.2 below.

TABLE 3.2 Statistically significant Relative Risks associated with each environmental variable

Variable	Significantly more	Significantly less
Rural areas	Social classes I and II (1.3)****	Asian parents (0.0)**** West Indian parents (0.1)**** Social class V (0.6)*** No father figure (0.7)** Mother smokes heavily (0.8)**
Poor urban areas	Asian parents (3.7)**** West Indian parents (2.6)**** Social class V (1.9)**** No father figure (1.8)**** Step-parent (1.5)** Mother aged < 25 (1.4)*** 3+ other children (1.3)**** Frequent household moves (1.2)**	Social classes, I, II, IIINM (0.5)**** Both parents from UK (0.8)****
Average urban areas	Social classes IIIM, IV, V (1.2)****	Asian parents (0.6)**** Social classes I and II (0.6)****
Well-to-do urban areas	Social classes I, II, IIINM (1.6)**** Mother aged 30–39 (1.1)**** Only 1 other child (1.1)***	No father figure (0.5)**** Step-parent (0.6)** Social classes IIIM, IV, V (0.6)**** 3+ other children (0.6)**** Mother aged < 30 (0.8)****
Moved house frequently (3+ in 5 yr)	Step-parent (2.7)**** Mother aged < 25 (2.0)**** Single parent (1.7)****	Neither natural parent (0.6)** Mother aged 30+ (0.7)****
Mother heavy smoker (20+ cigs/day)	No father figure (1.4)**** Step-parent (1.3)**	Both parents immigrant (0.2)**** Social class I, II, IIINM (0.8)****
Father heavy smoker (20+ cigs/day)	Social class V (1.3)*** Moved house 2+ (1.2)*** Poor or average urban area (1.2)****	Rural or well-to-do urban (0.8)***

Independent relative risks shown in brackets.
*$P < 0.05$; **$P < 0.01$; ***$P < 0.001$; ****$P < 0.0001$.

CHAPTER 4

The first months

by JEAN GOLDING and N. R. BUTLER

Introduction

In this chapter we shall be considering certain aspects of the child's early life, as recalled by the mother, and demonstrating the marked associations that many of the factors have with other variables, related to the parents' and the child's physical environment. It must be noted that we will not be dwelling on the associations between perinatal factors and their effect on the subsequent outcome in a prospective manner. Such a study is being carried out, but is outside the remit of the present volume. In the present study we will be doing the reverse—looking at the environmental situation at 5 and seeing in what ways the birth variables varied. Thus, when considering low birthweight, the analyses will not be aimed at discovering the aetiology of the condition, rather they will highlight the different environments in which the low birthweight survivor is most likely to be found.

Low Birthweight

The children of low birthweight in the 1946 cohort have been studied in some detail (Douglas, 1950, 1954, 1956, 1960; Douglas and Mogford 1953a, b; Douglas and Gear, 1976). The authors have shown that, whereas the growth and development of these children were reduced at early ages, by the time the children were 15 there were minimal differences compared with control children matched for social and other factors.

In Chapter 1 we showed that the proportion of children traced at 5 did not differ greatly with birthweight. Birthweight was recorded by the midwife, but the mothers of the study children were also asked the birthweight at the 5-year interview. There was a very high correlation between the mother's report and that recorded at birth, 95% being within 100 g of one another. Nevertheless, there were interesting differences: the mothers tended to report a slightly lower birthweight than that recorded by the midwife. In fact, the weight reported by the mother bears a closer relationship to the lowest reached by the infant in the days after delivery, than to the actual birthweight.

There are two ways in which we could have analysed the birthweight data: firstly, by taking the birthweight as recorded by the midwife at birth; or secondly, by taking that recalled by the mother. Either would have given similar results. For the analyses here we have taken the mother's report, as this is what most clinicians rely upon. It also meant that we had analysable information on the important but small group of 392 children for whom we had no birth data. Since the mother's recollection was in pounds and ounces, rather than grams, we have analysed our data in this way.

In all, 6.9% of mothers reported their infants to have been of *low birthweight* (under 5 lb 8 oz). As usual, there were differences between the sexes in birthweight distribution: boys being twice as likely to have been 9 lb or over at birth (Table 4.1).

TABLE 4.1 Birthweight distribution by sex of the child

Birthweight	Male	Female	All
Under 5 lb 8 oz	431	452	883
	(6.5%)	(7.4%)	(6.9%)
5 lb 8 oz–8 lb 15 oz	5521	5377	10,898
	(83.5%)	(87.6%)	(85.4%)
9 lb or over	662	312	974
	(10.0%)	(5.0%)	(7.7%)
All known	6614	6141	12,755
	(100.0%)	(100.0%)	(100.0%)

Chi-squared = 111, d.f. = 2, $P < 0.0001$.

At the time of the 5-year follow-up, the proportion of children who had been of low birthweight was slightly greater in urban areas (7.4%) than in rural areas (6.1%). Within urban areas, the proportion of low birthweight varied with the type of neighbourhood (Fig. 4.1); the children resident in 'poor' urban areas were twice as likely to have been of low birthweight than those living in 'well-to-do' areas.

Interestingly, there was no significant regional variation in the proportion of children who had been of low birthweight, but there was a slight trend with the number of household moves; the more times the child moved during the first 5 years, the more likely was he to have been of low birthweight.

Smoking during pregnancy is associated with an increased prevalence of low birthweight infants (Butler, Goldstein and Ross, 1972). Predictably, therefore, those women who were smoking heavily when the child

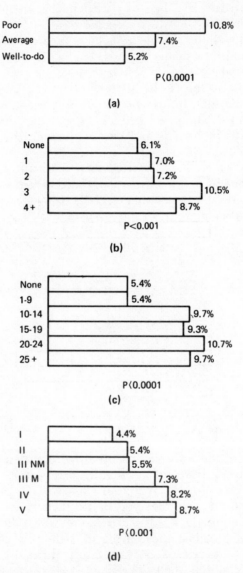

Fig. 4.1 Proportion of children who had been of low birthweight by (a) type of urban area, (b) number of household moves, (c) maternal smoking habit, (d) social class

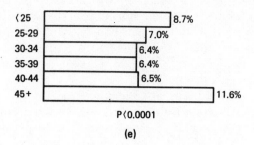

P⟨0.0001

(e)

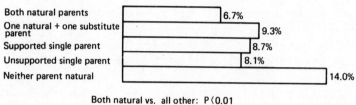

Both natural vs. all other: P⟨0.01

(f)

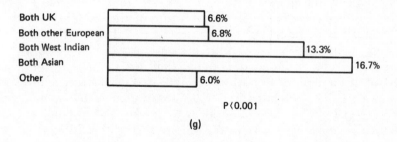

P⟨0.001

(g)

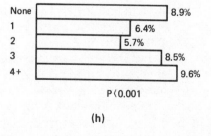

P⟨0.001

(h)

FIG. 4.1 *continued* (e) maternal age, (f) parental situation, (g) ethnic group of parents, (h) number of other children in the household

was 5 were almost twice as likely to have had a low birthweight baby as those mothers who were either non-smokers or very light smokers.

The proportion of children who had been of low birthweight also varied significantly with current maternal age, being lowest when the mother was aged between 30 and 44, and highest in the small group aged 45 and over.

The expected trend was also demonstrated in the prevalence of history of low birthweight with social class. Compared with social class I, there were proportionately twice as many low birthweight infants in social class V. There were also interesting variations with current parental situation, children living with both natural parents being least likely to have been of low birthweight. Among the small group of children living with neither natural parent, as many as 14% had a history of low birthweight.

Among the various ethnic groups, the children with West Indian or Asian parentage were twice as likely to have been a low birthweight baby as all other groups.

In regard to the number of siblings living in the same household, the distribution was V-shaped. The study child was slightly more likely to have been of low birthweight if he was an 'only' child, or one of a large family. There were, however, no differences in the pattern of maternal employment: the mother of a low birthweight infant was as likely to have worked during his pre-school years as the mother of a heavier child.

Standardisation has assisted in sorting out those factors that are independently associated with the presence of a low birthweight child. Analyses of the birth data of both the 1958 and the present study, had shown that although low birthweight appeared to be associated with low social class, this could be entirely explained by the fact that women of the lower social classes were more likely to smoke, and to be of reduced stature (Peters *et al.*, 1983). In the present survey of children studied at age 5, a similar phenomenon was seen—once the data had been standardised for maternal smoking behaviour and ethnic group, the association between low birthweight and social class disappeared, as did that with the type of neighbourhood, the number of household moves, the mother's age and parental situation.

The remaining significant factors are shown opposite (Fig. 4.2). Five-year-old children of mothers smoking ten cigarettes or more a day are nearly twice as likely to have been of low birthweight compared with children of mothers who were either non-smokers or smoked less than ten cigarettes a day. Children from Asian backgrounds were nearly two and a half times as likely to be of low birthweight, and those with West Indian parents were also at high risk.

The low birthweight infant, in general, is born at a disadvantage. He has either been delivered before the optimal time, or he has suffered

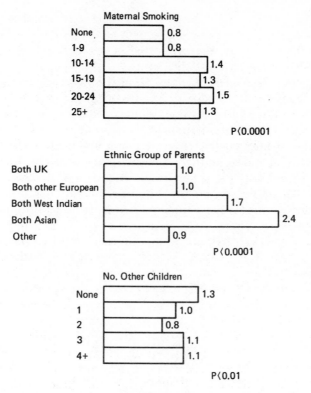

Fɪɢ. 4.2 Independent factors significantly associated with low birthweight

some growth retardation *in utero*. Not only is he more likely to have been at high risk of neonatal and post-neonatal death, he also will have been, on average, at increased risk of disease and disorder in the neonatal period. To have survived only to be reared in a smoky environment may in a sense be heaping 'insult upon injury'. In the rest of this volume we shall be showing the many ways in which the health and development of low birthweight infants differs from that of their *peers*.

Breast Feeding

A crucial decision affecting both mother and child is implemented during the first day or two after the child's birth and concerns the child's mode of feeding. It is probably taken partly in response to the child himself, but mainly in accord with the mother's received ideas, whether these were obtained at her own mother's knee, from school, the mass media, her own peers, the child's father or the health personnel with whom she has been in contact. There are known advantages in being breast fed, but it is also important to ascertain whether there are disadvantages. In later chapters we will be examining the data to see whether, in this study, the breast fed children had fewer behaviour disorders or reduced morbidity.

Information had been obtained from the midwives concerning the infant during the first 7 days of life. Chamberlain *et al.* (1975) showed that primiparous women in the age group 25–29 and those in social classes I and II were those most likely to attempt breast feeding. The actual type of hospital of delivery did not appear to have any effect.

At the 5-year follow-up the mother was asked whether the child had been breast fed, and if so for how long. Of the 12,981 responses, 37% of mothers claimed to have attempted breast feeding, but only 21% were still doing so at the end of 1 month, and only 11% had continued for 3 months or more. There was no sex difference in the proportions who had ever been breast fed, nor in the duration of breast feeding (Table 4.2).

TABLE 4.2   Duration of breast feeding by sex of child

Breast feeding	Male	Female	All known
Never	4254 (63.3%)	3928 (62.8%)	8182 (63.0%)
Yes < 1 month	1111 (16.5%)	982 (15.7%)	2093 (16.1%)
Yes 1–2 months	665 (9.9%)	629 (10.0%)	1294 (10.0%)
Yes 3 months+	692 (10.3%)	720 (11.5%)	1412 (10.9%)
All known	6722 (100.0%)	6259 (100.0%)	12,981 (100.0%)

Chi-squared = 6; d.f. = 3; N.S.

These results can be compared with population studies a quarter of a century earlier. In the Thousand Families study in Newcastle-upon-Tyne, 1947–1948, as many as 77% of the infants were being breast fed at the end of the first month, and 48% of all the mothers had breast fed for at least 3 months (Spence *et al.*, 1954). In the 1946 national cohort study (Douglas, 1950), similar but slightly lower proportions were found: 62% of all infants were breast fed at the end of the first month, and 44% for at least 3 months. Thus, compared with the 1946 cohort, infants in the present cohort were only a third as likely to have been breast fed for at least a month, and only a quarter as likely to have been fed for at least 3 months.

Although the Birth Survey had reported that fit low birthweight infants were as likely to be breast fed in the first week as the larger babies, when all survivors were grouped together there were significant differences. Of the 876 infants of low birthweight for whom information is available, only 24.1% had been breast fed at all, and only 5.4% had been breast fed for 3 months or more. These figures should be compared with 38.0% and 11.3% of infants weighing 5 lb 8 oz or more ($P < 0.0001$).

In the 1958 national cohort study, 69% of women attempted breast feeding, but only 43% were still breast feeding at the end of 1 month. There was, at this time, marked regional variation, mothers in Scotland and Wales being least likely to attempt or be successful at breast feeding, and those in London and the South of England being most likely to do so (Davie *et al.*, 1972). This finding was independent of the social class variation, with women in the upper social classes being more likely to breast feed than those in the lower social classes or with no father figure.

As in the 1958 cohort, the present study showed a very striking regional variation, with women in East Anglia, the South-East and South-West of England being twice as likely to breast feed as those in Wales, Scotland and the North of England (Fig. 4.3). Previous data on regional variations in breast feeding are hard to obtain, but Martin (1978) also showed that women in London and the South-East were more likely to breast feed than women resident in other parts of England and Wales. One small study from Glasgow found only 1% of Scottish mothers claiming to have breast fed their infants (Goel, House and Shanks, 1978).

Mothers living in rural areas were slightly more likely to attempt breast feeding than those in urban areas (42.1% vs 35.7%) and more likely to continue to do so for at least 3 months (13.2% vs 10.3%). Within urban areas (Fig. 4.4) women in the well-to-do neighbourhoods were more likely to attempt to breast feed. Proportionally twice as many women in these areas continued for 3 months or more compared with other urban residents. Differences were slight, however, compared to regional and social class differences. There was no association between breast feeding history and the number of times the child had moved house.

The children of mothers who were smoking at the time of follow-up were less likely to have been breast fed at all; there was a strong negative correlation with the number of cigarettes currently smoked, the difference between non-smokers and women smoking twenty-five or more cigarettes a day being almost two-fold. The trend was even more marked when children who had been breast fed for at least 3 months were considered, with a four-fold difference in the proportions relating to the groups of children with non-smoking mothers compared with those who smoked twenty-five or more cigarettes per day.

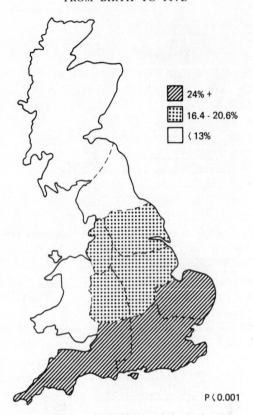

24% +

16.4 - 20.6%

⟨ 13%

P ⟨ 0.001

FIG. 4.3 Proportion of mothers who breast fed for at least a month, by region

Both the Newcastle study and that of Douglas showed little social class variation in the proportion of women attempting to breast feed, but that those of the non-manual social classes were more likely to prolong breast feeding after the 4th month than were those of the manual social classes. A similar pattern appeared in the 1958 data (Davie, Butler and Goldstein, 1972). More recently, however, with a relatively low proportion of women attempting to breast feed, the differences between the social classes have become marked (Martin, 1978; Coles, Cotter and Valman, 1978; Palmer, Avery and Taylor, 1979). The present study is no exception, the proportion of women who breast fed differed markedly across the social classes, mothers in social class I being over twice as likely to have attempted breast feeding as those in social class V. The differences were even more marked among those continuing after 3 months with a four-fold difference between social class I and V.

The study confirmed previous findings of a slightly lower rate of breast feeding among infants of younger mothers, but little trend

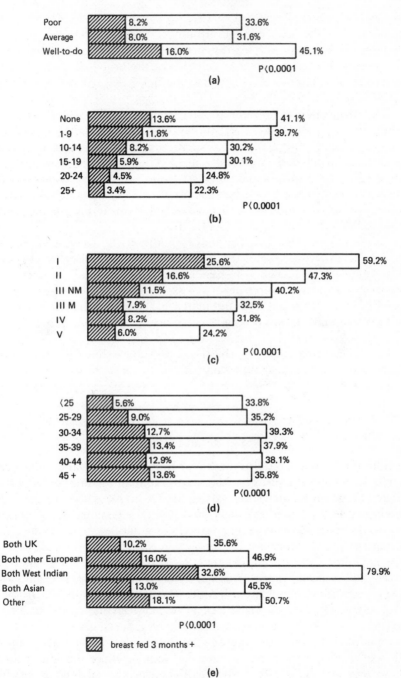

FIG. 4.4 Proportion of children who were breast fed by (a) type of urban area, (b) maternal smoking habit, (c) social class, (d) maternal age, (e) ethnic group of parents

thereafter (Martin, 1978; Palmer, Avery and Taylor, 1979). More marked were the differences in prolonged breast feeding (3 months or longer). Like earlier studies (Spence *et al.*, 1954), in comparison with mothers who were in their teens at delivery, the probability of prolonged breast feeding was twice as high if the mother was aged over 25 when the child was born.

The proportion of children to have been breast fed varied markedly with ethnic origin. As in other studies (Goel, House and Shanks, 1978; Palmer, Avery and Taylor, 1979), women who, together with their husbands, originated from the United Kingdom were least likely to breast feed, and those from the West Indies were most likely to do so. This is in spite of the fact that the latter were predominantly of social class IV and V. Some 80% of children of West Indian parents were breast fed, 33% for at least 3 months.

In addition to the findings above, mothers who were unsupported when the child was 5, and those who had had several other children, were significantly less likely to have breast fed. Such findings were to be expected from the strong negative associations found between breast feeding and both social class and maternal smoking habit. Nevertheless, indirect standardisation revealed that many of the factors were independently associated with breast feeding (Fig. 4.5). It can be seen that, all other things being equal, the children least likely to have been breast fed were those resident in Wales and Scotland, and those with mothers smoking heavily. Those most likely to have been breast fed were children of West Indian mothers and those of social class I.

Maternal Recall of Problems

The mother was asked, at the 5-year interview, whether as a baby the child had cried excessively, had had frequent feeding problems or frequent sleeping difficulties at night. Of those who answered the question, 13.3% stated that the child had had feeding problems, and 13.8% sleeping difficulties. These will be described in more detail in Chapter 6.

Altogether 1850 (14.3%) of the 12,954 children for whom the data were available were reported as having cried excessively as a baby. This problem was reported significantly ($P < 0.01$) more often for boys (15.2%) than girls (13.3%), although quantitatively the differences were small.

Children of low birthweight were substantially more likely to be remembered as crying excessively, as can be seen in Fig. 4.6. There were, however, no significant differences in the proportion of mother reporting excessive crying in their baby between those who had never breast fed and those who had attempted to breast feed (13.7% and

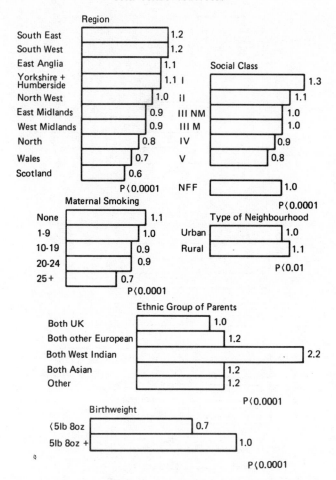

FIG. 4.5 Independent factors associated with a history of breast feeding (Relative Risks)

15.3%). There were significant differences, however, with the duration of breast feeding: mothers who had only breast fed for 2 months, or less, were more likely to remember their child as having cried excessively. It is possible to interpret these results in at least three ways: either mothers whose babies cried a lot ascribed the symptom to their inability to satisfy a hungry baby, and so changed to artificial feeding; or the mother, by ceasing to breast feed, caused distress in the baby; or thirdly, a stressful situation resulted in both the mother's milk supply ceasing and the baby's anxiety level increasing.

The only factor concerning the mother that bore any significant relationship to reports of crying in the baby was her age. In general, the younger the mother, the more likely was she to report that the baby had

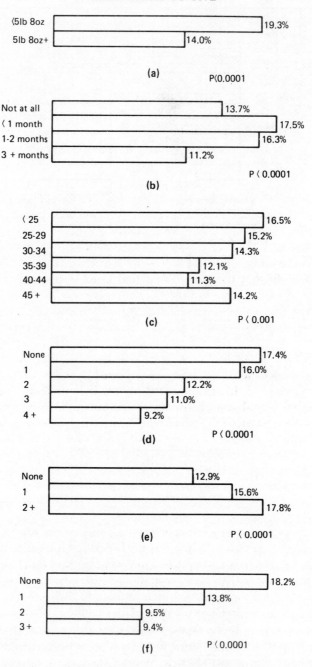

Fɪɢ. 4.6 Proportion of children said to have cried excessively as babies by (a) birthweight, (b) duration of breast feeding, (c) maternal age, (d) number of other children in the household, (e) number of younger children in the household, (f) number of older children in the household

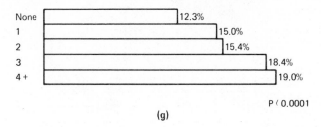

None   12.3%
1   15.0%
2   15.4%
3   18.4%
4 +   19.0%

P (0.0001

(g)

Fig. 4.6 *continued* (g) number of household moves

cried excessively. There were no significant relationships with social class, parental situation, ethnic group of the parents or maternal employment.

There was a strong variation, though, with the number of other children in the household—the more children the less likely the mother to have thought that the study child had cried excessively. Curiously there are two components to this: the more older siblings the child had, the less likely was he/she to have cried excessively, but the more younger siblings, the more likely was the child to be reported as having had this problem.

Perception of the child's early behaviour varied greatly with the number of household moves that had occurred by the time the child was 5. Interpretation of this finding is difficult. It is unlikely that we are measuring an actual causal association, although it may well be that moving house in the first months of life is upsetting to both the child and to the relationship between mother and child. Other possible explanations concern the character of the mother who moves house frequently. It is possible that she is less serene and, therefore, more likely to either perceive or promote problems in her baby.

There were regional differences too (Fig. 4.7): children resident in the South-East were apparently more likely to have cried to excess whereas those in Scotland, and the North, Wales and the South-West were least likely to have had this problem.

Indirect standardisation (Fig. 4.8), showed that there were five important and independent associations: the number of household moves; the number of other children in the household; the sex and birthweight of the study child; and whether the breast feeding had been attempted and abandoned before the child was 3 months old.

As stated previously, the mother's perception of problems of the child when it is very young is subjective. Nevertheless, the mother's memory of difficulties is probably a very pertinent guide to her later attitude to her young child.

As Sula Wolff (1981) postulates: 'Most mothers learn within the first

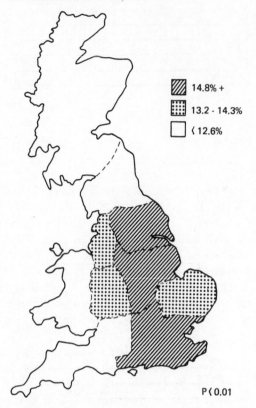

14.8% +

13.2 - 14.3%

< 12.6%

P < 0.01

FIG. 4.7 Proportion of children reported as having cried excessively as babies, by region

three months of their baby's life what to do to soothe him. The knowledge that they can satisfy his needs and stop him crying unites them with their infant more firmly. When, for whatever reason, a baby is irritable and difficult to soothe, his mother, deprived of these enjoyable experiences may spend less time with him . . .. This in turn frustrates the baby and increases his irritability.'

Even though the information on infant crying was collected after 5 years, our results are in remarkable accord with studies where the data were collected prospectively. Bernal (1972) showed, for example, that first-born babies cried more than second-born babies, and that this seemed to relate to the fact that the more experienced mother attended more quickly to her crying infant. The same study found that breast feeding was more often followed by bouts of crying than was bottle feeding, with mothers claiming to have given up breast feeding because the child was waking and crying 2 to 3 hours after a feed. The mothers interpreted this as a failure on their part to provide enough milk.

Apart from hunger, there are other reasons why an infant may cry.

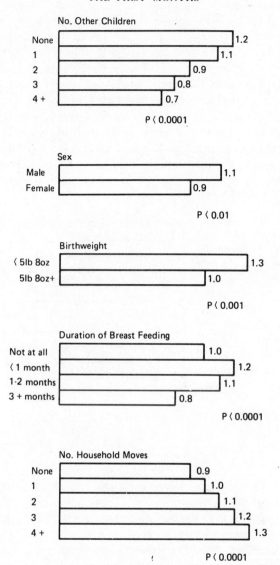

FIG. 4.8 Factors independently associated with reported crying as a baby (Relative risks)

These have been thought to include family tension, tiredness in the baby, colic and allergy. In these respects, it is interesting to note that there was little evidence to suggest that tension played an important part. There was no evidence of increased prevalence of crying if the mother was single, or the marriage was unstable and subsequently broke up. It is of interest to see in what ways the children, reported as having cried excessively as a baby, differed in regard to subsequent health and behaviour. We have only considered differences that are significant at the 1% level after standardisation for sex and social class.

The results are depicted in Fig. 4.9. The children with crying problems do appear to have had subsequent health problems. More children who had cried had squints and suspected hearing loss, more were said to have had headaches, stomach aches, and disorders of both the upper and lower respiratory tract. There were no significant associations with speech disorders, accidental injury, eczema or vision defect (other than squint). It is difficult to interpret these findings in any comprehensive fashion, although it is quite likely that many of the conditions were present during the first months of the child's life, and responsible for the crying response.

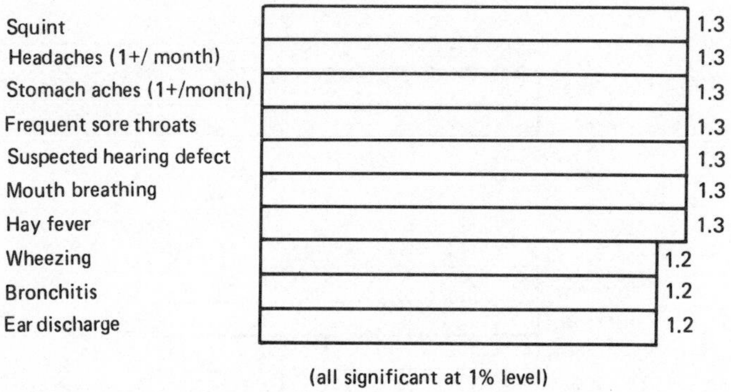

Squint	1.3
Headaches (1+/ month)	1.3
Stomach aches (1+/month)	1.3
Frequent sore throats	1.3
Suspected hearing defect	1.3
Mouth breathing	1.3
Hay fever	1.3
Wheezing	1.2
Bronchitis	1.2
Ear discharge	1.2

(all significant at 1% level)

FIG. 4.9 Relative Risk of other health outcomes in children reported as having cried excessively in early infancy (Relative Risk after standardisation for sex and social class)

Conclusions

1. Study children whose mothers smoked ten or more cigarettes a day were 75% more likely to have been of low birthweight than children whose mothers smoked less than ten per day.

2. Children of Asian and West Indian parents were more likely to have been of low birthweight. 'Only' children were more likely to have been of low birthweight. There was no independent association with social class.

3. Factors associated with the child having been breast fed were: non-manual social classes; West Indian parents; non-smoking mother; and residence in the South-East or the South-West of England.

4. Artificial feeding throughout was associated with low birthweight, manual social classes, a mother who smoked heavily and residence in Scotland, Wales or the North of England.

5. Excessive crying as a baby was reported more often in children who had been of low birthweight, those who had been breast fed for under 3 months and for those who had moved frequently. The more children the mother had had, the less likely were there to have been such problems.

6. Children who had crying problems were more likely to have had a variety of symptoms including stomach aches, headaches and respiratory disorders.

CHAPTER 5

Soiling and wetting

by JEAN GOLDING and G. TISSIER

Introduction

Although soiling (encopresis) or wetting, especially at night (enuresis), often has a profound psychological effect on both the parent and the child, they have never been considered as major reasons for health expenditure. These disorders are not thought to have far-reaching overt health consequences, but the long-term psychological effects have been largely uncharted.

Children who quickly learn the skills of keeping their pants dry by day and their beds dry at night save their mothers the energy and expense of endless washing and renewal of bedding. They will also be more acceptable than their 'occasionally wet' peers in playgroups and other types of pre-school educational and day care. The child who soils or wets is likely to be a source of embarrassment, if not frank irritation.

There is evidence (Shaffer, 1973) that failure to learn the habit patterns of dryness and bowel control is a disorder of development which may be related to genetic factors (Hallgren, 1957) or to social expectations. It may also reflect a greater frequency of environmental stress experiences (Douglas, 1973; Peckham and Essen, 1976). We shall be showing that although there is much overlap between the three symptoms (soiling, daytime wetting, bed-wetting), they do not exhibit identical epidemiological patterns.

Soiling

The 1946 cohort study found that by 18 months 86% of girls and 80% of boys had achieved bowel control, although a small proportion of each later started soiling again. The 1958 cohort mothers were asked in 1965 whether their children 'soiled by day after 4 years of age'. Overall, only 1.3% reported such a 'history', but there was a marked sex difference: 2% of boys compared with 0.6% of girls (Davie, Butler and Goldstein, 1972).

In the present study the question 'Does the child ever soil or make a mess in his/her pants?' was answered by the mother in the self-completion questionnaire. In all, 95.7% of the mothers of the 5-year-olds stated that this did not happen, 3.1% that it happened very occasionally (less than once a week), and only 1.2% that it occurred at least once a week (including twenty children who soiled 'every day', and another forty-three who soiled 'most days'). A striking difference between the sexes was apparent once more, with boys being nearly twice as likely to have this history than girls (Fig. 5.1).

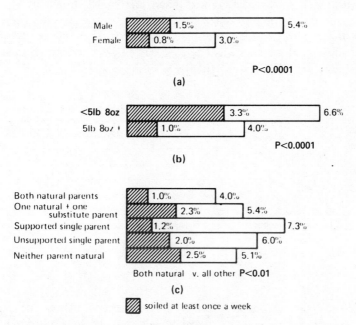

Male   1.5%   5.4%
Female   0.8%   3.0%

P<0.0001

(a)

<5lb 8oz   3.3%   6.6%
5lb 8oz +   1.0%   4.0%

P<0.0001

(b)

Both natural parents   1.0%   4.0%
One natural + one
   substitute parent   2.3%   5.4%
Supported single parent   1.2%   7.3%
Unsupported single parent   2.0%   6.0%
Neither parent natural   2.5%   5.1%

Both natural   v. all other   P<0.01

(c)

soiled at least once a week

FIG. 5.1 Proportion of children reported as soiling by (a) sex, (b) birthweight, (c) parental situation

There were no significant regional differences in the prevalence of soiling, nor was there any association with the type of neighbourhood, nor with social class. The symptom was as rare in children of mothers who had worked as in those who had been housewives throughout the child's life. The parents of the children who soiled were no more likely to smoke than the other parents. Nor was there a significant difference between the ethnic groups.

The children with a history of soiling had similar histories of household moves, and the same number of siblings as the children with no such history. Their mothers had the same age distribution too, but there were differences in children from different parental situations (Fig. 5.1). The prevalence of soiling was higher in all situations, other than those where there were two natural parents, but the association was most marked in single parent families.

There were also differences in the birth circumstances in that the prevalence of soiling was 50% greater if the child had been of low birthweight. The difference was even more pronounced if soiling at least once a week was considered, there being a three-fold difference in prevalence rates.

Analysis of the only three factors shown to be significantly associated with soiling showed that all the effects were independent of one another. The Relative Risks associated with each factor are shown in Fig. 5.2. Among the different parent groups, only the single parents showed a significant association—the combined Relative Risk for single supported and unsupported parents was 1.5 ($P < 0.01$)—i.e. children from such a background were 50% more likely to soil.

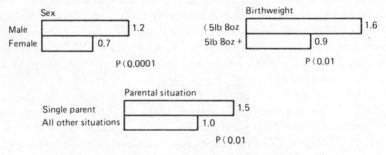

Fig. 5.2 Independent Relative Risks associated with soiling

There are said to be three types of encopresis (Anthony, 1957): (a) children who have never achieved bowel control; (b) children whose bowel control has relapsed; and (c) children whose faecal soiling alternates with constipation caused by purposeful retention of faeces. Anthony postulated that these disorders differed in their aetiology, but others have been unable to find differences in either personality structure, family constellation or method of toilet training (Carlson and Asnes, 1974; Bemporad *et al.*, 1978). Division into the three groups described above is currently being attempted by referring to general practitioners and hospital notes.

One of the unexpected findings in this study was the apparent lack of association with situations thought to be stressful to the child. The literature certainly suggests that traumatic events are likely to promote encopresis. Burns (1958), for example, reported a very high incidence of the disorder among children evacuated from London during World War II. Factors such as a change of environment, or the birth of a sibling, are said to be possible antecedents (Bellman, 1966; Levine, 1975), but we found no evidence for this in our study. There is confirmation in the literature, however, that loss of a parent is a common antecedent to the disorder (Olatawura, 1973; Bemporad *et al.*, 1978).

Daytime Wetting

In a longitudinal study of children in Nottingham, Newson and Newson (1968) showed that daytime wetting occurred regularly in 7% of 4-year-old children. The 1946 national cohort study found this to be the case for 3% of 6-year-olds (Douglas and Blomfield, 1956).

Similar to the question on soiling in the present study was enquiry concerning the frequency with which the children wet their pants during the day. It was apparent from the answers that this was more of a problem than soiling, with a positive history for the children of 1317 (10.1%) of the 13,048 mothers who answered the question. Of these, only forty (0.3% of the whole sample) claimed that such accidents happened every day. Eighty-eight (0.7%) said that they happened most days, and a further 104 (1.4%) stated that although not that frequent, they occurred at least once a week.

It is considered that regular diurnal enuresis should be differentiated from the large population of young children who have occasional accidents, and those who pass urine when they laugh. This disorder, known as giggle micturation, occurs predominantly among girls. In the present study there was a significant difference between the sexes, with girls about 40% more likely than boys to wet by day (Fig. 5.3). Unfortunately we were unable to differentiate the children with giggle micturation from the rest. The figure clearly shows that sex differences were of the same magnitude for the children wetting at least once a week, compared with those for whom it was a less frequent occurrence.

There was no overall association between birthweight and the prevalence of daytime wetting. If, however, attention is confined to children wetting fairly often (at least once a week), then there were significant differences, with the prevalence some 60% higher if the birthweight was low.

There were no significant associations with duration of breast feeding—nor were there marked regional differences, nor variation with type of neighbourhood, nor trend with social class, nor ethnic group. There was a slight increase in prevalence when the child was living with only one natural parent, but this was not statistically significant.

The mother who had taken a job was no more likely to have a child who wet by day, nor was any particular maternal age group at special

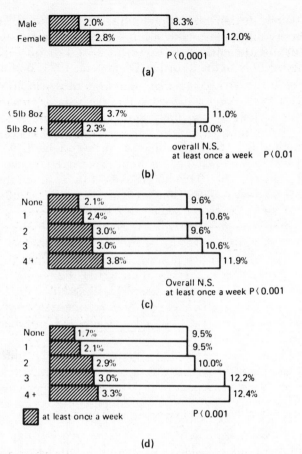

Fig. 5.3 Proportion of children reported wetting during the day by (a) sex, (b) birthweight, (c) number of household moves, (d) number of other children in the household

risk. There was, however, a trend between the prevalence of daytime wetting and the number of times the child had moved house. Figure 5.3 shows that this was only apparent for children who wet their pants at least once a week. There was a two-fold difference in the prevalence of wetting at least once a week between the group of children who had never moved house, and the group who had moved on at least four occasions.

There was also a positive association between the likelihood of wetting at least once a week and the number of other children in the household (Fig. 5.3). The child with at least four siblings was almost twice as likely to have this problem as was an 'only child'.

From the above it could be seen that, although there were certain distinct patterns exhibited by the children who wet by day at least once a week, there were no factors to distinguish those children who wet, but less often, apart from the fact that girls were more likely to be involved than boys.

We therefore restricted further analysis to those children who wet at least once a week. After standardisation, the association with household moves was no longer statistically significant, but associations with sex, birthweight and number of other children in household remained (Fig. 5.4).

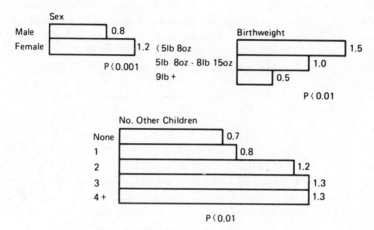

FIG. 5.4 Independent Relative Risks associated with wetting by day at least once a week

Thus, as with soiling, we have failed to show, for children who wet by day, differences that would be expected if a major cause of the disorder related to stress. One of the suggested causes of diurnal enuresis is an infected urinary tract. Certainly girls are more likely to have urinary infection than boys. Both Savage et al. (1969) and Berg et al. (1977) found that over half the girls with diurnal and noctural enuresis had bacteriuria—but it is not clear that the infections actually result in the lack of bladder control. Stansfield (1973) found that wetting tended to persist after the infection had been treated. Certainly within the present study a proportion of children will have had infections, but it is impossible in retrospect to indicate how many.

Wetting by day is closely related to both soiling and bed-wetting, although as many as 47% of children who wet by day have neither of the other two problems. Of those children who wet by day, but infrequently (less than once a week), 14% also soiled (Fig. 5.5). As many as a third of children who wet more often (more than once a week) also soiled, and more than half of these soiled fairly often (more than once a week).

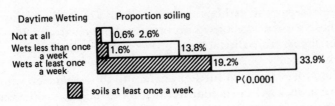

FIG. 5.5 Proportion of children who soil by frequency of daytime wetting

The association with bed-wetting is even stronger (Fig. 5.6). Of children who wet their pants at least once a week, 70% were reported to be bed-wetters, the vast majority of whom were wetting their beds at least once a week. This fact might suggest that a similar epidemiological pattern would be found for bed-wetting as we have demonstrated for wetting by day. In fact, as we shall show, very marked differences are apparent.

Bed-wetting

Involuntary emission of urine during sleep at night can be construed as a failure by the child to develop adequate cortical control over sub-cortical mechanisms. There are two major groups of theories and research into why this should be. In the first, physiological/behaviouristic, school of thought, enuresis is seen as the result of physiological immaturity or learning deficiency. In the second, psychodynamic, school, enuresis is seen as a response to environmental stress, usually considered to reflect an underlying emotional disturbance.

That the development of dryness has an overriding maturational component is self-evident. All relevant studies report an increasing percentage of children achieving dryness between the 1st year of life and at least 5 years of age.

Differences in the age of achieving dryness between sexes (Hallgren, 1957; Stein and Susser, 1967) and ethnic groups (Oppel et al., 1968) and consistency within family history (Hallgren, 1957) potentially point to genetically determined differences between individuals or groups of

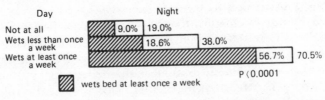

FIG. 5.6 Proportion of children who wet by night by frequency of daytime wetting

individuals in the age of maturation of bladder control. However, it is impossible to distinguish between genetic differences and co-varying cultural differences in such groups.

More significantly, a maturational influence is indicated in the finding (Zaleski et al., 1973) that children, aged from 4 to 14 years with nocturnal enuresis, have both structurally and functionally smaller bladder capacities than normal children. However, maturation deficiency cannot explain all cases of enuresis since, as Rutter et al. (1970) point out, dry children aged 4 years have smaller bladder capacities than wet children aged 7. Further, social class differences in the prevalence of bed-wetting emerge most strongly at ages where the maturational change can be presumed to be the least (Stein and Susser, 1967).

In our cohort study, 13,045 mothers answered the question as to whether their child currently wets the bed at night. In all, 78.1% claimed that he/she did not, 10.8% stated that the bed was wet only occasionally (defined as less than once a week), 3.9% recorded that it happened at least once a week, a further 4.3% said that it happened most nights, and another 2.7% that it was a nightly occurrence. Although, as we have shown, bed-wetting is closely related to daytime wetting and soiling, the majority of bed-wetters did not exhibit these other two symptoms. Indeed, of the 2791 children who wet their bed, 2148 neither soiled nor wet by day (Table 5.1).

The overall prevalence of bed-wetting of 21.8% may be compared with data from the other two cohorts. Douglas and Blomfield (1956) found that 12% of the children born in 1946 were still wetting their beds at age 4¼ years, but only 3.5% were wet several nights a week. Thus the earlier cohort appears to have had half the prevalence of frequent bed-wetting even though the data were collected at a slightly earlier age. The mothers of the children born in the 1958 cohort were merely asked in 1965 whether the child had ever wet by night after 5 years of age, the mother being instructed to ignore occasional mishaps: 11% of this population were reported to be bed-wetters. Some of the differences between cohorts could be due to the fact that the question was always asked in a slightly different way, but it is difficult to imagine that such an artefact could account for the two-fold difference in prevalence that we have shown between bed-wetting most days in the 1946 cohort and the 1970 one.

Both previous cohorts had shown that boys were more likely to wet their beds than girls. In this, the 1970 cohort was no exception: the 5-year-old boys were 40% more likely to wet their beds than their female contemporaries (Fig. 5.7).

The two previous cohorts have also shown that the prevalence of bed-wetting was higher in the manual social classes. In Fig. 5.7 we show that the same pattern prevails in the present study, with the lowest rate

TABLE 5.1 Numbers of children with various combinations of bed-wetting, daytime wetting and soiling

Bed wetting < 1 per wk	Bed wetting ≥ 1 per wk	Daytime wetting < 1 per wk	Daytime wetting ≥ 1 per wk	Soiling < 1 per wk	Soiling ≥ 1 per wk	Number of children
+	−	−	−	−	−	1128
+	−	−	−	+	−	165
+	−	−	−	−	+	25
+	−	+	−	−	−	45
+	−	+	−	+	−	9
+	−	+	−	−	+	28
+	−	−	+	−	−	12
+	−	−	+	+	−	6
+	−	−	+	−	+	1
−	+	−	−	−	−	1020
−	+	−	−	+	−	154
−	+	−	−	−	+	113
−	+	+	−	−	−	27
−	+	+	−	+	−	10
−	+	+	−	−	+	29
−	+	−	+	−	−	21
−	+	−	+	+	−	43
−	+	−	+	−	+	3
−	−	−	−	+	−	546
−	−	−	−	−	+	67
−	−	+	−	−	−	12
−	−	+	−	+	−	68
−	−	+	−	−	+	13
−	−	−	+	−	−	11
−	−	−	+	+	−	169
−	−	−	+	−	+	51
−	−	−	−	−	−	9359

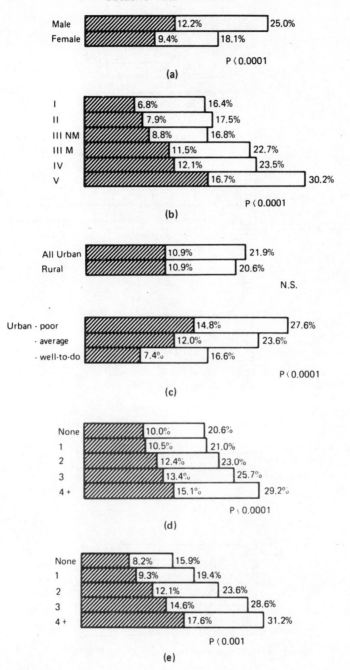

Fig. 5.7 Proportion of children reported as wetting by night by (a) sex, (b) social class, (c) type of neighbourhood, (d) number of household moves, (e) number of other children in the household (*continued on next page*)

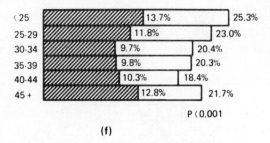

(f)

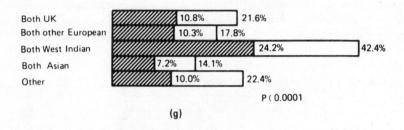

(g)

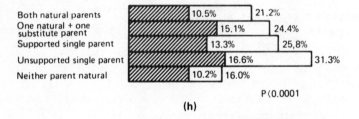

(h)

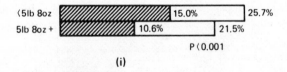

(i)

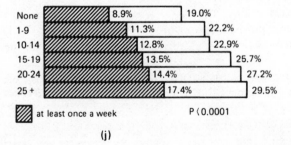

(j)

Fig. 5.7 *continued* (f) maternal age, (g) ethnic group of parents, (h) parental situation, (i) birthweight, (j) maternal smoking habit

reported when the child resided in a social class I household, and the highest in social class V. If attention is restricted to those children who wet their beds at least once a week, the trend with social class is even stronger.

There was no significant variation between the different regions of the country: nor did the rate differ between urban and rural areas. There was, however, a trend within the urban areas such that the rate was highest in 'poor' neighbourhoods, and lowest in the 'well-to-do' areas. These differences were, of course, largely to be expected from the social class distribution. There was a positive association, too, with household mobility: the more times the child had moved house, the more likely was he/she to wet the bed at the age of 5 (Fig. 5.7).

A strong, positive, linear association was also shown with the number of other children in the household. 'Only' children had a very low prevalence of bed-wetting, whereas children with four or more siblings had twice the risk.

Young mothers were slightly more likely to have children who wet their bed, but the small group of older mothers were also at increased risk. Whether the mother worked or not made little difference, however, to the prevalence of bed-wetting.

There was a strong association with the ethnic group of the parent(s). Not only was there a significant excess of children of West Indian parent(s) who wet their beds, but there were also significantly fewer children from Asian backgrounds with such a history.

An association was also found with the parental situation, the children of unsupported single parents having the highest prevalence (Fig. 5.7). Further breakdown of this group showed that among the forty-one children living with single fathers, the prevalence of bed-wetting was even greater at 46% overall and 15% wetting at least once a week. Children who were in residential care at the time of the study also had a high rate (6/10 known bed-wetters).

There had been no significant difference between children who had been breast fed and those who had been bottle fed, but, as with daytime wetting and soiling, there was a significant increase in prevalence of bed-wetting among infants of low birthweight (Fig. 5.7). The association was significant only for relatively frequent bed-wetters (i.e. at least once a week).

We noted with some surprise an association between bed-wetting and maternal smoking, the relationship being strongest for relatively frequent bed-wetting. The trend was such that the more cigarettes smoked by the mother, the higher the proportion of children who wet their beds.

As usual, the associations we have demonstrated are interactive. We have already indicated that standardisation by social class and the number of children in the household accounted for the fact that the children in poor urban areas were more likely to wet their beds. In similar ways the associations with maternal age, birthweight and the number of household moves were explained by other factors. The remaining significant independent associations are shown in Fig. 5.8.

As can be seen, there are fairly strong epidemiological patterns, with low social class and separation from a natural parent being of major importance. One previous study (Paulett and Tuckman, 1958) had suggested that household moves were often a common antecedent of enuresis, but our data agrees with those of Stein and her colleagues (1965) in finding no independent association.

Discussion

Although stress may be the reason why parental separation is associated with bed-wetting in many series, the relationship with social class is more likely to reflect differences in attitude and behaviour. However, which maternal attitudes are of importance here is less easy to define. Factors such as the encouragement of modesty, pressure for neatness, demands for compliance to instructions, etc., have not been found to relate to bed-wetting (Sears *et al.*, 1957; Newson and Newson, 1968). More important seem to be those factors which cluster around maternal warmth and the mother's satisfaction with her situation. Thus, Sears *et al.*, (1957) propose that the most important factor leading to the development of dryness is maternal warmth and that this variable depends largely on how content the mother is.

In the longitudinal study of the 1946 cohort, Douglas and Blomfield (1958) showed that the higher the social class the more likely were the mothers to start 'potty training' early. Rather surprisingly, even after allowing for social class, the activity was shown to work very efficiently— 49% of those 'potted' from the first 6 months of life were clean by the age of 1 year, compared with 29% of those whose 'potty training' had been postponed. At the age of 4¼ the incidence of encopresis was much higher in the group who had not been 'potted' until after the 6th month. The Newsons (1968) also showed that the women who were very concerned when their child was 12 months old, that their child should be fully trained, did have substantially more success than those mothers, who were only mildly concerned.

All British population studies have shown the same marked variation between bed-wetting and social class, whether they be relatively small single centre studies (Newson and Newson, 1968) or the large national cohorts (Douglas and Blomfield, 1958; Davie, Butler and Goldstein, 1972). The 1946 cohort analysis showed that, as with soiling, bed-wetting

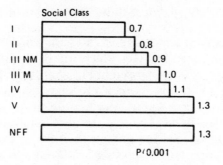

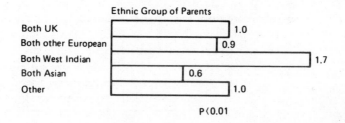

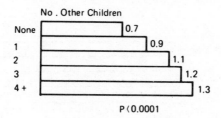

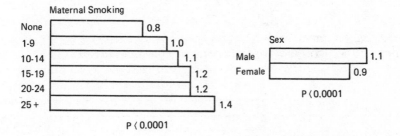

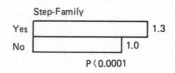

FIG. 5.8 Independent Relative Risks associated with frequent bed-wetting (at least once a week)

was more prevalent in the group which were later in starting 'potty training'.

A crucial question concerns health of the children with the various types of incontinence. Analyses which will be described in more detail later in the book are summarised in Figs. 5.9,10,11. Children who were soiling were significantly more likely than expected to complain of stomach aches, have a squint, vision problem or speech disorder.

Children with daytime wetting are also significantly more likely to have these four disorders, although the relative risks were of smaller magnitude. In addition, this group of children were more likely to have headaches.

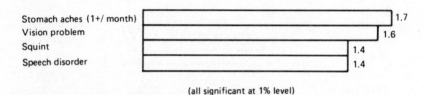

Stomach aches (1+/ month)   1.7
Vision problem   1.6
Squint   1.4
Speech disorder   1.4

(all significant at 1% level)

FIG. 5.9 Risk of other health outcomes in children who were soiling at 5 (Relative Risk after standardisation for sex and social class)

Vision problem   1.5
Squint   1.4
Speech disorder   1.4
Headaches (1+/month)   1.4
Stomach aches (1+/month)   1.4

(all significant at 1% level)

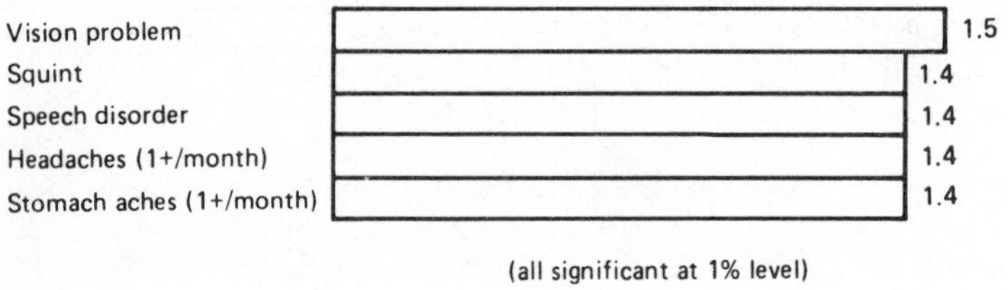

FIG. 5.10 Risk of other health outcomes in children who were wetting by day at 5 (Relative Risks after standardisation for sex and social class)

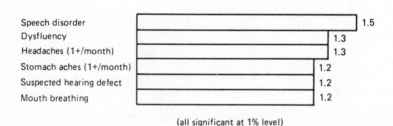

Speech disorder   1.5
Dysfluency   1.3
Headaches (1+/month)   1.3
Stomach aches (1+/month)   1.2
Suspected hearing defect   1.2
Mouth breathing   1.2

(all significant at 1% level)

FIG. 5.11 Risk of other health outcomes in children who were bed-wetting at least once a week at age 5 (Relative Risks after standardisation for sex and social class)

Bed-wetting was, however, not associated with squint or vision problems, although headache and stomach aches were again more prevalent in these children than would have been expected by chance. Bed-wetting was found more often in children with speech problems, including dysfluency. They were 20% more likely to breathe through their mouths and to be suspected of hearing difficulty. These findings suggest that bed-wetting might sometimes be associated with difficulties in communication. This will be discussed further in Chapter 8.

Conclusions

1. Soiling occurs more often among children of low birthweight and those living with a single parent. Boys are more likely to soil than girls.
2. Daytime wetting is more prevalent among girls, among children of low birthweight, and in families where there are two or more other children.
3. Bed-wetting was associated independently with the number of children in the household, low social class, number of cigarettes smoked by mother, lack of father figure, presence of a step-parent and West Indian families. Boys were more likely than girls to wet their beds. Asian children were significantly less likely to be reported as wetting their beds.

CHAPTER 6

Feeding and sleeping problems

by JEAN GOLDING

Introduction

We showed in Chapter 4 that children who were reported as crying excessively as babies were more likely to have had various medical disorders during their first 5 years. Closely linked with crying behaviour is the mother's assessment of her baby's feeding and sleeping requirements. Crying is frequently assumed to indicate that the child has been fed inadequately and often leads to changes in the food. This has been especially noted in breast fed infants, where the mother is unable to assess the actual quantity of milk consumed by the child.

Sleep, too, is frequently connected in the mother's mind with the total satisfaction of her baby's requirements. Mothers whose babies quickly learn to sleep through the night without waking are often excessively proud of the fact. Conversely, parents of a child who does not settle or wakes during the night feel both guilt and fatigue. Such a parental reaction has persisted for many decades since, in 1922, Sundell wrote that 'a sleepless baby is a reproach to his parents'.

The normal newborn baby takes about 3 months to settle into a rhythm whereby he is relatively wakeful during the day and sleeps more during the night. Only by 8 months, though, is there likely to be an uninterrupted period of sleep throughout the night (Anders and Weinstein, 1972). Factors which disturb this process have yet to be fully ascertained, but both feeding régimes and maternal anxiety have been implicated. On the other hand, a physical cause involving immature central nervous system responses has also been suggested. Bernal (1973) has shown that children who were wakeful as young infants tend to continue to be so throughout their early years.

Sleeping Problems in the Present Study

Of the 12,938 women who answered the question as to whether, as a baby, the child 'had had frequent sleeping difficulties at night', 1780

(13.8%) answered in the affirmative. Slightly more boys than girls were said to have had such problems (Fig 6.1).

Although the history of sleeping problems in the first months of life was reported proportionally more by mothers of low birthweight infants (16.5%) as compared with mothers of larger babies (13.6%), the difference was not statistically significant at the 1% level. There were statistically significant differences, however, with the duration of breast feeding (Fig. 6.1). Among the group where breast feeding had been attempted, but not continued beyond a month, there were 50% more children with such a history. It is not possible from the data available to us to determine any time sequence in this association. It could be that, because the child was not sleeping well, the mother decided to change from breast to bottle, or, alternatively, the baby whose mother stopped breast feeding in the first days or weeks might have reacted by having disturbed sleep patterns.

In contrast to many of the factors we shall consider in later chapters, there were no regional differences in the reported history of sleeping problems in the first 6 months of life. Prevalence of the problem appeared to have little relationship to the type of neighbourhood or the smoking history of the parents. There was a trend, however, with the number of household moves (Fig. 6.1). In general, the more times the child had moved house, the more likely was he to be reported as having had sleeping problems as a baby.

There were no significant associations with parental indicators such as ethnic group, parental situation, social class, maternal employment history or maternal age. Significant associations were apparent, though, with the number of other children in the household: the more children there were, the less likely the study child to be reported as having had sleeping problems as a baby. 'Only' children were at markedly increased risk of such a history.

In order to assess whether the factor we were indirectly considering was the experience of the mother, we examined the data for the number of children older than the study child—and hence the number of previous occasions on which the mother had had experience of coping with a young baby, prior to the birth of the study child. The same trend was seen (Fig. 6.1), the more previous children, the less likely the study child to have had such problems. No such trend was found with the number of younger siblings.

Indirect standardisation was carried out to assess those factors independently associated with an apparent history of sleeping problems as a baby. The association with household moves ceased to be statistically significant, but there remained highly significant associations with the number of children in the household, the duration of breast feeding, and the sex of the child. (Fig. 6.2).

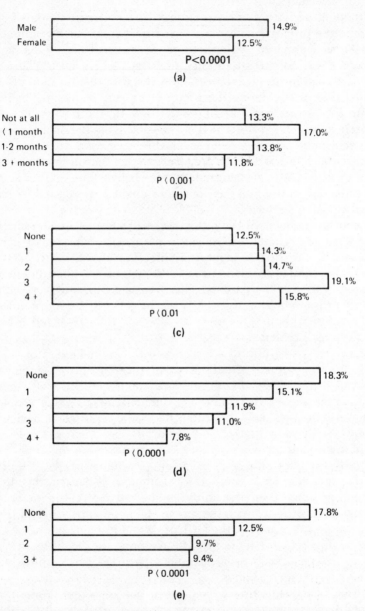

Fig. 6.1 Proportion of children reported as having had sleeping problems as a baby by (a) sex, (b) duration of breast feeding, (c) number of household moves, (d) number of other children in the household, (e) number of older children in the household

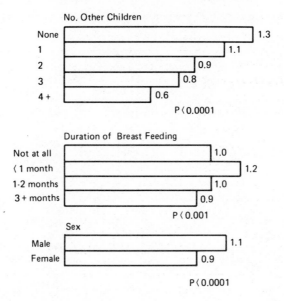

No. Other Children

None	1.3
1	1.1
2	0.9
3	0.8
4 +	0.6

P ⟨ 0.0001

Duration of Breast Feeding

Not at all	1.0
⟨ 1 month	1.2
1-2 months	1.0
3 + months	0.9

P ⟨ 0.001

Sex

Male	1.1
Female	0.9

P ⟨ 0.0001

FIG. 6.2 Factors independently associated with sleeping problems as a baby (Relative Risks)

In comparison with problems in their first 6 months of life, the 5-year-olds were almost twice as likely to have current sleeping problems. A quarter of the study children were involved. An enquiry was made into difficulties present at the time of interview. The most common of these concerned waking during the night (10.8%), difficulty getting off to sleep (8.8%), and waking early in the morning (7.2%). One child in twenty was said to have nightmares, but very few (less than 1 in 100) ever walked in their sleep.

Although there were no overall differences between the sexes in the proportion of children having any sleeping problems (Table 6.1), there was variation between the sexes in the type of problem. Girls were significantly more likely than boys to have difficulty getting off to sleep; boys were more likely than girls to wake early in the morning.

Several studies (Bax, 1980; Jones et al., 1978; Bernal, 1973) found that children with sleeping difficulties in infancy were at increased risk of sleeping problems later in childhood. This certainly appears to be upheld by our data, although it must be remembered that the history of early sleeping problems was obtained at the same time (though on a different questionnaire) as the report of current sleeping difficulties. In all (Fig. 6.3), 46% of children with sleeping problems as a baby were said to have sleeping difficulty at age 5, compared with 22% of the remainder (a two-fold difference in incidence). For children reported as having *severe* sleeping difficulties at 5, the differences were over six-fold.

TABLE 6.1   Proportion of children with various types of sleeping problem by sex

Sleeping problem*	Male	Female	All
Difficulty getting off to sleep***	543 (8.0%)	612 (9.7%)	1155 (8.8%)
Waking during the night	695 (10.3%)	718 (11.4%)	1413 (10.8%)
Waking early in the morning**	531 (7.9%)	409 (6.5%)	940 (7.2%)
Nightmares or night terrors	326 (4.8%)	323 (5.1%)	649 (4.9%)
Sleepwalking	44 (0.7%)	53 (0.8%)	97 (0.7%)
All with problems	1651 (24.5%)	1620 (25.8%)	3271 (25.1%)
No sleeping problems	5101 (75.5%)	4667 (74.2%)	9768 (74.9%)
All known	6752 (100.0%)	6287 (100.0%)	13,039 (100.0%)

*Categories not mutually exclusive.
**Differences between sexes significant: $P < 0.01$.
***Differences between sexes significant: $P < 0.001$.

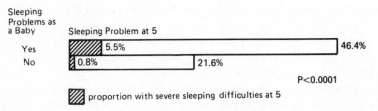

FIG. 6.3 Proportion of children having sleeping problems at age 5 according to whether they had had sleeping problems as a baby

Comparison of the types of sleeping problem present at 5 reveals that, for each, the proportion of children affected was greater among the group reported to have had sleeping problems as a baby (Table 6.2).

There was a certain amount of regional variation (Fig. 6.4), children in the South-East being most likely to have sleeping problems at 5, and those in Scotland and the West Midlands the least likely to do so.

As with earlier sleeping difficulties, sleeping problems among 5-year-olds did not vary significantly with birthweight. There was, however, once again, an association with the duration of breast feeding (Fig. 6.5). Children who had never been breast fed were the least likely to have current sleeping problems; those who had been breast fed, but only for a short time, were at greatest risk.

TABLE 6.2   Type of sleeping problem present at 5 by whether there had
been sleeping difficulties as a baby

| Type of sleeping problem* at 5 | Sleeping problem as a baby | | All known |
	Yes	No	
Difficulty getting off to sleep	331	804	1135
	(18.8%)	(7.3%)	(8.8%)
Waking during the night	419	976	1395
	(23.7%)	(8.8%)	(10.9%)
Waking early in the morning	260	664	924
	(14.7%)	(6.0%)	(7.2%)
Nightmares/night terrors	134	500	634
	(7.6%)	(4.5%)	(4.9%)
Sleepwalking	21	76	97
	(1.2%)	(0.7%)	(0.8%)
All with sleeping problems	819	2398	3217
	(46.4%)	(21.6%)	(75.0%)
No sleeping problems	946	8689	9635
	(53.6%)	(78.4%)	(75.0%)
All known	1765	11,087	12,852
	(100.0%)	(100.0%)	(100.0%)

*Not mutually exclusive.

There was evidence that children who had moved house were significantly more at risk of having sleeping problems, those who had moved four or more times being especially likely to have such attributes (Fig. 6.5). As found for reported sleeping problems in the babies, there were no associations with parental smoking habits or with the type of neighbourhood in which the family resided.

Prevalence of sleeping problems did not vary with social class, mother's age, maternal employment history, or parental situation. Children of Asian parents were, however, significantly less likely to have such problems than any of the other ethnic groups (Fig. 6.5). This is unlikely to be a reporting bias, since the proportion of Asian children said to have sleeping problems as a baby was almost identical to the rest of the population. There are at least two other possibilities: one is that the Asian expectation of 5-year-old behaviour differs from other groups, and thus the subjective threshold of what is a problem differs; the other is that 5-year-old Asian children genuinely do have a low prevalence of these difficulties.

There was a negative association between the number of children in the household and the prevalence of sleeping difficulties in the study child (Fig. 6.5). As shown with sleeping difficulties as a baby, the crucial

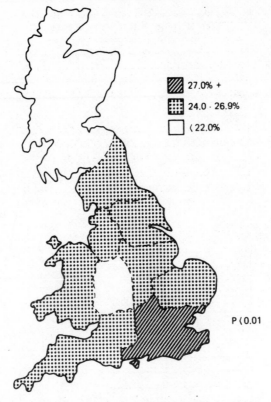

FIG. 6.4 Children with sleeping problems at age 5 by region

factor appeared to be the number of older, rather than younger, children.

Study of the inter-relationship of the factors shown to be associated with prevalence of sleeping problems at 5 revealed that the regional differences were the consequence of the regional variations in breast feeding and ethnic group, but that the other factors remained statistically significant. Relative Risks associated with each are depicted in Fig. 6.6.

Feeding Problems in the Present Study

More anxiety is expressed over their infant's feeding by mothers, in routine contacts with health visitors, that any other topic. In retrospect, though, the proportion of mothers reporting feeding problems when the child was a baby was, at 13.3%, very similar to the proportion reporting the child as having had frequent sleeping difficulties as a baby

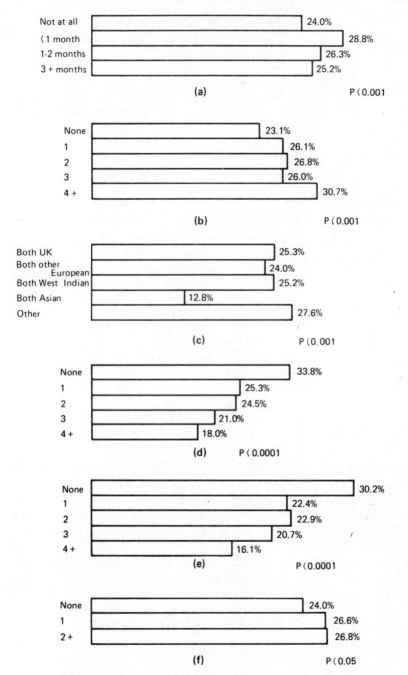

FIG. 6.5 Proportion of 5-year-old children with sleeping problems by (a) duration of breast feeding, (b) number of household moves, (c) ethnic group of parents, (d) number of other children in the household, (f) number of younger children in the household

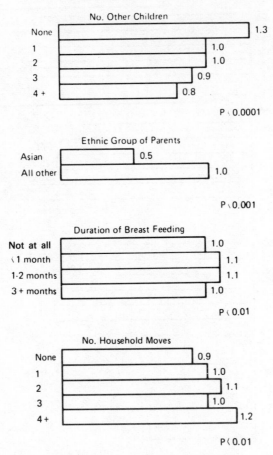

FIG. 6.6 Factors independently associated with sleeping difficulty at 5 (Relative Risks)

(13.8%). There was an association between the two symptoms: of the 1727 children with feeding difficulties as a baby, 670 (39%) had also had sleeping problems at that time.

The epidemiological associations with infant feeding problems are, as we shall show, very similar in many respects to those found for infant sleeping difficulties. Nevertheless, there are important differences. There were no differences between the sexes, but this time children of low birthweight were almost twice as likely to have feeding difficulties as a baby, compared with heavier infants (Fig. 6.7).

Not surprisingly, there was a strong association with breast feeding—the children who had been breast fed for 3 months, or more, were only half as likely to have had infant feeding problems as the rest of the population (Fig. 6.7). The reason is, of course, obvious. If there are no

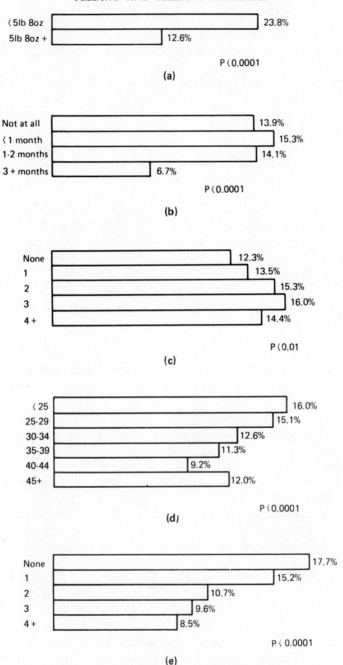

FIG. 6.7 Proportion of children reported to have had feeding problems as a baby by (a) birthweight, (b) duration of breast feeding, (c) number of household moves, (d) maternal age, (e) number of other children in the household

problems found in feeding by the breast, then the mother is more likely to continue breast feeding. If she is having difficulty feeding by the breast, she is more likely to change to the bottle. Overall, of children whose mothers had attempted to breast feed, 12.5% were said to have had feeding difficulties, compared with 13.9% of the children who had never been breast fed.

There were no differences between the regions, with the type of neighbourhood or the number of cigarettes smoked by the parents. There was, again, an association with the number of household moves. As can be seen in Fig. 6.7, children who had lived in the same house all their lives were less likely to have been said to have had feeding difficulties as a baby.

Although there were no differences with other social indicators such as social class and parental situation, the chance of the child having had feeding problems as a baby varied with the age of the mother—in general, the younger she was the more likely was the child to have had feeding problems.

The pattern seen with both infant sleeping and crying problems, in association with the number of children in the household, was also found for infant feeding problems (Fig. 6.7). 'Only' children and those with only one sibling were much more likely to have had such difficulties than children from larger families. Once again, it was the number of *older* children in the household that had the most association.

Indirect standardisation showed that the associations between infant feeding problems and both maternal age and household moves were the result of the strong association with the numbers of children in the household. Thus, there were only three factors that were independently associated with infant feeding problems: low birthweight, number of other children and. duration of breast feeding (Fig. 6.8).

By the age of 5, over a third (36.4%) of children were said to have eating or appetite problems, but in only 2.1% of children were there said to be severe problems. Two-thirds of the children with problems were said to be 'faddy', and most of the remainder were described as not eating enough. Only 1% of children in the study were thought to over-eat (Table 6.3). There were no differences between the sexes in the overall prevalence of feeding problems or in the particular types of problem.

In Fig. 6.3 we showed that children with sleeping problems when a baby, were twice as likely to have sleeping problems at 5, and six times more likely to have severe sleeping problems. There was also a relationship between infant feeding problems and the presence of feeding difficulties at 5—but this was not of the same magnitude (Fig. 6.9). Children said to have had feeding problems as a baby were only 44% more likely to have any feeding problems at 5, and only twice as likely to

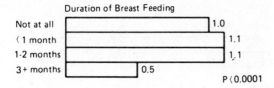

Duration of Breast Feeding

Not at all	1.0
< 1 month	1.1
1-2 months	1.1
3+ months	0.5

P < 0.0001

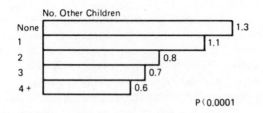

No. Other Children

None	1.3
1	1.1
2	0.8
3	0.7
4 +	0.6

P < 0.0001

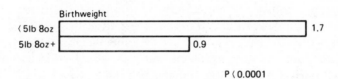

Birthweight

< 5lb 8oz	1.7
5lb 8oz +	0.9

P < 0.0001

FIG. 6.8 Factors independently associated with reported feeding problems as a baby (Relative Risk)

TABLE 6.3   Proportion of children with various types of eating or appetite problem by sex

Feeding problem*	Male	Female	All
Does not eat enough	769	751	1520
	(11.4%)	(12.0%)	(11.7%)
Over-eats	66	78	144
	(1.0%)	(1.2%)	(1.1%)
Faddy	1634	1515	3149
	(24.2%)	(24.1%)	(24.2%)
Other problem	72	83	155
	(1.1%)	(1.3%)	(1.2%)
All with problems	2412	2328	4740
	(35.7%)	(37.1%)	(36.4%)
No feeding problems	4347	3952	8299
	(64.3%)	(62.9%)	(63.6%)
All known	6759	6280	13,039
	(100.0%)	(100.0%)	(100.0%)

*Categories not mutually exclusive.

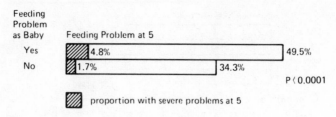

Fɪɢ. 6.9 Proportion of children with feeding problems at 5 according to history of feeding problems as a baby

have severe difficulties. The relationship was most pronounced in the group who, at 5, were described as not eating enough (Table 6.4).

Unlike the problems with feeding in the early months, the children of low birthweight were at no greater risk of eating or appetite problems at the age of 5. There was no difference either with the duration of breast feeding, the number of household moves, the type of neighbourhood, or parental smoking history. There was a statistically significant regional variation though, with Scotland (31.1%) and Wales (33.0%) having the lowest prevalences of problems and East Anglia (38.8%) and the North-West (38.9%) having the highest rates (Fig. 6.10).

There were no significant differences with maternal age or parental situation. Although there were significantly fewer children with feeding problems in social class V. (Fig. 6.11), there was no evidence of a linear

TABLE 6.4 Type of eating or appetite problem present at 5 by whether there had been feeding difficulties as a baby

| | Feeding problem as baby | | |
	Yes	No	All known
Does not eat enough	331	1174	1505
	(19.3%)	(10.5%)	(11.7%)
Over-eating	26	115	141
	(1.5%)	(1.0%)	(1.1%)
Faddy	514	2583	3097
	(30.0%)	(23.2%)	(24.1%)
Other problem	30	122	152
	(1.8%)	(1.1%)	(1.2%)
All with feeding problems	848	3822	4670
	(49.5%)	(34.5%)	(36.4%)
No feeding problem	866	7310	8176
	(50.5%)	(65.7%)	(63.6%)
All known	1714	11,132	12,846
	(100.0%)	(100.0%)	(100.0%)

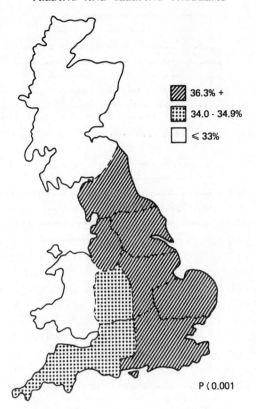

36.3% +

34.0 - 34.9%

≤ 33%

P ⟨ 0.001

FIG. 6.10 Children with feeding problems at age 5 by region

trend with social class. This exactly mirrored the finding for finicky children reported by Newson and Newson (1968).

There were significant differences by ethnic group due entirely to an excess of West Indian children with eating problems (Fig. 6.11). The excess was apparent both among children described as not eating enough (29% of West Indian children, 11% of the rest of the population), and among those who over-ate (4% of West Indians, 1% of the rest).

The strongest association was found, however, with the number of children in the household. The more children there were, the less likely was there to be a current eating or appetite problem.

Indirect standardisation showed that the regional and social class differences were due to their inter-relationships with the size of the family. The only significant factors independently associated with feeding problems at 5 were thus the number of other children in the family and whether the parents were West Indian (Fig. 6.12).

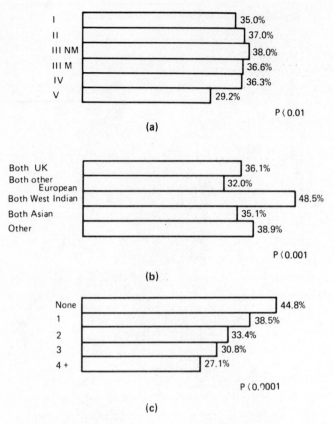

FIG. 6.11 Proportion of 5-year-old children with feeding problems by (a) social class, (b) ethnic group of parents, (c) number of other children in the household

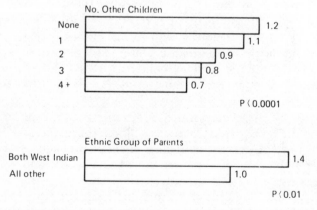

FIG. 6.12 Factors independently associated with eating or appetite problems at 5 (Relative Risk)

Other Health and Behaviour Problems

The question as to whether feeding and sleeping problems are meaningful in relation to other health outcomes is addressed in later chapters. They show that feeding problems as a baby were associated with a large number of other findings (Fig. 6.13). Predominant among these were associations with stomach aches or vomiting at the age of 5. The feeding problems encountered early in life may well have been associated with factors such as colic which continued during the child's pre-school life. In retrospect, children with disorders of vision and speech, those with headaches or respiratory symptoms, were all at increased risk of having had early feeding difficulties. It is impossible to determine from our data whether these problems were objectively associated. It is quite possible that when a child has a variety of symptoms throughout his life, early problems will be recalled more readily. Only a study collecting data prospectively could attempt to answer such a question.

In contrast with the associations found with early feeding problems, those current at 5 were only related to four other conditions (Fig. 6.14).

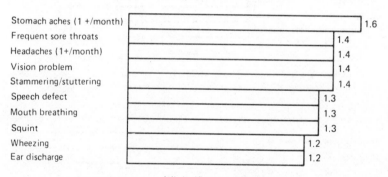

(all significant at 1% level)

FIG. 6.13 Risk of other health outcomes in children with feeding problems as a baby (Relative Risks after standardisation for sex and social class)

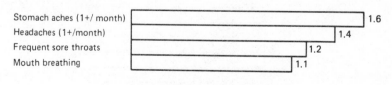

(all significant at 1% level)

FIG. 6.14 Risk of other health outcomes in children with eating or appetite problems at 5 (Relative Risks after standardisation for sex and social class)

Two of these are concerned with pain in the gastro-intestinal tract and may be responsible for feeding reluctance.

The pattern of associations with infant sleeping problems differs again (Fig. 6.15). Here the significant risks are mainly associated with the respiratory tract.

By the age of 5, conditions associated with sleeping problems had changed (Fig. 6.15). Allergic disorders and painful conditions tended to predominate. Children who had had hospital admissions were not affected by sleeping problems, but like Richman (1981) we found an association with previous accidental injury.

Feeding problems, whether as a baby or at 5, were not related to wetting or soiling behaviour at 5 (Table 6.5). In spite of the fact that enuresis is thought by many to be a symptom of sleep disorder (Anders and Weinstein, 1972), we found only 20% more children than expected

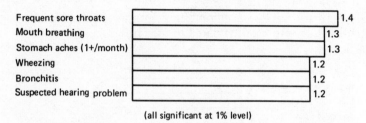

Fig. 6.15 Risk of other health outcomes in children with a history of sleeping problems as a baby (Relative Risks after standardisation for sex and social class)

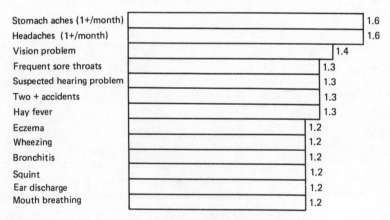

Fig. 6.16 Risk of other health outcomes in children with sleeping problems at 5 (Relative Risks after standardisation for sex and social class)

TABLE 6.5 Children with feeding and sleeping problems, who also had wetting and soiling problems, compared with numbers expected after standardising by sex and social class

| | Sleeping as a baby | | Sleeping at 5 | |
	Observed	R. Risk	Observed	R. Risk
Wets bed at least once a week	196	1.0	402	1.2**
Wets by day	178	1.0	443	1.4****
Soils	83	1.1	184	1.4****

| | Feeding as a baby | | Feeding at 5 | |
	Observed	R. Risk	Observed	R. Risk
Wets bed at least once a week	215	1.2*	463	0.9
Wets by day	194	1.1	502	1.1
Soils	84	1.2	222	1.1
Sleeping problem as a baby	670	2.9****	780	1.2****
Sleeping problem at 5	575	1.4****	1529	1.3****

to be both eneuretic and to have a sleep problem. Interestingly, there was a stronger relationship between sleep disorders and both daytime wetting and soiling.

Conclusions

1. Children with sleeping difficulties in early infancy are more likely to be first or second born, to have been breast fed for a short period of time, and to be male.
2. Those who have sleeping problems at 5 were twice as likely to have had sleeping problems as a baby. They, too, were more likely to have been breast fed for a short time, and to be first or second born. Children of Asian parents were significantly less likely to have had sleeping problems.
3. Feeding problems in early infancy were more prevalent among low birthweight babies. Children with older siblings and those who had been breast fed for at least 3 months were significantly less likely to have had the problem.
4. Feeding difficulty at 5 was also least in families where there were older siblings. West Indian children were more likely to be reported as having feeding problems.

CHAPTER 7

Temper tantrums and other behaviour problems

by JEAN GOLDING and D. RUSH

Introduction

Few studies have attempted to estimate the prevalence of behaviour problems in British pre-school children. Richman, Stevenson and Graham (1975) found a prevalence of 7% moderate or severe and 15% mild behaviour problems in 3-year-olds in a London borough. Jenkins, Bax and Hart (1980) asked mothers of 4½-year-olds living in North London whether they were worried about their child's behaviour. Doctors assessed their replies, and the children themselves. In all, 7% of the children were judged to have moderate or severe behaviour problems. The authors noted that the commonest complaints included the occurrence of temper tantrums.

Temper Tantrums

A temper tantrum is usually considered to be a sign of frustration in the child—the tantrum itself does little, however, to solve the problem against which the protest is being made. The noise produced can be at such a pitch that the mother is likely to be driven to anger herself. If in a public place, parental anxiety and embarrassment can compound the issue, and the long-term results can be a further sundering of a possibly already compromised parent–child relationship.

In the present study, in contrast with feeding and sleeping problems which showed relatively little variation with the social background or physical environment, we shall show that temper tantrums vary markedly across different population groups.

On the self-completion questionnaire, the mother was asked to state the frequency with which her child had had temper tantrums within the past year. Of the 12,324 who replied, 59% declared that the child had not had a tantrum, 18% that there had been tantrums, but not as often as once a month, a further 10% had had tantrums, but not as often as once a week, and 13% had had tantrums at least once a week.

Overall, more boys were reported as having temper tantrums than girls, but as Fig. 7.1 shows, this was marked only for children having them frequently (at least once a week): 15% of boys compared with 10% of girls had tantrums as often as this. Indeed, preliminary analysis indicated that it was this group of children that showed most marked associations with the other factors that we shall be discussing. For the sake of brevity, therefore, we shall confine our attention to the group of children, who had had a temper tantrum at least once a week.

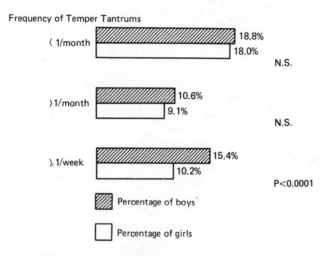

FIG. 7.1 Proportion of children said to have had temper tantrums in past year by sex of child

Parental factors

There was a U-shaped variation with maternal age—the risk to children of both young and elderly mothers being greatest (Fig. 7.2). There was also a marked increase in prevalence of frequent temper tantrums in all instances where the child was living with a single parent (whether supported or not), and where the household included a step-parent (Fig. 7.2). Almost one in five children in these situations had this history, compared with one in eight of the children who either lived with their natural parents, or who were adopted or fostered.

A very strong trend was shown with social class (Fig. 7.2), the children from the manual social classes being at far greater risk of temper tantrums than those from the non-manual classes. Indeed, there was a four-fold difference in rates between social classes I and V.

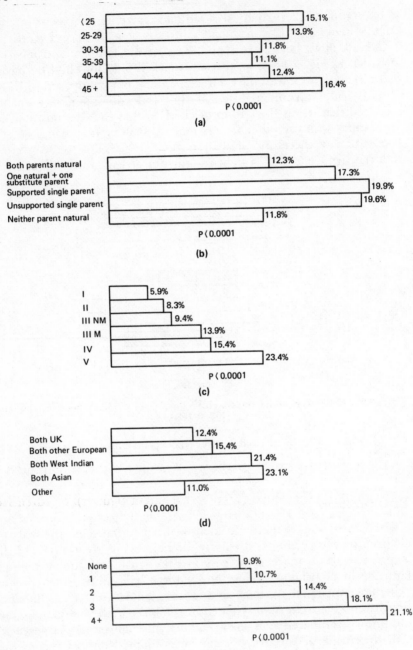

Fig. 7.2 Proportion of children having temper tantrums at least once a week by (a) maternal age, (b) parental situation, (c) social class, (d) ethnic group of parents, (e) number of other children in the household

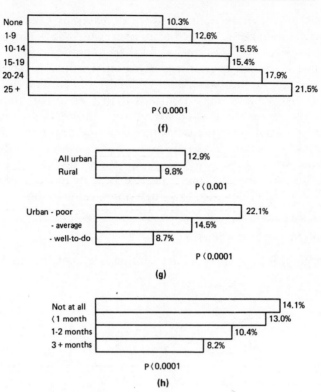

FIG. 7.2 *continued* (f) maternal smoking habit, (g) type of neighbourhood, (h) duration of breast feeding

There was no increase in the risk of frequent temper tantrums if the mother had worked during the child's life, but there was a marked variation with the ethnic group of the parent figure(s). Children from West Indian or Asian backgrounds had almost twice the risk as children with parents from the United Kingdom.

The environment

Unlike feeding and sleeping problems, which were negatively associated with the number of children in the household, there was a strong positive association with temper tantrums (Fig. 7.2). Proportionately, twice as many chidren from households with at least four other children had frequent tantrums, compared with 'only' children or those where there was only one sibling.

As shown with bed-wetting, there were strong trends with maternal smoking. Mothers who were very heavy smokers (twenty-five or more cigarettes per day) were almost twice as likely to have a child with frequent temper tantrums as the mother who was a non-smoker.

The number of times the child had moved house was of no importance in the aetiology of frequent temper tantrums, but there were significant geographical associations. Children in rural areas appeared to be far less likely to have tantrums than their urban counterparts. Within urban areas there was a strong trend in prevalence, with one in five children from 'poor' areas having this history compared with one in seven children from 'average' and one in eleven children from 'well-to-do' areas. As shown in Fig. 7.3, there was a large continuous area, comprising the Midlands, the North of England, Yorkshire and Humberside, where particularly high rates were found.

Birthweight and breast feeding

Children of low birthweight were at increased risk: the prevalence of

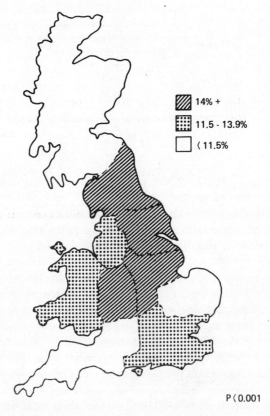

14% +

11.5 - 13.9%

< 11.5%

P < 0.001

Fig. 7.3 Proportion of children with temper tantrums at least once a week, by region

frequent temper tantrums among this group was 16% compared with 12.5% among children who had been heavier babies. There was a strong negative association with duration of breast feeding (Fig. 7.2). Altogether, the prevalence of frequent temper tantrums was 11% among children who had ever been breast fed, compared with 14% of children who had always had artificial feeds. The longer the mother had continued to breast feed, the less likely was the child to have had frequent tantrums at the age of 5.

Inter-relationships

Clearly, it is likely that certain relationships described above have arisen as the result of others. In fact the U-shaped association with maternal age was due to the fact that both young and old mothers were more likely to live in those urban areas where temper tantrums were common. In similar ways it was possible to 'explain' associations with the ethnic group of the parents, duration of breast feeding, birthweight, and the presence of a step-parent. The remaining significant factors are shown in Fig. 7.4.

The crucial factors independently associated with increased risk of frequent temper tantrums appear to be low social class or absence of father figure, three or more other children in the household, residence in Yorkshire, the Midlands or the South-East of England, or in a poor urban area. Mothers smoking heavily are especially likely to have a child with frequent temper tantrums—but whether either is directly a consequence of the other is impossible to say from these data.

Wetting and soiling, feeding, sleeping and infant problems

There was an increased prevalence of temper tantrums among children exhibiting any of the forms of incontinence: if they soiled, their risk of frequent temper tantrums was increased by two-fifths, and if they wet their beds at least once a week the rate was increased by three-quarters.

As we showed in Chapter 5, boys are more likely to soil and wet the bed than girls. They are also 50% more at risk of having frequent temper tantrums. Because of this, it is anticipated that more children would be expected to have two of the conditions together than a crude computation from prevalence data would indicate. Similarly, since bed-wetting shows the same trend with social class, with relatively high prevalences in social class V, one would expect there to be more children who both wet the bed and have temper tantrums for this reason alone.

Standardisation for sex and social class does reduce, but does not obliterate, the size of the associations: children with any type of

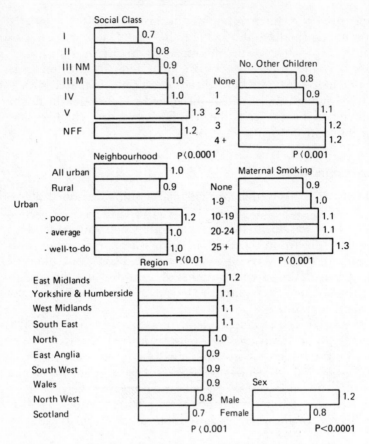

Fig. 7.4 Independent Relative Risks of frequent temper tantrums

incontinence are at least 40% more likely to have temper tantrums than their peers of identical sex and social class (Table 7.1). Children reported as having crying, feeding or sleeping problems as a baby were also more likely to be reported as having frequent temper tantrums. The Relative Risk was highest for those children who were said to have had infant crying problems (1.5). Positive associations were also found among children with current feeding or sleeping problems—their likelihood of having frequent temper tantrums was between 20% and 40% in excess of that expected. As we shall show, however, far more dramatic associations were found, with most of the other behaviour characteristics of the child.

Other Behaviour Problems

The mother was asked, on her self-completion questionnaire, to put a

TABLE 7.1 Number of children reported to have both frequent temper tantrums (at least once a week) and feeding, sleeping or incontinence problems compared with the number expected after standardisation for social class and sex of child

Reported behaviour	Number Also With Frequent Temper Observed	Tantrums Expected	Observed Expected
Wets bed at least once a week	275	188.6	1.5*****
Wets by day	212	155.4	1.4*****
Soils	107	76.1	1.4****
Feeding problems at 5	673	564.7	1.2*****
Sleeping difficulties at 5	539	393.2	1.4*****
Feeding problems as a baby	278	209.4	1.3*****
Sleeping problems as a baby	292	219.5	1.3*****
Crying problems as a baby	333	227.8	1.5*****

cross against each of nineteen statements according to whether they 'certainly applied, applied somewhat, or did not apply' to the study child. The numbers of replies to each description are shown in Table 7.2.

The most infrequent of the descriptions was that of twitches, mannerisms, or tics which were said to apply certainly to less than 1% of the population of 5-year-olds. This can be compared with over 2% who replied positively to a similar question in the 7-year-old follow-up of the 1958 cohort (Davie, Butler and Goldstein, 1972). This would suggest that either the prevalence of such symptoms has decreased between the cohorts, or that the stresses encountered between the ages of 5 and 7 result in an increase in the prevalence of these signs. In contrast, the replies to the questions denoting aspects of hyperactivity (restless, squirmy or fidgety, unable to settle) resulted in very similar rates to those found in the preceding cohort. Similar rates were also found for the children described as irritable.

Direct comparison is not advisable for any of the other items as they were not asked in an absolutely identical manner in the two cohorts. Nevertheless, there would appear to have been fewer mothers in 1975 reporting that their 5-year-old children were rather solitary, miserable, or tearful, often worried, or frequently fighting with other children than did mothers of 7-year-olds in 1965. On the other hand, similar proportions were said to bite their nails, and rather more of the 5-year-olds were said to suck their thumbs and destroy their own or other's belongings. These are probably all age rather than cohort effects.

In order to see ways in which the behaviour characteristics could be grouped together, factor analyses were carried out. The results indicated that there were three interesting groups:

The difficult child: characterised as destroying belongings, frequently fighting, taking things belonging to others, being disobedient, telling lies, and bullying. Such a child is also inclined to be irritable and to have frequent temper tantrums.

The troubled child: is often worried, rather solitary, fearful or afraid, fussy or over-particular. This child is likely also to be described as miserable or tearful.

The hyperactive child: not unexpectedly is likely to be described as very restless, squirmy or fidgety, and unable to settle.

In order to assess whether children who fell into one of these categories were more likely than expected to display the characteristics of the other groups, the inter-group correlation coefficients were calculated. A correlation coefficient of 1 would mean that all children in one group would also be in the other; a coefficient of -1 would imply that no children in one group were included in the other, and 0 would

TABLE 7.2 Description of behaviour as applied to the study child

Description	Doesn't apply %	Applies somewhat %	Certainly applies %	All replied N = 100.0%
Often destroys own or others' belongings	77.0	18.8	4.2	12,977
Frequently fights with other children	63.8	32.0	4.2	12,991
Irritable. Is quick to 'fly off the handle'	54.3	34.2	11.5	12,985
Sometimes takes things belonging to others	79.5	18.6	1.9	12,979
Is often disobedient	30.4	60.1	9.5	12,984
Often tells lies	66.0	31.8	2.2	12,991
Bullies other children	84.5	14.0	1.5	13,000
Often worried, worries about many things	65.1	29.4	5.5	12,966
Tends to do things on his own—rather solitary	55.0	35.8	9.2	12,960
Often appears miserable, unhappy, tearful or distressed	77.6	19.9	2.5	12,983
Tends to be fearful or afraid of new things or new situations	64.0	29.4	6.6	12,985
Is fussy or over-particular	59.5	31.2	9.3	12,979
Very restless. Often running about or jumping up and down, hardly ever still	31.1	40.0	28.9	12,985
Is squirmy or fidgety	56.8	31.6	11.6	12,892
Cannot settle to anything for more than a few moments	65.4	27.6	7.0	12,983
Not much liked by other children	94.1	4.5	1.4	12,962
Has twitches, mannerisms or tics of face or body	96.2	3.1	0.7	12,964
Frequently bites nails or fingers	71.2	17.4	11.4	13,001
Frequently sucks thumb or finger	71.0	11.9	17.1	13,006

mean that no more were in both than would be expected. The actual correlation coefficients were:

Difficult × troubled: 0.28
Difficult × hyperactive: 0.47
Troubled × hyperactive: 0.22

These may be interpreted as showing that there is some relationship between all three groups: children with one type of 'deviant' behaviour being more likely than expected to exhibit one of the others. The closest association was between the 'difficult' behaviours and those denoting hyperactivity.

Sex differences

In the rest of this chapter we shall discuss only those children described by their mothers as certainly having the problem. There are major differences between the sexes in many of the characteristics (Fig. 7.5). Boys were far more likely than girls to exhibit all the characteristics of the 'difficult' child—being especially more at risk of fighting and destructive behaviour.

Boys were also more likely to exhibit hyperactive behaviour. There was little to choose between the sexes in regard to the symptoms indicative of the 'troubled' child—apart from the fact that girls were significantly more likely to be described as fussy or over-particular. There was also a preponderance of girls with, what were once called, 'bad habits'—i.e. thumb sucking and nail biting. Similar sex variation has been reported from America (Macfarlane, 1954).

Social class differences

As in the 1958 study, there were strong associations with social class for each of the 'certain' descriptions (Fig. 7.6). There was an increasing prevalence with falling social class in all but one behaviour problem: for thumb sucking, the reported prevalence in social class I was twice that in social class V. When a similar pattern was found in the 1958 cohort, it was suggested (Davie, Butler and Goldstein, 1972), that thumb sucking might be associated inversely with the prevalence of using dummies or comforters. Unfortunately, data on the use of dummies were not collected in this survey, but others have shown that the use of dummies is more prevalent in the lower social classes (Newson and Newson, 1968).

Relationship with temper tantrums

In order to assess whether children with frequent temper tantrums

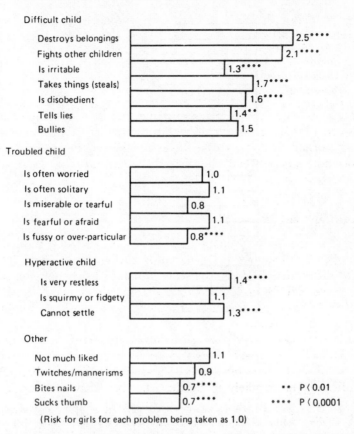

FIG. 7.5 Ratio of prevalence of behaviour problems in boys compared with that in girls

exhibit the other behaviour characteristics more often than expected by chance, it is obviously important to standardise by both sex and social class. The results are shown in Table 7.3 and it is clear that any child with temper tantrums has over three times the risk of each of the characteristics of a 'difficult' child, about twice the risk of a hyperactive characteristic, and 80% more likely to have a description typical of a 'troubled' child. The only attribute that did not occur among children with tantrums more often than would be expected was thumb sucking.

Discussion

Analysis and interpretation of the behavioural characteristics described in the latter part of this chapter is fraught with difficulty. Maternal assessments of these factors are subjective and likely to be influenced by the mother's physical and mental state, her affection for

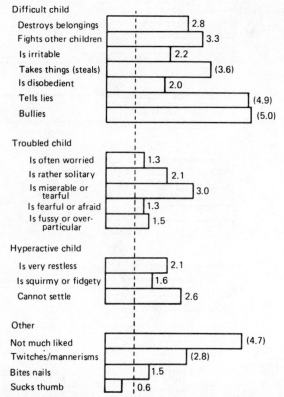

FIG. 7.6 Ratio of prevalence of behaviour problems in the lower social classes (IV and V) compared with that in the upper social classes (I and II)

the child, and ways in which his behaviour differs from that of his siblings. In comparison, information on events and the frequency with which they happen is likely to be far more reliable—especially if these events are such that they are immediately recognisable and unlikely to be forgotten or ignored. Such items include temper tantrums as well as the wetting and soiling histories described in Chapter 5.

Temper tantrums and other behaviour traits have been shown to be more frequent in the lower social classes in other studies (Newson and Newson, 1968; Davie, Butler and Goldstein, 1972). The Newsons pointed out that some of the associations may be related to parental behaviour. For example, in their Nottingham study the mothers in the lower social classes were more likely to lie themselves, they were also more liable to tell their own child, if hit by another, to retaliate and hit that child back.

TABLE 7.3   Number of children reported to have both frequent temper tantrums (at least once a week) and other behaviour characteristics compared with the number expected after standardisation for social class and sex of child

Behaviour trait	Number also having temper tantrums			Total obs.
	Obs.	Exp.	Obs./Exp.	Total exp.
Difficult child				
Destroys belongings	238	79.1	3.0	
Fights other children	236	80.4	2.9	
Is irritable	710	203.3	3.5	
Takes things (steals)	112	35.3	3.2	3.1
Is disobedient	498	168.7	3.0	
Tells lies	105	41.6	2.5	
Bullies	90	28.9	3.1	
Troubled child				
Is often worried	168	88.6	1.9	
Is rather solitary	263	158.2	1.7	
Is ᵢmiserable or tearful	131	43.9	3.0	1.8
Is fearful or afraid	190	107.8	1.8	
Is fussy or over-particular	260	150.5	1.7	
Hyperactive child				
Is very restless	861	492.7	1.7	
Is squirmy or fidgety	423	192.5	2.2	1.9
Cannot settle	282	124.3	2.3	
Miscellaneous				
Not much liked	59	25.7	2.3	
Has twitches/mannerisms	25	12.3	2.0	1.3
Bites nails	262	180.0	1.5	
Sucks thumb	253	243.4	1.0	

Another factor thought to be of particular importance in the aetiology of temper tantrums is an inability to communicate. In Chapter 8 we shall be looking at the way in which the children who stammer and stutter, and those who have other speech difficulties fare in this respect. We shall show that children with temper tantrums are indeed significantly more likely to have speech disorders. These associations are small, however, when compared with those with headaches and stomach aches. Figure 7.7 shows the size of the significant associations with headaches and stomach aches. It can be seen that children with either of these symptoms are over twice as likely to have temper tantrums at least once a week.

The findings in the present study of positive associations with maternal smoking and urban living raise many questions concerning the effect of pollutants on the child on the one hand—and the effect of

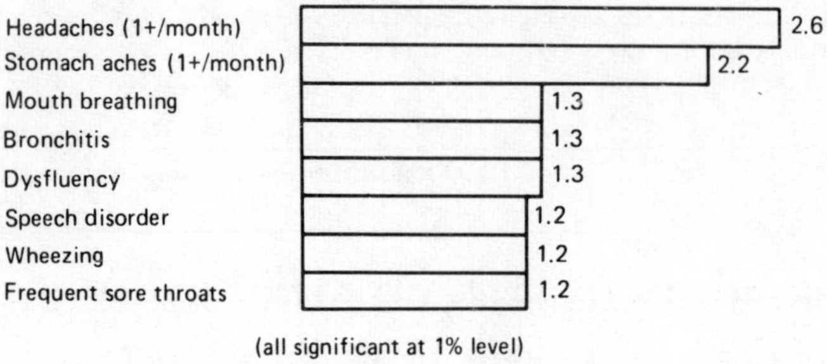

Headaches (1+/month) — 2.6
Stomach aches (1+/month) — 2.2
Mouth breathing — 1.3
Bronchitis — 1.3
Dysfluency — 1.3
Speech disorder — 1.2
Wheezing — 1.2
Frequent sore throats — 1.2

(all significant at 1% level)

FIG. 7.7 Risk of other health outcomes in children with temper tantrums at least once a week (Relative Risks after standardisation for sex and social class)

stress on the other. These are topics to which we shall return throughout this volume.

Conclusions

1. Frequent temper tantrums are independently associated with the male sex, low social class, lack of a father figure, residence in a poor urban environment, with the number of siblings the child has, and the number of cigarettes the mother smokes. There was a strong regional variation in prevalence.

2. Children with temper tantrums are more likely to have other adverse behaviour traits, especially those associated with the difficult child.

CHAPTER 8

Disorders of speech and language

by MARY PATERSON and JEAN GOLDING

Introduction

Speech defects present in the 7-year-old child have been shown not only to be closely correlated with poor educational attainment at that time (Butler, Peckham and Sheridan, 1973), they also have a poor prognosis for later attainment (Sheridan and Peckham, 1978). Barely intelligible speech may have other drawbacks which are psychological rather than intellectual. The child who cannot communicate easily is liable to suffer from symptoms of frustration which may result in severe behaviour problems.

The aetiology of speech delay or disorder is unclear. Shaw (1977) suggested that babies who were irritable and/or cried excessively were at increased risk of language delay. She suggested that the baby's behaviour results in damage to the bond with the mother, who subsequently becomes less responsive to the infant's needs.

Dysfluency

Stammering is the name normally reserved for speech dysfluency which exhibits characteristics such as phoneme, syllable and/or word repetitions, sound prolongations and/or difficulty in initiating utterances.

As very young children often exhibit this type of behaviour in the course of developing language and practising its use, it would be wrong to label these as stammerers at this stage. It is true, that in some cases, early dysfluent behaviour can lead to stammering later, but it is often felt that treating and drawing attention to 'normal dysfluency' early in life may exacerbate the problem. This is often why children with dysfluent speech are not usually given therapy until around the age of 7 or 8. Nevertheless, they may attend a speech therapist so that their parents may be counselled and the situation reviewed from time to time.

Speech dysfluency is thought to have a multiple aetiology, combining psychological, environmental and physiological components. There is also substantial evidence for a genetic involvement—the concordance among monozygotic twins being very high compared with dizygotic twins (Chakravartti *et al.*, 1979).

In the present study the health visitor asked the mother whether the child had 'ever had a stammer or stutter or other difficulty with speech' and for each was given the options: 'No', 'Yes in past but not now', 'Yes now—mild', 'Yes now—severe'. Throughout the rest of this chapter we shall refer to the children reported to have stammered or stuttered as having speech dysfluency. Altogether 6% of the children were said to have had this condition—a similar proportion to that recorded for the 7-year-olds in the 1958 cohort (Butler, Peckham and Sheridan, 1973). Of these, half were no longer suffering from the problem by the age of 5. Of the remainder, the vast majority (95%) were described as mild.

The boys in the 1958 cohort were almost twice as likely as the girls to have a history of speech dysfluency by the age of 7 (Davie, Butler and Goldstein, 1972). The present study is similar (Fig. 8.1). There were differences between the sexes too in the persistence and severity of the problem. Of the boys who had such a history, 52% still had the problem, whereas only in 43% of the girls had the problem persisted. Among the eighteen children who had severe current dysfluency, thirteen were boys.

Children of low birthweight were not at increased risk of speech dysfluency, nor was breast feeding associated with the onset of the condition. There was no evidence of a significant trend with social class, but there were statistically significant associations with maternal age (Fig. 8.1). The prevalence of dysfluency was greatest among children of the youngest group of mothers.

There were no differences with the parental smoking habits or between the different ethnic groups—nor did the prevalence of speech dysfluency differ among the group of children whose mothers had been employed. There were significant differences with parental situation though, the greatest prevalence being found among the small group of children who had been adopted or fostered.

'Only' children were far less likely to have had dysfluent speech than children with siblings. Although there was no trend, in overall proportions with such a history, between children with just one sibling and those with four or more; the children with fewer siblings were more likely to have grown out of the habit. In Fig. 8.1 it can be seen that the number of younger siblings is much more strongly associated than the number of older siblings. It is thus possible that the speech dysfluency might often have arisen on the advent of a new baby in the household.

Traumatic events in the form of household moves were also associated with dysfluent speech (Fig. 8.1). The child who had moved more than once had a higher prevalence, especially of current dysfluency.

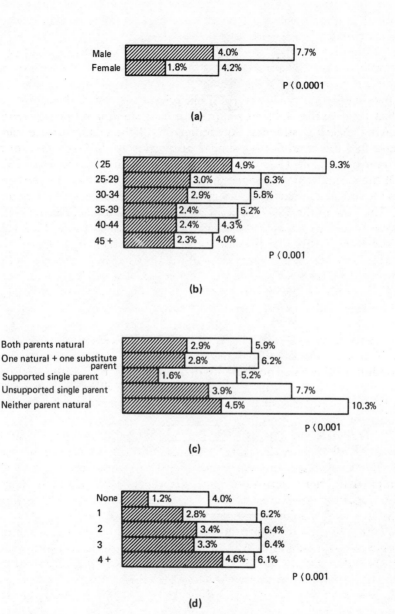

FIG. 8.1 Proportion of children with a history of speech dysfluency (stammer/stutter) by (a) sex of child, (b) maternal age, (c) parental situation, (d) number of other children in the household (*continued on next page*)

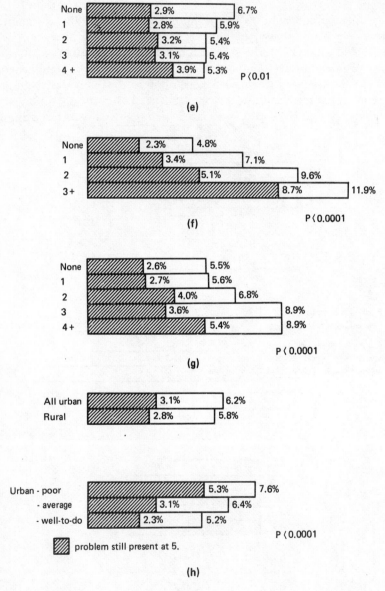

Fig. 8.1 *continued* (e) number of older children in household, (f) number of younger children in household, (g) number of household moves, (h) type of neighbourhood

There were no significant differences between the regions, nor did the prevalence in urban areas differ significantly from that in rural areas. Nevertheless, within urban areas there were profound differences, with highest rates in the poor urban areas. The variation was especially pronounced for children with current dysfluency.

Since dysfluency that resolves in the early years is almost considered part of normal development, we confined the indirect standardisation process to analyse information pertaining to dysfluency present at the age of 5. Figure 8.2 illustrates the statistically significant findings. The highest relative risks were associated with maternal youth, having four

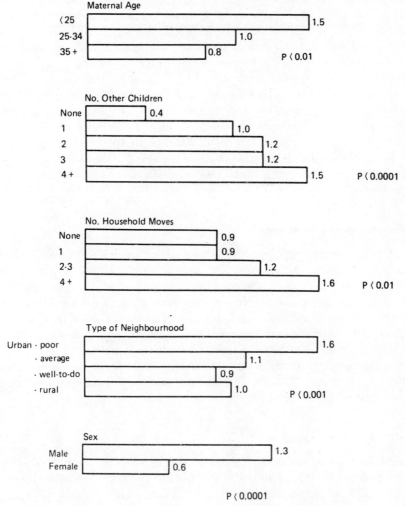

Fig. 8.2 Relative Risks independently associated with current dysfluency

or more siblings, moving house at least four times, and residing in a poor urban neighbourhood. There was no significant association with parental situation after maternal age and the number of siblings had been taken into account.

Speech and Language Disorders

The term 'other speech difficulty' used in this survey covers a wide range of problems, including articulation problems, either due to developmental delay, or of organic aetiology, such as deafness, cleft palate, cerebral palsy, or macroglossia. Although it was only speech difficulties that were to be recorded, it became clear that there were quite a number of the children for whom language problems had been described. In the rest of this chapter we shall refer to all children said to have had 'other speech difficulties' as having 'speech problems'.

Ten percent of the children were said to have, or to have had, speech problems and three-quarters of these were still present when the child was 5. As many as 113 children were said to have severe defects. Although there was overlap between the categories 'stammering/ stuttering' and 'other speech disorders', only 89 children had a history of both disorders (i.e. only 11% of children with speech dysfluency and 6.5% of children with speech problems'). Table 8.1 shows that only eight children currently had both severe dysfluency and severe speech problems.

Severe speech problems

Of the 113 children reported to have severe speech problems, 35 were also reported as being mentally handicapped. In all, eight of the children had Down's Syndrome, two were reported to be autistic, five had cerebral palsy and twelve were reported as having other congenital malformations. Five children had clefts of lip and/or palate and a small group (8) were reported to be both mentally and physically handi-capped. In all 83% (92 of the 113 children) had both speech and language problems while only 19 children had speech problems alone. (In a further two children we had insufficient information to ascertain the type of problem.)

Mild speech problems

In contrast with the children with severe problems, the majority of those with mild difficulty had speech problems alone (65%) and only a third had speech difficulties in association with language problems. Eighteen percent of the children with mild problems had dental

TABLE 8.1 Numbers of children with speech dysfluency (stammer or stutter) by the numbers with speech problems

Speech dysfluency	Speech problems					
	None recorded	Yes in past	Yes now mild	Yes now severe	Not known	All
None recorded	11,054	332	839	99	3	12,327
Yes—in past	371	11	18	1	3	404
Yes now—mild	319	6	39	5	2	371
Yes now—severe	9	0	1	8	0	18
Not known	2	0	4	0	9	15
All	11,755	349	901	113	17	13,135

sigmatism (lisp) while in a further 5% from the 'mild' category there were physical causes for their problems (e.g. short frenulum linguae, macroglossia, small mandible).

The epidemiological associations found with speech problems

In spite of the multiple aetiologies, the proportion of children with speech problems as a whole did differ from the rest of the population in a number of respects. As with speech dysfluency, boys were more likely to have problems (Fig. 8.3).

Children who had been breast fed did not differ from those who had been bottle fed in their risk of speech problems. Low birthweight infants were at greater risk though (Fig. 8.3). The increase in risk was apparent among children who had had a problem in the past and those who were currently affected. The differences were most marked when the child had severe problems (2.2% of the 883 low-birthweight children, 0.8% of the remainder).

There were no differences with social class, parental situation or the maternal employment history. There were significant differences, however, with ethnic group of parents—children form West Indian and 'other' parentage being most likely to have had speech problems.

As with speech dysfluency, 'only' children were least likely to have speech problems. Children with two or more siblings were twice as likely to be affected (Fig. 8.3). For speech dysfluency we were able to show a marked association with the number of younger siblings, but there is no such effect here.

There was no geographic variation in the prevalence of speech problems. Unlike children with speech dysfluency those with speech or language problems were not found significantly more often among children who had moved house frequently or those resident in poor urban areas. There was, however, a significant association with maternal smoking; the more cigarettes she smoked, the more likely the child to have had speech problems.

Confining attention to children with speech problems present at 5 we found that the statistically significant factors related to the sex of the child, the number of other children in the household and the maternal smoking habit. Once these had been taken into account, there was no remaining significant association with birthweight, and ethnic group. The magnitude of the relative risks associated with the three factors is shown in Fig. 8.4.

Speech Therapy

In comparison with the cohort seen 12 years earlier, the proportion of

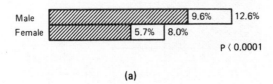

(a)

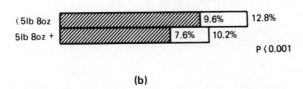

(b)

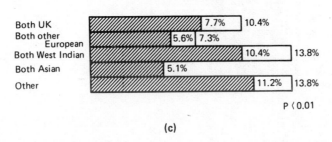

(c)

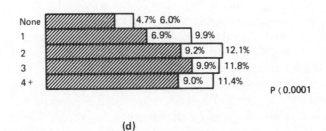

(d)

FIG. 8.3 Proportion of children with a history of speech problems by (a) sex of child, (b) birthweight, (c) ethnic group of parents, (d) number of other children in the household
(*continued on next page*)

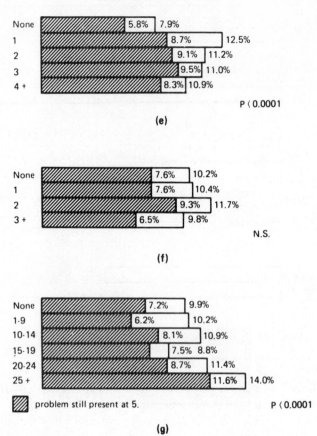

None ▨ 5.8% | 7.9%
1 ▨ 8.7% | 12.5%
2 ▨ 9.1% | 11.2%
3 ▨ 9.5% | 11.0%
4 + ▨ 8.3% | 10.9%

P ⟨ 0.0001

(e)

None ▨ 7.6% | 10.2%
1 ▨ 7.6% | 10.4%
2 ▨ 9.3% | 11.7%
3 + ▨ 6.5% | 9.8%

N.S.

(f)

None ▨ 7.2% | 9.9%
1-9 ▨ 6.2% | 10.2%
10-14 ▨ 8.1% | 10.9%
15-19 ▨ 7.5% 8.8%
20-24 ▨ 8.7% | 11.4%
25 + ▨ 11.6% | 14.0%

▨ problem still present at 5.

P ⟨ 0.0001

(g)

FIG. 8.3 *continued* (e) number older children in the household, (f) number of younger children in the household, (g) maternal smoking habit

children receiving speech therapy had greatly increased. Butler, Peckham and Sheridan (1973) report that by the age of 7, only one in forty of the 1958 cohort had seen a speech therapist. In our study, by the age of 5, one in twenty-three had been seen.

Nevertheless, of the 113 children with severe speech difficulties at 5, at least thirty-five (31%) had never seen a speech therapist. Among children with mild speech problems at 5, over 70% had never seen a speech therapist, and among children with speech dysfluency, 88% had not been seen.

Since children with speech problems and/or speech dysfluency are more likely to be male, it is not surprising (Fig. 8.5) that more boys than girls are referred for speech therapy.

Although children of low birthweight were only 25% (Fig. 8.3) more

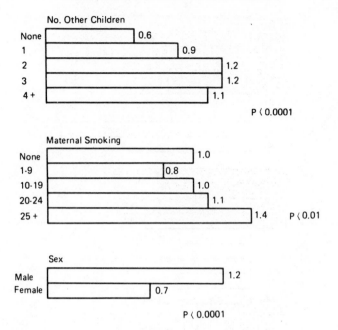

No. Other Children

None	0.6
1	0.9
2	1.2
3	1.2
4 +	1.1

P ⟨ 0.0001

Maternal Smoking

None	1.0
1-9	0.8
10-19	1.0
20-24	1.1
25 +	1.4	P ⟨ 0.01

Sex

| Male | 1.2 |
| Female | 0.7 |

P ⟨ 0.0001

FIG. 8.4 Relative Risks independently associated with current speech and language disorders

likely to have had speech problems, we found that these children were 50% more likely to have had speech therapy (Fig. 8.5).

The children of smoking mothers were not more likely to have been referred to a speech therapist, even though they had more speech problems. There was no association between uptake of speech therapy and maternal age, social class, parental situation, maternal employment or ethnic group of the parents. There was an association with the number of other children in the household which closely mirrored the prevalence of speech problems (Fig. 8.5), with children with two or three siblings being most likely to see a speech therapist. Children from larger families were less likely to see a therapist though, in spite of the fact that they had an equally high prevalence of problems.

In spite of the fact that there were no regional differences in the prevalence of dysfluency or speech problems, there was significant variation in the proportion of children who had seen a speech therapist (Fig. 8.6).

The highest rates were in London and the South-East of England (5.3%) with the West Midlands and South-West both with 4.8%, and Wales with 4.6%. The lowest rates were found in Yorkshire and Humberside (3.2%), Scotland (3.3%), the North-West of England (3.3%) and the East Midlands (3.4%).

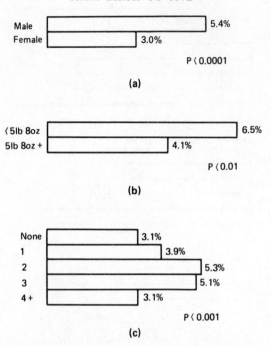

FIG. 8.5 Proportion of children seen by a speech therapist by (a) sex of child, (b) birthweight, (c) number of other children in the household

The 7-year follow-up of the 1958 cohort also found wide geographical differences in the use of speech therapy, and that regions with the poorest clinical speech test results were those least likely to have used speech therapists. At that time, the areas with lowest rates of speech therapy were the North, North-West, Yorkshire and Midlands. In our survey, a similar pattern prevailed even though the proportion receiving speech therapy in the later cohort had more than doubled in some of these areas.

The factors independently associated with whether a pre-school child received speech therapy in 1975 are illustrated in Fig. 8.7. The greatest risk is associated with low birthweight and is probably due to the fact that low birthweight infants are more likely to be screened regularly and, if problems exist, to attend multidisciplinary assessment centres.

Hearing Difficulty and Speech Problems

One of the prerequisites for the normal development of speech and language is adequate hearing. Yet of the children with speech problems a large proportion had never had any sort of hearing assessment. This varied from 24% of children with current severe problems to 36% of

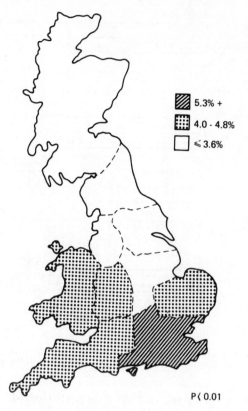

FIG. 8.6 Proportion of children seen by speech therapist by region

those with mild problems. Of those who did have hearing assessments, the majority were only screened once or twice.

Most of the screening was carried out by doctors and health visitors. Many of the children were screened in the first 12 months, when the type of screening carried out was a distraction test. This type of screening test is a fairly crude method which only detects whether the child is responsive to sound or not. Often, it is only if the response to this test is dubious that further investigation follows. Children who respond well to this test are often not assessed again until just before they go to school, and for some, the time interval is even greater. Health visitors play a vital role in 'picking up' any babies whose hearing may be suspect, for further testing.

A child who passes his distraction test at around 9 months may suffer intermittently with hearing loss due to transient conditions, such as otitis media, or he may have a loss in specific frequencies which will inevitably interfere with the development of speech and language. It may only be

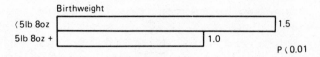

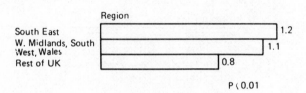

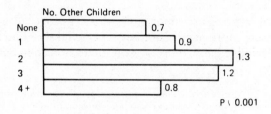

FIG. 8.7 Factors independently associated with receipt of speech therapy (Relative Risks)

with pure tone audiometry that these types of problems can be fully detected.

It is disturbing that in our study there were fourteen children with severe speech problems who had neither had a hearing assessment nor been seen by a speech therapist. In addition, 25% of the children with mild speech problems had such a history. This would indicate that quite a high proportion of children with established speech and/or language problems may be of school age before their problems are investigated. Entry into school at 5 with these problems will be likely to have a deleterious effect on their later educational attainment, as Butler, Peckham and Sheridan (1973) found. The drawbacks may not end there; problems with communication often lead to symptoms of frustration, resulting in behaviour problems.

Behaviour Problems

It has been known that children with speech problems are likely to have emotional and behaviour problems. Obviously, however, the preponderance of boys among children with many of the obvious behaviour disorders means that one would expect to find a clustering of behaviour problems in these children. In Table 8.2 we have documented the numbers of children who had dysfluency or speech problems in association with other individual behaviour problems. These numbers have been compared with those that would have been expected from the sex distributions of each. (The method is similar to the one employed with temper tantrums, but this time there has been no need to control for social class.)

In spite of a previous report (Shaw, 1977) that subsequent speech difficulties were more prevalent than expected if the child had cried a lot or been an irritable baby, there was no such association among our large

TABLE 8.2 Numbers of children with history of speech disorder together with other behaviour attribute compared with the numbers expected after standardising for sex

Child's history	Dysfluency Observed	R. Risk	Other speech problem Observed	R. Risk
Wets bed (1+ per week)	118	1.3**	220	1.5****
Wets by day	90	1.2	178	1.4****
Soils	49	1.4	88	1.4****
Sleeping problems as a baby	127	1.2	200	1.1
Sleeping problems at 5	219	1.1	370	1.1
Feeding problems as a baby	148	1.4****	225	1.3***
Feeding problems at 5	304	1.1	522	1.1
Temper tantrums (1+ per week)	137	1.4***	210	1.2**
Destroys belongings	51	1.4	110	1.8****
Fights	53	1.5**	77	1.3
Is irritable	128	1.4***	200	1.3**
Takes things	23	1.5	49	1.8****
Is disobedient	106	1.3**	189	1.4****
Tells lies	29	1.6	50	1.6***
Bullies	18	1.5	24	1.1
Is often worried	67	1.6***	73	1.0
Is rather solitary	96	1.3**	157	1.3**
Is miserable or tearful	35	1.8***	48	1.4
Is fearful or afraid	79	1.5***	124	1.4***
Is fussy or over-particular	86	1.2	117	1.0
Is very restless	239	1.0	472	1.2***
Is squirmy or fidgety	128	1.4***	238	1.5****
Cannot settle	81	1.4**	153	1.6****
Crying problem as a baby	140	1.2	220	1.1
Not much liked	20	1.8**	27	1.4
Has twitches/mannerisms	6	1.1	16	1.6
Bites nails	118	1.4***	162	1.1
Sucks thumb	132	1.0	246	1.1

**P < 0.01; ***P < 0.001; ****P < 0.0001.

population. Nevertheless, children with speech problems did appear to be more likely to have had feeding difficulties as a baby. This was not unexpected since the articulator's primary function is feeding. Infants who have poor sucking and feeding ability often have poor kinaesthetic awareness and subsequently may have poor speech patterns.

The most dramatic associations were with those factors indicative of a 'difficult' child. The correlations were strongest among the children with other speech defects, the children with stammering or stuttering being more likely to exhibit signs of troubled behaviour.

Bed-wetting has been frequently reported in association with stammering/stuttering. Our data shows that children with a history of dysfluency were 33% more likely to be wetting their beds than children with no such history. The association was strongest though for children with other speech defects. There were no associations with feeding and sleeping problems at 5—but children who had dysfluency were at increased risk of being nail biters. This finding was also reported for the 1946 cohort (Douglas and Blomfield, 1956).

We shall be discussing other problems associated with speech dysfluency and speech problems in later chapters, but our findings are summarised in Figs. 8.8 and 8.9. Children with speech dysfluency are at

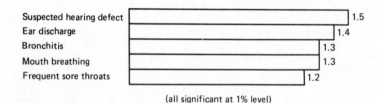

(all significant at 1% level)

FIG. 8.8 Risk of other health outcomes in children with history of speech dysfluency (Relative Risks after standardisation for sex and social class)

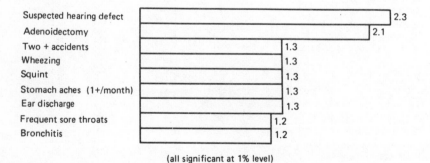

(all significant at 1% level)

FIG. 8.9 Risk of other health outcomes in children with a history of speech problems (Relative Risks after standardisation for sex and social class)

50% increased risk of hearing difficulty and 40% of otitis media. They are more likely, too, to have had frequent sore throats, bronchitis and to breathe through their mouths.

The associations with speech problems are far greater though (Fig. 8.9). These children were twice as likely to have had hearing problems and to have had an adenoidectomy. They were also substantially more likely to have complained of a number of symptoms.

Conclusions

1. History of speech dysfluency (stammering/stuttering) was most prevalent in boys, in children who had younger siblings, in those who had moved house frequently, those in poor urban areas, and with young mothers.
2. Speech disorders were positively associated with maternal smoking and the number of other children in the household. Boys were more likely than girls to have such problems.
3. Speech therapy varied with sex and region. Low birthweight infants were more likely to have speech therapy as were children with two or three siblings.
4. Children with dysfluency or speech problems were at increased risk of many types of behaviour problems.

CHAPTER 9

Headaches and stomach aches

by JEAN GOLDING and N. R. BUTLER

Recurrent pains in children are remarkably common. Apley, Mac-Keith and Meadow (1978) estimated that the prevalence of limb pains lay between one in twenty-four and one in five children, abdominal pains between one in nine and one in six, headaches affected about one in seven children, with migraine rather less common (from one in twenty-five to one in eight). The authors felt that in view of the similarities and inter-relationships between the pains, between the children who suffer them and between their families, the conditions could profitably be grouped together. They stated that they could all be reactions to emotional stress.

The psychosomatic label tends to be attached when physical investigations have failed to reveal any abnormality. Nevertheless, it is quite possible that this is merely a failure to develop or apply the appropriate tests, especially to young children who are frequently incapable of describing their symptoms adequately.

There is now an increasing body of evidence to suggest that young children can have migraine, and some indeed have abdominal migraine. Either symptom can be the result of allergic reaction, particularly to food, or a consequence of tension or stress. Information on the prevalence of headaches and stomach aches in the 5-year-old children in our cohort is examined below with the aim of seeing whether any coherent epidemiological patterns emerge.

Headaches

In the present study mothers were asked whether the child had had headaches within the past year, and were given the response options: 'Never', 'Yes, but less than once a month', 'Yes, at least once a month', and 'Yes, at least once a week.' Of the 12,448 responses, 65% claimed that the child had not had a headache during the 12 months, 29% had had headaches, but not as often as once a month, a further 5% at least once a month, but less than once a week, and only 1% (156 children) had headaches as frequently as once a week.

Since interest lies in the children who have recurrent headaches, we shall henceforth concentrate on the group of 759 children who had had headaches at least once a month. Although there were slightly more girls than boys involved, the differences were not statistically significant. Low birthweight infants were at no greater risk, and there were no differences between children who had been breast fed and those who had only had cow's milk.

There were no significant differences in the prevalence of headaches within different parental situations: the child of a single parent or the one with a step-parent was no more or less likely to have had this symptom. There were no significant variations with maternal age, or history of employment, but there was a strong association with social class (Fig. 9.1), children in the manual social classes having rates at least 50% greater than children in the non-manual classes.

There were also marked ethnic differences, with the children of West Indian and Asian parents being more likely to have had headaches than their European peers.

There were significant differences between the prevalence of headaches in the child and the number of cigarettes smoked by the mother. Figure 9.1 shows, however, an inconsistent pattern, with no convincing trend. Nevertheless, the children with the highest prevalence of headaches were those whose mothers were the heaviest smokers.

In view of the strong social class trend, it was not surprising that there were differences with type of neighbourhood (Fig. 9.1). Although there were no significant differences between the prevalence of headaches in urban as opposed to rural areas, within urban areas there was a trend with the rate in poor urban areas being nearly twice that in well-to-do urban areas.

There were no differences in the prevalence of headaches with the numbers of household moves, but Wales and Scotland had rates significantly different from the rest of Britain—the Welsh rate being markedly higher and the Scottish rate lower (Fig. 9.2).

In order to assess which results were responsible for the others, indirect standardisation was carried out. We found that the social class variation was responsible for the associations between headache and type of neighbourhood, ethnic group of parents and maternal smoking habit. There remained only the regional variation which was not 'explained' by social class, and the social class variation which was not the result of the regional distribution (Fig. 9.3).

Stomach Aches

Similarly phrased to that on headaches was a question concerned with the frequency with which the child had had stomach aches or vomited.

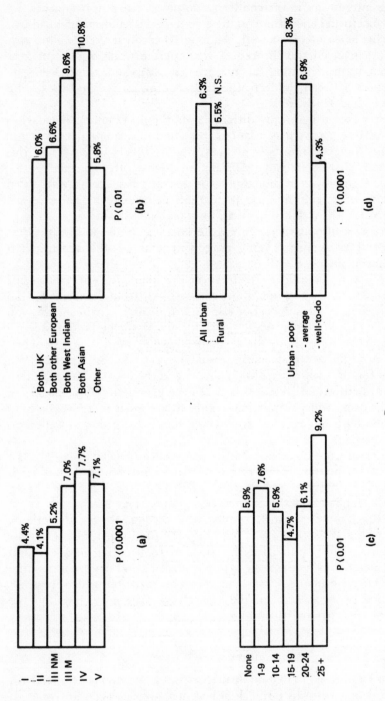

FIG. 9.1 Proportion of children having headaches at least once a month by (a) social class, (b) ethnic group of parents, (c) maternal smoking habit, (d) type of neighbourhood

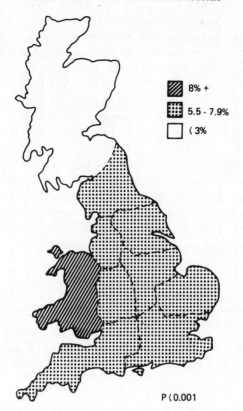

P ⟨ 0.001

FIG. 9.2 Proportion of children to have headaches at least once a month by region

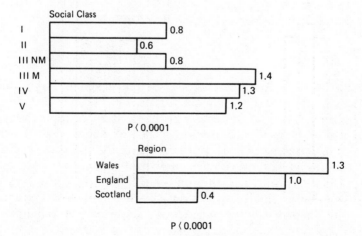

FIG. 9.3 Relative Risks associated with headaches after indirect standardisation

Of the 12,503 responses, 41% stated that the child had not had either in the previous 12 months, and 49% that the child had had stomach aches but never as often as once a month. Of the 10% that had had stomach aches more frequently, nearly a third (323 children) had them at least once a week. For the remainder of this chapter we shall discuss the differences between the group of 1228 children who had had the pains at least once a month, and the remainder. As with headaches, there was an excess of girls in this group, but this was not statistically significant at the 1% level.

There was a high correlation between headaches and stomach aches. Of the children who had had headaches, 38% (four times the expected proportion) also had had stomach aches. Conversely, of the children who had had stomach aches, 24% (four times the expected proportion) had had headaches (Table 9.1). Nevertheless, the majority of children in each group had had only one of the symptoms.

TABLE 9.1 The numbers of children reported to have had headaches at least once a month by the number reported to have had stomach aches or vomited at least once a month

Stomach aches at least 1 per month	Headaches at least 1 per month		All known
	Present	Absent	
Present	269	873	1142
	(23.6%)	(76.4%)	(100.0%)
Absent	438	10,589	11,027
	(4.0%)	(96.0%)	(100.0%)
All known	707	11,462	12,169
	(5.8%)	(94.2%)	(100.0%)

$P < 0.0001$.

We have already shown that social class was related to the prevalence of headaches, but there was no such trend with the probability of the child having stomach aches. As with headaches, there were no differences in the history of stomach aches with maternal age, parental situation, maternal employment or ethnic group of parents. There was again an unusual pattern with the number of cigarettes smoked by the mother (Fig. 9.4); this time the non-smokers and light smokers were more likely to have children with stomach aches than those who smoked between ten and twenty-four cigarettes a day—but the highest prevalence was found among the small group of children with mothers who were very heavy smokers.

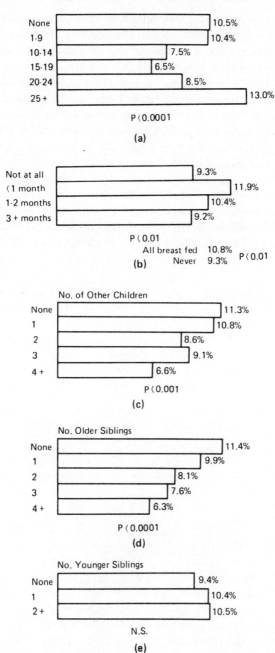

FIG. 9.4 Proportion of children to have stomach aches at least once a month by (a) maternal smoking habit, (b) duration of breast feeding, (c) number of other children in the household, (d) number of older children in the household, (e) number of younger children in the household

Children who had been of low birthweight were not more likely to have had stomach aches, but there was an association with breast feeding (Fig. 9.4). Children who had been breast fed were slightly, but significantly, more likely to have stomach aches, the group that had been breast fed for the shortest time having the greatest prevalence.

As with headaches, regional differences were marked. Again Scotland had a reported prevalence far lower than anywhere else in Britain, and once again Wales had one of the highest rates (Fig. 9.5). The highest prevalence was found in the East Midlands, where 12.6% of children were said to have had stomach aches at least once a month.

The other major association was found with the number of other children in the household. Although this factor had not been associated with headaches, there was a strong trend with prevalence of stomach aches—the more children in the household, the less the likelihood that the mother would claim the child had the disorder (Fig. 9.4). When the

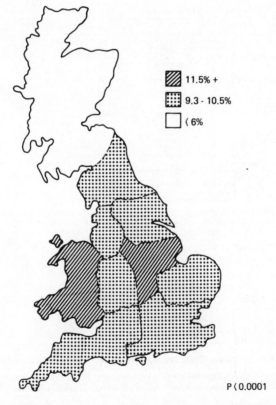

11.5% +

9.3 - 10.5%

⟨ 6%

P ⟨ 0.0001

FIG. 9.5 Proportion of children to have stomach aches or vomiting at least once a month by region

analysis split the siblings into those older and younger than the study child, it became immediately apparent (Figs. 9.4d,e) that the crucial factor was the number of older children. This pattern is reminiscent of that shown for the feeding and sleeping problems demonstrated in Chapter 6.

After indirect standardisation, the regional, maternal smoking and sibling associations remained statistically significant, but that between stomach aches and breast feeding ceased to be significant (Fig. 9.6).

Behaviour Problems

Children with headaches or stomach aches were at increased risk of

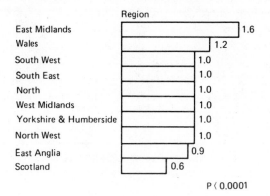

Region

East Midlands	1.6
Wales	1.2
South West	1.0
South East	1.0
North	1.0
West Midlands	1.0
Yorkshire & Humberside	1.0
North West	1.0
East Anglia	0.9
Scotland	0.6

P ⟨ 0.0001

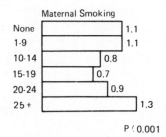

Maternal Smoking

None	1.1
1-9	1.1
10-14	0.8
15-19	0.7
20-24	0.9
25+	1.3

P ⟨ 0.001

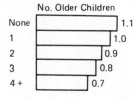

No. Older Children

None	1.1
1	1.0
2	0.9
3	0.8
4 +	0.7

P(0.0001

FIG. 9.6 Relative Risks associated with stomach aches and vomiting at least once a month

many behaviour problems (Table 9.2), but in no instance did the size of the relationship approach that found between the two symptoms themselves. The greatest association was with temper tantrums—children who had tantrums at least once a week were over twice as likely as expected to have headaches or stomach aches. Almost all the other behaviour characteristics were also over-represented among children with intermittent pains. It is possible that rather than real associations

TABLE 9.2 Number of children with various behaviour problems to be reported as having headaches or stomach aches at least once a month

Child's history	Headaches		Stomach aches	
	Observed	R. Risk	Observed	R. Risk
Wets bed (1+ per week)	107	1.3**	160	1.2**
Wets by day	102	1.4***	167	1.4****
Soils	44	1.4	85	1.7****
Sleeping problems as a baby	126	1.2*	223	1.3***
Sleeping problems at 5	264	1.6****	585	1.6****
Feeding problems as a baby	141	1.4****	256	1.6****
Feeding problems at 5	339	1.4****	430	1.6****
Temper tantrums (1+ per week)	185	2.6****	274	2.2****
Destroys belongings	58	1.8****	86	1.7****
Fights	51	1.6**	75	1.5**
Is irritable	152	1.7****	215	1.5****
Takes things	27	1.9***	43	1.9****
Is disobedient	118	1.6****	188	1.6****
Tells lies	34	2.0***	40	1.5*
Bullies	17	1.5**	23	1.3
Is often worried	104	2.5****	148	2.2****
Is rather solitary	110	1.6****	150	1.3***
Is miserable or tearful	51	2.6****	63	2.1****
Is fearful or afraid	84	1.6****	138	1.7****
Is fussy or over-particular	113	1.6****	164	1.4****
Is very restless	266	1.2***	459	1.3****
Is squirmy or fidgety	138	1.6****	231	1.7****
Cannot settle	91	1.7****	149	1.8****
Crying problem as a baby	140	1.3**	231	1.3****
Not much liked	28	2.6****	25	1.5
Has twitches/mannerisms	10	1.8	24	2.7****
Bites nails	113	1.3**	182	1.3***
Sucks thumb	134	1.1	242	1.2*
Dysfluency	59	1.3	93	1.3*
Other speech defect	98	1.2*	161	1.3**

Relative risk given the presence of behaviour problem.
*$P < 0.05$; **$P < 0.01$; ***$P < 0.001$; ****$P < 0.0001$.
Headaches standardised for social class.

they might reflect a maternal reporting bias in that the mother who finds one fault or defect in the child will automatically find many others.

Elsewhere in this volume we shall show that children with repeated accidents and those with more than one hospital admission are at increased risk of headaches. Figure 9.7 summarises those results that are significant at the 1% level. There is little to implicate allergic reactions as major components of these headaches, since the children were not at increased risk of eczema or hay fever, and only 20% more likely to have ever wheezed.

Stomach aches are usually more likely than headaches to be investigated by the medical profession, with a view especially to precluding appendicitis. Nevertheless, this group of children was not more likely to have been admitted to hospital. They were, however, at risk of various respiratory symptoms, speech and hearing problems (Fig. 9.8). In addition, they had increased rates of the predominantly allergic disorders—eczema, wheezing and hay fever.

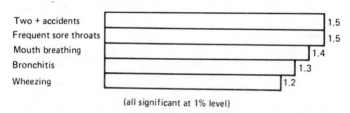

FIG. 9.7 Risk of other health outcomes in children with headaches at least once a month (Relative Risks after standardisation for sex and social class)

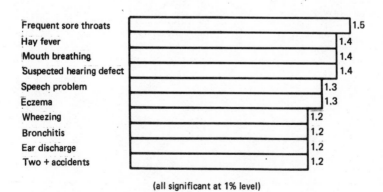

FIG. 9.8 Risk of other health outcomes in children with stomach aches at least once a month (Relative Risks after standardisation for sex and social class)

Discussion

Thirty-seven years ago there were strong conflicts of opinion as to the aetiology of abdominal pain in childhood. These ranged from Menninger (1947): 'the alimentary tract mirrors the emotions better than any other body system', to Maitland-Jones (1947): 'the abdominal expression of psychological discomfort is unknown in the child.'

Certainly the analysis of our own study had confirmed that children with headaches and those with stomach aches are at increased risk of a wide range of behaviour problems. These children are also more likely to have suffered ill health in various forms. What is not clear from the data is whether any component of environmental stress is responsible for these conditions. Stress is notoriously difficult to measure, but one method which is relatively objective looks at associations with so-called 'life events'. Among young children, life events would include the birth of a sibling, the loss of a parent or a household move. All three of these events were shown to be associated with speech dysfluency, but there is little evidence to support the hypothesis that children with headaches or stomach aches come from such backgrounds. If stresses there are, they would appear to arise within the child rather than be imposed from without.

Conclusions

1. Children with headaches are more often to be found in the manual social classes. Children in Wales have a high rate and those in Scotland a very low rate.
2. Scotland has a low prevalence of stomach aches or vomiting, and Wales and the East Midlands have a high rate. The fewer children in the family, the greater the prevalence of reported stomach ache.
3. Children with headaches and those with stomach aches have an increased risk of all types of behaviour problem (except thumb sucking), and many other disorders.

CHAPTER 10

Accidents

by JEAN GOLDING

Introduction

Although the word 'accident' implies a random event, all forms of injury to the child, whether traumatic, or the consequence of such events as ingesting poisons, being bitten by animals or insects, burnt, scalded or the lodging of some solid article within the child's body (e.g. swallowed safety pin, or a bead stuck up a nostril), will be included in this chapter. These have been included regardless of whether the injuries were self-inflicted, caused by others, or more truly accidental. The only stringent criterion was that the injury resulted in medical treatment.

Over the past 50 years there has been a dramatic fall in the childhood death rate, due to the drop in fatal infections largely consequent upon improved nutrition, better housing and improved sanitation (McKeown, 1979). The death rate due to trauma did not show a similar fall and consequently became more and more important. By 1966, in seventeen of twenty-one European countries, the leading cause of death in the age group 1–5 was trauma (Havard, 1974).

Not only are accidents the major causes of death in early childhood, they are responsible for a substantial proportion of hospital admissions, attendance at casualty and general practitioner surgeries, with all the consequent anxiety to both family and child, and work to the health personnel.

In our own cohort, seventeen of the 16,334 livebirths (one in one thousand) had died from violence of various types between the time of delivery and follow-up at the age of 5. This is comparable with six deaths in 5386 legitimate singletons (one in nine hundred) born in the 1946 cohort (Douglas and Blomfield, 1958) and sixteen of 16,811 children (one in one thousand) born live in 1958 (unpublished). The details of the seventeen deaths in our cohort are listed in Table 10.1. At least three of these were non-accidental injury.

There was striking social class distribution in the traumatic deaths described, there being six (35%) children of social classes IV and V and a

141

TABLE 10.1 Deaths to children in the study due to trauma (only deaths under 5 years of age included)

Study number	Social factors	Injuries causing death	Mechanics	Age at death
1	Unmarried 20-year-old mother, no antenatal care, baby delivered at home by herself	Stab-wounds to heart	Unknown	1 day
2	—	Head injury—blow	Murder	8 months
3	—	Multiple injuries	Car hit van in which he was travelling	3 months
4	Unmarried mother	Fractured skull	Collision between car and motor bike combination in which baby was travelling	6 months
5	Unemployed father of social class V, mother had monoplegia due to CVA at 16 years	Not known	Road traffic accident	10 months
6	Social class IV, West Indian parents in Inner London	Carbon monoxide poisoning	House fire	9 months
7	Social class V, mother aged 18	Carbon monoxide poisoning	Fire at house after candles lit during power cut	22 months
8	5th child of 28-year-old widow	Burns	Fire at home while mother out shopping. Baby unattended, cause of fire unknown	12 months
9	4th child	Hanging	Shirt caught in side of cot	13 months
10	—	Fractured skull, bilateral retinal haemorrhages, bruises on trunk	Mother claimed spent hours rocking and banging her head—open verdict	15 months
11	Social class V, living in caravan	Fractured skull	Father unloading tyres from a lorry when one fell onto child	2 years
12	—	Blood supply to brain halted	Door fell across neck of child	2 years
13	Step-parent	Lacerations of small intestines; covered in massive bruises	Step-father had beaten her and thrown her downstairs—convicted of manslaughter	2 years
14	Social class V	Fractured skull	Pedestrian hit by car towing caravan	4 years
15	Social class IV	Cerebral haemorrhage	Pedestrian hit by coach	4 years
16	—	Contusion of brain and spinal cord	Pedestrian hit by car	3 years
17	Mother separated from her husband	Multiple injuries	Road traffic accident	4 years

further four (24%) whose mothers were unmarried, widowed or separated from the child's natural father at birth. These figures should be compared with 20% and 7% respectively, from the population at birth (Chamberlain *et al.*, 1975). An increased incidence of traumatic death among children in the lower social classes has been well documented for England and Wales (Adelstein and White, 1976), but little attention appears to have been paid to the increased risk among children born outside marriage.

Case Ascertainment Among Children Followed Up at 5

The survey included detailed questions on the medical history questionnaire (page 379), concerning accidents to the child. These were to be listed in chronological order with details of where each accident had occurred, the injuries received, the place to which the child had been taken and the treatment given. Only details of those accidents serious enough to require medical advice or treatment were requested. Altogether there were 7887 such accidents to 5703 (43%) of the children in the sample.

Residual Handicaps Due to Accidental Injury

What is remarkable at this age group is that as far as could be ascertained there were only eight children who had residual handicaps at the age of 5, as the result of accidental injury. Two of these had scarring from burns: one of these children had touched wires in a street lamp, resulting in a severe deep burn to his fingers and the palm of his hand. The other had been involved in a fire in a field outside his home and had scars from 30% burns to feet, legs, hands and face.

Two children had amputated fingers—one had caught his hand in a door, the other in a drain. The majority of major disability was caused, however, by road traffic accidents. In one, the child had been a passenger in his mother's car when 15 months old. The car had skidded when another car pulled up suddenly in front. The child was presumably not in a safety harness for he suffered a severe head injury and now has hearing and speech defects and is thought to be mentally retarded. Another child had fallen off a milk float, which then ran over his abdomen. He had severe internal injuries including a ruptured diaphragm and is now without one of his kidneys and his spleen. Two other children were knocked down by cars. One had a spinal injury and is now paraplegic, the other has a severe hearing defect.

Age Differences

Death and disability as a result of an accident is extremely rare when one considers the prevalence of accidents. Altogether in this survey 5703 (43.4%) of the 5-year-olds had had at least one accident requiring medical treatment.

Table 10.2 demonstrates the fact that accidents were comparatively rare during the first year of life, and that the peak frequency occurred during the third year. A comparison of the distribution of deaths with the number of accidents shows, however, that the deaths are over-represented in the first year of life.

TABLE 10.2   Case fatality rate by age at accident

Age of child at accident	Total number of accidents*	Number of deaths	Case fatality rate per 1000 accidents
Under 12 months	621	6	9.7
12–23 months	1954	4	2.0
24–35 months	2191	3	1.4
36+ months	3091	4	1.3
All known**	7857	17	2.2

*Including deaths.
**In thirty cases age at accident not recorded.

Not unexpectedly, the risk of each type of injury varied with age (Fig. 10.1), the infants under 12 months being at low risk of all injuries compared with infants in their 2nd year. Nevertheless, the pattern did vary—more children had head injuries, superficial injuries and foreign bodies in various orifices in their 3rd and 4th years, whereas the peak incidence for fractures, burns and scalds and for ingestions of various substances was in the 2nd year.

Accident Repeaters

The distribution of accidents per child is shown in Table 10.3 and compared with the distribution that would have been expected were accidents purely random phenomena. The difference between the two distributions is highly significant ($P < 0.0001$). This would imply that some children do have more accidents than would be expected by chance. In fact the number of children who had three or more accidents in their first 5 years of life was 50% more than expected and the number having five or more accidents was five times that expected by chance. The maximum number of accidents per child was nine (one case).

Sex differences

All studies of accidental injury in the under-5s have found an overall

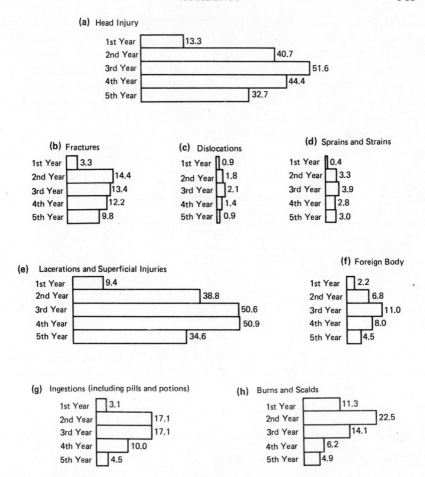

FIG. 10.1 Incidence per 1000 children of various types of injury in each year of life

excess of boys (Clements, 1955; Douglas and Blomfield, 1958; Miller *et al.*, 1960; Tokuhata *et al.*, 1974; Murdock and Eva, 1974). Ours is no exception: 48% of the boys had had at least one accident, compared with 38% of girls. There was a steady trend in sex ratio: the more accidents the child had had, the more likely was he to be male (Fig. 10.2). Twice as many boys as girls had had three or more accidents.

Preliminary analyses suggested that children who had had a single accident differed little from children who had had no accidents. Profound differences existed, however, in the group of children who had had more than one accident, as we shall show in the remainder of this chapter.

TABLE 10.3   The distribution of accidents per child compared with that expected by chance, assuming a Poisson distribution

Total number of accidents per child	Number of children Observed	Expected
0	7432	7205.0
1	4116	4326.6
2	1137	1299.1
3	346	260.0
4	75	39.0
5	22	4.7
6	3	0.5
7	2	0.1
8+	2	—
Total children	13,135	13,135.0

$\Sigma\ (O - E)^2/E\ =\ 205;\ \text{d.f.}\ =\ 5;\ P\ <\ 0.00001.$

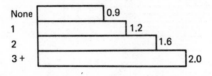

P < 0.0001

FIG. 10.2 Male/female sex ratio according to number of accidents recorded per child

Variations in family characteristics

It has been suggested that the family background is of major importance in the aetiology of accidents, but results have been conflicting. Some authors have suggested that the accident rate is increased in single-parent families (Spence *et al.*, 1954; Husband, 1975), but others have been unable to demonstrate such an effect (Murdock and Eva, 1974).

In this study we found that there was some suggestion that, although children living with a single parent were at no greater risk of repeated accidents, those living with a step-parent were at increased risk (Fig. 10.3).

In spite of the marked trend in mortality with social class, several authors have reported little difference in the *prevalence* of accidents (Douglas and Blomfield, 1958; Murdock and Eva, 1974; Sibert, 1975). We too found no difference among accidents in general, but among accident repeaters we did find a slight excess in prevalence among the

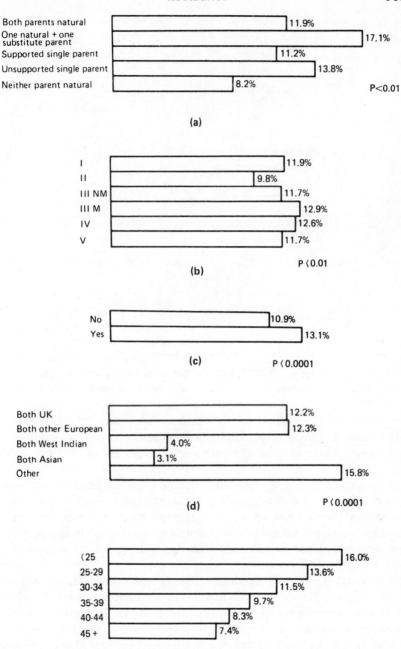

FIG. 10.3 Proportion of children to have had two or more accidents by (a) parental situation, (b) social class, (c) whether mother had worked during child's life, (d) ethnic group of parents, (e) maternal age (*continued on next page*)

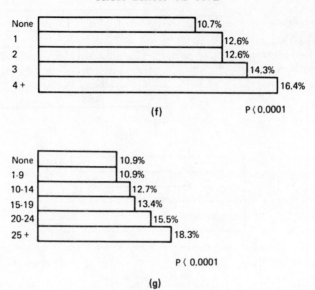

(f)   P ⟨ 0.0001

(g)

FIG. 10.3 *continued* (f) number of household moves, (g) maternal smoking habit

manual social classes (Fig. 10.3). Nevertheless, the trend is far from convincing, and the significance is due to a low rate in social class II.

Several authors have been unable to find a relationship between the child's liability to accidents and the number of children in the family (Brown and Davidson, 1978; Backett and Johnston, 1959; Douglas and Blomfield, 1958). We too found little to suggest that the presence or absence of siblings was of importance in the genesis of accidents in this age group.

After studying the backgrounds of one hundred children in Belfast, who had had accidents as pedestrians, Backett and Johnston (1959) reported that children of working mothers were more prone to such events. No such association was found with accidents in either the 1946 cohort study (Douglas and Blomfield, 1958) or a prospective population study in Inner London (Brown and Davidson, 1978). We found, however, that children of women who had worked at all during the child's life were at increased risk of being accident repeaters (Fig. 10.3).

We have not been able to find any reports in the British literature concerning the accident rate according to ethnic background of the child. In our study there was a highly significant variation: children of Asian or West Indian parents apparently had fewer accidents than the other groups (Fig. 10.3). It could be that these children had had genuinely fewer accidents, it is possible that the maternal conception of an injury warranting medical attention was of higher degree, or that comprehension of the question was impaired. The difficulties involved in interpreting ethnic differences will be discussed fully in a later section.

The proportion of children having more than one accident also varied markedly with maternal age, children born to teenage mothers being twice as likely to be accident repeaters as children born to women of 35 or more (Fig. 10.3). The age of the mother does not appear to have been considered by other authors, which is surprising in view of this strong association.

Variation with the environment

There was a highly significant difference between regions in the proportion of children with more than one accident (Fig. 10.4). Children living in the North and North-West of England have a greater likelihood of such a history, and those in East Anglia have a low risk.

Havard (1974) stated that the majority of pedestrian casualties to

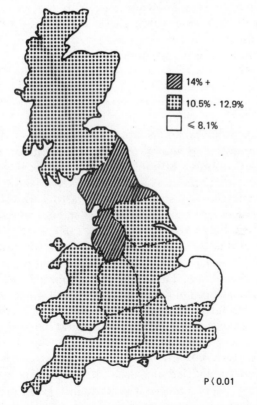

14% +

10.5% - 12.9%

≤ 8.1%

P ⟨ 0.01

FIG. 10.4 The variation in the proportion of children with a history of at least two accidents by region

children under 4 occur in urban areas. Although we have not yet analysed the data according to whether the injury occurred in the street, the proportion of children having had at least two accidents was certainly far greater in urban (12.7%) than rural (9.4%) areas ($P < 0.001$). Within towns and cities, though, the prevalence of multiple accidents did not vary significantly with the type of neighbourhood.

In the Newcastle Thousand Families study (Miller *et al.*, 1960) an association was found between accidents in the under 5s and overcrowding in the household. This was confirmed by Husband (1975) in a study of a small general practice population, but in the present study there was no indication of increased risk of accidents when the household was technically over-crowded.

One of the most striking findings, however, was a positive association with the number of times the family had moved since the child's birth (Fig. 10.3). This was such that one in six of the children who had moved at least four times had had at least two accidents compared with one in ten of the children who had never moved.

There was an even stronger association with maternal smoking habit. As can be seen from Fig. 10.3, there was a strong dose–response relationship: the more cigarettes smoked, the greater the risk of the child having two or more accidents.

Inter-relationships

We have shown that accidents among young children are more likely to occur if the mother is young, living in a poor urban area, or when there have been a number of household moves. We showed in Chapter 3, however, that young mothers were more likely to move often and live in poor urban areas. To ascertain which factors were independently associated with accident repeaters, indirect standardisation was carried out, and the results are depicted in Fig. 10.5.

It can be seen that the major associations were with maternal youth, employment and smoking habit, the ethnic group of the parents and the type of neighbourhood. These factors accounted for the regional variation and the associations with social class and number of household moves. After standardisation there were still more accident repeaters than expected when the child had a step-parent, but this was statistically significant only at the 5% level.

Maternal 'stress' has been thought to be associated with childhood accidents, whether identified in terms of paramenstrual tension (Dalton, 1970), illness or preoccupation (Backett and Johnston, 1959), mild psychiatric disorder as measured by a questionnaire (Brown and Davidson, 1978), the presence of so-called life events (Brown and

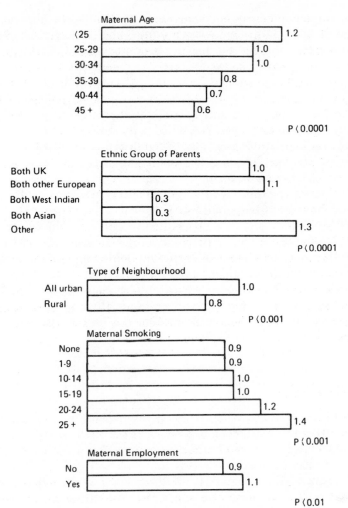

Fig. 10.5 Independent significant associations with children with two or more accidents (Relative Risks)

Davidson 1978; Padilla *et al.*, 1976) or a combination of these (Sibert, 1975).

Although we had not administered a life events questionnaire to the mothers in our survey, we did collect data on several items that would have been considered life events: viz. household moves; the birth of subsequent children; loss of a father, or advent of a new father figure; starting or stopping work. As already shown, accident repetition was positively associated with the number of household moves, but only because of the stronger association with maternal age. There did not appear to be any association between accidents and the birth of subsequent siblings. Certain of our findings could, however, support the hypotheses that there are associations between accidents in the pre-school child and maternal employment, or the advent of a step-parent.

The child

The child was at no greater risk of being an accident repeater if he/she had been of low birthweight or had been breast fed. Nor were children with reported feeding, sleeping or crying problems as a baby at increased risk of this outcome.

In the literature various types of personality characteristics of accident repeaters have been pinpointed varying from the determined, daring, fearless personality described by Husband (1975) to the hyperactive, 'aggressive–impulsive' and 'passive–anxious' characters shown by Margolis (1971) to be associated with repeated poisoning. Medical examination of the 1946 cohort at the age of 6 showed that those who had had two accidents were more likely to have good eyesight and hearing but to have mothers who were more worried about their general behaviour and 'bad habits' such as nail biting (Douglas and Blomfield, 1956).

In our study there were differences in the pattern of behaviour of the children who had had at least two accidents when compared with that expected from the sex and social class distribution (Table 10.4). Accident repeaters were significantly more likely to be described as disobedient, destructive or to fight other children. In addition to these, the factors that were most associated with accident repeaters were those which indicate hyperactivity (unable to settle, restless, squirmy or fidgety). In addition, children who had more than one accident were more likely to bite their nails.

As we described in Chapter 6, children who had repeated accidents were more likely to have sleeping difficulties at 5—the greater the severity of the problem, the more likely the child to have had two or more accidents (Fig. 10.6). No particular type of sleeping problem predominated.

Sleeping problems could well be a consequence of a traumatic event. The other association which could be explained causally was that found with headaches. The more often the child had had headaches in the past year, the more likely was he/she to have had at least two accidents (Fig. 10.7). We intend to ascertain whether the association was with head injuries in particular.

Apart from the association with headaches and the obvious fact that children who have accidents are more likely to be admitted to hospital, there were few other major associations (Fig. 10.8). Children with speech problems were found to have had more accidents than expected, but the

TABLE 10.4   Health and behaviour attributes of children who had had two or more accidents

Child's history	Children with 2+ accidents Observed	Relative Risk
Wets bed (1+ per week)	202	1.1
Wets by day	171	1.1
Soils	78	1.1
Sleeping problems as a baby	239	1.1
Sleeping problems at 5	487	1.3****
Feeding problems as a baby	243	1.2*
Feeding problems at 5	579	1.0
Temper tantrums (1+ per week)	235	1.2*
Destroys belongings	99	1.4**
Fights other children	96	1.3**
Is irritable	206	1.1
Takes things	40	1.3
Is disobedient	211	1.3****
Tells lies	46	1.2
Bullies	30	1.2
Is often worried	87	1.0
Is solitary	140	0.9
Is miserable or tearful	55	1.4*
Is fearful or afraid	97	0.9
Is fussy or over-particular	148	1.0
Is restless	558	1.2****
Is squirmy or fidgety	244	1.3****
Is unsettled	160	1.4****
Crying problem as a baby	256	1.1
Not much liked	22	1.0
Has twitches/mannerisms	12	1.0
Bites nails	230	1.3****
Sucks thumb	263	1.0
Dysfluency	96	0.9
Other speech defect	216	1.3***
Headaches (1+ per month)	138	1.5****
Stomach aches (1+ per month)	179	1.2**

(Expected numbers after standardisation for sex and social class.)
*P < 0.05; **P < 0.01; ***P < 0.001; ****P < 0.0001.

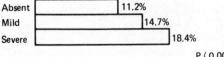

FIG. 10.6 Proportion of children to have had two or more accidents by severity of sleeping difficulty at 5

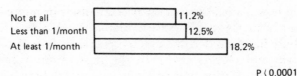

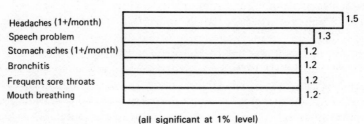

FIG. 10.7 Proportion of children to have had two or more accidents by frequency of headaches in 12 months prior to interview

FIG. 10.8 Risk of other health outcomes in children with two or more accidents (Relative Risks after standardisation for sex and social class)

meaning of this association was not clear. Other associations, although significant, carried a Relative Risk of only 1.2.

Non-accidental Injury

No analysis of accidents to small children would be complete without a discussion of non-accidental injury. Apart from the three or possibly four fatalities we have recorded, there was sufficient evidence in the records of forty-four children to suspect that they had been victims of child abuse. This gives a rate of 3.3 per 1000. For forty of these children there were records of hospital inpatient or outpatient episodes involving injuries. For the remaining four children there was evidence from clinic records of suspected child abuse.

One of the striking, though not unexpected, characteristics of this group of children was the number of other problems reported. Eleven had emotional problems of sufficient severity to be considered handicapping. Fourteen had suffered from some form of fit, turn or convulsion. Three were certainly mentally retarded and a further two were suspected of being so. Five were also suspected of neurodevelopmental delay. The association between child abuse or neglect and reduction of intellectual potential has been well documented in the past (Buchanan and Oliver, 1977).

Obviously, it is not possible, in retrospect, to determine accurately how many of the developmental problems in this group arose as the result of abuse, and in how many instances the problem itself prompted a violent reaction in a parent. Certainly an association between congenital defects and child abuse has been documented by several authors (Hunter *et al.*, 1978; Baldwin and Oliver, 1975). In the present study four of the children suspected of being abused had congenital defects of sufficient severity to warrant treatment (one spina bifida with hydrocephalus, one with a polycystic kidney, one with an extra digit on a hand and a foot, and one with talipes valgus).

Perhaps surprisingly, only nine of the children with suspected child abuse had been recorded as having more than two episodes involving injury. Thus, the prevalence of recognised abuse among the children with multiple accidents was of the order of only 2%.

It seems likely that there is a great overlap in the epidemiological background of children who genuinely have accidents as opposed to those injured deliberately. For example, stress has also been noted to be an important factor in families who have a history of child abuse (Justice and Duncan, 1976; Friedrich and Boriskin, 1976; Cater and Easton, 1980), as has parental neuroticism (Smith, Hanson and Noble, 1973) and general ill-health (Lynch, 1975). Unfortunately, the information available does not enable us to examine such overlap in detail in this study. Nevertheless, it will be of interest to ascertain the outcome of the forty-four children at the next follow-up to see whether, as they grow older, their behaviour and intellectual problems improve.

Discussion

It is not the purpose of this chapter to describe physical ways in which accidents could be prevented—whether in the design of homes or playgrounds, health education of the parents, insistence on restraining straps in cars, or the use of child-proof containers. All play their part, and have been described already at some length (Hall, 1974; Jackson, 1977; Department of Prices and Consumer Protection, 1979).

The unique feature of this study lies in the fact that we have been able to study some of the factors that distinguish children who had a high frequency of accidents from those of their peers who did not.

As suggested by previous authors, aspects of the mother appear to be the most important factors that we have been able to examine, although the temperament of the child probably also has a bearing on this. We shall shortly be able to examine the data in time-related sequences. It is possible that children who have had several accidents are more likely then to become hyperactive, tense or miserable. It seems somewhat more plausible, though, that these characteristics are themselves prodromal of accidental injury.

Similarly, it seems unlikely that the mother starts smoking heavily as a result of her child's pattern of accidents. It is more possible that the mother, who is preoccupied with her aches and pains, anxieties and tensions, is more likely to smoke heavily and less likely to supervise her child adequately.

In the *Pickwick Papers*, Mr. Micawber said:

> 'Accidents will occur in the best-regulated families: and in families not regulated . . . they may be expected with confidence and borne with philosophy.'

Although we have no information on whether siblings of accident repeaters themselves have more accidents, we can say with some certainty that there are children who, probably as the result of their innate temperament, may be expected to have one accident after another. It is likely that this pattern is complemented by maternal attitudes and the opportunities the child has. We must, nevertheless, agree with Cynthia Illingworth (1974) when she said:

> 'Unquestionably, many poisonings and accidents are due to carelessness, but the more carefully one takes the history of what actually happened the more one feels that those writers who merely blame the parent for carelessness, and assume with proper care all these accidents would be avoided, either have no children of their own, or, if they have had children, have forgotten their capacity for getting into trouble.'

It will be fascinating to add information from the next 5 years to this cohort. Will the children who have already identified themselves as accident repeaters grow out of this habit, will they continue to have accidents or will they present with other forms of deviant behaviour— slow learning or emotional maladjustment? As the younger mothers get older and more experienced, will the risk of accidents to their children diminish?

Conclusions

1. Boys are more likely to have accidents than girls.
2. Certain children have more accidents than would be expected by chance. These accident repeaters are more likely to be boys than girls.
3. Accident repetition is found more often: (a) the younger the mother; (b) in urban areas; (c) when the mother has been employed; and (d) when the mother smokes heavily. Accident repetition is rarely reported among children of Asian or West Indian parents.

4. Children who were accident repeaters were reported to be significantly more likely to be disobedient, destructive and to fight other children. They exhibited characteristics of hyperactivity, and were more likely to have headaches than expected.

CHAPTER 11

Wheezing and asthma

by JEAN GOLDING and N. R. BUTLER

Introduction

Respiratory difficulty in young children is one of the most common yet disturbing disorders with which a parent may have to cope. This is especially true of those disorders characterised by the child making the abnormal and distressing sounds best described as wheezing.

Although it is true that a child with asthma will have attacks of wheezing, among children who have wheezed there is no consensus as to which children have asthma and which do not. Jones (1976) begins his comprehensive book on asthma in children with the sentence: 'Asthma is a disease which commands attention because it is common, although the incidence is in dispute, morbidity is high, views on management are contradictory, and a definition defies even the erudite.'

It is therefore with great caution that we present the results of a study based merely on the parental answers to a questionnaire. A similar method has, however, been used to examine epidemiological associations of asthma and other wheezing during early childhood by Leeder *et al.* (1976b). They followed over 2,000 children through the first 5 years of life, and identified 3.2% of children as having had episodes of wheezing, said by the parents to be asthma, and 22.5% with episodes of wheezing not said to be asthma. They showed that the two groups were different in terms of their pulmonary function when, at the age of 5, a sample of children said to have asthma had peak expiratory flow rates (PEFR) significantly lower than that of the children with other wheezing problems, who themselves had a lower mean PEFR than children who had never wheezed.

Case Ascertainment

In her interview the health visitor was instructed to ask the mother whether the child had ever 'had one or more attacks or bouts in which he/she had wheezing on the chest'. Of the 12,977 mothers who answered this question, 21% (2702) replied in the affirmative. In addition, one child had died in status asthmaticus at the age of 2½.

The different causes ascribed by the parent to the wheezing attacks in our survey are shown in Table 11.1. The categories are mutually exclusive, the pecking order being from top to bottom: thus, a child who had one attack of wheezing with bronchitis and another of wheezing with croup would have been counted only in the 'wheezing-with-croup' group. It can be seen that 10% of all children with wheezing were said to have asthma, giving a population frequency of 2.1%. A further 2.3% had croup, and another 5% of the population had been reported as having had bronchitis with wheezing. The remainder had no diagnosis attached to their attacks of wheezing.

For the rest of this chapter we will be examining the attributes of just two groups: the 270 children followed, and said to have asthma; and the 2432 who had had attacks of wheezing, not ascribed to asthma. These two groups will be compared with the 10,275 children whose mothers stated that they had never had an attack of wheezing.

TABLE 11.1   The various diagnoses ascribed by the parent to the children who had a history of wheezing

Diagnosis ascribed by parent	Children with wheezing Number	%
Asthma	270	2.1
Croup	303	2.3
Bronchitis	649	5.0
Wheezing only	1455	11.2
Wheezing, but diagnosis not stated	25	0.2
All children with wheezing	2702	20.8
All children with known wheezing history	12,977	100.0

Age at First Attack

Some 8% of all the children had had a history of wheezing in the first 12 months of life. Thereafter, the rate of first attacks of wheezing seemed fairly steady at about 3% per year. The distribution of ages of first attack are shown for the two sub-groups in Table 11.2. There is little of note to distinguish between them, the age at first attack of the children with asthma was very similar to the other children with a history of wheezing. Some 40% of each group had had their first attacks during the first year of life.

Table 11.2   Age at first attack of wheezing

Age	Asthma	Other wheezing	All wheezing
Under 12 months	100	930	1030
	(38.5%)	(41.6%)	(41.2%)
1 year	45	343	388
	(17.3%)	(15.3%)	(15.5%)
2 years	57	320	377
	(21.9%)	(14.3%)	(15.1%)
3 years	33	332	365
	(12.7%)	(14.8%)	(14.6%)
4 years	25	314	339
	(9.6%)	(14.0%)	(13.6%)
All known	260	2239	2499
	(100.0%)	(100.0%)	(100.0%)

In the 12 months prior to interview (i.e. while the child was aged 4) 1284 children had at least one wheezing attack. Of these, half (639) had only one attack, 247 had two and the remainder had three or more. Fifty-six were said to have 'many' attacks—one child had had sixty-six. Children with the label asthma accounted for only a quarter (104/398) of the children who had had three or more attacks.

During the 5 years of the life of the children in the study there had been 473 hospital admissions associated with wheezing involving 322 children. Among these there were 117 admissions to 65 children labelled as being asthmatic. The maximum number of admissions per child was nine.

Sex, Birthweight and Breast feeding

There was a highly significant difference between the sexes (Fig. 11.1) in that the children who had had asthma were 70%, and those with other wheezing attacks were 30% more likely to be male than were the children with no history of wheezing. The male predominance is in accord with that found in all studies of wheezing in this age group (Henderson et al., 1979; McNicol and Williams, 1973).

Children who were of low birthweight were slightly more likely to have had a history of wheezing and of asthma than their contemporaries of higher birthweight.

Linking back to the information collected at birth, we found that 5.8% of children with subsequent asthma and 3.4% of children with other wheezing recorded had had respiratory problems in the neonatal period compared with 2.2% of controls ($P < 0.001$). The respiratory problems included the respiratory distress syndrome.

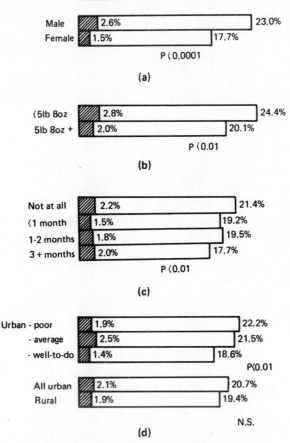

Fig. 11.1 Proportion of children who had ever wheezed by (a) sex of child, (b) birthweight, (c) duration of breast feeding, (d) type of neighbourhood (*continued on next page*)

Salk and Grellong (1974) had also shown an increased incidence of neonatal respiratory distress syndrome in thirty asthmatic children (17%) compared with 2% of their sixty controls.

It has often been suggested that breast feeding is likely to protect children against allergic disorders such as asthma. In this study children who had wheezed were indeed significantly less likely to have been breast fed—and there was evidence to support the hypothesis that the longer the child had been breast fed, the lower the chance that wheezing had occurred (Fig. 11.1). For children with asthma, although there was a slightly lower rate among those who had been breast fed, this was not statistically significant, and there was no sign of a trend with duration of breast feeding.

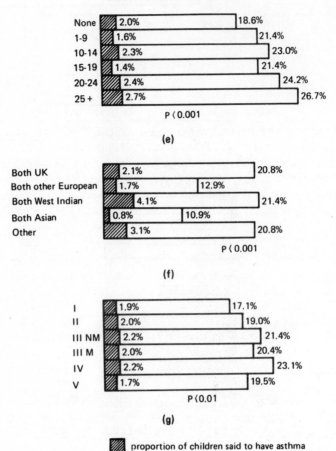

FIG. 11.1 *continued* (e) maternal smoking habit, (f) ethnic group of parents, (g) social class

The Environment

In the 7-year follow-up of the 1958 cohort, strong regional variation in the prevalence of asthma was found, with the highest rates in Wales, and the lowest in Scotland (Davie, Butler and Goldstein, 1972). In the present cohort we, too, have found a strong regional variation in the proportion of children ever to have wheezed (Fig. 11.2). The highest rates were found in Wales (24.6%) and South-West of England (23.6%), and the lowest in Scotland (17.6%).

There were no significant differences between the prevalence of wheezing and the number of household moves; nor was wheezing significantly more prevalent in urban as opposed to rural areas (Fig. 11.1). Nevertheless, there were differences in the type of urban area.

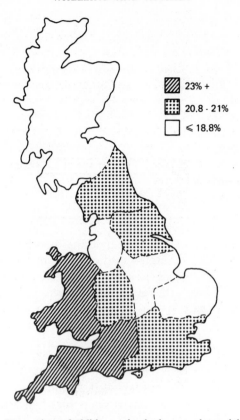

23% +

20.8 - 21%

≤ 18.8%

FIG. 11.2 Proportion of children who had ever wheezed by region

Children in the well-to-do areas were slightly less likely to have had wheezing attacks, or to be labelled asthmatic, than the children in the less salubrious areas.

There was a stronger association with the maternal smoking habit at 5 (Fig. 11.1): children whose mothers smoked were more likely to have a history of wheezing. In general, the more cigarettes the mother smoked, the more likely was the child to have wheezed. A similar relationship was not apparent for the children with asthma. Nor was there any relationship between the paternal smoking habit and wheezing or asthma.

The Parents and Siblings

Children of single parents or step-parents were at no increased risk of wheezing or asthma—nor were there significant differences with the age of the mother or the number of other children in the household. There were significant differences, however, in the reported history in relationship to the ethnic group of the parents. Children of Asian parents, together with those from Europe, were significantly less likely ever to have wheezed, whereas those of West Indian parents were at least as likely to have this history as their peers with parents from the United Kingdom.

There was also a significant variation with social class (Fig. 11.1), but there was no clear evidence for a trend. This is in contrast with findings for asthma in some other studies (Peckham and Butler, 1978; Leeder *et al.*, 1976; Hamman *et al.*, 1975; Graham *et al.*, 1967), where children in social classes I and II were over-represented.

Inter-relationships

Indirect standardisation showed that the association with maternal smoking accounted for the initial findings with breast feeding, the type of neighbourhood and social class. There was still an excess of wheezing among children of low birthweight, but this was only significant at the 5% level. The major factors were region, ethnic group and the maternal smoking habit (Fig. 11.3).

Family Medical History

During the interview the mother of the child was asked whether she herself, the child's father, or any siblings had had asthma, hay fever, eczema or convulsions. In retrospect, the paternal history was probably unreliable, since the father was rarely present at interview. We, therefore, present figures only for the mother and siblings.

As can be seen from Figs. 11.4 and 11.5, there were strong positive associations between family history of asthma or eczema and wheezing in the child. The association was not solely accounted for by the children in the study who were said to have asthma. There was a greater likelihood of the child wheezing if the mother had hay fever, but if the sibling had hay fever the index child was apparently at little excess risk.

The Child's Behaviour

In order to assess whether there were significantly more problems in the child who had a history of wheezing it was necessary to standardise for sex. The significant results are shown in Table 11.3. The only way in which the small group of children said to have asthma differed significantly from other children with the same sex distribution concerned their ability to be frequently worried. Nevertheless, this only applied to 26 of the 270 children with asthma.

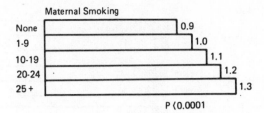

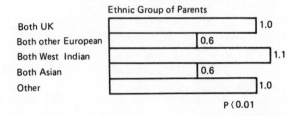

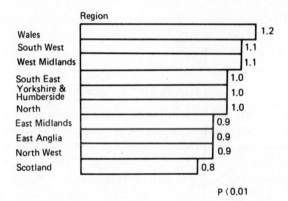

FIG. 11.3 Factors independently associated with wheezing (Relative Risks)

Among all children with a history of wheezing there was also an excess of children said to worry, as well as an excess of those described as squirmy, restless, irritable, destructive and likely to take things belonging to others. In addition, they were also more likely to have frequent temper tantrums. Although highly significant, the sizes of these associations were fairly small, with Relative Risks rarely exceeding 1.2.

One of the more striking findings was that the children who had ever wheezed were more likely to have been said to have had problems in their first months of life—these concerned crying, feeding and sleeping difficulties. There were also more children with sleeping difficulties at 5.

From the results in Table 11.3, and analyses presented in subsequent chapters, it is possible to assess ways in which health of children who

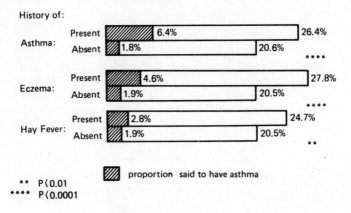

FIG. 11.4 Proportion of children who had ever wheezed according to maternal history of asthma, hay fever, or eczema

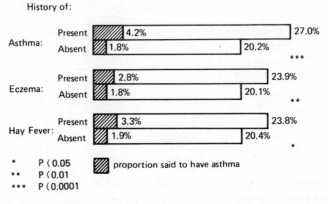

FIG. 11.5 Proportion of children who had ever wheezed according to sibling history of asthma, eczema or hay fever

wheezed differs from expectation. The significant results are shown in Fig. 11.6. Lower respiratory conditions (bronchitis and pneumonia) head the list. The association with bronchitis was expected, since wheezing often occurs during attacks of bronchitis. Children with wheezing were twice as likely to have hay fever, but only 50% more at risk of having eczema. As discussed in Chapter 9, children who had wheezed were more likely to have headaches or stomach aches. Whether this implies that all three disorders are psychosomatic responses to stress, or that all are allergic responses to environmental stimuli, must remain open to debate.

TABLE 11.3 Numbers of children with a history of wheezing and a history of asthma compared with the numbers expected after standardising for sex

Child's history	All with wheezing Observed	R. Risk	All with asthma Observed	R. Risk
Wets bed (1+ per week)	319	1.1	18	0.6
Wets by day	285	1.1	26	1.0
Soils	142	1.2	13	1.1
Sleeping problems as a baby	443	1.2**	46	1.2
Sleeping problems at 5	778	1.2****	75	1.1
Feeding problems as a baby	416	1.2**	46	1.3
Feeding problems at 5	1021	1.0	113	1.2
Temper tantrums (1+ per week)	400	1.2***	36	1.0
Destroys belongings	154	1.3***	14	1.1
Fights other children	125	1.1	14	1.1
Is irritable	380	1.2***	41	1.3
Takes things	72	1.4**	5	0.9
Is disobedient	303	1.2	32	1.2
Tells lies	77	1.3	6	2.0
Bullies	50	1.2	6	1.4
Is often worried	188	1.3***	26	1.8**
Is solitary	287	1.2	15	0.6
Is miserable or tearful	83	1.2	4	0.6
Is fearful or afraid	209	1.2	24	1.3
Is fussy or over-particular	269	1.1	19	0.8
Is restless	371	1.2***	32	1.0
Is squirmy or fidgety	860	1.1**	84	1.1
Is unsettled	216	1.1	18	0.9
Crying problem as a baby	456	1.2***	53	1.4
Not much liked	18	0.9	1	0.5
Twitches/mannerisms	44	1.2	6	1.6
Bites nails	450	1.0	51	1.2
Sucks thumb	316	1.1	24	0.8
Dysfluency	193	1.1	21	1.0
Other speech defect	353	1.3****	33	1.1
Headaches (1+ per month)	188	1.2**	21	1.4
Stomach aches (1+ per month)	298	1.2**	32	1.3
2+ Accidents	332	1.0	37	1.1

*$P < 0.05$; **$P < 0.01$; ***$P < 0.001$; ****$P < 0.0001$.

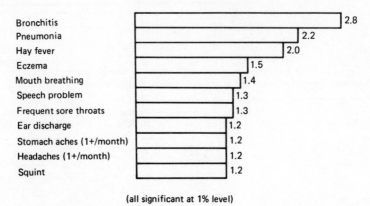

(all significant at 1% level)

FIG. 11.6 Risk of other health outcomes in children with wheezing at least once a week (Relative Risks after standardisation for sex and social class)

Discussion

As mentioned earlier, the reported prevalence of asthma in early childhood depends largely on the definitions used, and the method of ascertainment. In the literature, reported prevalence has varied from 0.85% in Finland (Peltonen, Kasanen and Peltonen, 1955), through 2.0% on the Isle of Wight (Graham *et al.*, 1967), and 2.1% in Birmingham (Morrison-Smith, 1961) to 4.8% in Aberdeen (Dawson *et al.*, 1969). In the present study we have relied on the mother's perceived diagnosis of asthma, and this must depend on her physician's criteria for diagnosis of asthma, his perception of whether such a label might cause distress, and the mother's own experience. In order to obviate such biases we have, therefore, concentrated on all children who have had episodes of wheezing.

Leeder and his associates (1976) stated that the relationship between attacks of wheezing accompanying acute lower respiratory infection and wheezing precipitated by allergens, emotional stress or exercise, is particularly difficult to define. They showed that children who had had pneumonia or bronchitis during their first year were twice as likely to have later wheezing attacks than the children without such a history. It is feasible that damage to the lungs during such attacks, or earlier during the neonatal period, may make the child more susceptible to allergens later in infancy. Nevertheless, it must be pointed out that the typical epidemiological associations of infection (late birth order, low social class, over-crowding) have not been demonstrated in the group of children with wheezing. These children typically have parents with asthma or eczema, are of the male sex, have had a respiratory disorder in the neonatal period, and live in Wales, or the South and West of England.

During the first six months of life the children who were to become asthmatic were more likely to have had crying, sleeping and feeding problems. The question immediately arises as to whether the children who later had wheezing attacks were actually having more problems at this age; whether, in retrospect, the mother of a child who had wheezing attacks during his pre-school years envisaged him as having been troublesome all his life; or could it be that the child who, presented with these early problems, was really complaining about his relationship with his mother? Certainly there is a strong association between later asthma and early mother/child separation (Golding and Butler, 1984a), and this would suggest the possible importance of the psychological consequences of a failure in the mother–infant bonding process.

Breast feeding is said to be of physical benefit to the infant. It has been shown to be associated with lower incidences of allergic and respiratory diseases in several populations (Chandra, 1979; Saarinen et al., 1979), although consensus of findings is not always apparent. In the present study, there was an association between bottle feeding and increased risk of wheezing, but this appeared to be due entirely to the strong association with maternal smoking habit.

As Jones (1976) argues so cogently, there are major difficulties in trying to decide in retrospect the order in which psychological and psychosomatic factors have played a part. That children with attacks of wheezing should have nightmares and be described as fearful or afraid is hardly surprising: one could almost consider it a normal reaction to a life punctuated with frightening periods when the child is fighting for every breath.

McNicol et al. (1973) examined a group of 315 children with asthma and concluded that in only a small group of severely affected patients was there any evidence of abnormal behaviour patterns. In our whole study only eight asthmatic children were said to have a profound emotional or behavioural problem by the age of 5. Indeed, perhaps the most striking finding is how slight the differences in behavioural characteristics are between these children and the rest of the population. The most striking differences are in the proportion of children with sleeping problems, which is understandable, and those described as restless, squirmy or fidgety or with the stigma of the 'Difficult' child. There was certainly no excess of those traditional signs of stress: bed-wetting and speech dysfluency.

As in previous analyses we have a strong dose-dependent relationship with maternal smoking. Unlike accidents, it is feasible to postulate a direct irritant effect of the smoke on the child's respiratory system—but it is equally possible that smoking in the mother is merely a marker of a stressful situation. This is clearly an area in which more detailed studies are warranted.

Conclusions

1. Children who have a history of wheezing are most prevalent in Wales, West Midlands, and the South-West of England. There is a significantly lower rate of wheezing in Scotland.
2. The more cigarettes the mother was currently smoking, the more likely was the child to have wheezed. Children of Asian or Other European parents were less likely to have a history of wheezing.

CHAPTER 12

Eczema and hay fever

by JEAN GOLDING and TIM PETERS

Introduction

Allergic or hypersensitive disorders are defined as abnormal and varied reactions which occur 'following a contact with substances or agents which normally do not cause symptoms in other individuals. For instance, drinking cow's milk, or eating eggs, fish, nuts etc. does not produce any adverse effect in the majority of humans, but in a few, ingestion of any such foodstuff is followed within minutes by a series of characteristic symptoms and signs' (Kuzemko 1978). Among these are asthma, eczema and hay fever.

Estimates of prevalence of allergic disorders in the population has varied with the means of ascertainment and definitions used. In the preceding chapter we described the difficulties inherent in defining whether a child had asthma or not, and felt that by taking all who had had a wheezing attack we would possibly be nearer the truth than if we only took children for whom the mother had attached the label, 'asthma'. There was a ten-fold difference between the two estimates of prevalence that we could have taken.

Eczema also has problems of definition, and it is unfortunate that we did not enquire more searchingly as to whether the child had had skin conditions that might have been considered to be eczema by a dermatologist. In the event, we only asked whether the child had ever had eczema and assumed that the mother and health visitor would be able to answer accurately and consistently. This seems unlikely in view of the fact that clinicians themselves frequently disagree.

The definition of hay fever is far less prone to argument. It is characterised by attacks of sneezing, usually with streaming eyes, and mostly seasonal in occurrence. The most frequent cause of the disorder is an allergic reaction to different types of pollen.

There are well-documented familial associations. It has been reported that about 50% of children born to a parent with an allergic disorder will themselves develop some form of allergy by the age of 4.

One of the suggestions that has been made concerning the prevention of such disorders has concerned breast feeding. It has been reported that the child who is completely breast fed for the first 3–5 months of life is less likely to develop eczema (Blair, 1969; *British Medical Journal*, 1976). The mechanism has been thought to be related to specific antibodies present in breast milk, such as the immunoglobulin IgA, which may be of importance in preventing absorption of antigens (Goldman and Smith, 1973; Walker, 1975). Nevertheless, it is also true that sensitising allergens can be excreted in human milk and actually cause the reaction that the breast feeding was aimed at preventing. Egg white is a case in point (Donnally, 1930). This substance is a frequent cause of childhood eczema.

Prevalence

The mother was asked by the health visitor whether the child had ever had: (a) eczema and (b) hay fever or sneezing attacks. In all, 1539 of the 12,555 children with known history were said to have had eczema (12.3%), but far fewer children (549 of 12,521 or 4.4%) were said to have had hay fever or sneezing attacks.

It can be seen from Table 12.1 that the age of the appearance of these disorders differed somewhat. Among all children said to have had eczema, the age of the first appearance was said to be before the age of 4 in almost 90%, whereas, for hay fever, only 71% of the children had started sneezing before the age of 4.

There were differences, too, in the proportion of children where the condition had resolved. Of the 1374 children who had eczema before the age of 4, only a third continued to have the disease in the following

TABLE 12.1 Five-year-old children reported as having had eczema or hay fever before or after their 4th birthday

Onset	Last occurrence	Eczema	Hay Fever
Before 4	Before 4	905 (7.2%)	170 (1.4%)
Before 4	After 4	469 (3.8%)	219 (1.7%)
After 4	After 4	165 (1.3%)	160 (1.3%)
Never	—	11,016 (87.7%)	11,972 (95.6%)
All known		12,555 (100.0%)	12,521 (100.0%)

year, whereas over 55% of those 389 children who had had hay fever before their 4th birthday continued to do so in the following year.

Epidemiological Associations with Eczema

The proportion of boys who had had eczema (12.3%) was identical to the proportion of girls (12.3%), but there was a significant association between birthweight and eczema. Children of low birthweight seem to be at a substantially reduced risk of having this disorder (Fig. 12.1), compared with their heavier contemporaries.

In view of the doctrine that atopic disease in children can be partly prevented by breast feeding, the associations we found with duration of breast feeding are particularly dramatic. Figure 12.1 shows that, contrary to prediction, the *longer* the mother breast fed, the higher was the proportion of children reported to have had eczema. These findings were not due to the mother being more likely to breast feed if there was a history of atopic disorder in the family, since the 1970 infants were born before this hypothesis was widely known.

There were geographical differences in the prevalence of eczema (Fig. 12.2). The highest prevalences were in the South-East (14.7%) and the South-West (13.8%). The lowest rates were found in Scotland (8.3%), Wales (9.3%) and the North of England (9.5%).

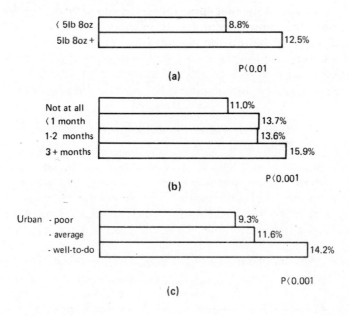

FIG. 12.1 Proportion of children reported to have had eczema by (a) birthweight, (b) duration of breast feeding, (c) type of urban neighbourhood (*continued on next page*)

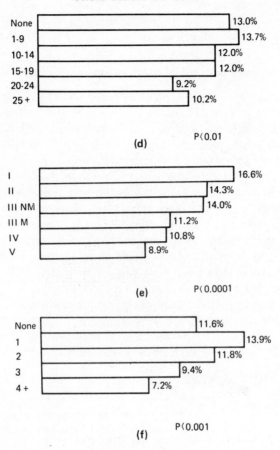

Fɪɢ. 12.1 *continued* (d) maternal smoking habit, (e) social class, (f) number of other children in the household

In the 1958 cohort there was also a significant variation with region (Davie, Butler and Goldstein, 1972). Using roughly the same groupings as in Fig 12.3, the corresponding rates for eczema after the first year of life were: in the South and South-West: 7.20%; in the Midlands, East Anglia, and Yorkshire: 5.21%; in Wales, Scotland, the North and North-West of England: 4.82%. Thus, the pattern was similar across the two studies.

There were proportionately fewer children in urban areas as opposed to rural areas reported as having had eczema, but the differences were not statistically significant. There were, however, statistically significant associations between the types of neighbourhood among the urban children. As can be seen from Fig. 12.1, the proportion of children reported to have eczema in the well-to-do urban areas was some 50%

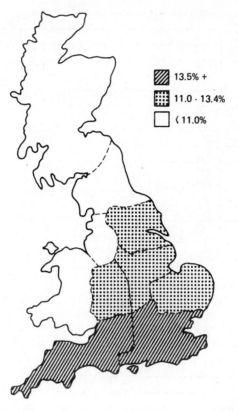

13.5% +

11.0 - 13.4%

< 11.0%

P < 0.0001

FIG. 12.2 Proportion of children in each region reported as having had eczema

greater than in the poorer urban areas. There was no association with the number of times the child had moved house.

There was a significant negative association with maternal smoking habits (Fig. 12.1). The prevalence of eczema among mothers who smoked heavily was significantly less than mothers who smoked little (one to nine cigarettes a day), or among non-smokers.

There were no differences in the prevalence of eczema with maternal age, ethnic group of parents, or parental situation. Children of mothers who had worked at any time during their lives were at no more risk than those of mothers who had not worked at all since the child was born. There were, however, major differences in the social class distribution of children with eczema (Fig. 12.1). There was a strong negative trend, with children in social class I having a rate almost twice that found in social class V.

It is conceivable again that this social class association might be an anomaly associated with the definition of the term eczema, or it could be a real effect. To examine the first suggestion, we turned to data from the 1958 cohort study. At age 7, the mother was asked 'Has your child ever had eczema?', and the results by social class bore a very close similarity to those that we have shown: the rate of eczema in social class I was over twice that reported for social class V. In addition, however, there was an examination of the child by a clinical medical officer. He was asked whether he had found signs of eczema on examination. Overall, eczema was found in 2.5% of the population, but the rate did indeed vary from social class I where the rate was 4.2% to social class V where it was 2.0%. This would suggest that the social class variation in the 1958 cohort was genuine and not due to different perception of the disorder between manual and non-manual social classes.

The number of other children in the household was also associated with eczema: the more children there were, the less the condition was reported (Fig. 12.1).

Inter-relationships

We have shown statistically significant variations between a history of eczema and maternal smoking, urban neighbourhood, social class, breast feeding, number of other children in the household, region and birthweight. Indirect standardisation revealed that the associations with breast feeding, maternal smoking and type of neighbourhood were secondary to the others, and were not statistically significant once the standardisation had taken account of region, social class, birthweight and the numbers of other children in the household. The magnitude of the latter effects is shown in Fig. 12.3.

Epidemiological Associations with Hay Fever

As already noted, relatively few children were reported as having had hay fever by the age of 5. Because of the smaller numbers involved, the chance of finding significant associations is much reduced. Nevertheless, there was a highly significant sex difference in the prevalence of hay fever (Fig. 12.4). The boys in the study were 40% more likely than the girls to have had a history of this disorder.

There was no difference in the prevalence of reported hay fever among children of low birthweight, but, as with eczema, the longer the mother breast fed, the higher were the proportions of children with hay fever.

We showed that eczema is more likely to have been reported in the South and South-West of England. The same is true of hay fever (Fig. 12.5). Once again, Scotland and the North have among the lowest prevalences.

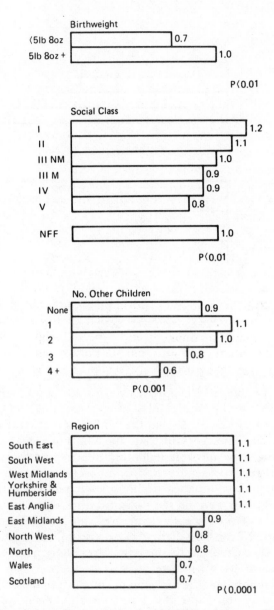

Fig. 12.3 Factors independently associated with childhood eczema (Relative Risks)

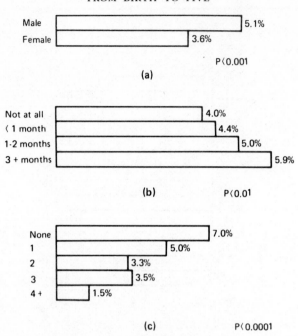

FIG. 12.4 Proportion of children reported to have had hay fever by (a) sex of the child, (b) duration of breast feeding, (c) number of other children in the household

As with eczema, we were able to confirm that a similar pattern had been found in the 1958 cohort (Davie, Butler and Goldstein, 1972): among children in the South and South-West of England the incidence was 7.2%; in Wales, East Anglia, the Midlands and North-West it was 5.1%; and in Scotland, Yorkshire and the North of England it was 4.3%.

None of the other environmental indicators was associated with hay fever. Thus, there was no variation in prevalence with the type of neighbourhood, the number of household moves, or the maternal smoking habit. Nor were there social class differences or variation with the parental situation, the mother's age, her employment history or ethnic group. Nevertheless, there was a strong association with the number of other children: the more children there were, the less likely the child was to have had hay fever (Fig. 12.4).

There were only four factors significantly associated with hay fever: sex of the child; breast feeding; region; and the number of other children in the household. Indirect standardisation showed that the breast feeding effect was due to the regional and sibling associations. Figure 12.6 shows the three remaining independent associations: the incidence of hay fever in the first 5 years is twice that in Scotland if the

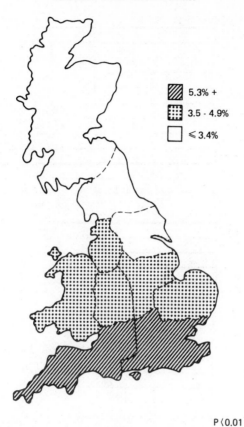

FIG. 12.5 Proportion of children reported to have had hay fever by region

child lives in the South or South-West of England; and the 'only' child
appears to have four times the incidence of the child in a very large
family (four or more other children).

Children in the Household

For both eczema and hay fever, we have found a significant decrease
in risk with the number of other children in the family. In order to
ascertain whether the associations are with the number of older or
younger siblings, we looked at each variable again. The results are
shown in Fig. 12.7. It seems clear that both the number of older and the
number of younger children in the household have a similar effect, the
total number of children being, perhaps, the most relevant.

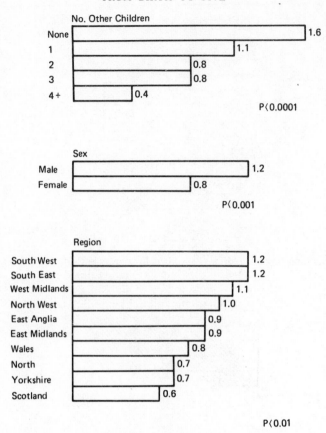

FIG. 12.6 Factors associated with hay fever (Independent relative risks)

Familial Associations

The health visitor had asked the mother whether she, the natural father, or any of the siblings had ever had asthma, hay fever or eczema. We have not presented data on the father's medical history as there appeared to be some under-reporting. Indeed, the mother was unlikely to know whether her husband had, for example, had eczema as a child. We therefore confine our analysis to the history of atopic disorders in the mothers and siblings of the study children.

From Fig. 12.8 it can be seen that the study children were some 50% more likely to have eczema if either the mother, or a sibling, has had asthma or hay fever, but they were almost three times more likely to have eczema if one of these relatives also had eczema.

The children of mothers who had a history of asthma or eczema were almost twice as likely to have hay fever compared with the rest of the

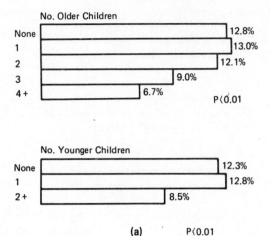

FIG. 12.7a Proportion of children with eczema by numbers of older and younger siblings

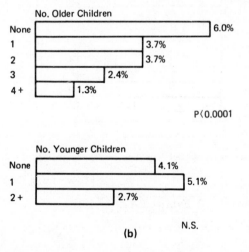

FIG. 12.7b Proportion of children with hay fever by numbers of older and younger siblings

cohort. If their mother had had hay fever then the child was nearly three times as likely to have developed hay fever by the age of 5. For hay fever the relationships with sibling history were similar, but not all of the same order of magnitude.

Behaviour and Other Conditions

Children with eczema and hay fever differed little in their behaviour patterns from others of similar sex and social class distributions (Table

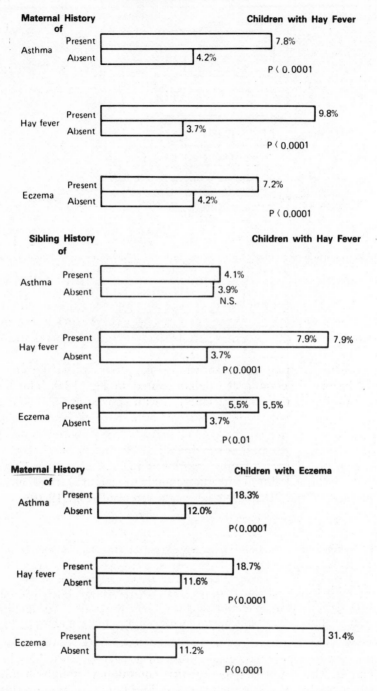

Maternal History of   **Children with Hay Fever**

Asthma   Present   7.8%
Absent   4.2%
P < 0.0001

Hay fever   Present   9.8%
Absent   3.7%
P < 0.0001

Eczema   Present   7.2%
Absent   4.2%
P < 0.0001

Sibling History of   **Children with Hay Fever**

Asthma   Present   4.1%
Absent   3.9%
N.S.

Hay fever   Present   7.9%   7.9%
Absent   3.7%
P < 0.0001

Eczema   Present   5.5%   5.5%
Absent   3.7%
P < 0.01

Maternal History of   **Children with Eczema**

Asthma   Present   18.3%
Absent   12.0%
P < 0.0001

Hay fever   Present   18.7%
Absent   11.6%
P < 0.0001

Eczema   Present   31.4%
Absent   11.2%
P < 0.0001

Continued on next page

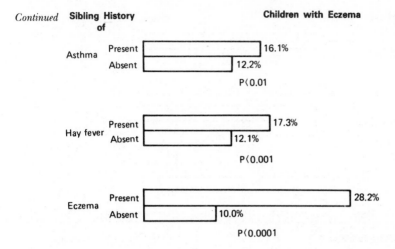

FIG. 12.8 Proportion of children with eczema, asthma, or hay fever according to familial history of asthma, hay fever or eczema

12.2). The only differences related to sleeping problems among children with either condition, crying problems as a baby (hay fever), being often worried (hay fever), fearful or afraid (eczema), and thumb sucking (eczema).

The other conditions significantly more likely to occur in children who have a history of eczema are demonstrated in Fig. 12.9. The most striking finding is the fact that children with eczema are almost three times as likely to have hay fever but only 50% more likely ever to have wheezed. More children than expected had a history of both eczema and bronchitis, mouth breathing, hearing disorder and stomach aches.

The same factors were found more often in children with hay fever. In addition, these children were more likely to have had frequent sore throats and to have had their adenoids removed (Fig. 12.10).

Discussion

In 1937 Sir F. Truby-King stated in his book *Feeding and Care of Baby* that 'breathing and living in impure air predisposes the child to eczema, as does lack of exercise, constipation, over-feeding, over-clothing, washing in hard water, and excessive exposure of the face to sunlight and wind'. The evidence for any of these statements is not available. Indeed, very few epidemiological studies on eczema appear to have been carried out. This is probably because the condition, although obviously annoying and distressing to the patient and his family, does not result in death and only occasionally in hospital admission. The same can be said

TABLE 12.2 Observed and expected numbers of children with eczema and hay fever to have other disorders

Child's history	Eczema		Hay fever	
	Observed	R. Risk	Observed	R. Risk
Wets bed (1+ per week)	169	1.0	58	0.9
Wets by day	167	1.1	57	1.0
Soils	61	0.9	23	0.9
Sleeping problems as a baby	229	1.1	82	1.0
Sleeping problems at 5	471	1.2****	184	1.3***
Feeding problems as a baby	217	1.1	93	1.2
Feeding problems at 5	605	1.1	238	1.1
Temper tantrums (1+ per week)	192	1.1	78	1.1
Destroys belongings	55	0.9	15	0.6
Fights other children	56	0.9	29	1.1
Is irritable	181	1.1	83	1.2
Takes things	30	1.1	14	1.3
Is disobedient	153	1.1	60	1.1
Tells lies	36	1.1	10	0.8
Bullies	18	0.8	11	1.2
Is often worried	104	1.3	46	1.5**
Is solitary	118	0.9	63	1.2
Is miserable or tearful	41	1.1	12	0.8
Is fearful or afraid	130	1.3**	51	1.3
Is fussy or over-particular	153	1.1	61	1.2
Very restless	437	1.0	171	1.0
Is squirmy or fidgety	183	1.1	77	1.2
Cannot settle	106	1.1	49	1.2
Crying problem as a baby	254	1.2	106	1.3**
Not much liked	20	1.0	8	1.0
Twitches/mannerisms	13	1.2	5	1.2
Bites nails	176	1.0	53	0.8
Sucks thumb	337	1.3****	103	1.1
Dysfluency	105	1.1	38	1.0
Other speech defect	170	1.1	57	1.0
Headaches (1+ per month)	106	1.2	40	1.4
Stomach aches (1+ per month)	184	1.3***	63	1.4**
2+ Accidents	209(184.2)	1.1	62	0.9
Wheezing	468	1.5****	243	2.0****
Eczema	—		174	2.6****
Hayfever	174	2.7****	—	

**P < 0.01; ***P < 0.001; ****P < 0.0001.
Expected numbers: for eczema after standardising for social class; for hay fever after standardising for sex.

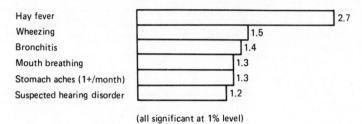

FIG. 12.9 Risk of other health outcomes in children with eczema (Relative Risks after standardisation for sex and social class)

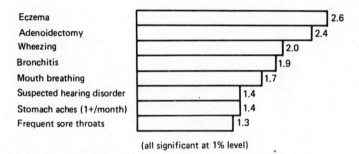

FIG. 12.10 Risk of other health outcomes in children with hay fever (Relative Risks after standardisation for sex and social class)

for hay fever. The present cohort study, therefore, offers a valuable data source, from which perhaps old hypotheses can be discarded and new ones generated.

From the information presented here and in the previous chapter, there is no evidence to confirm the hypothesis that prolonged breast feeding protects against allergic diseases. Indeed, initial analyses had suggested that on the contrary, the longer the breast feeding the more likely the child was to have had eczema (Golding, Butler and Taylor, 1982). Further analysis here has demonstrated that this finding was the result of an artefact due to the fact that the regional and social population most likely to breast feed are also those most likely to report eczema in the child. We have shown that the association is regional and social class dependent only.

Interpretation of our results is bedevilled by questions of definition. In spite of this, we can compare our data with other population studies where enquiry has been made in a similar manner. Retrospective enquiry of a twin population in Sweden (Edfors-Lubs, 1971) showed a steady increase in reported prevalence of childhood eczema with cohort:

Year of birth	% childhood eczema
1886–1895	1.2
1896–1905	1.7
1906–1915	2.4
1916–1925	2.6

There has certainly been an increase in prevalence between the two national cohort studies. By the age of 7, 7.6% of children in the 1958 cohort were reported as having had eczema compared with 12.3% of the 1970 cohort who had had the disorder by the age of 5. This is in contrast with the figures for hay fever. These have remained fairly static: 5.5% of 7-year-olds born in 1958; 4.4% of 5-year-olds born in 1970.

Clues as to possible meanings for the apparent increase in eczema may be found from the social class distribution. In both cohorts children from the upper social classes were more likely to have had eczema than those from the manual social classes. Medical examination of the 1958 cohort children indicated that this was a genuine association. Further analysis of our data (Peters, 1985) has shown that the component of social class responsible for the association is the educational qualifications of the parents. Parents who were university graduates were most likely to have a child with eczema. It is still possible that we are dealing with a problem of semantics: the more educated the parents, the more likely they may be to attach the label 'eczema' to a skin lesion. On the other hand, it may be that these parents are more likely to behave towards their children and their homes in a different way, or, finally, there may be a genetic link between eczema and intelligence. These are all avenues we intend to explore.

Conclusions

1. Children with eczema are found significantly less often in low social classes, in large families and in Scotland, Wales, the North and North–West of England. Children of low birthweight are less likely than expected to develop eczema.
2. There is evidence that the prevalence of eczema has risen since the previous cohort study.
3. Hay fever is 50% more prevalent in boys than girls. It is found most in the South–East and South–West of England, but is uncommon in Scotland. The prevalence of hay fever falls with the number of children in the household.

CHAPTER 13

Squints and vision defects

by JEAN GOLDING and N. R. BUTLER

Squint

The inability to see clearly is relatively common. Nevertheless, it is important that visual defects are identified as early as possible in order that long-term damage can be prevented. This is especially true of squints.

A squint is a deviation of the visual axes. There are three mechanisms by which a squint may occur: first, the motor-apparatus that rotates the eye may be damaged; secondly, there might be a defect in the sensory component of the reflex arc, for instance, caused by an eye which has poor sight; and thirdly, there may be defect in the central component of the reflex arc (*British Medical Journal*, 1974). The first of these is uncommon in childhood, the defect in the second is confined to the visual apparatus, but the third is located in the brain itself (Douglas, 1963). If congenital in origin, an early straightening operation is usually the method of choice. If associated with the lazy eye syndrome, then the better eye may be covered by a patch to force the child to use the other eye. Glasses may also be prescribed to correct a convergent squint, and orthoptic exercises carried out to encourage the eye towards stereoscopic vision.

In a study of the children in the 1958 cohort who had a squint on clinical examination at 7, Alberman, Butler and Gardiner (1971) found that the group included proportionally more children with cerebral palsy, or mental subnormality, than the rest of the population. In addition, children with squints were twice as likely to be clumsy, and 50% more likely to have unintelligible speech. The authors found that even when the clumsy and mentally subnormal children were excluded, the remaining children with squints tended to have reading problems and difficulties in copying designs. The prevalence of squint did not vary in the 1958 cohort with age at examination. The condition was said to have been present at examination in 3.5% of the 7-year-olds (Alberman, Butler and Gardiner, 1971) and 3.4% of the 11-year-olds (Pearson and

Peckham, 1972). In addition, squint had been said to be present prior to the 7-year examination for another 3.9% of the children.

The present 1970 cohort study of 5-year-olds did not include a medical examination, and we have to rely on the mother's report. In all, 973 of the 13,005 children for whom information was available were said to have had a squint, but in half of these (483 children) the problem was no longer present. Thus, although 7.5% of the children had had a squint, by the age of 5 only 3.8% still had the problem. These figures are in remarkable accord with those from the earlier cohort.

Of the 935 children with squint, 93.4% had attended for advice. Over a third of these were told that no treatment was necessary (Table 13.1). Of the remainder, a wide variety of treatments was given, usually in combination with one another. Of those given treatment, two-thirds were prescribed glasses, 45% had a patch over their good eye, 30% were given exercises, and a third of the children had had an operation.

TABLE 13.1   Treatment given to children who had a history
of squint

Treatments (not mutually exclusive)	Number of children	
Operation	172	(18.4%)
Exercises	150	(16.0%)
Glasses	336	(35.9%)
Patch over eye	223	(23.9%)
Treatment given—type not stated	31	(3.3%)
Number given treatment	503	(53.8%)
Advised no treatment needed	370	(39.6%)
Never attended for treatment or advice	62	(6.6%)
All known	935	(100.0%)

As in the 1958 cohort, there were no differences between the sexes in the proportion of children who had ever had a squint, but those who had been of low birthweight were substantially more likely to have had this problem (Fig. 13.1). There was also a significant variation with duration of breast feeding, but no evidence of a linear trend. Children who had never been breast fed were no more or less likely to have a squint than those who had been breast fed for up to 2 months of age, but there were proportionally fewer children with squints among the groups who had been breast fed for 3 months or more.

There were no statistically significant differences between the regions, nor did the incidence of squint vary with the type of neighbourhood. Nevertheless, among families who moved house frequently there were more likely to be children with a squint.

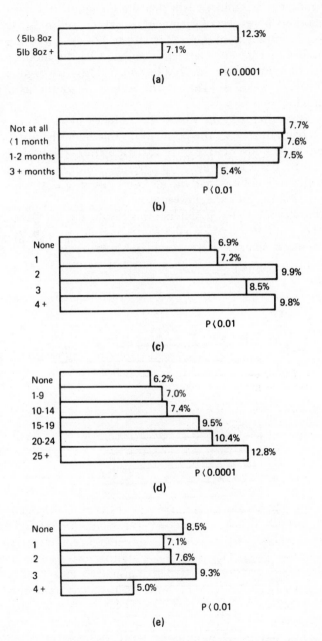

FIG. 13.1 Proportion of children ever having had a squint by (a) birthweight, (b) duration of breast feeding, (c) number of household moves, (d) maternal smoking habit, (e) number of other children in the household

The mothers of children who had had a squint did not differ from other mothers in respect of their ages, social class, ethnic group, parental situation or employment status. There was, however, a strong trend with the number of cigarettes currently smoked by the mother (Fig 13.1). Children of mothers who smoked heavily (twenty-five or more cigarettes a day) were twice as likely to have had a squint as children of non-smoking mothers.

The only other way in which the families of children with squint differed from the rest of the population concerned the number of other children in the household. Figure 13.1e illustrates the findings. It can be seen that there was no evidence of a trend—children with no siblings, or those with three siblings, had the highest rates of squints, those with four or more siblings had the lowest rate.

Standardisation failed to explain this result (Fig. 13.2), but it must be pointed out that if the two small groups of children with either three or four or more siblings were combined there would no longer be a statistically significant association between squint and the number of children in the household.

Figure 13.2 also demonstrates the fact that the major variables

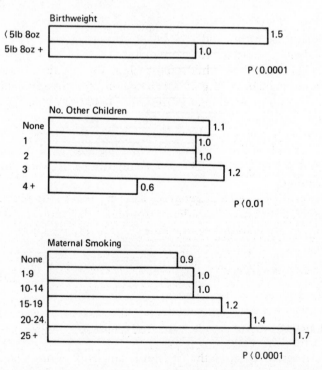

FIG. 13.2 Factors independently associated with squint (Relative Risks)

associated with squint were the birthweight of the child and the number of cigarettes smoked by the mother. These factors were responsible for the associations with duration of breast feeding and the number of household moves.

Vision Problems Other than Squint

A study from Sweden has shown that unless vision screening has been carried out in young children, significant numbers of defects will escape detection (Kohler and Stigmar, 1978). These include amblyopia and myopia. Thus, since our present study did not include a vision test, we may well be underestimating the extent of the problem. The results of the tests on the children when they reached the age of 10 will be especially valuable.

Nineteen children had severe vision problems (Table 13.2). These included two children of very low birthweight who had retrolental fibroplasia, three with cerebral palsy, one of whose defect was due to meningitis. Two children had had cancer (one retinoblastoma, one Wilm's tumour), the association between Wilm's tumour and aniridia having been documented previously (Shannon *et al.*, 1982). It is apparent from the list that severe visual defect has many different physical associations. Only one case was thought possibly to be associated with rubella (case 8): a child with bilateral cataract, whose mother had been a rubella contact during pregnancy.

In all, 451 of the 12,547 children for whom the question was answered had a vision problem, giving an incidence of 3.6%. In 146 children the problem was said to be no longer present. For 173 (38%) of the children with vision defects, a history of squint was also recorded.

Children with vision problems were equally distributed between the sexes, but, as with squint, children who had been of low birthweight were at increased risk (Fig. 13.3). There were no differences with duration of breast feeding.

There was no evidence of geographical variation in the prevalence of visual defect, but there was evidence to suggest that more children than expected were to be found among those who had moved house on many occasions.

Mothers of children with defective vision did not differ from other mothers in respect of their age, employment history, social class, ethnic group or parental situation. The only statistically significant differences were found with the mother's smoking habits (Fig. 13.3). Mothers whose children had defective vision were more likely to smoke, and smoke heavily, when the child was 5 years old.

Standardisation showed that a significant association remained between vision problems and both low birthweight and a large number of

TABLE 13.2 Children with major vision problems

Case number	Visual defect(s)	Other abnormalities	Possible aetiology	Social factors
1	Albino Horizontal nystagmus and strabismus Partially sighted	—	Familial albinism (2 siblings also affected)	Asian parents Poor home conditions Baby delivered at home unattended Mother a non-smoker
2	Totally blind—Leber's amaurosis	—	?	Social class I Parents are non-smokers
3	Severe myopia Wears glasses	Conductive hearing defect (grommet inserted age 4)	?	Single mother Smokes 20 cigarettes per day
4	Congenital vertical and horizontal nystagmus for near and distant vision Special schooling recommended	—	—	Baby delivered at home Social class II Mother a non-smoker
5	Fine pendular nystagmus	Educationally backward Suspected hearing difficulty Eczema Mild speech difficulty	? Congenital	Mother smokes 30 cigarettes per day
6	Severe visual loss left-eye Squint repair at 18 months Eye patch prescribed 4 years Squint still present	—	—	Mother smokes 7 cigarettes per day
7	Optic atrophy With glasses: Vision: R 4/60 L 6/36 Convergent right strabismus	Spastic quadriplegia Mentally backward Arrested hydrocephalus Bronchitis	Perinatal: Low birthweight (1780 g) Cerebral signs and apnoeic attacks	Parents refuse to recognise the child has problems Mother smokes 20 cigarettes per day
8	Bilateral cataract Bilateral squint Squint operation at 3 years Cataract aspiration at 5 years	Febrile convulsion at 15 months	Perinatal: Low birthweight (1390 g) Tube fed, Cyanotic attacks or Rubella (mother Rubella contact)	Parents both nurses Mother smokes 30 cigarettes per day
9	Atrophic retinal choroiditis Bilateral nystagmus and hypermetropia	Cerebral palsy (L. hemiplegia)	Congenital: Mother had severe febrile illness in first months of pregnancy	Parents separated at birth Little antenatal care Mother a non-smoker
10	Blind Hypoplastic optic nerves Extensive cerebral	Microcephaly with encephalocele—lesion closed in neonatal period	Congenital	Mother is non-smoker

11	Damaged left optic nerve	Congenital Diackian Diamond anaemia Pneumococcal meningitis 3 years Spastic paraplegia Mental retardation Died aged 5 years	Post meningitis	Social class IV Mother a non-smoker
12	Left eye removed (retinoblastoma) Partially sighted right eye	—	Cancer	Mother smokes 10 cigarettes per day
13	Cataract right eye—discovered only at age 4 Very poor vision	Restless	?	Mother smokes 13 cigarettes per day
14	Blind in right eye—first identified at 4 years 'Findings suggestive of toxocara'	Slightly backward	Infection	Three younger siblings Mother a non-smoker
15	Alternating squint Vision defect Refuses to wear glasses	Multicystic left kidney removed 5 weeks Frequent falls—four accidental injuries Bumps on head—referrals to outpatients for observation—suspected child abuse Whooping cough 8 months	? Congenital	Mother smokes 30 cigarettes per day
16	Retrolental fibroplasia Blind in one eye Partially blind in other	Pneumonia Slightly backward	Perinatal: Low birthweight (1250 g) Respiratory distress Nursed in incubator	Maternal smoking 20 cigarettes per day Father psychiatrically ill
17	Right cataract (op. 20 m) Blind in right eye Left eye normal	Severe eczema	?	Mother a non-smoker
18	Bilateral cataracts Extremely shortsighted Aniridia	Right Wilm's tumour Educationally subnormal Microcephaly Birthweight 4 lb 10 oz Nursed in incubator	Congenital	Home delivery Mother smokes 7 cigarettes per day
19	Retrolental fibroplasia	Severe speech problem Mental handicap	Perinatal: Birthweight 2 lb 6 oz Jaundice Hypothermia (92°F) Respiratory distress Extensive bruising	Three older siblings Mother was shot in 1972 by father Father now in prison Parents divorced Mother smokes 20 cigarettes per day

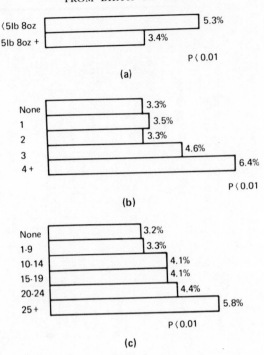

FIG. 13.3 Proportion of children with a vision problem (other than squint) by (a) birthweight, (b) number of household moves, (c) maternal smoking habit

household moves (Fig. 13.4). The association with maternal smoking was not statistically significant once these two factors had been taken into account.

Health and Behaviour of the Children

Ways in which the behaviour of children with squint differ from their contemporaries are shown in Table 13.3. They were reported as having been more likely to have had feeding and crying difficulties in early infancy. In addition, they were more likely to have many of the attributes of the 'difficult' child—being more destructive, bullying and disobedient. They were over twice as likely to have twitches or mannerisms and were at increased risk of wetting by day and soiling.

Apart from these behaviour differences there was little to distinguish between the health of these children (Fig. 13.5). They were somewhat more likely to have had a history of mouth breathing and wheezing, but no more at risk of hearing problems or other atopic or respiratory disorders than expected.

Children with other vision problems showed a different pattern (Fig.

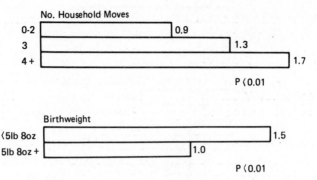

Fig. 13.4 Factors independently associated with vision problems (Relative Risks)

13.6). Unlike the children with squint, they were more likely to have had pneumonia and be suspected of hearing difficulties. Behaviour traits common to children with squint, and those with other vision problems, were wetting by day, soiling, risk of being fearful or afraid when presented with new situations, having sleeping problems at 5, being disobedient, and having a history of feeding problems as a baby.

Prescription of Glasses

One of the factors that may influence behaviour of children with vision problems concerns whether or not they have been prescribed glasses. Children with glasses are often afraid of breaking them and aware that they are different from others. They often get teased by other children and are given nick-names such as 'square eyes', 'the owl', 'four eyes', etc.

Of the 5-year-old study children, 474 had been prescribed glasses, but fifty-three of these children (11%) were said no longer to wear them.

Glasses had been prescribed for 36% of the children who had had a squint, and for half (222) of the 451 children with vision problems. These figures include 111 children who had both squint and vision problems. Figure 13.7 shows that about two-thirds of the children who had both squint and vision problems had been prescribed glasses, two-fifths of those who had vision problems alone, and a third of children with squint, but, apparently, no vision problem.

As might be expected, there was a relationship between birthweight and the prescribing of glasses. Proportionally almost twice as many low birthweight children had worn glasses (Fig. 13.8) as those who weighed 5 lb 8 oz or more at delivery.

There was a statistically significant variation with the duration of breast feeding. Nevertheless, as can be seen from Fig. 13.8, the pattern

TABLE 13.3 Health and behaviour of children with squint, vision problems or who wear glasses compared with numbers expected after standardisation for sex and social class

Child's history	Squint		Vision problem		Glasses	
	Observed	R. Risk	Observed	R. Risk	Observed	R. Risk
Wets bed (1+ per week)	118	1.1	57	1.2	57	1.1
Wets by day	132	1.4***	69	1.5***	59	1.2
Soils	59	1.4**	31	1.6**	25	1.3
Sleeping problems as a baby	149	1.1	71	1.2	62	1.0
Sleeping problems at 5	292	1.2**	160	1.4****	127	1.1
Feeding problems as a baby	162	1.3**	81	1.4**	73	1.2
Feeding problems at 5	386	1.1	175	1.1	176	1.0
Temper tantrums (1+ per week)	145	1.2*	68	1.3	65	1.1
Destroys things	65	1.6***	23	1.2	33	1.7**
Fights other children	48	1.2	19	1.0	23	1.2
Is irritable	128	1.1	58	1.1	47	0.8
Takes things	26	1.4	9	1.1	9	1.0
Is disobedient	133	1.5****	60	1.4**	60	1.3*
Tells lies	29	1.4	8	0.8	9	0.9
Bullies	23	1.6*	7	1.1	11	1.6
Is often worried	60	1.1	31	1.3	18	0.7
Is rather solitary	87	1.0	44	1.1	41	1.0
Is miserable or tearful	35	1.4*	17	1.5	16	1.4
Is fearful or afraid	92	1.5***	46	1.6**	40	1.3

Is fussy or over-particular	91	1.0	39	0.9	43	1.0
Is very restless	286	1.0	122	1.0	143	1.1
Is squirmy or fidgety	133	1.2*	61	1.2	73	1.4**
Cannot settle	98	1.5***	43	1.4*	49	1.5**
Crying as a baby	173	1.3**	72	1.1	65	1.0
Not much liked	11	0.8	9	1.4	6	0.9
Twitches/mannerisms	15	2.1**	3	0.9	4	1.2
Bites nails	127	1.2	59	1.2	67	1.3
Sucks thumb	177	1.1	97	1.3*	83	1.0
Dysfluency	79	1.3*	29	1.1	33	1.1
Other speech defect	128	1.3**	62	1.3*	58	1.1
Headaches	74	1.3*	38	1.5*	33	1.2
Stomach aches	110	1.2*	49	1.2	43	1.0
2+ Accidents	119	1.0	48	0.9	54	0.9
Wheezing	237	1.2**	110	1.2	100	1.0
Eczema	122	1.1	63	1.2	44	0.8
Hay fever	45	1.1	25	1.3	19	1.0
Vision problem	173	5.2****	173	—	222	13.6***
Squint	—	—		5.2****	363	10.3****

*$P < 0.05$; **$P < 0.01$; ***$P < 0.001$; ****$P < 0.0001$.

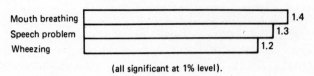

FIG. 13.5 Risk of other health outcomes in children with a squint (Relative Risks after standardisation for sex and social class)

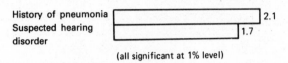

FIG. 13.6 Risk of other health outcomes in children with a vision problem (Relative Risks after standardisation for sex and social class)

Squint	Vision problem	Proportion with glasses	
Yes	Yes		64%
No	Yes		40%
Yes	No		32%

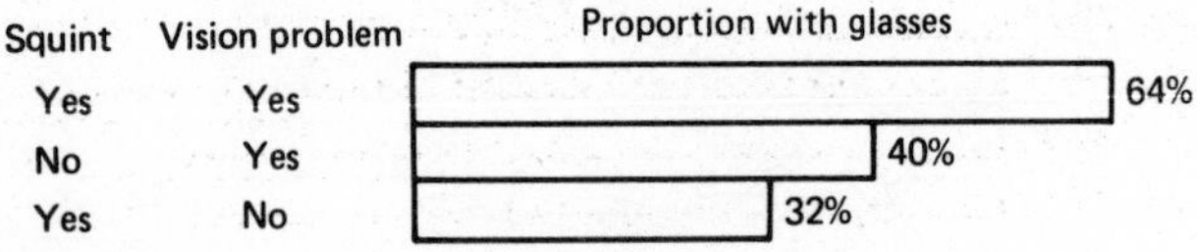

FIG. 13.7 Proportion of children prescribed glasses according to whether child had a squint or other vision problem

was bizarre—children being most likely to have glasses if they had either never been breast fed, or they had been breast fed for between 1 and 2 months.

There were no other statistically significant differences apart from that found with maternal cigarette smoking. This was very similar to that found for squint; the more cigarettes the mother currently smoked, the more likely was the child to have had glasses.

Standardisation (Fig. 13.9) demonstrated that the associations between the prescription of glasses and low birthweight, maternal smoking habit and duration of breast feeding were independent of one another.

The behaviour of children prescribed glasses did not differ much from children without glasses. Children with glasses were more likely to be described as destructive (R. Risk 1.7), to be squirmy or fidgety (R. Risk 1.4) or to be unable to settle (R. Risk 1.5). They were not significantly more likely to display those other characteristics shown in Table 13.3 to be associated with both vision problems or squint—viz. daytime wetting, soiling, sleeping problems, being fearful or afraid, twitching, or having a history of feeding or crying problems as a baby. This might mean that, once given glasses, a child's behaviour is likely to improve, or that children with behaviour problems are unlikely to be prescribed glasses to treat their vision problems.

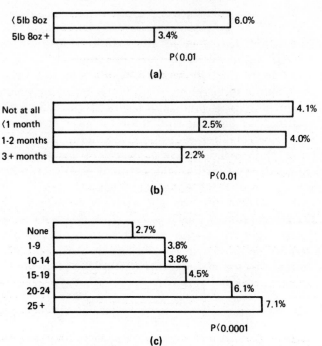

FIG. 13.8 Proportion of children prescribed glasses by (a) birthweight, (b) duration of breast feeding, (c) maternal smoking habit

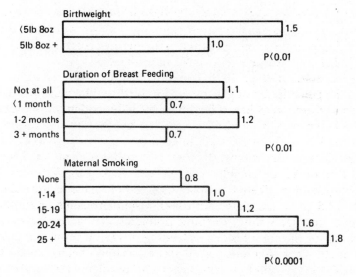

FIG. 13.9 Factors independently associated with the child wearing glasses

Discussion

One of the major findings in this study confirms previously reported associations—viz. an increased incidence of squint and vision problems in infants of low birthweight. Alberman, Benson and Evans (1982) showed that children of birthweight of 2000 g or less were significantly more likely to have both mild and severe vision defects than their matched controls. We have shown that low birthweight was a feature in four of the nineteen children with very severe defects, but also that mild and moderate abnormalities were at least 50% more prevalent than expected in children of birthweight less than 2500 g (5 lb 8 oz). This finding was equally true of squint.

We have shown a profound trend between the prevalence of history of squint and maternal smoking habit at 5. It is possible that this association reflects a teratologic effect—the mothers smoking heavily when their child is 5 tend to be those who smoked heavily during pregnancy. It is conceivable that this has affected that part of the brain governing the central component of the reflex arc.

Conclusions

1. Squint is more prevalent among children who have been of low birthweight and whose mothers smoke.
2. Vision defect was also more apparent among low birthweight infants.
3. Children with squint were more likely to have speech problems, to wheeze and breathe through their mouths, as well as have many behaviour problems.
4. As well as having more behaviour difficulties, children with vision problems were more likely to have had pneumonia and be suspected of hearing difficulty.

CHAPTER 14

Bronchitis and pneumonia

by JEAN GOLDING

Introduction

Although apparently simple, the question 'Has your child ever had bronchitis?' begs many questions. The paediatrician would distinguish between at least four different types: acute bronchitis which often follows an upper respiratory tract viral infection, and rarely lasts more than a week; recurrent bronchitis with chronic cough in a catarrhal child; wheezy bronchitis with recurrent episodes of coughing and wheezing, the term sometimes being used synonymously with asthma; and acute bronchiolitis which typically occurs in winter epidemics in infants under 12 months of age, and is often associated with the respiratory syncytial virus (Valman, 1980a). In contrast, pneumonia is a much more straightforward clinical diagnosis.

Factors said to be associated with bronchitis or pneumonia in the early years of life have included atmospheric pollution (Douglas and Waller, 1966), gas cooking in the home (Melia *et al.*, 1977), parental cigarette smoking (Colley, Holland and Corkhill, 1974), the number of siblings in the household (McCall and Acheson, 1968), low social class (Spence *et al.*, 1954; Colley, 1976) and deficient maternal care (Miller *et al.*, 1960).

Prevalence

In the 1946 cohort, Douglas and Blomfield (1958) reported that 29% of children had had a lower respiratory tract infection in the first 2 years of life alone.

In the present study the incidence was much lower: 17.1% (2165 children) had had bronchitis at some stage during their first 5 years. Of these, 45.2% (978) had had an attack during the 12 months preceding the interview. Pneumonia was comparatively rare: only 1.6% (205) of the children had such a history, and in only fifty (24%) of these had an attack occurred in the preceding 12 months. In all, 116 of the children with bronchitis had also had pneumonia.

There were slight sex differences in the proportions of children who had had either pneumonia (116 boys, 90 girls) or bronchitis (1241 boys, 924 girls). In both cases there were 25% more boys than girls. This is in accord with the findings from many other studies (Watkins et al., 1979; Leeder et al., 1976a). Because numbers with bronchitis were greater, statistical significance was reached only for this group (Fig. 14.1).

Birthweight and Breast Feeding

Watkins and colleagues (1979) found no birthweight differences in the reported prevalence of bronchitis and/or pneumonia in the first year of life, but a study of hospital admissions (McCall and Acheson, 1968) showed an increased rate of admissions for bronchitis/pneumonia in the first year among low birthweight infants. Follow-up studies of very low birthweight infants have shown high rates of lower respiratory tract infection (Pape et al., 1978). In the present study we are unable to split the information by age of occurrence, but there was no excess of bronchitis under 5 years among infants of low birthweight.

In contrast, there was a strong association between low birthweight and a subsequent history of pneumonia (Fig. 14.2); children who had weighed under 2500 g at birth were over twice as likely to have had pneumonia as their heavier contemporaries.

Restricting their attention to attacks of bronchitis in the first year of life, Watkins, Leeder and Corkhill (1979) found a negative association between lower respiratory tract infection and breast feeding. We, too, found a reduced prevalence of both bronchitis and pneumonia in infants who had been breast fed (bronchitis: 15.4% breast fed vs 18.2% not breast fed, $P < 0.001$; pneumonia: 1.2% vs 1.9%, $P < 0.01$). There was a significant negative trend with duration of breast feeding for bronchitis but not for pneumonia (Fig. 14.1).

Parents and Siblings

Death from pneumonia between the ages of 1 and 4 is strongly related to social class (Adelstein and White, 1976), as are infant hospital admissions for lower respiratory tract infections (McCall and Acheson, 1968). Among population studies of history of bronchitis or pneumonia in early childhood, whether or not based on hospital admissions, a similar trend with social class has been demonstrated (Douglas and Blomfield, 1958: Miller et al., 1960; Colley and Reid, 1970).

In the present study there were also strong associations with social class: for bronchitis there was a steady increase in the proportion of children who had had the disorder as the social class became lower (Fig. 14.1). For pneumonia there was a significant difference between prevalences in the non-manual (1.1%) as compared with the manual

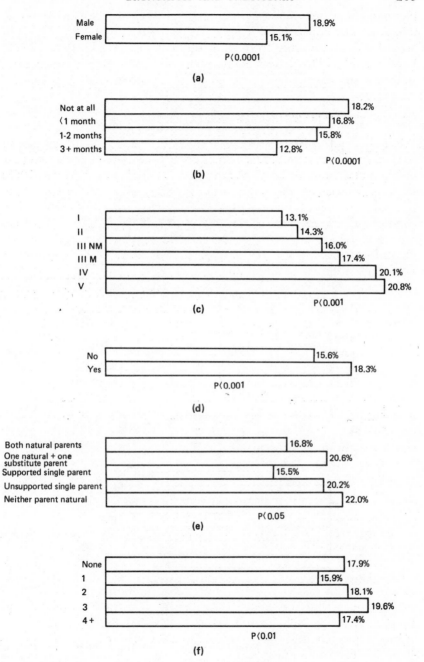

Fig. 14.1 Proportion of children ever to have had bronchitis by (a) sex of the child, (b) duration of breast feeding, (c) social class, (d) whether mother had worked during child's life, (e) parental situation, (f) number of other children in the household
(continued on next page)

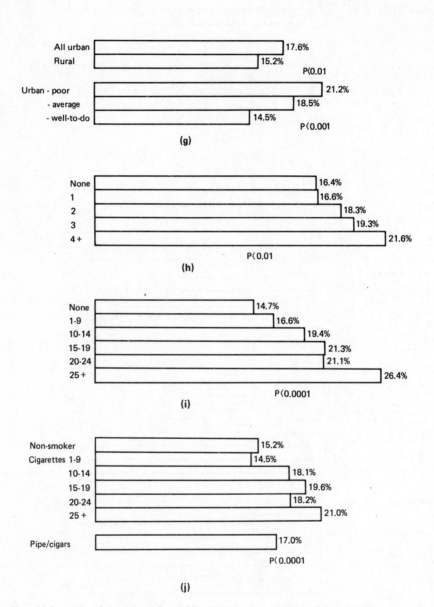

FIG. 14.1 *continued* (g) type of neighbourhood, (h) number of household moves, (i) maternal smoking habit, (j) paternal smoking habit

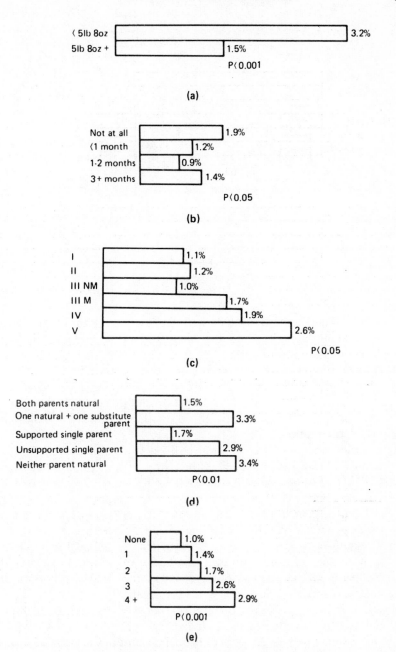

FIG. 14.2 Proportion of children ever to have had pneumonia by (a) birthweight, (b) duration of breast feeding, (c) social class, (d) parental situation, (e) number of other children in the household (*continued on next page*)

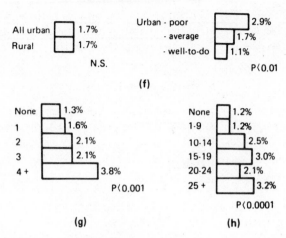

FIG. 14.2 *continued* (f) type of neighbourhood, (g) number of household moves, (h) maternal smoking habit

(1.8%) groups ($P < 0.01$), but little evidence for a linear trend (Fig. 14.2).

Like McCall and Acheson (1968) in Oxford, we found no relationship between the mother's age and the likelihood of a child having had bronchitis or pneumonia. We did, however, find that children of mothers who had ever worked were more likely to have had bronchitis (Fig. 14.1). The figures for pneumonia were in the same direction but not statistically significant (1.8% of children of mothers who had worked compared with 1.4% of those whose mothers remained full-time housewives throughout).

The child who was living with both natural parents at 5 was significantly less likely to have had either bronchitis or pneumonia than children in other situations (bronchitis: 16.8% vs 19.7%, $P < 0.001$; pneumonia: 1.5% vs 2.8%, $P < 0.01$). As can be seen in Figs. 14.1, 14.2, children who appear to have been most at risk were, in order, those not living with a natural parent, those living with a step-parent and those with a single unsupported parent. It is worth noting that this is one of the few occasions on which children who had been adopted or fostered appeared to be worse off than other groups, but it is also important to note that the numbers involved are very small.

There were no significant differences between the ethnic groups. Previous studies (Leeder *et al.*, 1976a; Colley, Holland and Corkhill, 1974) have found increased rates of bronchitis and pneumonia with the number of siblings. In this study, too, there were significant associations with the number of other children in the household (Figs. 14.1, 14.2). The variation with bronchitis, however, showed no sign of a linear trend; the lowest rates were found when there was either only one sibling or four or more. With pneumonia, however, there was a strong linear trend—the risk to children living in households with at least four other children was almost three times that of the 'only' child.

The Physical Environment

There was a strong regional variation in the history of bronchitis (Fig. 14.3), though not with pneumonia. The greatest proportion of children

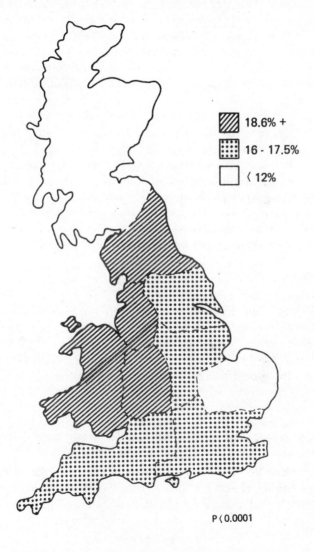

18.6% +

16 - 17.5%

⟨ 12%

P ⟨ 0.0001

FIG. 14.3 Proportion of children reported to have had bronchitis, by region

said to have had bronchitis was found in Wales (22.4%), and the lowest was in Scotland (10.8%). Intuitively, the fact that the rate in Scotland was so low was surprising, especially since there is a greater proportion of lower social class households there than in the rest of the country. Are the Scottish children really less likely to have had bronchitis, or is there a greater reluctance to apply such a label to the child? There is some evidence that the death rate from respiratory disorders in boys in the age group 1–4 were somewhat lower in Scotland than in England and Wales (Colley, 1976), but hospital admission rates between the two areas are roughly identical (Snook, 1977). That there is an increased rate in Wales had been reported by Colley and Reid (1970), and confirmed by Yarnell and St. Leger (1981).

Like Colley and Reid (1970) we found that children resident in urban areas were more likely than those in rural areas to have had bronchitis. There were no such differences with regard to pneumonia.

Within urban areas there were strong associations between both disorders and the type of area (Fig. 14.1, 2), rates being highest in the poor and lowest in the well-to-do urban areas.

There were also positive associations between each condition and the number of times the child had moved house (Fig. 14.1,2). The association was particularly strong for pneumonia—children who had moved frequently were over twice as likely to have had the disorder as those who had not moved at all.

Strong associations have been found both in Britain and in New Zealand between the prevalence of a history of bronchitis or pneumonia and parental smoking habit (Colley, Holland and Corkhill, 1974; Fergusson, Horwood and Shannon, 1980).

The British study noted that the risk was much increased if both parents smoked, compared with one parent, but did not appear to have determined whether the smoking habit of the mother was more associated with an adverse history than the smoking habit of the father. This was examined by the New Zealand longitudinal study. It was found that maternal smoking was the important association—once this had been taken into account, paternal smoking had no significant effect (Fergusson, Horwood and Shannon, 1980).

In the present study, also, there were strong associations between maternal smoking and both bronchitis and pneumonia (Figs.14.1, 14.2), with a dose–response effect being evident. There was no significant association between paternal smoking and a history of pneumonia—but there was a positive association for bronchitis (Fig. 14.1j).

Inter-dependence

Of all the various factors shown to be associated with bronchitis and pneumonia, it is important from a preventative point of view to assess which associations are the direct consequence of others— and which still hold when all others have been taken into account.

For bronchitis, we found that the initial associations with breast feeding, number of siblings, type of neighbourhood and number of household moves were the result of their close association with social class and maternal smoking habit. Paternal smoking was also explained in this way. The remaining statistically significant associations are shown in Fig. 14.4. The number of cigarettes smoked by the mother, sex of the child, maternal employment, lower social class and the region of the country all had significant effects.

Since half the children with pneumonia had also had bronchitis, one might have expected a similar pattern to emerge after standardisation. On the contrary, there is only one factor in common: maternal smoking habit. The other variables found to be important (Fig. 14.5) were the number of other children in the household, the number of household moves and the child's birthweight.

Other Problems

After making allowance for their sex and social class distribution, the children with a history of bronchitis were no more likely to be incontinent at age 5 than children without such a history (Table 14.1), nor were they more likely to have had feeding difficulties—either as a baby or at the time of interview. They were, however, at 20% increased risk of having had sleeping problems (both as a baby and at the time of interview). The children with bronchitis were more likely to have nightmares (6.4% vs 4.6%), and to wake early in the morning (9.7% vs 6.7%) or during the night (13.9% vs 10.2%). The children who had had bronchitis were also significantly more likely to display characteristics of the 'difficult' child, and of the 'troubled' child.

In interpreting the information concerning the children with pneumonia, it must be remembered that, because of the small numbers involved, only very large differences will be statistically significant. Apart from their wheezing history, the only way in which children who had had pneumonia differed substantially from the rest of the population concerned their propensity to suck a thumb or finger (Table 14.1). The likelihood of this behaviour increased by 70%.

As expected, both pneumonia and bronchitis occurred more frequently in children with a history of wheezing. Frequently, of course, in such children the infection will have been accompanied by wheezing. Of all children who had ever had bronchitis, 60% also had a history of wheezing. Of all children who had pneumonia, 52% had a history of wheezing.

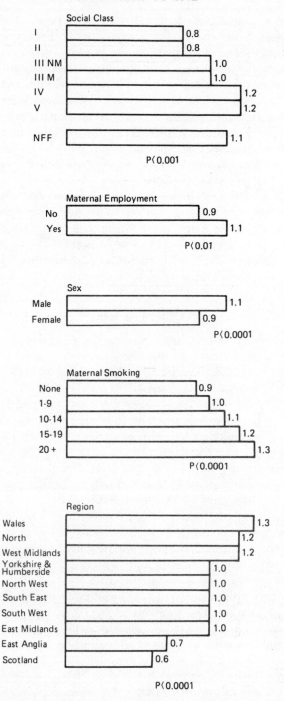

Fig. 14.4 Factors independently associated with history of bronchitis (Relative Risks)

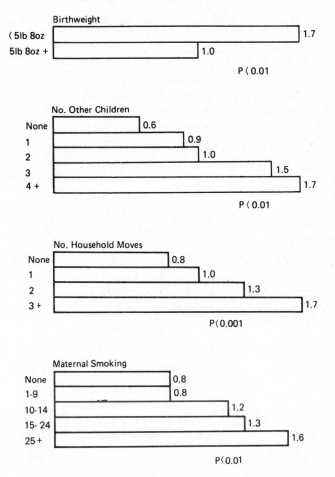

Fig. 14.5 Factors independently associated with a history of pneumonia (independent Relative Risks)

Children with a history of bronchitis were also at increased risk of disorders of the upper respiratory tract, including hay fever. They were more likely, too, to have had hearing and speech difficulties, including dysfluency (Fig. 14.6).

Children with a history of pneumonia had a somewhat different pattern of associations (Fig. 14.7). They were twice as likely as expected to have vision problems, and more than twice as likely to have had a tonsillectomy.

Discussion

Most epidemiological studies have obtained their information by

TABLE 14.1 Number of children with various behaviour and other problems to be reported as having bronchitis or pneumonia compared with numbers expected after standardisation for sex and social class

Child's history	Bronchitis		Pneumonia	
	Observed	R. Risk	Observed	R. Risk
Wets bed (1+ per week)	274	1.1	31	1.1
Wets by day	246	1.2	22	1.4
Soils	105	1.1	11	1.0
Sleeping problems as a baby	361	1.2***	29	0.9
Sleeping problems at 5	638	1.2****	64	1.3
Feeding problems as a baby	327	1.1	28	1.0
Feeding problems at 5	796	1.0	75	1.0
Temper tantrums (1+ per week)	358	1.3****	35	1.1
Destroys belongings	136	1.4***	16	1.2
Fights other children	109	1.1	14	1.1
Is irritable	331	1.3****	10	1.9
Takes things	58	1.3	10	1.9
Is disobedient	256	1.2**	27	1.1
Tells lies	65	1.3	10	1.7
Bullies	48	1.4	7	1.7
Is often worried	153	1.3**	14	1.2
Is solitary	257	1.3***	27	1.3
Is miserable or tearful	79	1.4**	10	1.9
Is fearful or afraid	166	1.2	21	1.5
Is fussy or over-particular	228	1.1	17	1.0
Is very restless	699	1.1	77	1.1
Squirmy or fidgety	302	1.2**	36	1.4
Cannot settle	188	1.2	21	1.2
Crying problem as a baby	382	1.2****	33	1.1
Not much liked	43	1.3	6	1.8
Twitches/mannerisms	21	1.3	2	1.3
Bites nails	269	1.1	24	1.2
Sucks thumb	337	1.0	45	1.7***
Dysfluency	178	1.3***	9	0.5
Other speech defect	281	1.2**	34	1.3
Headaches (1+ per month)	170	1.3***	17	1.4
Stomach aches (1+ per month)	237	1.2**	25	1.4
2+ Accidents	333	1.2***	26	0.8
Wheezing	1295	2.8****	106	2.1****
Eczema	355	1.4****	24	1.0
Hay fever	165	1.9****	12	1.5
Vision problem	86	1.2	15	2.1**
Squint	186	1.2	24	1.6*
Bronchitis	—	—	116	3.4****
Pneumonia	116	3.4****	—	—

**P < 0.01; ***P < 0.001; ****P < 0.0001.

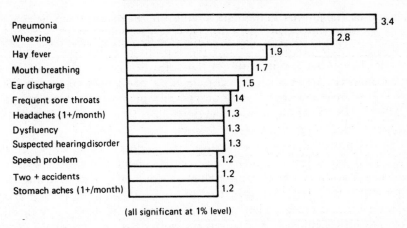

FIG. 14.6 Risk of other health outcomes in children with bronchitis (Relative Risks after standardisation for sex and social class)

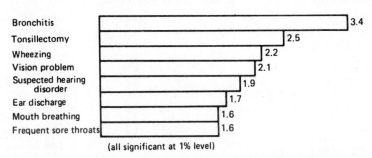

FIG. 14.7 Risk of other health outcomes in children with pneumonia (Relative Risks after standardisation for sex and social class)

questioning the mother as to whether the child had ever had bronchitis or pneumonia. There is a tacit assumption that she will have the requisite knowledge to make such diagnoses. A prospective general practice study compared diagnoses of lower respiratory tract illness in all infants under 12 months of age with the responses to a questionnaire administered to the mother. Of the 404 mothers included, thirty-three claimed that their child had had bronchitis or pneumonia, but the general practitioners had recorded these diagnoses for 116 of the children (only twenty-one were reported by both mother and general practitioner). The authors (Watkins et al., 1982) state that 'we know that because of considerable inter- and intra- doctor variation in the interpretation of the symptoms and signs of respiratory illness, little value can be placed on the diagnostic labels of G.P.s'. Nevertheless, they also note that, although not identical to the general practitioner's diagnoses, the mother does identify children, the majority of whom have had a lower respiratory tract infection, and who, if other follow-up studies are replicated, will have reduced pulmonary function (Leeder *et al.*, 1976c). Indeed, other studies have shown that among adolescents who had been given such a history in their pre-school years there are greatly increased risks of respiratory symptoms (Holland, Bailey and Bland, 1978), including winter cough (Colley, Douglas and Reid, 1973) and impeded lung function (Woolcock *et al.*, 1979).

Justification for use of maternal history taking, therefore, lies in the long-term evidence that one is measuring a meaningful entity, as well as the fact that this is the way most clinicians obtain a medical history for their patients. Given, therefore, the various *caveats*, it is interesting to try to interpret our results. The most crucial factor is the strong relationship for both bronchitis and pneumonia with maternal smoking. It is generally assumed that there is a direct causative mechanism—the inhalation of the smoke causing irritation to the bronchioles and increased susceptibility to infection. Is this necessarily so? The association is equally strong between maternal smoking and both childhood accidents and temper tantrums. This is a topic to which we shall return in Chapter 21.

Conclusions

1. Children in the lower social classes and those living with a single parent are at increased risk of having had bronchitis. There are strong regional differences, with Scotland having the lowest risk and Wales the highest. The more cigarettes the mother smoked, the more likely the child was to have had bronchitis. Boys were more often affected than girls.
2. The risk of pneumonia was higher when the child had been of low birthweight. The more children in the household, the more likely the study child was to have had pneumonia. The more household moves, the more likely pneumonia was to have occurred. Children of mothers smoking ten or more cigarettes a day were at increased risk.

CHAPTER 15

Sore throats, ear discharge and mouth breathing

by JEAN GOLDING and N. R. BUTLER

Sore Throats

Since tonsillectomy is the commonest surgical procedure to be carried out on children, it is perhaps surprising that little epidemiological research has been carried out on the conditions leading to the operation. The most frequently quoted such condition is recurrent sore throat.

Family studies by Brimblecombe and his colleagues (1958) indicated that sore throats in childhood were less common than acute coryza or nasal catarrh and, in comparison with the latter two disorders, sore throat with respiratory illness was less likely to be seasonal in character or to be passed from one member of the family to another. Interestingly, they found that children who had already had a tonsillectomy were as likely to have sore throats as those who had not had the operation.

In Wales, Griffiths (1979) carried out a study over a 6-month period of all members of his general practice consulting for problems relating to the ear, nose and throat. Of the 206 consultations relating to the throat, 120 were for the condition he described as tonsillar adenitis (sore throat, enlarged glands, a temperature and little else). He, too, showed that there was little evidence for seasonal variation, but that the peak incidence was in 3–4-year-olds.

In our study, 2623 (20.7%) of 12,699 mothers who answered the question stated that their child had had 'repeated sore throats requiring medical attention'. Approximately a quarter (749) of these had had sore throats in the year before interview and not before that, another quarter (581) had had the condition but not in the past year, and the remainder (10.1% of all the children) had had repeated sore throats both before and after their 4th birthday (Fig. 15.1).

Purulent Ear Discharge

Otitis media is an infection with variable manifestations. Typically, pus

215

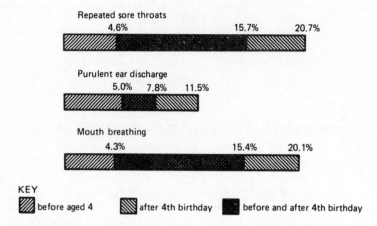

Fig. 15.1 Proportion of children to have had repeated sore throats, purulent ear discharge or mouth breathing by age at occurrence

fills the middle ear and the manifestations may be acute pain, hearing loss and purulent ear discharge. Resolution may occur in days, months or even longer. Over time the discharge changes in character, and may then resemble serum, mucus or even glue.

Even after the symptoms of otitis media have cleared up, the long-term damage may be marked. An MRC study followed up 403 children who had had acute otitis media and tested their hearing using audiograms. Those with signs of hearing loss were tested again at a later date. The study showed that 17% of children who had had acute otitis media had a loss of 20 decibels or more in at least two frequencies compared with 4.5% of controls of the same age and sex. These findings were apparent within a year of the episode and over 3 years after it (Fry et al., 1969).

In all, 1451 (11.5%) of the 12,591 children for whom the data were available were reported as having had purulent ear discharge. The problem was obviously less likely to be a long-standing one than for sore throats (Fig. 15.1); only a quarter of the children with such a history had had the disorder both before and after their 4th birthday. Although boys were slightly more likely than girls to have the history, the differences were not statistically significant (12.1% vs 10.9%).

Mouth Breathing

Indicative of chronic catarrh or the 'adenoidy' child is one who breathes through his mouth rather than his nose. In our study, the mothers were asked if the child had had 'habitual snoring or mouth breathing'. This was recorded for 2539 (20.1%) of 12,653 children. As can be seen in Fig. 15.1, the condition appears slow to resolve: of those 2042 children who had had the condition in the first 4 years of life, only a third had stopped mouth breathing by the time they were 4 years old.

Sex differences

Boys were more likely than girls to have frequent sore throats (Fig. 15.2) and to breathe through their mouths or snore (Fig. 15.3), but there were no differences between the sexes in the likelihood of the condition resolving.

Birthweight and Breast Feeding

The children of low birthweight in the 1946 cohort had an increase in the prevalence of frequent colds in the first 2 years of life (Douglas and Blomfield, 1958). Although we found an increased rate of pneumonia in the low birthweight infants in this study, there were no statistically significant differences in the prevalence of the three symptoms of upper respiratory tract disorder.

In Newcastle-upon-Tyne, Miller and his colleagues (1960) found no association between respiratory illness and duration of breast feeding. In the present study in contrast to the pattern found with lower respiratory infection, there was no *reduction* in the prevalence of any of the three upper respiratory symptoms among children who had ever been breast fed, but there was significant variation between repeated sore throats and duration of breast feeding (Fig. 15.2). This shows an excess of sore throats among infants fed for under a month, and a dearth among those fed for over 3 months.

Parents and Siblings

Both the 1946 cohort study (Douglas and Blomfield, 1958) and the longitudinal study in Newcastle (Miller *et al.*, 1960) found no social class variation in the prevalence of respiratory illness. We, too, found no difference between social classes in the reports of sore throats or purulent ears, but there was a variation in the children said to breathe habitually through their mouths (Fig. 15.3). Children from the non-manual social classes were significantly less likely to be reported as having had this trait.

The prevalence of both sore throats and mouth breathing varied with the age of the mother (Figs. 15.2, 15.3). In general, the older she was, the less likely the child was to have had the condition.

There were significant associations between habitual mouth breathing and the parental situation (Fig. 15.3). Children living with both natural

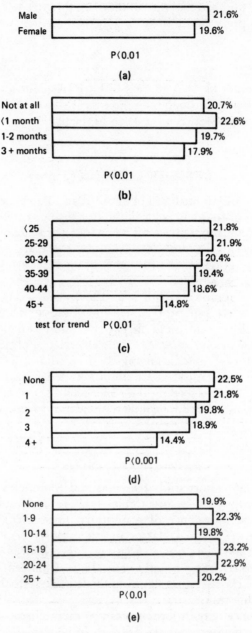

Fig. 15.2 Proportion of children to have a history of having had repeated sore throats by (a) sex of child, (b) duration of breast feeding, (c) maternal age, (d) number of other children in the household, (e) maternal smoking habit

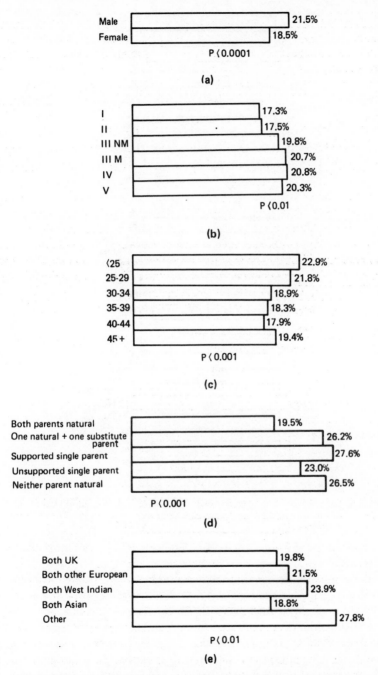

FIG. 15.3 Proportion of children with a history of having had habitual mouth breathing by (a) sex of child, (b) social class, (c) maternal age, (d) parental situation, (e) ethnic group of parents *(continued on next page)*

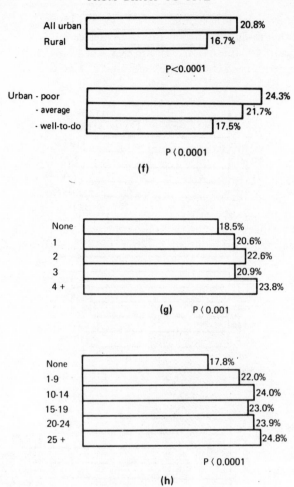

Fig. 15.3 *continued* (f) type of neighbourhood, (g) number of household moves, (h) maternal smoking habit

parents were at least risk, but in all other situations they were more likely to be affected.

Maternal employment was in no way related to any of the conditions, but the ethnic group of parents was associated with reports of mouth breathing (Fig. 15.3). Children with West Indian parents were at increased risk—but those of the 'other' group (largely of mixed parentage) were at even greater risk.

Neither mouth breathing nor discharging ears were related to the numbers of other children in the household, but there was a strong significant, negative association with sore throats. As can be seen from Fig. 15.2, the more children in the household, the less likely was the study child to have had frequent sore throats. This curious finding is the reverse of that demonstrated by most infections, but is in accord with the Newcastle study (Miller *et al.*, 1960) where it was found that the more persons in the household, the less likely was the child to have a respiratory illness.

The Physical Environment

Statistically significant regional differences were found for sore throats (Fig. 15.4). As with bronchitis, the highest rates were found in Wales (24.2%). Also high was the Scottish rate (22.4%), in marked contrast with the findings for bronchitis where Scotland had a very low rate. Purulent ear discharge followed a roughly similar geographical pattern, but failed to reach significance at the 1% level.

Although the prevalence of habitual mouth breathing did not vary

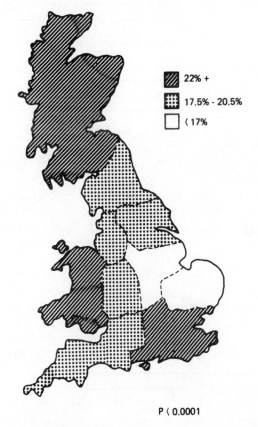

22% +

17.5% - 20.5%

< 17%

P < 0.0001

Fig. 15.4 Proportion of children with a history of frequent sore throats by region

with region, there were pronounced differences with type of neighbour-hood in which the child resided (Fig. 15.3). Not only was such a history far more common in urban areas, within urban areas there was a marked trend, the poorer the area the more likely was the child to breathe through his mouth or snore. Nevertheless, the rate in the well-to-do urban areas was still higher than that found in rural areas.

For both sore throats and mouth breathing there was evidence of a trend with the number of occasions on which the child had moved house—the more times the child had moved, the more likely was he to have had the condition, but statistically the association was significant only for children with mouth breathing (Fig. 15.3).

There was only one factor with which similar epidemiological patterns were found for all three entries—and that concerned the smoking habit of the mother (Figs. 15.2, 15.3, 15.5). Nevertheless, convincing evidence of a dose–response trend was only apparent with mouth breathing. There, the difference in prevalence between children of non-smoking, as opposed to smoking, mothers was marked.

Inter-relationships

Indirect standardisation procedures showed that associations between repeated sore throats and maternal age, number of household moves and maternal smoking habit were secondary to the major associations with region and number of children in the family (Fig. 15.6). This stresses more than ever the atypical epidemiological nature of the disorder. Why should the disorder appear to be less common in families where there are more children, and hence more infections likely to be introduced into the family?

In Chapter 18 we shall be examining epidemiological associations with tonsillectomy. In particular, we shall be examining the hypothesis that regions with high risks of sore throats will be those with high rates of tonsillectomy. The negative association between sore throats and the

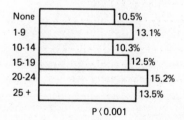

FIG. 15.5 Proportion of children with a history of having had ear discharge by maternal smoking habit

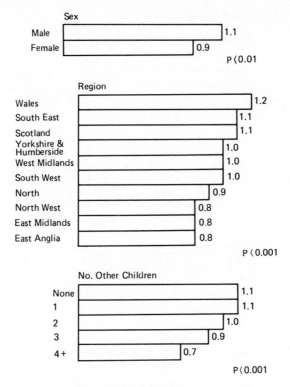

FIG. 15.6 Independent Relative Risks associated with frequent sore throats

number of children in the household is related to the number of older rather than younger children (Fig. 15.7). In view of the fact that infections are more likely to be introduced to the family of a pre-school child by his elder siblings who attend school, this is even more unexpected.

There was only one significant epidemiological association with discharging ears: that with maternal cigarette smoking (Fig. 15.8). The lack of a trend with social class had been shown in the two previous national cohorts (Douglas and Blomfield, 1958; Davie, Butler and Goldstein, 1972), but we have been unable to ascertain whether any previous study has looked to see whether smoking mothers are more likely to have children with discharging ears.

In contrast, habitual snoring or mouth breathing exhibited many strong social associations—relatively few of which, however, persisted after standardisation (Fig. 15.9). Thus, maternal age, social class and parental situation associations were explained by the type of neighbourhood and maternal smoking. In addition, there were significant variations with ethnic group and sex of the child.

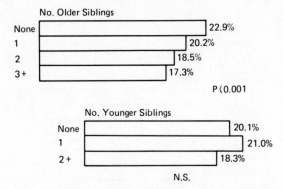

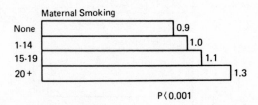

Fig. 15.7 Proportion of children with repeated sore throats by numbers of older and younger siblings

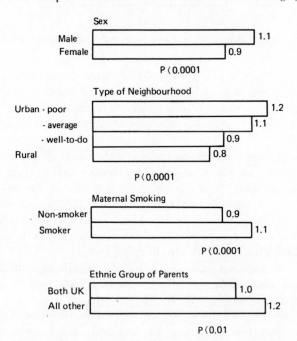

Fig. 15.8 Independent Relative Risks associated with discharging ears

Fig. 15.9 Independent Relative Risks associated with habitual mouth breathing

The data could be interpreted as showing two components, one constitutional and one environmental. The sex and ethnic group differences would perhaps form part of the constitutional variation—and the association with both maternal smoking and type of neighbourhood would be suggestive of a reaction to atmospheric pollution.

Other Attributes of the Children

There have been a number of reports relating chronic otitis media in early childhood to various adverse developmental outcomes, such as speech defects (Needleman, 1977; Lehmann et al., 1979; Howie, 1980) and disturbed behaviour (Hersher, 1978). In a recent review of the literature, Paradise (1981) concluded that available evidence pointed away from, rather than toward, a causative relationship. He suggested that early surgical interference would probably do more harm than good, but that it is important for special adjustments to be made by parents to their children while they have slight hearing loss.

In the present study, the children who had had suppurating ear discharge were more likely to have behaviour problems, but these were no greater in magnitude than those children who had a history of habitual mouth breathing or snoring (Table 15.1).

Indeed, the behaviour patterns were different for each symptom. Children with frequent sore throats were more likely to have sleeping and feeding difficulties—in infancy as well as at 5; they were more likely to have features of the 'troubled' child and the hyperactive child. In contrast, children with ear discharge were more likely to be 'difficult', but those who breathed through their mouths were at increased risk of each behaviour syndrome.

Children with each of the symptoms were significantly more likely to have each of the other two. They were all at twice the risk of having a hearing defect suspected (Fig. 15.10), and children with speech problems or dysfluency were over-represented in each group.

As the figure shows, children with each of these relatively minor symptoms are at increased risk of many other disorders. Hearing problems are the most obvious, and these will be discussed in the next chapter.

Conclusions

1. Twenty-one percent of children had had repeated sore throats requiring medical attention. Boys were affected more than girls. The more older children in the household the less likely was the study child to be affected. There were strong regional

TABLE 15.1 Number of children with various behaviour and other problems to be reported as having frequent sore throats, ear discharge or mouth breathing compared with the numbers expected after standardisation for sex and social class

Child's history	Sore throats		Ear discharge		Mouth breathing	
	Observed	R. Risk	Observed	R. Risk	Observed	R. Risk
Wets bed (1+ per week)	253	0.9	183	1.2	337	1.2**
Wets by day	283	1.1	159	1.1	279	1.1
Soils	131	1.2	72	1.2	117	1.1
Sleeping problems as a baby	462	1.4****	229	1.2	451	1.3****
Sleeping problems at 5	817	1.3****	427	1.2***	777	1.2****
Feeding problems as a baby	452	1.4****	236	1.2***	421	1.3****
Feeding problems at 5	1099	1.2****	559	1.1	1014	1.1**
Temper tantrums (1+ per week)	377	1.2***	205	1.2	421	1.3****
Destroys belongings	115	1.1	86	1.4**	161	1.4****
Fights other children	131	1.2	78	1.3	146	1.3**
Is irritable	346	1.2**	201	1.2**	400	1.3****
Takes things	57	1.2	45	1.7***	67	1.3
Is disobedient	281	1.2	171	1.2**	330	1.3****
Tells lies	64	1.1	51	1.6***	93	1.6****
Bullies	45	1.2	34	1.6**	59	1.5**
Is often worried	208	1.5****	104	1.3**	182	1.3***
Is solitary	268	1.2	151	1.1	307	1.3****
Is miserable or tearful	84	1.3**	50	1.4	89	1.4**
Is fearful or afraid	203	1.2**	132	1.4***	201	1.2**
Is fussy or over-particular	302	1.3****	130	1.0	299	1.3****

	Sore throats		Ear discharge		Mouth breathing	
Very restless	851	1.2****	437	1.0	904	1.2****
Squirmy or fidgety	376	1.3****	209	1.3***	408	1.4****
Cannot settle	217	1.2**	127	1.3**	246	1.4****
Crying problem as a baby	470	1.3****	243	1.2**	472	1.3****
Not much liked	48	1.3	28	1.4	45	1.2
Twitches/mannerisms	19	1.0	13	1.3	28	1.5
Bites nails	311	1.1	180	1.1	319	1.1
Sucks thumb	449	1.1	274	1.1	419	1.0
Dysfluency	189	1.2**	126	1.4****	197	1.3**
Other speech defect	315	1.2**	205	1.3****	395	1.5****
Headaches (1+ per month)	219	1.5****	107	1.3	207	1.4****
Stomach aches (1+ per month)	338	1.5****	164	1.2**	332	1.4****
2+ Accidents	384	1.2****	202	1.1	367	1.2**
Wheezing	671	1.3****	369	1.2****	719	1.4
Hay fever	141	1.3**	71	1.1	184	1.7****
Eczema	320	1.1	198	1.2	373	1.3****
Vision problem	92	1.0	65	1.3	100	1.1
Squint	189	1.0	121	0.9	215	1.4****
Bronchitis	595	1.4****	331	1.4****	619	1.5****
Pneumonia	63	1.6***	39	1.7***	65	1.6***
Sore throats	—	—	487	1.7***	1035	2.0****
Ear discharge	487	1.7****	—	—	453	1.6***
Mouth breathing	1035	2.0****	453	1.6****	—	—

$*P < 0.05$; $**P < 0.01$; $***P < 0.001$; $****P < 0.0001$.

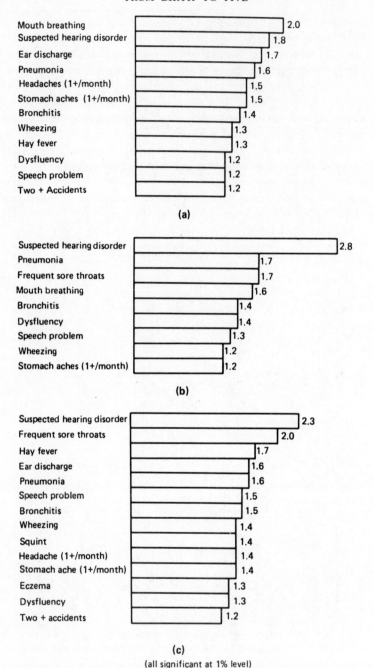

(a)

(b)

(c)

(all significant at 1% level)

FIG. 15.10 Risks of other health outcomes in children with (a) frequent sore throats, (b) discharging ears, and (c) mouth breathing (Relative Risks after standardisation for sex and social class)

differences—children in Wales, Scotland and the South-East being the most affected.

2. Twelve percent of the children had purulent ear discharge. The prevalence was higher, the more cigarettes the mother smoked.

3. Twenty percent of children were said to habitually breathe through their mouths or snore. The prevalence was higher in boys than in girls. Children of immigrant parents and those whose mothers smoked were at greater risk of such a history. Urban residents were more affected than those living in rural areas, the poorer the urban area the greater the prevalence.

4. The children with these three disorders had high rates of differing behaviour disorders and morbidity. Associations with suspected hearing difficulty were especially high.

CHAPTER 16

Hearing disorders

by JEAN GOLDING and N. R. BUTLER

Introduction

Hearing loss in a child may be transient, or permanent, over all tones, or only affecting a certain range. Causes of profound hearing loss (Fraser, 1964) include rubella in pregnancy, dominant or recessive genes, post-natal infection (especially meningitis) or accidental injury— but the majority of mild and moderate cases in the childhood population are associated with frequent upper respiratory tract infections, enlargement of the adenoids (leading to persistent mouth breathing), frequent ear infections and 'glue ear'.

Whether deafness is an even worse misfortune than blindness is a moot point. Love (1911) considered deafness to be 'a much worse misfortune. For it means loss of the most vital stimulus—the sound of the voice—that brings language, sets thoughts astir'. A child's hearing loss can go unrecognised for months or years. Because these are the vital years when the art of communication is developed, it is important to identify the hearing loss as early as possible so that treatment can be carried out.

Failure to detect and treat the condition may result in fairly intractable speech disorders—with consequent emotional and educational deficiencies.

From evidence found at the necropsies of inner ears of severely asphyxiated neonates, it has been suggested that survivors of birth asphyxia would be at risk of profound hearing loss (Hall, 1964). Other suggestions concerning perinatal factors influencing the genesis of hearing deficits include the influence of incubator noise on the cochlea of the newborn (Douek et al., 1976) and high serum bilirubin levels (Crabtree and Gerrard, 1950). Follow-up of survivors of severe birth asphyxia (D'Souza et al., 1981), or very low birthweight (<1500 g) infants (Abramovich et al., 1979), had revealed a greater incidence of deafness than in the general population, involving about 10% of the population.

The children from the 1958 birth cohort were given clinical hearing tests, as well as audiometric tests, at the age of 7. In all, almost 6% of the children were found to have significant hearing impairment (Sheridan, 1972), and in a third of these the loss was moderate bilateral or severe. Children with such marked defects were also more likely to have speech defects and vision defects, to be clumsy and 'maladjusted' (Peckham, Sheridan and Butler, 1972).

Prevalence

Neither clinical hearing test nor audiometry were carried out at the age of 5, although they have been subsequently. At the 5-year interview the health visitor asked the mother whether the child had ever had 'hearing difficulty (suspected or confirmed)'.

Altogether, of the 12,629 children for whom the question was answered, 1055 (8.4%) had been thought to have had a hearing difficulty at some stage of their lives. In half of these (512) the disorder was stated to have been present during the 12 months prior to interview. Scrutiny of a random one in ten of the questionnaires revealed that a professional agency (ENT departments in hospitals, hearing assessment clinics, etc.) had been consulted over the hearing loss in over 80% of the cases. Whilst this does not mean that all these children had a significant impairment, it implies that there was sufficient doubt to lead to investigation.

The relationship between purulent ear discharge and habitual mouth breathing was strong. Among the 1055 with hearing loss a third had had discharging ears, and nearly half had been, or were, habitual mouth breathers.

Of all 1055 children thought to have had a hearing loss, only twenty-three (one in forty-six) was considered at the age of 5 to have a severe defect. These will be discussed in more detail at the end of the chapter.

Sex, Birthweight and Breast Feeding

In spite of reports of increased incidence of sensorineural deafness in very low birthweight or pre-term infants (Abramovich et al. 1979; Schulte and Stennert, 1978), there was no evidence to suggest that low birthweight infants in this study were at increased risk. Obviously, however, when we are able to assess the severity of loss from audiograms, the results may be different. More boys than girls, however, were thought to have a hearing loss (Fig. 16.1).

There was an unexpected relationship with breast feeding. Children who were breast fed were more likely to have been suspected of having had a hearing loss than those who had been fed artificially throughout.

Parents and Siblings

In the previous chapter we showed that there were no social class differences in the prevalence of ear discharge, but that there was a strong positive association between social class and mouth breathing—the lower the social class, the greater the prevalence. In contrast, prevalence of suspected hearing loss shows the opposite pattern, the lower the social class, the less likely the perceived problem.

Can this be an objective reality, or is it a subjective bias? Are upper

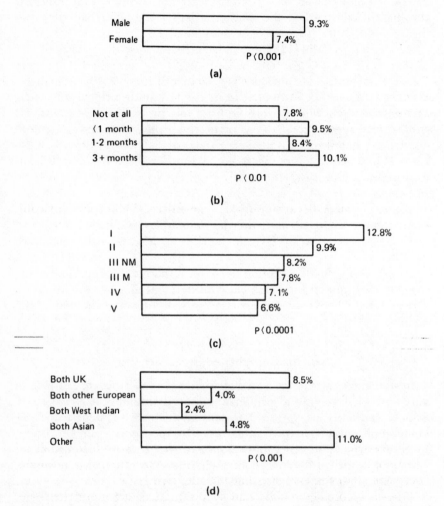

FIG. 16.1 Proportion of children suspected to have had some hearing difficulty by (a) sex of child, (b) duration of breast feeding, (c) social class, (d) ethnic group of parents

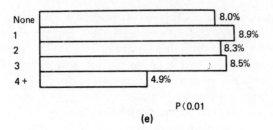

(e)

P ⟨0.01

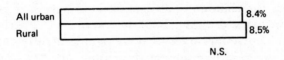

N.S.

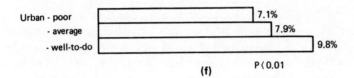

(f) P ⟨0.01

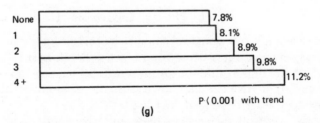

P ⟨0.001 with trend

(g)

FIG. 16.1 *continued* (e) number of other children in the household, (f) type of neighbourhood, (g) number of household moves

social class parents more likely to suspect and investigate a transient hearing loss, whereas the lower social class parents ignore it?

Suspicion of hearing difficulties was not associated with the age of the mother or whether she had been employed or not. Nor was there any relationship with the parental situation—children living with a single parent were not at increased risk.

There was, however, a marked variation with ethnic groups. As Fig. 16.1 indicates, children whose parents are West Indian, Asian or from elsewhere in Europe were far less likely to have suspected any hearing difficulty. Could this again be a lowered index of suspicion among these parents—or are the children really less likely to have had periods of deafness? As we showed in Fig. 15.3, they were no less likely to have persistent mouth breathing, nor were there significant differences in the prevalence of ear discharge among the ethnic minority groups.

In view of the above findings one might have postulated that the more children there were in the household, the less likely a mother was to notice the hearing loss. In fact, there was a significant difference in the proportion of children with hearing loss according to the number of other children in the household (Fig. 16.1), but we found no evidence for a trend. There was merely a significantly reduced prevalence among children with four or more siblings.

The Physical Environment

Once again the regional variation (Fig. 16.2) is highly significant—the highest reported rates being found in the South-East (10.7%) and the South-West (10.0%), and the lowest rate (3.5%) in Scotland. This pattern was different from that shown for the symptoms of the upper respiratory tract described in Chapter 15.

There were no differences between urban and rural areas in the prevalence of suspected hearing difficulties, but as would have been expected from the social class distribution, the parents in well-to-do urban areas were more likely to identify such a problem than those in average or poor areas (Fig. 16.1).

The number of times the child moved house is greatest among the residents of the poor urban areas. Since these areas show a lower risk of hearing loss, one might have anticipated that suspected hearing loss would be negatively associated with the number of household moves. In fact, the reverse was apparent: the more moves, the greater was the chance that the child had been thought to have had hearing loss.

In spite of positive associations between maternal smoking and certain respiratory symptoms, there was no straight-forward relationship between maternal smoking habit and hearing loss.

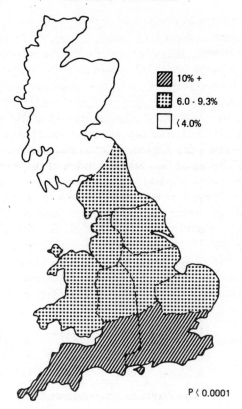

▨	10% +
▦	6.0 - 9.3%
☐	⟨4.0%

P ⟨ 0.0001

FIG. 16.2 Proportion of children who had been reported as having had hearing difficulties by region

Inter-relationships

Independent standardisation (Fig. 16.3) showed that the predominant associations were with region and social class. Once those were taken into account, the associations with breast feeding and type of neighbourhood became statistically insignificant. There were still statistically significant variations, however, with the ethnic group of the parents and the number of children in the household.

In this study we have been measuring the proportion of children suspected of having hearing loss. There are three components that will influence our results—(a) the real incidence of hearing loss in our study population; (b) the mother's perception of the real loss; (c) the mother's suspicion of hearing loss which is imagined rather than real. All will, of course, be influenced by the hearing tests administered by health visitors at various stages of the child's first 5 years.

Obviously, it is better to err on the side of being ultra-suspicious in

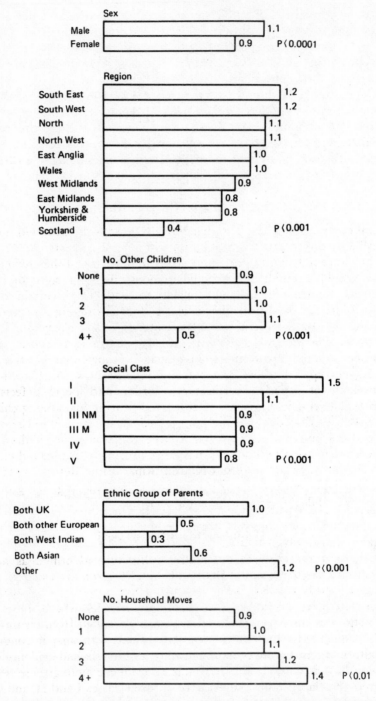

Fig. 16.3 Independent Relative Risks associated with suspected hearing loss

order to identify all the children who really do have hearing defects. It is tempting to suggest that this is indeed what is happening to children in social class I, and that, in comparison, the children in the more deprived groups (lower social classes, ethnic minorities, large families) are not so aware of those possibilities.

The positive finding with the number of household moves does not wholly fit this hypothesis. Nevertheless, a similar association was found with habitual mouth breathing, and it could be that these children are genuinely more likely to have a hearing loss. Alternatively, it could be that with each household move the child is examined by a different health visitor, and so a real loss is more likely to be detected.

Behaviour and Other Morbidity

In comparison with all study children, those with suspected hearing difficulty differed in their behaviour in several respects (Table 16.1). They were not significantly more likely to have any of the attributes of the 'troubled' child, but they did demonstrate some signs of hyper-activity (squirmy or fidgety; unable to settle) and certain of the characteristics of a 'difficult' child (stealing, destroying and disobedi-ence). Of course, the disobedient child may be suspected, for that reason, of being deaf; conversely, the deaf child may be more likely to disobey unintentionally, due to his inability to comprehend instructions.

As anticipated, there were strong relationships with health and development, especially respiratory disorders and speech defects (Fig. 16.4). The two-fold increase in suspected hearing loss among children with speech disorders was not unexpected. As mentioned in Chapter 8, the disturbing finding was that a large proportion of children with speech defects had *not* been suspected of hearing difficulty and had not had their hearing tested. Children with vision defects were also substantially more likely to have hearing loss, making this group of sixty-two children especially handicapped.

Children Identified as Deaf

There were twenty-three children who were identified as having severe hearing difficulties. Details of these children are listed in Table 16.2.

Three of the children were born into families where there were already deaf members, two had presumably resulted from trauma, two after meningitis and four were associated with major congenital malformations. Of the remaining twelve infants, six had evidence of an atypical perinatal period. There was no evidence among these twenty-three of social class bias: seven were of social classes I and II, and seven of social classes IV and V.

TABLE 16.1 Numbers of children with various behaviour and other problems also to have had (known or suspected) hearing difficulty compared with those expected after standardising for sex and social class

Child's history	Hearing difficulty Observed	Relative Risk
Wets bed (1+ per week)	139	1.2**
Wets by day	126	1.2
Soils	57	1.3
Sleeping problems as a baby	178	1.2**
Sleeping problems at 5	332	1.3****
Feeding problems as a baby	167	1.2
Feeding problems at 5	426	1.1
Temper tantrums (1+ per week)	145	1.2
Destroys belongings	62	1.5**
Fights other children	47	1.1
Is irritable	143	1.2
Takes things	30	1.6**
Is disobedient	135	1.4***
Tells lies	30	1.4
Bullies	13	0.9
Is often worried	71	1.3
Is solitary	105	1.1
Is miserable or tearful	35	1.4
Is fearful or afraid	88	1.3
Is fussy or over-particular	90	1.0
Very restless	326	1.1
Squirmy or fidgety	174	1.5****
Cannot settle	94	1.4**
Crying problem as a baby	194	1.3***
Not much liked	19	1.4
Has twitches/mannerisms	11	1.5
Bites nails	116	1.0
Sucks thumb	222	1.2**
Dysfluency	94	1.5***
Other speech defect	253	2.3****
Headaches (1+ per month)	76	1.3
Stomach aches (1+ per month)	133	1.4****
2+ Accidents	143	1.1
Wheezing	244	1.1
Eczema	157	1.2**
Hay fever	66	1.4**
Vision defect	62	1.7****
Squint	97	1.3*
Bronchitis	229	1.3****
Pneumonia	30	1.9***
Repeated sore throats	360	1.8****
Ear discharge	326	2.8****
Mouth breathing	462	2.3****

*P < 0.05; **P < 0.01; ***P < 0.001; ****P < 0.0001.

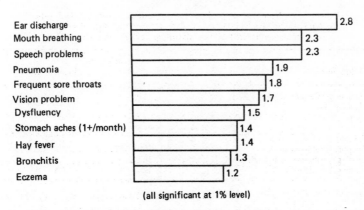

(all significant at 1% level)

FIG. 16.4 Risk of other health outcomes in children with suspected hearing disorders (Relative Risks after standardisation for sex and social class)

It should be remembered, though, that these were the children for whom hearing defects had been detected. Elsewhere we have shown (Butler *et al.*, 1982) that only 40% of children in the cohort were screened with audiometry at school entry, and 13% had still not been tested by the age of 10. Analysis of the audiometric tests carried out on the 10-year-olds for this study should show the size of the group of children with actual hearing defects that were not identified by the age of 5.

Conclusions

1. By the age of 5, 8% of children were suspected of having hearing difficulty. Half of these breathed through their mouths, and over a third had had purulent ear discharge. Boys were more often affected than girls.
2. Children from social classes I and II were more likely to have such a history, whereas children with immigrant parents were at low risk. Families with a large number of children (four or more, apart from the study child) were unlikely to suspect a hearing loss.
3. There was a marked regional variation, with Scottish children being least likely to be thought to have hearing loss, and those in the South-East and South-West of England the most likely to have such a history. The more often the child moved house, the more likely he was to be suspected of hearing deficit.

TABLE 16.2 Listing of all children recognised at interview as having severe hearing loss

Case number	Hearing defect and treatment (where known)	Other defects	Presumed aetiology	Social class, social and other factors
1	Partial loss	—	N.K.	III M
2	Conductive loss; Grommet in right ear 4 years	Severe myopia	N.K.	Single parent family
3	Low tone loss External ear anomalies (bat ears, accessory auricle) Wears hearing aid	Cleft palate Cleft lip Hypoplastic mandible	Congenital	III M
4	Bilateral conductive deafness	—	N.K.	III M
5	Bilateral—partial hearing Myringotomy 2 years	Speech defect Slightly backward	RTA at 22 months—bleeding from left ear	IV, 'difficult father', unemployed frequently Lacks parental supervision (5 RTAs) Sister has hearing loss after severe infection 'Good capable but harassed mother'—kept short of money by husband
6	Partial hearing, wears aid, admitted for investigations 15 months and 3½ years	Speech defect	Familial	II, mother and sister both partially deaf
7	Congenital deformity of left pinna + inner ear atresia Cosmetic operation on ear at 2 years Adenoidectomy, irrigation right ear Wears hearing aid	Low birthweight	Congenital	II
8	Perforated ear drums—bilateral (for possible grafting in future)	Speech defect Low birthweight	Perinatal (3 weeks in incubator)	III M step-father
9	Moderate bilateral loss	Speech defect Social + emotional retardation (severe birth asphyxia)	Perinatal	IV

No.	Audiological findings	Associated features	Aetiology	Social class / comments
12	High frequency loss (wears hearing aid)	Low birthweight / Speech defect / Hyperactive	Perinatal (incubator 6 weeks)	II
13	'Profoundly deaf' Wears aid, attends school for deaf	Speech defect / Slightly backward	N.S.	I
14	Absent right auditory meatus Deaf in right ear	Mild speech defect	Congenital	II
15	Hearing difficulty Adenoidectomy Grommets inserted 4 years	Speech defect / Slightly backward	N.S.	V
16	Bilateral loss (30dB) Ear discharge	Speech defect / Dysfluency	Fall on head at 3 months	IV
17	'Deaf'	Athetoid cerebral palsy / Myoclonic jerks / No speech / Low birthweight / Gestation 31 weeks	Perinatal (severe jaundice)	III M
18	Partial hearing Ear infection (hospital admission at 2 years)	Low birthweight / Microcephaly / Mental retardation / Very little speech	Perinatal (in SCBU 14 days)	III M, unemployed
19	Bilateral deafness	Speech defect	Meningitis 3 months	IV
20	Adenoidectomy Fluid drained left ear Sinuses washed Wears hearing aid	Speech difficulty (mild) / Slightly backward	Familial	I, elder sibling also wears hearing aid
21	'Nerve deafness' Wears aid	Speech disorder (in past) / Low birthweight	Perinatal	I
22	Partially hearing (diagnosed 9 months)	Speech difficulty	Familial	Single parent, sibling totally deaf
23	Partially hearing (45dB) At special school, hearing aid fitted 1973, hearing improved by 1975	Speech difficulty (in past) / Twin I	N.S.	III M, step-father, child failed to keep appointments

RTA = Road traffic accident
SCBU = Special care baby unit.

CHAPTER 17

Hospital admissions

by JEAN GOLDING and MARY HASLUM

Introduction

Admission to hospital for a child can be stressful to the family as well as the child. There are many ways in which a hospital admission may occur, the majority of which will fall into one of the following four categories: (a) major illness for which hospital treatment is imperative; (b) illness which, for social or psychological reasons, is best treated in hospital; (c) instances where the diagnosis is in doubt, but the child requires to be kept under observation while investigations are carried out; (d) surgery for relatively minor problems.

Admissions falling into category (d) are usually easy to identify. They include tonsillectomies and other ENT procedures, cosmetic surgery, etc. Nevertheless, in retrospect, it is not easy to distinguish between admissions for reasons (a), (b) or (c). Thus an admission for diarrhoea and vomiting might have been a severe case of gastro-enteritis, the child being almost moribund, or it may have been fairly mild—admission having occurred because the mother was thought to be incompetent or home circumstances inappropriate, or it might have been thought that the child had a metabolic disorder and needed to be admitted for investigation.

Thus, it would be dangerous to interpret information on hospital admissions as an index of ill health in the population. They are presented here merely as events that occurred in a population of children.

Number of Admissions

Of the 13,135 study children, over a quarter (3350) had been admitted to hosptial before the age of 5, 7% (925) had had at least two admissions, and one in forty (342) had been in hospital on three occasions or more. The dubious credit for the maximum number of admissions went to a child with spina bifida who was admitted to hospital thirty-three times.

Admission of children to hospital before the age of 5 is more frequent

242

today than two decades ago, 25.5% in the 1970 cohort compared with 18.5% in the 1946 cohort (Douglas and Blomfield, 1958). Although the length of each stay has generally been reduced, the proportion of children who experience long or multiple admissions is no less (Wadsworth, 1983).

There were differences between the sexes (Fig. 17.1), with more boys than girls admitted. Boys were 60% more likely to have been admitted on two or more occasions.

Throughout this volume, low birthweight children have been noted as being at increased risk of many diverse disorders, including pneumonia, squint and bed-wetting. It is not unexpected, therefore, that there is a marked difference in hospital admissions. Among low birthweight infants, two-fifths had hospital admissions, compared with a quarter of the children who weighed over 2500 g at birth (Fig. 17.1). The low birthweight group were more than twice as likely to have had two or more admissions than their heavier contemporaries.

There was a trend with the duration of breast feeding: the longer the child had been breast fed, the less likely he was to have been admitted to hospital (Fig. 17.1). Children with multiple admissions showed a pattern similar to those with a single admission.

As shown in Fig. 17.2, there were significant regional differences: children living in Scotland, Wales and the North-West were more likely

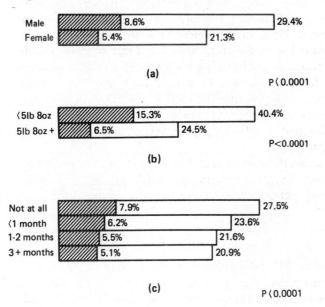

Fig. 17.1 Proportion of children to have been admitted to hospital by (a) sex of child, (b) birthweight, (c) duration of breast feeding (*continued on next pages*)

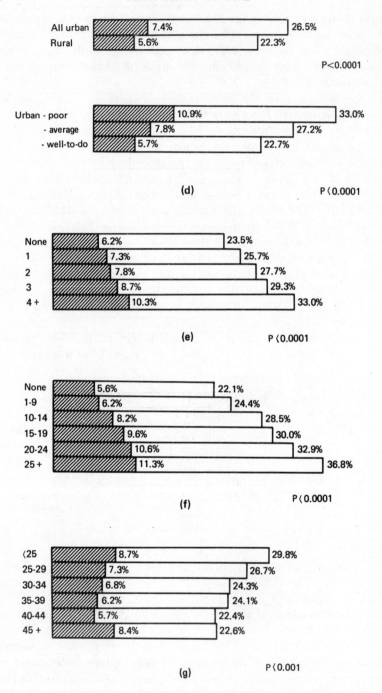

FIG. 17.1 *continued* (d) type of neighbourhood, (e) number of household moves, (f) maternal smoking habit, (g) maternal age

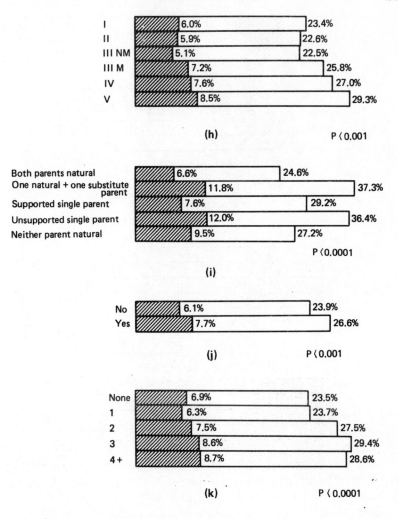

FIG. 17.1 *continued* (h) social class, (i) parental situation, (j) whether mother was employed during child's life, (k) number of other children in the household

to have been admitted, and those in East Anglia were least likely to have had such a history.

Children living in urban areas were more likely than those in rural areas to be admitted to hospital. Within urban areas there was a significant trend, children in poor areas being 50% more likely to have at least one admission than those in well-to-do areas, and twice as likely to have more than one admission.

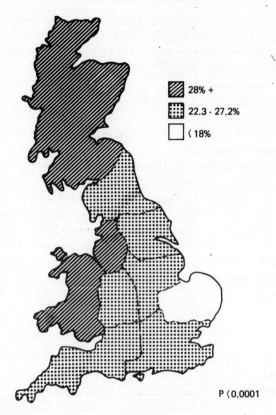

28% +

22.3 - 27.2%

< 18%

P < 0.0001

FIG. 17.2 Proportion of children to have been admitted to hospital by region

There was a significant trend, too, with the number of times the child had moved house. Figure 17.1 shows that the more moves, the more likely the child was to have been admitted.

Maternal cigarette smoking has been increasingly demonstrated as an important association of various types of morbidity in our study children. Hospital admissions show a similar pattern—the more cigarettes the mother smokes, the more likely the child is to be admitted to hospital (Fig. 17.1). The trend was strongest for multiple admissions; in comparison with children of non-smokers, those with mothers smoking twenty-five or more cigarettes a day were twice as likely to be admitted on at least two occasions.

There was also a trend with maternal age. As shown in Fig. 17.1, the younger the mother, the more likely was the child to have been admitted to hospital.

There were social class differences, but little evidence for a linear trend (Fig. 17.1). Children in the non-manual classes were least likely to have been admitted, but children of social class I did not have the lowest risk. Among the manual classes, however, there was a trend with children in social class V being most likely to have been admitted.

Differences in admission rate with parental situation were far more pronounced than those with social class. Children whose natural mothers were either single and unsupported or living with a step-father were 50% more likely to have been admitted at all, and nearly twice as likely to have had multiple admissions when compared with children with both natural parents.

Children whose mothers had been employed were also more likely to have been admitted to hospital. Nevertheless, although statistically significant, the increase in risk was fairly small.

Of the thirteen variables examined, only one (ethnic group of parents) showed no relationship with the chance of the child having a hospital admission. There was a significant association with the number of children in the household (Fig. 17.1). In general, if the study child lived in a household with two or more children, he was more likely to have been admitted to hospital.

Inter-relationships

As shown in Chapters 2, 3 and 4, the variables considered here are strongly related to each other. Indirect standardisation was used to determine which of our findings could be explained in terms of the others.

We found that the association remained with low birthweight, sex of the child, the mother's smoking habit, the parental situation, number of other children in the household and region. The magnitude of associations is depicted in Fig. 17.3. They were able to explain the findings we had originally demonstrated with maternal age, social class, maternal employment, type of neighbourhood, number of household moves and duration of breast feeding.

In attempting to interpret these results it is interesting to try to relate the factors to the different causes for hospital admission we postulated at the start of this chapter. It is probable that the associations with low birthweight and sex, which persist after standardisation for social factors, are indicators of real differences in the incidence of major morbidity. Differences between regions may well relate to differences in provision of beds or admitting policy for particular conditions, rather than differences in morbidity, but it is likely that the associations with parental situation may indicate a policy of admission of children in such situations. The association with maternal smoking could either indicate an increased morbidity among the children of smoking mothers, or that such mothers have other attributes which suggest to the clinician that the

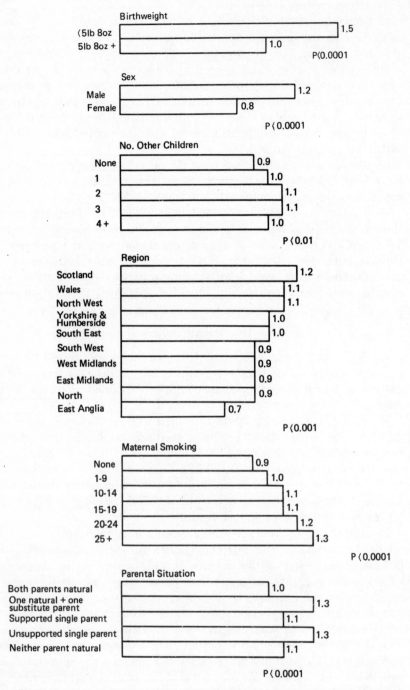

Fɪɢ. 17.3 Factors independently associated with children who have had hospital admissions (Relative Risks)

child would be better nursed in hospital. It is of note that a similar relationship between maternal smoking and childhood hospital admissions was found in Finland by Rantakallio (1978). She had collected the information on maternal smoking at the end of pregnancy and followed the infant's progress. The association she found with maternal smoking was independent of birthweight.

Evidence from Israel also supports our findings. Winter and Lilos (1974) carried out multivariate analyses to assess which factors would predict hospital admission by the age of 2. They, too, found low birthweight, number of previous children and the male sex to be independently associated—the association with large families being the most significant statistically.

Behaviour Problems in Children Admitted to Hospital

Analysis of the 1946 data showed clearly that a single short admission to hospital in the first years of a child's life was not associated with later emotional or behavioural disturbance, but that repeat admissions, or single admissions of more than a month in length, were related to subsequent emotional disturbance and later delinquency (Douglas, 1975; Wadsworth, 1979). The findings were confirmed by the Isle of Wight study (Quinton and Rutter, 1976). The relationship was increased the longer the length of hospital stay. At the time in which the 1946 cohort was having its early hospital experiences, the hospital environment was far different from that prevailing today. There were few children's wards, little or no awareness of a child's need to play, vigorous emphasis on the neatness of the ward and visiting often restricted to only once or twice a week.

In the 1970s there were large numbers of children's wards in general hospitals, many with policies of unrestricted visiting and the opportunity for the mother to stay overnight with her child. It is, therefore, of great interest to observe the mother's awareness of such policies and her attitudes towards them.

From information provided in the maternal self-completion form we were able to assess these attitudes. Altogether 80% of the mothers disagreed with the statement 'It's best not to visit children under 5 in hospital, because it's too upsetting for the child.' Nevertheless, although it was only a small proportion (5%) who strongly agreed, this represented 652 mothers—and hence 652 children, who presumably would not be visited by their mothers if they were admitted to hospital. There was, however, evidence that attitudes changed with experience in that the more often the child had been admitted, the more likely the mother was to disagree strongly with the statement. Nevertheless, there were thirty-seven children who had had at least three hospital admissions and whose mothers agreed that the children should not be visited.

When it came to the question of unlimited visiting, opinions were almost equally divided: 43% of the population thought that it was 'unreasonable to expect hospitals to upset their routine by allowing unlimited visiting in children's wards'. As many as 29%, however, disagreed strongly with this opinion, the mothers whose children had had multiple admissions being slightly more likely to fall into this category.

Concerning the reaction of the child to the experience, the balance of opinion was that the 'children who get upset in hospital soon get over it afterwards'. Such a concept, in direct opposition to Douglas's long-term findings, was most strongly held by women residing in Scotland and Wales, and least apparent in those from the South of England. There was a strong social class trend, with women from social class V almost four times as likely to agree strongly with the statement compared with women from social class I. There was, however, only a very small variation with maternal age: the women who were over 30 when their child was born were slightly more likely to subscribe to this view.

The communication problems between the mother and the hospital medical practitioners were tested in the reactions to the statement: 'The trouble with hospital specialists is that they never have time to explain all their patients would like to know.' As many as 41% of the mothers strongly agreed and a further 27% mildly agreed.

The numbers of children who had been admitted to hospital, and had various behaviour traits, are compared with numbers expected in Table 17.1. It can be seen that children who had had just one admission differed little from expectation, the only ways in which they differed at the 1% significance level being in an increased prevalence of bed-wetting, being miserable or tearful and having twitches or mannerisms. In contrast, the children who had had more than one admission were

TABLE 17.1   Number of children with hospital admissions to have had other behaviour and health problems compared with numbers expected after standardisation for social class and sex

Child's history	One hospital admission		Two+ hospital admissions	
	Observed	R. Risk	Observed	R. Risk
Wets bed (1+ per week)	327	1.2**	147	1.4***
Wets by day	240	1.0	131	1.4****
Soils	114	1.1	79	1.9****
Sleeping problems as a baby	380	1.1	166	1.3**
Sleeping problems at 5	663	1.1	262	1.2
Feeding problems as a baby	394	1.2****	189	1.5****
Feeding problems at 5	869	1.0	367	1.1

Continued

Table 17.1 continued

Child's history	One hospital admission		Two+ hospital admissions	
	Observed	R. Risk	Observed	R. Risk
Temper tantrums (1+ per week)	342	1.1	153	1.2**
Destroys belongings	121	1.1	70	1.6***
Fights other children	121	1.1	65	1.4**
Is irritable	300	1.1	148	1.3**
Takes things	56	1.1	38	1.9****
Is disobedient	246	1.0	138	1.4****
Tells lies	69	1.2	37	1.6**
Bullies	39	1.0	26	1.6
Is often worried	150	1.1	53	1.0
Is rather solitary	248	1.1	116	1.3**
Is miserable or tearful	87	1.4**	43	1.7***
Is fearful or afraid	169	1.0	81	1.3
Is fussy or over-particular	226	1.0	101	1.2
Is very restless	747	1.0	333	1.2**
Is squirmy or fidgety	285	1.0	155	1.4****
Cannot settle	198	1.1	106	1.5****
Crying problem as a baby	406	1.2**	187	1.4****
Not much liked	43	1.2	27	1.9***
Twitches/mannerisms	30	1.6**	10	1.4
Bites nails	290	1.1	105	1.0
Sucks thumb	402	1.0	152	1.0
Dysfluency	158	1.0	60	1.0
Other speech defect	291	1.1	173	1.7****
Headaches (1+ per month)	143	1.0	83	1.5***
Stomach aches (1+ per month)	237	1.0	100	1.2
2+ Accidents	393	1.3****	207	1.7****
Wheezing	564	1.1*	311	1.6****
Eczema	303	1.1	116	1.1
Hay fever	94	0.9	56	1.4**
Vision problem	106	1.3*	61	1.9****
Squint	246	1.4****	151	2.2****
Bronchitis	494	1.2****	262	1.7****
Pneumonia	70	1.8****	80	5.2****
Repeated sore throats	608	1.3****	280	1.5****
Ear discharge	328	1.2***	154	1.5****
Mouth breathing	600	1.3****	302	1.6****
Suspected hearing disorder	246	1.3***	176	2.4****

*P < 0.05; **P < 0.01; ***P < 0.001; ****P < 0.0001.

exhibiting a large number of negative behaviour characteristics at the age of 5. These included the enuresis/encopresis triad, all the traits exhibited by the 'difficult' child, and those of the hyperactive child. In addition, they were thought to be 'not much liked', miserable or tearful and rather solitary.

Thus, our data confirm that a single short hospital admission is unlikely to be associated with subsequent behaviour problems in the child. This conclusion cannot be extrapolated to single admissions of more than 2 week's duration. From the information presented in Table 17.1 there is substantial *prima facie* evidence that multiple hospital admissions are associated with increased risk of behaviour disorder. Further analysis is currently in progress.

There are ways of interpreting the data other than by deducing a causal effect. Firstly, in the analysis as presented here, we have been unable to eliminate children whose admissions were actually related to their behaviour problem. Secondly, we have taken no account of the fact that the various disorders, which result in hospital admission, may also be likely to result in behaviour deviance. Finally, we have not yet standardised for other social factors, which we have shown to be associated with both hospital admission and various behaviour traits. Such standardisation may well illuminate many of the significant associations demonstrated in Table 17.1.

This work is being carried out at present and the evidence so far suggests that the associations between the length of time a child spends in hospital and subsequent behaviour disorder is robust and remains, after taking sex, social circumstances, birthweight, and age at admission into account (Haslum, in preparation). Other influences, however, remain to be considered. Douglas (1975) found that children admitted to hospital during the first 5 years of life were more likely to come from large families and to have parents who took little interest in the child's school work.

In addition, it has been suggested that some procedures are associated with distress and are related to later behavioural disturbance. Stacey *et al.* (1970) found such a relationship in children after discharge for tonsillectomy but Davenport and Werry (1970) failed to confirm this. Sibinga and Friedman (1971) found evidence which led them to suggest that the immobilisation associated with fractures had an effect on language delay and articulation problems.

Douglas (1975) also looked at reasons for admission. He found no evidence for the relationship suggested by Sibinga and Friedman. There was little difference in the reasons for admission between the disturbed and non-disturbed children in the 1946 cohort, except that admissions for infections and allergies were twice as common in the disturbed children. He also found, however, that children admitted for infections and allergies were twice as likely to have experienced multiple admissions as other children admitted to hospital.

The associations which he found between admission for an operation and later behaviour disturbance were not consistent. Delinquency, for example, was more likely to follow if the admission was not for an operation, whereas 'troublesome behaviour' identified at age 15 by teachers was more likely if the initial admission was for an operation.

There is a small amount of evidence in our data to suggest that the reasons for admission may have a bearing on later behavioural disturbance, but the results are equivocal and require much further work.

So far our analyses of the consequences of hospital admission on children's behaviour is restricted to age 5. We await the results of the analysis of outcome at 10, particularly in view of the disturbing finding from Douglas's work. He found that children with admissions of duration of a month or more before the age of 5 were more likely to be rated as disturbed at ages 13 and 15 by their teachers; they were also more likely to show delinquent behaviour as evidenced by being cautioned by the police or sentenced by the courts, and they were more likely to develop unstable job patterns on leaving school.

It should be remembered, however, as Quinton and Rutter (1976) point out, that the increase in numbers of children with behaviour disorders, which is associated with hospital admissions, contributes only 1 or 2% to the total number of disturbed children in the population.

Educational Attainment in Children Admitted to Hospital

Douglas also found that prolonged or repeated admissions were associated with reading difficulties in adolescence. In the 1946 cohort, children with this experience of hospital admissions performed less well on the Watts–Vernon Reading Test at age 15 than those who had not been admitted to hospital or had had only short admissions. Admission to hospital before age 5 appeared to be crucial; admission after this age had little or no effect on subsequent reading performance.

Analyses of our data, taking sex and social circumstances into account, shows a small but highly significant association between periods of stay in hospital of 2 weeks or longer and poor performance on the English Picture Vocabulary Test and a Copying Designs Test at age 5 (Haslum, in preparation). This implies that the detrimental effect of a long stay in hospital during the preschool period on indices of development, as disparate as vocabulary and visuo-motor co-ordination, is apparent at the beginning of a child's formal school career.

Other Disorders

Interestingly, although dysfluency (stammering) is reputed to be associated with stressful situations, children who had been admitted to hospital (either once or more than once) did not appear to have had an increased risk of the disorder. In contrast (Table 17.1), children with other speech disorders were significantly more likely to have had multiple hospital admissions. This relationship is unlikely to be causal. It is likely that the other problems associated with the speech disorders, such as cerebral palsy and hearing difficulty, are responsible for the multiple admissions.

Most of the symptoms and conditions considered were found to be significantly associated with multiple hospital admissions; many of these would have been responsible for at least one of these admissions.

In the case of squint, hearing disorders, frequent sore throats, mouth breathing and ear discharge the admissions would generally be for cold surgery. Cases of pneumonia, bronchitis, wheezing and accidental injury would be more likely to result in emergency admissions.

It is difficult, however, to understand immediately why children with headaches would be more likely to have multiple admissions. It is possible that the answer lies in the child rather than the condition. We showed in Chapter 9 that children with headaches were more likely to have many other conditions present.

Conclusions

1. Children admitted to hospital were more likely to be male and to have been of low birthweight. The proportion of children admitted to hospital increased with the number of cigarettes smoked by the mother and the number of siblings in the household. Children from single-parent or step-parent backgrounds were more likely to be admitted than those living with both natural parents.
2. Admission to hospital varied with region, being highest in Scotland, Wales and the North-West of England, and lowest in East Anglia.
3. Children who had been admitted on two or more occasions showed evidence of behaviour disorder.

CHAPTER 18

Operations

by JEAN GOLDING

Introduction

Surgical procedures, involving as they do the administration of anaesthetic and an unconscious period with the awakening to the shock of pain, must be particularly traumatic to a young child. Some of these procedures are of debatable efficacy, but are among the commonest reasons for hospital admission. In this chapter we propose to discuss the ways in which the four most common operations vary in regard to environmental and social variables.

Tonsillectomy and Adenoidectomy

From its advent in the last century, tonsillectomy became increasingly popular until it became regarded as a panacea for a large variety of childhood illnesses. Nevertheless, tonsils have usually been removed for one of two reasons: chronic infection or hypertrophy (Mawson, Adlington and Evans, 1967). Nevertheless, Wright (1978) has shown that tonsils removed under the clinical diagnoses of recurrent sore throat, chronic tonsillitis and 'unhealthy' tonsils do *not* show acute inflammation, although the tissue is in a highly reactive state. Interpretation of this finding is still awaited.

The tonsils are, normally, the site of synthesis of the immunoglobulins, particularly IgG. Swelling of this area could merely be the result of increased activity due to the response to infection elsewhere in the body. If this were so, removal of the tonsils would lower the body's resistance to infection (Wood, 1973).

The removal of the adenoids is also of potential danger. The procedure tends to be carried out to eliminate nasal obstructive symptoms and prevent recurrent otitis media (Kjellman *et al.*, 1978). The tissue removed in the operation is also lymphoid and has the same potential disadvantages as tonsillectomy. Levels of antibodies after tonsillectomy (with and without adenoidectomy) have shown a fall in

IgG and in antibodies to various viral infections (Veltri *et al.*, 1972) including polio (Ogra, 1971). Reduction in the immune status might be responsible for the finding from America of an increased risk of subsequent Hodgkin's disease in tonsillectomised children (Vianna *et al.*, 1980).

Whether the benefits of the operations outweigh the disadvantages has been a moot point for some considerable time, but assessment is difficult and the perfect study has yet to be carried out (Venters and Bloor, 1974). Two randomised studies have been carried out in Britain. McKee (1963) compared episodes of illness in children who had had a tonsillectomy shortly after presentation with a group who exhibited the same (relatively minor) reasons for surgery, but for whom no operation was carried out. The only difference between the two groups lay in a significant decrease in sore throats, otitis media and nasal catarrh in the children who had the operation. A similar study was carried out by Mawson, Adlington and Evans (1967, 1968) who found no decrease in catarrh, cough or otitis media in the group who had had a tonsillectomy, but a significant reduction in sore throats, mouth breathing and snoring in the year after the operation. In both studies it was notable that differences between cases and controls diminished markedly over time, and were barely distinguishable after 2 years.

Possibly as a result of the controversy, the tonsillectomy rates fell between the two earlier cohorts (Calnan, Douglas and Goldstein, 1978). Of the children born in 1946, 2.5% had had a tonsillectomy by the age of 4, and 25.7% by the age of 11. For the 1958 cohort the comparable rates were 1.7% and 20.1%. The reduction in tonsillectomy rates was most apparent in the Midlands and the South of England; Scotland had the highest rate in 1946, and fell only from 30% to 27% between 1957 and 1968 when the children in each cohort were aged 11.

In both cohorts children in the non-manual social classes were most likely, and those in social class V were least likely to have the operation. There were also similar trends in each cohort in regard to birth rank—the more elder siblings, the less likely the child was to have the operation.

In the present study 282 children (2.2%) had had a tonsillectomy (with or without an adenoidectomy) and 146 (1.1%) had had an adenoidectomy (without a concomitant tonsillectomy). Twenty-eight children fell in both categories, having had a tonsillectomy on one occasion and an adenoidectomy on another. The sex differences are shown in Fig. 18.1. It can be seen that although boys were more likely than girls to have had either operation, the differences were only statistically significant for adenoidectomy.

There were no significant differences between the tonsillectomy rate and social class. Nevertheless, as in the other two cohorts, the rate was

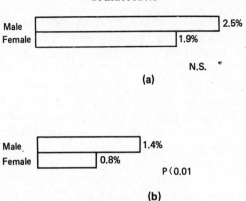

FIG. 18.1 Proportion of children of either sex to have had (a) a tonsillectomy, (b) an adenoidectomy

higher in the non-manual than the manual social classes (2.6% and 2.0%). Again, the association with the number of other children in the household was not statistically significant, but the trend was in the same direction as in the earlier studies: only 1% of children with four or more siblings had had their tonsils removed compared with 2.3% of those who had two or fewer siblings. Unlike a report from France (Said *et al.*, 1978), we were unable to demonstrate an increased risk of operation if the parents smoked.

It is interesting to compare the findings for tonsillectomy with those for frequent sore throats reported in Chapter 15. In both, boys were more affected than girls; Scotland had high rates of both repeated sore throats and tonsillectomy; there were similar negative trends with the number of siblings. Thus, the epidemiological pattern of repeated sore throats reflected that found for tonsillectomy.

Adenoidectomy without tonsillectomy was negatively related to social class (Fig. 18.2), the higher the social class the more likely the child was to have had his adenoids removed.

To our surprise, there was only one factor that differed significantly between children who had had a tonsillectomy and those who had

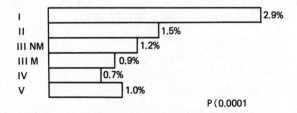

FIG. 18.2 Proportion of children to have had an adenoidectomy by social class

not—and that concerned the region in which the child resided. As in the previous cohort studies, the rate was highest in Scotland (Fig. 18.3). The lowest proportion of children with a history of tonsillectomy was found in East Anglia, with 0.8%.

There were also significant regional differences in adenoidectomy, with Scotland having the highest rate (Fig. 18.4). Wilson (1978) has confirmed from national data that in 1974 more children (25–30%) in Scotland would have had their tonsils removed than children in England and Wales (under 20%). In comparison, in the same year in the United States the proportion was substantially higher (38%). Wilson also pointed out that the numbers of children having adenoidectomy (without tonsillectomy) in Scotland rose in the period 1967–1973, while the number of adenotonsillectomies fell.

In contrast to the similarity between the epidemiological patterns

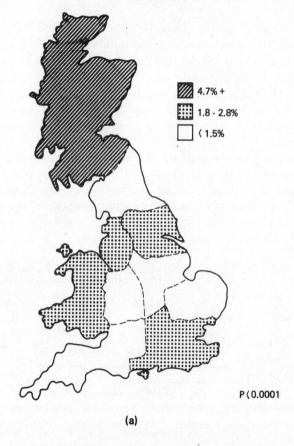

4.7% +

1.8 - 2.8%

⟨ 1.5%

P ⟨ 0.0001

(a)

Fig. 18.3 Proportion of children in each region who had had (a) a tonsillectomy
(*continued on next page*)

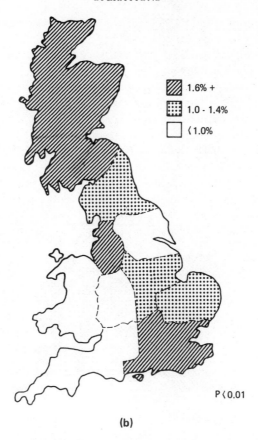

1.6% +

1.0 - 1.4%

<1.0%

P<0.01

(b)

FIG. 18.3 *continued* (b) an adenoidectomy

noted for tonsillectomy and repeated sore throats, that with adenoidectomy did not mirror the findings for mouth breathing or ear discharge. A strong association with social classes I and II was apparent for suspected hearing disorders, as discussed in Chapter 16. The geographical distributions are not similar, however. Scotland had the lowest rate of suspected hearing problems but the highest rate of adenoidectomies.

It may surprise the cynic that the epidemiological pattern displayed by each operation bears some relationship to the pattern of the conditions for which the operations are generally recommended. There is evidence, nevertheless, that factors other than an objective assessment of his condition have considerable bearing on whether the child has either operation. There are at least three people involved in the decision-making process. Firstly, the mother has to decide that the condition warrants a consultation with her general practitioner. He then has to

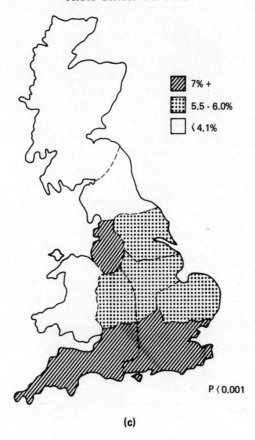

7% +

5.5 - 6.0%

⟨ 4.1%

P ⟨ 0.001

(c)

Fig. 18.3 *continued* (c) circumcision (proportion of boys)

make the decision as to whether to refer to an ENT consultant. In a proportion of cases this may be after overt pressure from the mother, but this is likely to be relatively rare (between 2–4%, Venters and Bloor, 1974). More subtle pressure, with the parent bringing the child repeatedly to the surgery for minor ailments, may well be more effective. Certainly, Robinson (1971) found that children were more likely to be taken to the family doctor frequently if the mother felt that taking out tonsils was good for the child's health regardless of whether they were infected. Policies for referral to the surgeon vary from one general practitioner to another. Once referred to the surgeon, Backett and his colleagues (1966) found that some 90% of children would be placed on the waiting list for operation. Thus, it is likely that it is variations in parental and general practitioner attitudes that are responsible for the regional and social class variations we have shown, rather than differences in the policies of the ENT surgeons.

Circumcision

In a cogent article entitled 'The Fate of the Foreskin', Gairdner (1949) questioned the validity of routine circumcision in the young boy. Since then the procedure has become relatively rare, and is now carried out mainly for religious reasons or because there is a specific medical indication.

The dramatic fall in prevalence of circumcision is illustrated well using data from the two earlier cohort studies (Calnan, Douglas and Goldstein, 1978). By the age of 12 months, 17.5% of the boys in the 1946 cohort had been circumcised compared with 4.6% of the 1958 cohort. The rates of circumcision after 1 year of age showed little change between the two studies (5.2% and 5.3% had been circumcised between the ages of 1–11 years). This presumably indicates that circumcision for medical reasons has stayed at a constant rate.

In the present study 389 (5.9%) of the boys had been circumcised, half of the operations having been carried out during admission to hospital. Once again, the data mirrored that of the 1958 cohort in regional variation. In both studies the highest rates were found in the South and the lowest rate in Scotland (Fig. 18.3). In addition to this regional variation, there was a statistically significant association with the type of neighbourhood. Figure 18.4 shows that children resident in either

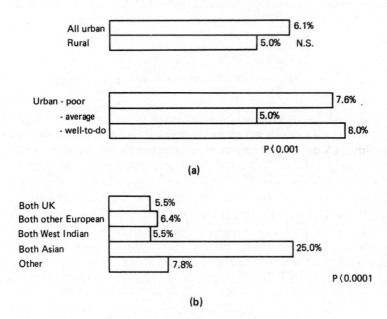

FIG. 18.4 Proportion of boys circumcised by (a) type of neighbourhood and (b) ethnic group of parents

urban-poor or urban-well-to-do areas were more likely to be circumcised than those living in urban-average or rural areas.

There were no other significant associations with environmental variables. The present study did not confirm the findings of the other cohorts (Calnan, Douglas and Goldstein, 1978) of a trend with social class, with the boys from the non-manual classes being more likely to have been circumcised. In the 1970 cohort 50% more of the boys in social class I were circumcised, but there was no trend thereafter. There was, however, a strong association with ethnic group of the parents (Fig. 18.4), due to the fact that a quarter of Asian boys had been circumcised.

The ways in which these factors relate to one another has been described earlier. Standardisation (Fig. 18.5) showed that the association with region was independent of ethnic group and type of neighbourhood variables, and that the chance of a boy in Scotland or the North of

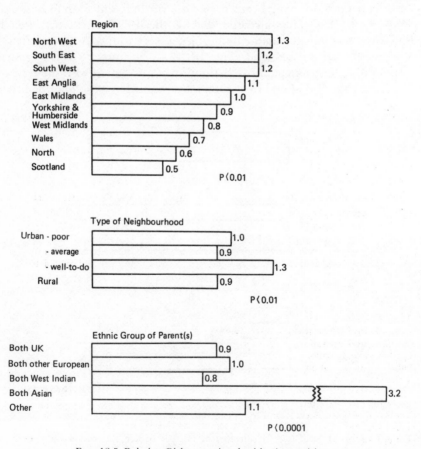

FIG. 18.5 Relative Risks associated with circumcision

England being circumcised was only half that of a child living in the South-East or South-West. The relationship with Asian background remained after standardisation, but this accounted for the original increased rate in boys living in poor urban areas. There remained an association, however, with well-to-do urban areas which presumably indicates a cultural effect.

Hernia Repair

Two hundred and twenty children (1.7%) had had a hernia repair by the age of 5. The majority of these were associated with inguinal hernias (Table 18.1). There were, as found in other studies, marked sex differences (Fig. 18.6), boys being over four times as likely than girls to have had such an operation.

Among the other twelve variables examined, only one, birthweight, was associated with hernia. Children of low birthweight had over twice the rate of hernia repair compared with children weighing 2500 g or more.

Behaviour and Health Problems

It has been suggested that removing a child's tonsils may be considered to be a belligerent act on the part of some parents towards a child who is not conforming. There is, however, no evidence from the present study that young children who had had their tonsils removed have behaviour problems (Table 18.2). It is impossible from the data we have available to assess whether the tonsillectomy was responsible for any improvement in the health of our children. As expected, there were significantly more children with hearing disorders and symptoms of the

TABLE 18.1 Numbers of operations of each type carried out on study children admitted to hospital (procedures carried out in the hospital of birth have not been included)

Operation	Number carried out
Adrenal, thyroid or thymus operation	1
Lymph gland operation	7
Cardiac catheterisation	19
Other heart operation	13
Tracheostomy	6
Other intrathoracic respiratory operations	1
Laryngoscopy or other respiratory operations	5
Tooth extraction/abscess drainage	9
Salivary gland	1
Tongue tie	11

Continued

Table 18.1 continued

Operation	Number carried out
Repair of cleft lip/palate	39
Other tongue/palate operation	3
Oesophageal atresia operation	2
Pyloric stenosis operation	23
Appendectomy	32
Inguinal hernia repair	137
Umbilical hernia repair	22
Other hernia repair	58
Other operation to stomach or intestine	20
Anal operation	8
Spleen operation	3
Laparotomy	3
Circumcision	178
Orchidopexy	11
Hydrocele operation	16
Hypospadias/epispadias operation	11
Other genital operation	5
Female genital operation	1
Renal operation	16
Other urinary tract operation	7
Drainage of abscess	38
Plastic surgery	35
Skin operation	35
Operation to nails	3
Congenital dislocation of the hips operation	12
Talipes operation	8
Other operation on a joint	2
Operation on a bone	10
Operation on a tendon/muscle	7
Other musculo-skeletal operation	24
Grommets or myringotomy	109
Other ear operation	14
Nose or sinus operation	13
Tonsillectomy and adenoidectomy	227
Adenoidectomy only	90
Other throat operation	2
Squint operation	199
Other eye ball operation	4
Lacrimal gland operation	9
Other eye operation	11
Operation to brain	7
Operation to spinal cord	6
Other nervous system operation	3
Operation for skull fracture	2
Open reduction fracture	4
Other reduction fracture	9
Operation for dislocation	2
Repair of laceration	17
Removal of foreign body	17
Operation—type unclear	20
Radiological procedure	6

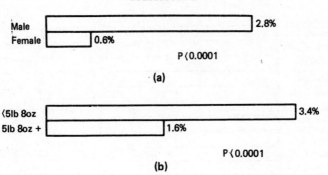

FIG. 18.6 Proportion of children to have had a hernia repair by (a) sex of child and (b) birthweight

TABLE 18.2 Number of children with tonsillectomy or adenoidectomy to have had behaviour or health problems compared with those expected after standardisation for sex and social class

Child's history	Tonsillectomy		Adenoidectomy	
	Observed	R. Risk	Observed	R. Risk
Wets bed (1+ per week)	35	1.1	22	1.5
Wets by day	35	1.3	16	1.2
Soils	20	1.6*	9	1.4
Sleeping problems as a baby	48	1.2	29	1.5*
Sleeping problems at 5	81	1.2	43	1.2
Feeding problems as a baby	35	0.9	25	1.3
Feeding problems at 5	109	1.1	62	1.2
Temper tantrums (1+ per week)	33	0.9	22	1.3
Destroys belongings	12	1.0	4	0.7
Fights other children	11	0.9	6	1.0
Is irritable	26	0.8	15	1.0
Takes things	8	1.5	4	1.6
Is disobedient	25	0.9	14	1.1
Tells lies	8	1.3	2	0.7
Bullies	1	0.2	0	0.5
Is often worried	16	1.1	9	1.2
Is rather solitary	30	1.2	13	1.1
Is miserable or tearful	6	0.9	3	1.0
Is fearful or afraid	18	1.0	7	0.8
Is fussy or over-particular	30	1.2	12	1.0
Is very restless	88	1.1	48	1.2*
Is squirmy or fidgety	31	1.0	25	1.6*
Cannot settle	24	1.2	14	1.5*
Crying problem as a baby	54	1.4*	30	1.5*
Not much liked	5	1.3	3	1.8
Twitches/mannerisms	2	1.0	3	3.4*
Bites nails	28	0.9	13	0.9
Sucks thumb	53	1.1	34	1.3

Continued

Table 18.2 continued

Child's history	Tonsillectomy		Adenoidectomy	
	Observed	R. Risk	Observed	R. Risk
Dysfluency	14	0.8	6	0.7
Other speech defect	51	1.7	32	2.1****
Headaches (1+ per month)	15	0.9	10	1.3
Stomach aches (1+ per month)	32	1.2	19	1.4
2+ Accidents	41	1.2	18	1.0
Wheezing	62	1.1	38	1.3
Eczema	38	1.2	27	1.5*
Hay fever	20	1.7*	16	2.4***
Vision problem	16	1.7*	8	1.6
Squint	19	0.9	11	1.0
Bronchitis	49	1.0	28	1.2
Pneumonia	11	2.5**	2	0.9
Repeated sore throats	214	3.8****	55	1.9****
Ear discharge	71	2.3****	59	3.6****
Mouth breathing	183	3.3****	105	3.8****
Suspected hearing disorder	101	4.4****	84	6.4****

$*P < 0.05$; $**P < 0.01$; $***P < 0.001$; $****P < 0.0001$.

upper respiratory tract who had had either a tonsillectomy or an adenoidectomy. Children with speech problems were also twice as likely to have had an adenoidectomy. The strongest associations, however, were with suspected hearing disorder. Children who had had tonsillectomy were over four times as likely, and children with adenoidectomy six times more likely, to have been suspected of having a hearing problem.

The only unexpected findings were an excess of adenoidectomies among children with hay fever, and more than twice as many as expected having a history of both pneumonia and tonsillectomy. Returning to the case notes revealed that the majority of these children (9/11) had had pneumonia some time before the operation. Thus, the pneumonia had not occurred in association with, or shortly after, the tonsillectomy.

Children who had been circumcised or had had a hernia exhibited little in the way of behaviour disturbance or other morbidity (Table 18.3). Of the eighty-eight assessments made, only one was statistically significant at the 1% level. This concerned an association between hernia

TABLE 18.3 Numbers of children with hernia repairs or boys circumcised also to have behaviour or health problems compared with numbers expected after standardisation for sex

Child's history	Hernia repair		Circumcision	
	Observed	R. Risk	Observed	R. Risk
Wets bed (1+ per week)	27	1.0	36	0.8
Wets by day	20	1.0	27	0.9
Soils	15	1.4	21	1.0
Sleeping problems as a baby	42	1.3	62	1.1
Sleeping problems at 5	56	1.0	99	1.1
Feeding problems as a baby	35	1.2	48	0.9
Feeding problems at 5	86	1.1	137	1.0
Temper tantrums (1+ per week)	30	1.0	64	1.1
Destroys belongings	16	1.4	30	1.3
Fights other children	11	1.0	21	1.0
Is irritable	24	0.9	45	0.9
Takes things	8	1.7	9	1.0
Is disobedient	26	1.1	43	1.0
Tells lies	6	1.1	15	1.5
Bullies	3	0.8	4	0.6
Is often worried	7	0.6	24	1.1
Is rather solitary	17	0.8	34	0.9
Is miserable or tearful	12	2.3**	12	1.4
Is fearful or afraid	12	0.8	25	1.0
Is fussy or over-particular	20	1.1	30	1.0
Is very restless	80	1.2	125	1.0
Is squirmy or fidgety	25	1.0	55	1.2
Cannot settle	14	0.9	29	1.0
Crying problem as a baby	44	1.0	64	1.1
Not much liked	4	1.3	4	0.7
Twitches/mannerisms	3	1.9	1	0.4
Bites nails	22	1.0	36	1.0
Sucks thumb	40	1.2	59	1.1
Dysfluency	18	1.1	24	0.8
Other speech defect	25	1.0	44	0.9
Headaches (1+ per month)	14	1.1	25	1.1
Stomach aches (1+ per month)	18	0.9	44	1.3
2+ Accidents	26	0.9	58	1.0
Wheezing	36	0.7	88	1.0
Eczema	19	0.7	59	1.3*
Hay fever	6	0.6	26	1.4
Bronchitis	38	1.0	90	1.3*
Pneumonia	6	1.6	9	1.4
Repeated sore throats	53	1.2	100	1.2*

Continued

Table 18.3 continued

Child's history	Hernia repair Observed	Hernia repair R. Risk	Circumcision Observed	Circumcision R. Risk
Ear discharge	23	0.9	51	1.1
Mouth breathing	51	1.1	102	1.3*
Suspected hearing disorder	24	1.3	39	1.1
Tonsillectomy	10	1.9*	14	1.5
Adenoidectomy	10	3.5****	10	1.9*
Hernia repair	—		12	1.1

*P < 0.05; **P < 0.01; ***P < 0.001; ****P < 0.0001.

operations and the child being described as miserable or tearful. In the absence of other supporting evidence it seems likely that this is one of those results that occurs by random chance. There was no evidence that circumcision was likely to have an adverse effect on the behaviour of the boys in the survey.

In spite of the lack of association with various causes or morbidity there was an inter-child relationship between the operations. Children who had had a tonsillectomy or an adenoidectomy were more likely to have also had a hernia operation or to have been circumcised. The largest association was between adenoidectomy and hernia operation, with a relative risk of 3.5. There is no obvious explanation for this finding.

Conclusions

1. Two percent of the study children had had a tonsillectomy. There was strong regional variation, Scotland having the highest rate.
2. Adenoidectomy (without tonsillectomy) had been carried out in 1% of the children. Those of social classes I and II were most likely to have had the operation. Boys had a higher rate, and there was strong regional variation.
3. Six percent of boys had been circumcised. The rates were highest in the South of England and lowest in Scotland. Twenty-five percent of boys living with Asian parents had been circumcised. Boys living in well-to-do urban areas were more likely to have been circumcised.
4. Hernia repairs had been carried out on 220 children. Boys were four times as likely as girls to have had the operation. Low birthweight infants were twice as likely to be involved.

CHAPTER 19

Use of the preventative health services

by JEAN GOLDING and N. R. BUTLER

Introduction

It has long been felt among members of the health profession that 'the availability of good medical care tends to vary inversely with the need for it in the population served' (Hart, 1971). Brimblecombe (1975) made a similar statement, but put a rather different emphasis on the causal mechanism: 'better-off families whose need is generally least make the optimal use of the services provided, while the poorer families whose need is commonly greatest make the least use of available resources'.

Both views have been challenged for the population in general. Collins and Klein (1980) showed that for different types of morbidity and disability the lower social classes were as likely to contact their general practitioner as the upper social classes. The main cause for concern, however, as far as the child health services are involved, is in the areas of screening and preventative health care. Under these heads we shall include visits to the child health clinic, the birth follow-up clinic and the dentist, take-up of immunisation and the role of home visiting by the health visitor.

Wynn (1976) feels that a major purpose of home visiting lies in the education of parents in child management. Mothers will often be more willing to ask advice of a health visitor in the privacy of her own home, rather than in a busy child health clinic. Indeed, Owen and Porters (1975) showed that more intensive home visiting is often needed and greatly appreciated by inexperienced or disadvantaged mothers.

There has been much discussion in the medical press concerning the role of the child health clinic. Henrickse (1982) promoted a stormy response when he reviewed the results he had obtained after examining 252 children routinely in the child health clinic. He found only one previously undetected abnormality of any consequence, and suggested that the system was not cost effective. In the correspondence that resulted from his article, Simpson (1982) reported the results from her own survey: in examining 632 children, sixteen had been found to have

269

previously undetected conditions of consequence (including congenitally dislocated hips, speech and hearing disorders).

Bryant (1982) pointed out, however, that it would be a mistake to assume that screening was the only function of child health clinics. The Court Report (1978) had recommended that expert opinion and advice should be made freely available in answer to parental concern. The functions of the child health clinic are closely allied to those of the health visitor and have been described by Nowotny (1976). It is the health visitor who is notified of the birth and she is expected to visit the mother at home in the first weeks after delivery. She will, at this visit, describe the functions of the clinic, and invite the mother to attend. As well as coming for developmental checks, it is the health visitor's task to explain to the parents that the clinic is for parental reassurance, advice on feeding and general support. Immunisation may be carried out either at the clinic or by the general practitioner. Increasingly, too, mothers tend to bring the child for advice on minor illnesses and infections, although the clinic doctor is normally unable to prescribe drugs.

Attendance at a child health clinic clearly will depend on the way in which the concept is explained to the mother, the welcome she obtains at her first visit, the geographical position of the premises in relation to the family home and the hours of opening, especially if the mother works. Nevertheless, Hart, Bax and Jenkins (1981) have shown that it is possible to achieve a 97% attendance rate in an inner city area by paying attention to such details and motivating the mother. When such efforts are not made, the attendance rate is low. Zinkin and Cox (1976) showed that children at high risk of developmental problems are those least likely to attend child health clinics. They are also more likely to move house frequently, thus making difficult any home visiting the health visitor might attempt.

Previous Cohort Studies

Prior to 1948, care provided by hospitals or general practitioners to children would have to be paid for, charges being based on what families could reasonably afford. The child welfare clinics and health visiting services were free, however. Nevertheless, only two-thirds of children in the 1946 cohort had attended a welfare centre in the first year of life.

In all, 28% of mothers had not taken their children to clinic within the first 4 years of life, but this proportion varied with social class. Forty percent of social class I and II children had never used the clinics, nor had 50% of agricultural workers, presumably due to their geographical isolation. First born children were proportionally most often taken to welfare centres.

Children in the 'upper' social classes were visited at home by health visitors less often than children of manual workers. Nevertheless, home visiting by health visitors did not appear wholly to compensate for the lack of clinic visits. In spite of the fact that later born children were less likely to attend clinics, they were not more likely to be visited at home. Children of agricultural workers, however, though less likely to visit a clinic, did receive frequent home visits. Douglas and Blomfield (1958) noted that 'there was general tendency for mothers who used one service fully, to use them all, and for those who neglected one to neglect them all'. This was apparent for antenatal and post-natal care as well as infant welfare clinics and health visitor home visits.

In the 1958 cohort, three out of four children had attended a clinic in the first year of life, but only 56% did so after the first year (Davie, Butler and Goldstein, 1972). Children from social class III were the most likely to attend, and there were strong regional differences. Residents in Scotland and the North of England were significantly less likely to attend than children living in Wales or the South of England.

In the earlier study of Newcastle-upon-Tyne (Miller et al., 1960), it was also found that the social class III mothers were the most likely to attend child health clinics. Those children who were first or second born, those who were legitimate and those with a reasonable standard of maternal care were also more likely to attend.

The Present Study

In 1975 mothers were asked whether the study child had (a) been seen by the health visitor at home; (b) been to a child health clinic; and (c) been to a birth follow-up clinic. For each question the ages at which the child was seen were documented. Unfortunately, the question on the birth follow-up clinic was not completed as well as the rest of the items on the questionnaires; about 4000 mothers failed to answer it. The variation in response to each question with regard to basic environmental and social variables is documented in the microfiche appendix tables for the interested reader.

As shown in Table 19.1, some 93% of mothers had been visited at home by the health visitor during the first 6 months of the child's life, and only 2.3% had never had a health visitor visit the home during the child's life. In contrast, 10% of the children had never been taken to a child health clinic. Birth follow-up clinics, in contrast, are not thought of as important in the preventive health field, but as many as 1843 children had been seen here—presumably by paediatricians. These visits would form an important means for screening for abnormality in a presumably high-risk population. Geographical and social factors which appear to be associated with uptake of each of these facilities are described below.

TABLE 19.1 Number of study children who had been seen at home by a
health visitor, been to a child health clinic and/or a birth follow-up clinic

Attendance	Home health visitor visit	Child health clinic	Birth follow-up clinic
Never	286	1194	7254
	(2.3%)	(10.2%)	(79.7%)
Under 6 months	11,397	8956	1651
	(93.1%)	(76.8%)	(18.2%)
Only after 6 months	589	1515	192
	(4.6%)	(13.0%)	(2.1%)
All known	12,272	11,665	9097
	(100.0%)	(100.0%)	(100.0%)

Children Not Visited at Home in the First Six Months

In all, 875 children had not been visited at home by the health visitor
in the first 6 months. In theory there are many reasons why a health
visitor might have failed to visit—ranging from maternal refusal to allow
access to the mother having moved from the area.

There was little difference between the social classes in the proportion
who had not been visited. Children of young mothers were as likely to
have been visited as were those whose mothers were older. There were
strong differences, however, in the parental situation (Fig. 19.1):
children who, by the age of 5, were living with either a single
unsupported parent, a step-parent or neither natural parent, were least
likely to have received such a visit.

There was also considerable variation with the ethnic group of the
parent(s). Children of immigrant parents were less likely to have
received a visit from a health visitor in the first 6 months of life, this
being especially true for those from an Asian background.

There were no differences in health visitor home visits if the child was
of low birthweight, nor was there any association with the duration of
breast feeding. There were, however, strong environmental differences.
Figure 19.2 depicts the strong regional variation. Home visiting appears
to have been most efficient for families resident in Wales, Yorkshire,
East Anglia and the North of England, and least available for those
living in London and the South East.

There were no differences overall between urban and rural areas in
the proportion who received home visits, but children living in poor
urban areas were less likely to have had such a history.

The strongest association, however, was found with the number of
household moves (Fig. 19.1). There is a marked trend; the more times

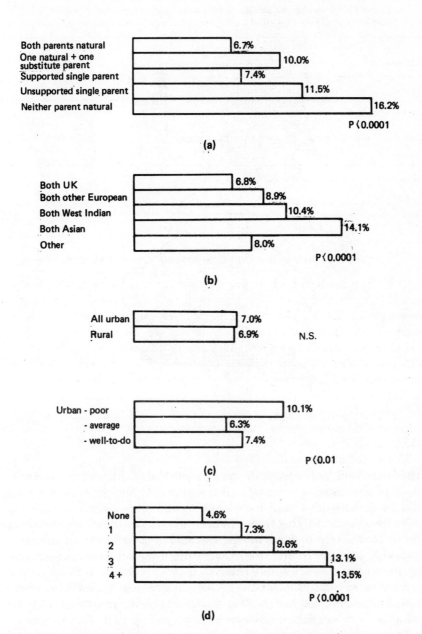

FIG. 19.1 Proportion of children *not* visited at home by the health visitor in the first 6 months by (a) parental situation, (b) ethnic group of parents, (c) type of neighbourhood, (d) number of household moves

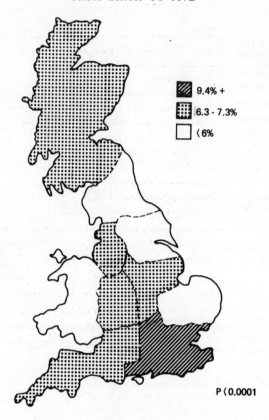

FIG. 19.2 Proportion of children not visited at home by the health visitor in the first 6 months by region

the household had moved, the more likely the health visitor was not to have paid a home visit in the first 6 months. Although we do not have details of the dates at which the child moved house, it is likely that the association indicates that those children who move house frequently are those most likely to have moved during the first weeks of life. It is probable that the health visitors were often unable to obtain the new address of the mother and child.

Indirect standardisation was carried out to assess whether any of the associations depicted in Figs. 19.1 and 19.2 could be responsible for one another. The significant results are shown in Fig. 19.3. The association with poor urban areas was due to the strong variation with region and the number of household moves. The association with West Indian and European immigrant families was also accounted for by other factors, but that with Asian families remained. If it is a true finding, this is disturbing, as it is likely that the Asian mothers are least aware of the

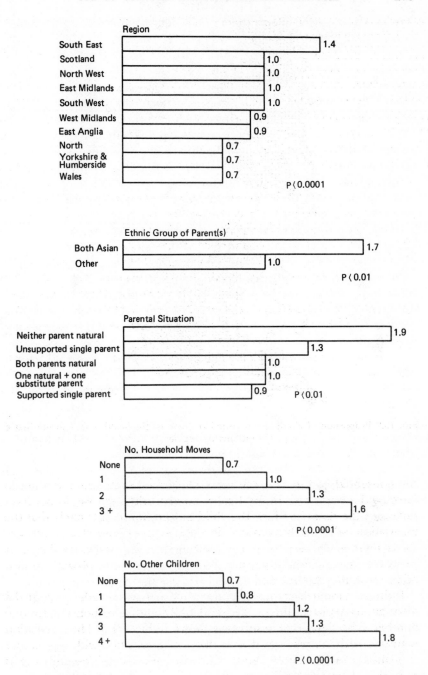

FIG. 19.3 Relative Risks of child not being visited by health visitor in first 6 months

health services available to them and would benefit from information, advice and support.

Child Health Clinic Attendance

In this section we shall describe the factors associated with non-attendance at a child health clinic. Such a history was found for 1194 children (10% of the population). As we have already noted, reasons for non-attendance at a child health clinic may be many. The clinic is certainly an important area for the screening of developmental problems, and the giving of immunisation. Nevertheless, it is not the only way in which the child may be screened or immunised, and this must be remembered in interpreting the results.

It was encouraging to note that children of low birthweight and hence, as we have shown, of increased risk of developmental problems, were those who were more likely to be taken to the clinic (Fig. 19.4). In addition, mothers who breast fed were more likely to attend, especially if they breast fed only for a short period of time. Presumably, these mothers started attending because they were having problems feeding their baby and needed the health visitor's advice and the reassurance of seeing the baby gain weight.

Although not associated with failure to be visited by a health visitor, there was strong evidence to suggest that non-attendance at a child health clinic was strongly associated with the number of children the mother had. Figure 19.4 shows that mothers who had at least two other children were those most likely not to attend a clinic. Mirroring this finding was the fact that the younger mothers were more likely to attend the clinic and the older mothers were least likely to do so.

Once again, there was no significant variation with social class, but there was a strong association with the parental situation at 5. We have already shown that the single unsupported mothers were more likely not to have been visited at home by a health visitor in the first months of life. Fig. 19.4 indicates that this group was also more likely not to attend child health clinics. This was also true of the single supported and step-parent families; many of the latter presumably would have gone through a single parent phase at some stage during the child's early life.

One of the other factors that best predicted the mother who did not take her child to a clinic was the amount she smoked at the time of interview. Mothers who were heavy smokers were those most likely to have never taken the child to a clinic.

Although there were, again, differences in region and type of neighbourhood, they differed from those demonstrated with failure of a health visitor to call. Figure 19.5, shows that Scotland exhibited quite a different use of such a service than the rest of Great Britain. Almost one in five children in Scotland had never attended a child health clinic, compared with one in ten overall. London and the South East had shown a marked increase over the rest of the country in failure of the health visitors to make home visits, but there was no indication from our data to indicate reduced attendance at child health clinics in those regions.

There was, however, evidence that the finding of the 1946 cohort of decreased clinic attendance in rural areas was still apparent 24 years later. Figure 19.4 shows one in six children resident in rural areas had

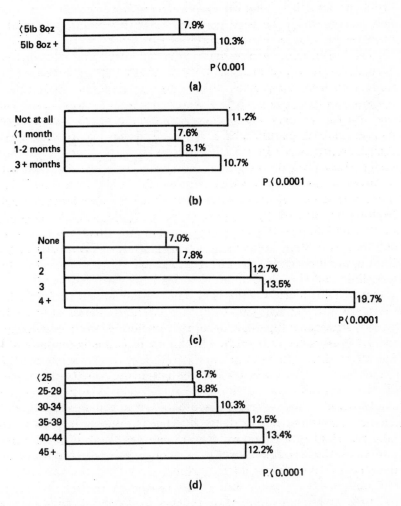

Fig. 19.4 Proportion of children never to have attended a child health clinic by (a) birthweight, (b) duration of breast feeding, (c) number of other children in the household, (d) maternal age (continued on next page)

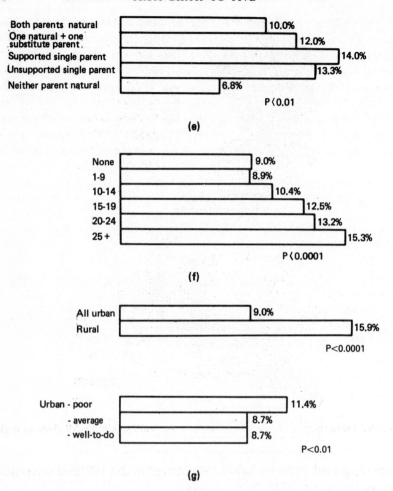

(e)

(f)

(g)

FIG. 19.4 *continued* (e) parental situation, (f) maternal smoking habit, (g) type of neighbourhood

never been to a child health clinic compared with one in eleven from urban areas.

In spite of the finding that the households who had moved frequently were less likely to have been visited by a health visitor, they were no less likely to be non-attenders at a child health clinic.

Of all the eight factors shown to be initially associated with failure to attend a child health clinic, four were found to be the result of the associations with the other four. Thus associations with both maternal age and birthweight were due to the strong association between non-attendance and the number of other children in the household. The variation with both duration of breast feeding and parental

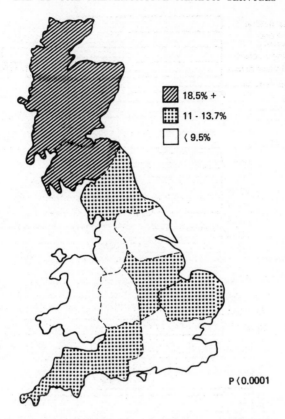

18.5% +

11 - 13.7%

⟨ 9.5%

P ⟨0.0001

FIG. 19.5 Proportion of children never to have attended a child health clinic by region

situation ceased to be statistically significant at the 1% level once other factors had been taken into account.

The factors that independently predict failure to attend a child health clinic include region, rural area, maternal cigarette consumption and number of other children in the family (Fig. 19.6). The strongest associations were with: at least four other children in the household (relative risk 1.8), residence in Scotland (1.6), residence in rural area (1.5) and a mother who smoked twenty-five or more cigarettes per day (1.4).

Birth Follow-up Clinic

There is little in the literature concerning the proportion of children seen at a birth follow-up clinic. In the present survey, we were somewhat surprised to find that as many as 1843 had attended such a clinic. As anticipated, children of low birthweight were proportionally far more

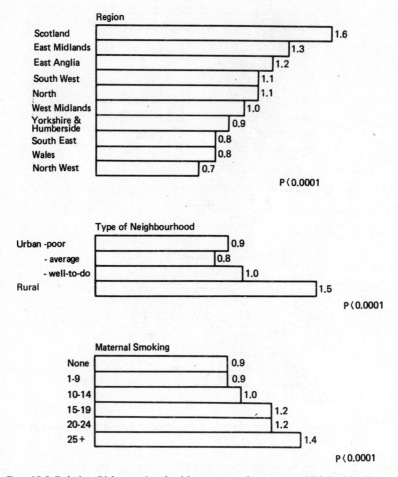

Fig. 19.6 Relative Risk associated with non-attendance at a child health clinic

likely to have been followed up in this way (Fig. 19.7). Nevertheless, numerically, far more infants of normal birthweight were seen (431 of low birthweight, 1358 of birthweight 5lb 8oz or over).

Children seen at such clinics were less likely to have been breast fed, more likely to be an only child or from an immigrant family. They were also more likely to have either a single parent or to have been fostered or adopted by the time they were 5.

Children from urban areas were more likely to have attended a follow-up clinic than those from rural areas. There was a trend within urban areas such that children from poor urban areas were those most likely to be involved (Fig. 19.7). In addition, children who had moved house frequently were also more likely to have been seen at a birth follow-up clinic.

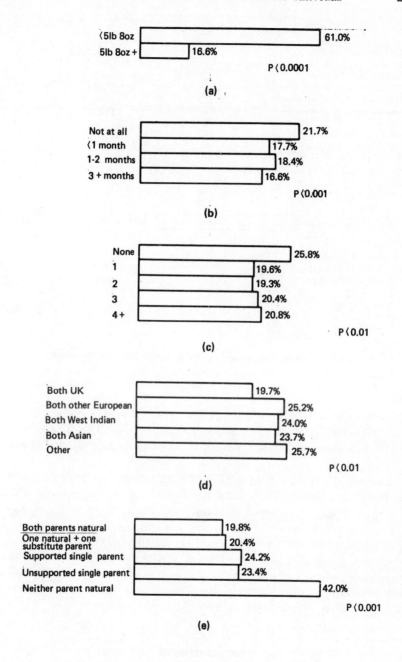

Fig. 19.7 Proportion of children seen at birth follow-up clinic by (a) birthweight, (b) duration of breast feeding, (c) number of other children in the household, (d) ethnic group of parents, (e) parental situation (*continued on next page*)

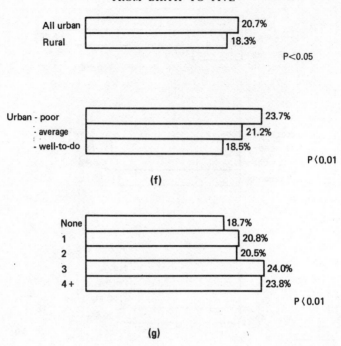

FIG. 19.7 *continued* (f) type of neighbourhood, (g) number of household moves

Finally, there were significant regional differences. Children in East Anglia were least likely to go to such a clinic (Fig. 19.8). Those in the Midlands were also less likely than the rest of Britain to attend birth follow-up clinics.

The results, thus far, suggested that birth follow-up clinics might well be identifying children socially and medically at risk. The finding that they were following up more children from the poor urban areas, more children of immigrant parents and more who were destined to move house frequently was initially encouraging. Indirect standardisation, however, showed that all these findings were due entirely to the fact that there were more children of low birthweight in these groups. Indeed, only low birthweight ultimately discriminated between those seen and those not seen at the birth follow-up clinic (Fig. 19.9).

Dental Health

Dental caries is a progressive disease, but is treatable if caught in its early stages. To make this possible, it is recommended that the child's teeth be examined at intervals of 6 months or so. That the problem is

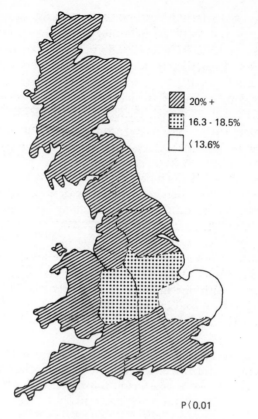

Legend:
- 20% +
- 16.3 - 18.5%
- ⟨ 13.6%

P⟨0.01

Fig. 19.8 Proportion of children seen at birth follow-up clinic by region

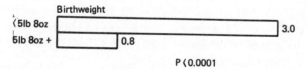

Birthweight

⟨5lb 8oz ————————————————— 3.0

5lb 8oz + ——— 0.8

P⟨0.0001

Fig. 19.9 Factors independently associated with attendance at a birth follow-up clinic

large is obvious from the population studies that have been carried out in Britain. Examination of 5-year-olds in Hereford found that four out of five had dental caries, and 13% of the children had at least *ten* teeth decayed, extracted or filled (Izon, Pullen and Scivier, 1978). The average number of decayed teeth was 4.82.

Hereford water was not fluoridated at the time of the survey. Nor was fluoridation employed in Grimsby and Hull when Fallon and Watson (1982) examined the teeth of 5-year-olds. They found slightly less decay with a mean of 3.2 affected teeth per child and 6% of children having ten or more decayed teeth. In Scunthorpe, however, where the water had a relatively high fluoride level (0.85 ppm), less than 1% of children had ten or more affected teeth, and the mean number of decayed teeth was 1.6 per child.

Dental behaviour varies with social class, the upper social classes being far more likely both to take their children to the dentist and to ensure that they brush their teeth (Beal and Dickson, 1974). Conversely, children in the lower social classes were those most likely to eat sweets, and those most likely to have dental caries.

Both Asian and West Indian parents are less likely than those from the United Kingdom to take their children to the dentist. Nevertheless, West Indian children are more likely to brush their teeth and less likely to have dental caries (Beal and Dickson, 1975).

The 1958 cohort showed that by the age of 7, 23% of children had never been taken to the dentist. There was the anticipated trend with social class; one in six children from social class I had never seen a dentist compared with one in three of social class V (Davie, Butler and Goldstein, 1972). Children in Scotland and the South of England were more likely to have visited a dentist than children in Wales and the rest of England.

On examination, 10% of the 7-year-olds in that cohort had at least ten decayed, missing or filled teeth. There was a social class trend—6.5% of social class I children were so affected compared with 11% of social class IV. Children from Scotland were more likely to have decayed teeth.

The present study

By the age of 5, of the 12,395 children for whom we have information, three-quarters had been seen by a dentist at least once, and 3938 (32%) had had treatment of some sort. The group of children who had *never* been seen by a dentist were of interest, and differed from the rest of the population in a number of ways.

Although there were no sex differences in the likelihood of a child failing to be seen by a dentist, there were significant birthweight differences (Fig. 19.10). Children of low birthweight were more at risk in this respect.

That symbol of maternal health behaviour, the duration of breast feeding, was strongly and inversely associated with failure to take the child to a dentist. The shorter the time the mother had fed from the breast, the less likely that the child visited the dentist.

As with all the other factors relating to the health behaviour, there were strong regional differences. Children who lived in Scotland (30.5%) were more likely not to visit the dentist and those who lived in

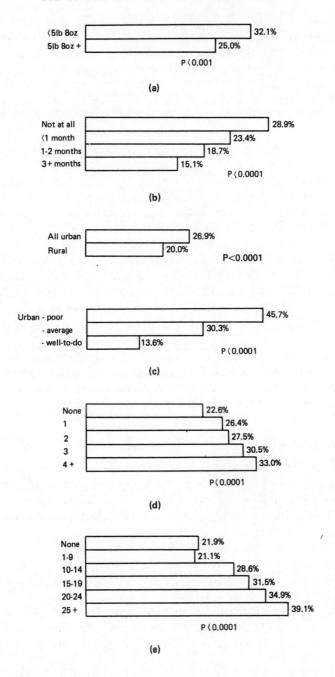

Fig. 19.10 Proportion of children *never* seen by a dentist by (a) birthweight, (b) duration of breast feeding, (c) type of neighbourhood, (d) number of household moves, (e) maternal smoking habit (*continued on next page*)

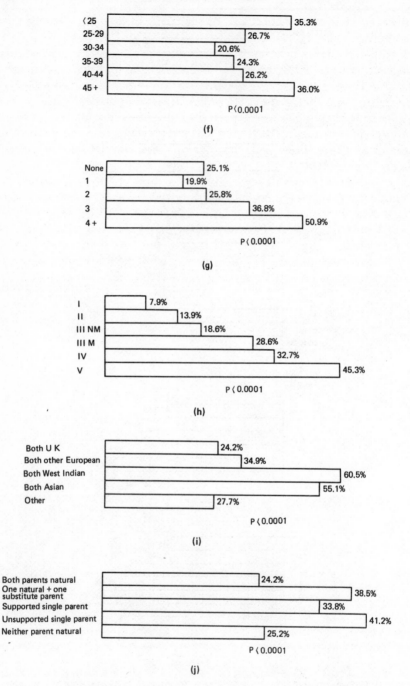

Fig. 19.10 *continued* (f) maternal age, (g) number of other children in the household, (h) social class, (i) ethnic group of parents, (j) parental situation

the South East (18.4%) or South West (14.3%) of England were the most compliant (Fig. 19.11).

Although access to a dentist is probably easier in urban than in rural areas, it was evident that a greater proportion of children in urban areas had never been to a dentist. There was a pronounced trend with the type of urban area. Children in poor urban areas were those at greatest risk.

Presumably families who repeatedly move house are less likely to have a local dentist. Figure 19.10 demonstrates the fact that the more often the child moved house, the more likely was it that he had never been seen by a dentist.

As we have shown in several chapters throughout this volume, the smoking habit of the mother is a strong predictor of health behaviour. Dental behaviour conformed to this pattern (Fig. 19.10)—the mothers who smoked most were those most likely to refrain from taking the child to a dentist.

Maternal age, and the number of children in the household, were also strongly associated with dental health. Mothers who were in their 30s at

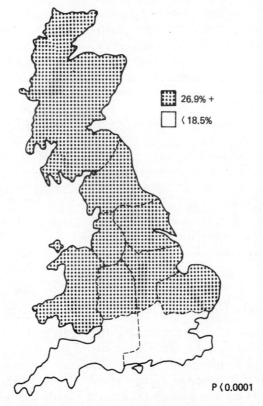

26.9% +

< 18.5%

P < 0.0001

FIG. 19.11 Proportion of children *never* seen by a dentist by region

the time of the 5-year follow-up were those whose behaviour most conformed to that recommended. Children of both younger and older mothers were more likely never to have visited the dentist (Fig. 19.10). The child who had a single sibling was at least risk of never visiting a dentist. Thereafter, the more children in the family the more likely was the child not to have visited a dentist.

As in other studies, we found a strong social class relationship. Figure 19.10h shows that very few children in social class I had failed to visit a dentist, but that there was a strong trend thereafter. Nearly half the children in social class V had never visited a dentist.

Children of Asian and West Indian parents were at even greater risk of having no dental examination (Fig. 19.10i). Two-thirds of the children in these groups were involved. In addition, those children who were living with a single parent or those with a step-parent were more likely to fail in this respect.

Clearly, of the eleven factors significantly associated with failure of the child to visit a dentist, many occurred as a result of others. Indirect standardisation showed that six factors were responsible for the other findings. These were: region; type of neighbourhood; number of household moves; number of other children in the household; presence of a father figure; and social class. Once these had been taken into account, the associations with birthweight, duration of breast feeding, ethnic group, maternal age and maternal smoking habit failed to reach statistical significance. Figure 19.12 shows that the highest Relative Risks associated with non-attendance at a dentist occur with children from large families (four or more siblings), and those living with a single mother.

As dental treatment can only have a preventative role if decay is caught early, it is distressing that groups known to be at most risk of decay, such as the lower social classes, are those least likely to go to a dentist. The problems are probably increasing as time goes on. In our latest follow-up of this cohort we have found that children in the lower social classes are those most likely to consume those items most likely to promote decay—viz. chocolates and sweets (Haslum, Golding and Morris, 1983).

The Health and Behaviour of the Children

In an analysis of data concerning the 1946 cohort, Douglas and Blomfield (1958) found it difficult to assess the efficacy of the child welfare services in promoting health. This was due to the fact that a relatively large proportion of the best attenders were mothers of 'weakly' children. It is of interest though to examine the 1970 cohort data to see whether children born 24 years later exhibit the same characteristics.

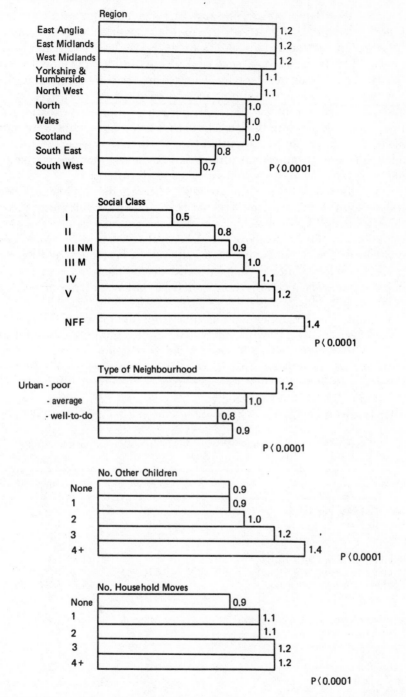

Fig. 19.12 Factors independently associated with failure to visit a dentist (Relative Risks)

Table 19.2 demonstrates the ways in which children seen in a birth follow-up clinic differ in regard to their medical and behavioural history. Taking associations significant at the 1% level or greater, it can be seen that children seen at such clinics were considerably more likely to have had behaviour problems as a baby (crying, feeding and sleeping), to have sleep problems continuing at 5, to have speech disorders, squint and other vision problems, to have respiratory symptoms (wheezing, hay fever, pneumonia, sore throats and mouth breathing). They were more likely to have been admitted to hospital, especially for an adenoidectomy. Connected with this may be the fact that they were more likely to have been suspected of hearing disorders.

These findings are not unexpected. The fact that a child has been followed up in this way implies that he has been considered at risk of developmental problems—whether because of low birthweight, short gestation or abnormal signs in the neonatal period. The findings confirm that such follow-up examinations are reaching children with certain problems, but are unable to address the question as to whether being seen at such a clinic is more beneficial than attendance at a normal child health clinic.

In Table 19.3 it can be seen that that group of children who were not visited at home by a health visitor in the first 6 months of life did not differ significantly from the rest of the population in respect of the variables we have listed. In contrast, the children who had not been taken to a child health clinic were significantly different from the rest of the population in several respects. This confirms the finding from the 1946 cohort that children with problems are more likely to be taken to a

TABLE 19.2   The health and behaviour of children seen in a birth follow-up clinic

Child's history	Observed	Relative Risk
Wets bed (1+ per week)	235	1.2*
Wets by day	205	1.1
Soils	96	1.2*
Sleeping problems as a baby	313	1.3****
Sleeping problems at 5	691	1.5****
Feeding problems as a baby	369	1.5****
Feeding problems at 5	691	1.0
Temper tantrums (1+ per week)	249	1.1
Destroys belongings	99	1.3*
Fights other children	85	1.1
Is irritable	226	1.1
Takes things	42	1.2
Is disobedient	199	1.1
Tells lies	50	1.2
Bullies	36	1.3

Continued

Table 19.2 continued

Child's history	Observed	Relative Risk
Is often worried	103	1.0
Is solitary	191	1.1
Is miserable	56	1.2
Is fearful or afraid	149	1.2*
Is fussy or over-particular	201	1.2*
Is squirmy or fidgety	242	1.2*
Restless	557	1.1
Unsettled	138	1.1
Crying as a baby	332	1.3****
Twitches/mannerisms	22	1.6*
Not much liked	30	1.2
Sucks thumb	298	1.0
Bites nails	195	1.0
Stammers/stutters	110	1.0
Other speech problem	254	1.3****
Headaches (at least 1 per month)	121	1.1
Stomach aches (at least 1 per month)	204	1.2*
2+ Accidents	217	1.0
History of wheezing	458	1.2****
History of eczema	213	1.0
Hay fever	107	1.4***
Vision problem	85	1.3**
Squint	192	1.4****
Bronchitis	340	1.1*
Pneumonia	52	1.8****
Repeated sore throats	425	1.2**
Ear discharge	230	1.1
Mouth breathing	414	1.2**
Suspected hearing disorder	179	1.2**
One hospital admission	424	1.2****
2+ hospital admissions	241	1.8****
Tonsillectomy	43	1.1
Adenoidectomy	37	1.8****
Circumcision	51	0.9
Hernia repair	38	1.2

Relative Risk = observed/expected, the expectation having derived from standardisation by social class.
*$P < 0.05$; **$P < 0.01$; ***$P < 0.001$; ****$P < 0.0001$.

TABLE 19.3 The health and behaviour of children who (a) were not visited at home under 6 months by a health visitor, (b) never attended a child health clinic, or (c) never went to a dentist

Child's history	No health visitor home visit		Never child health clinic		Never dentist	
	Observed	R. Risk	Observed	R. Risk	Observed	R. Risk
Wets bed (1+ per week)	87	0.9	142	1.1	448	1.2****
Wets by day	73	0.8	123	1.0	339	1.0
Soils	30	0.8	50	1.0	160	1.2*
Sleeping problems as a baby	116	1.0	111	0.7****	397	0.9
Sleeping problems at 5	198	0.9	233	0.8***	712	0.9*
Feeding problems as a baby	123	1.1	94	0.6****	407	1.0
Feeding problems at 5	313	1.0	353	0.8***	1148	1.0
Temper tantrums (1+ per week)	96	0.9	132	0.9	496	1.2**
Destroys belongings	43	1.2	38	0.8	190	1.3***
Fights other children	30	0.8	49	1.0	187	1.2***
Is irritable	92	0.9	104	0.8**	457	1.2**
Takes things	20	1.2	18	0.8	90	1.3*
Is disobedient	82	1.0	94	0.8	366	1.1*
Tells lies	23	1.2	29	1.1	120	1.5****
Bullies	11	0.8	16	0.9	70	1.3
Is often worried	45	1.0	44	0.7*	188	1.1
Is solitary	79	1.0	109	1.0	383	1.2***
Is miserable or tearful	20	0.9	14	0.5**	105	1.2
Is fearful or afraid	53	0.9	62	0.8	241	1.1
Is fussy or over-particular	84	1.0	90	0.8	390	1.3****
Very restless	237	1.0	288	0.8**	1065	1.1**
Is squirmy or fidgety	94	0.9	97	0.7***	415	1.1
Cannot settle	53	0.9	69	0.8	289	1.2**
Crying problem as a baby	139	1.1	121	0.7***	429	1.0
Not much liked	14	1.2	20	1.2	65	1.3
Twitches/mannerisms	5	0.8	4	0.5	28	1.1

Bites nails	99	1.0	109	0.8	412	1.1
Sucks thumb	136	0.9	198	1.0	401	0.8****
Dysfluency	51	1.0	66	0.9	225	1.1
Other speech problem	97	1.1	107	0.9	346	1.0
Headaches (1+ per month)	65	1.3*	52	0.8*	212	1.1
Stomach aches (1+ per month)	86	1.1	69	0.6****	287	1.0
2+ Accidents	104	1.0	127	0.9	377	1.0
Wheezing	176	1.0	238	1.0	670	1.0
Eczema	105	1.0	118	0.8	273	0.8****
Hay fever	30	0.8	45	0.9	94	0.7**
Vision problem	34	1.1	31	0.8	94	0.9
Squint	61	0.9	71	0.8	234	1.0
Bronchitis	134	0.9	172	0.9	580	1.1
Pneumonia	19	1.4	19	1.0	70	1.3*
Repeated sore throats	159	0.9	185	0.8***	588	0.9
Ear discharge	102	1.1	130	1.0	307	0.9
Mouth breathing	164	1.0	176	0.8***	615	1.0
Suspected hearing disorder	85	1.2	75	0.8*	193	0.8
One hospital admission	162	1.0	201	0.9	627	1.1
2+ hospital admissions	69	1.1	81	1.0	258	1.1
Tonsillectomy	25	1.3	17	0.7	53	0.8
Adenoidectomy	18	1.8*	16	1.2	15	0.5**
Circumcision	29	1.1	42	1.2	89	1.0
Hernia operation	12	0.8	20	1.0	62	1.2

*P < 0.05; **P < 0.01; ***P < 0.001; ****P < 0.0001.

child health clinic since, in each instance, non-attenders were less likely than expected to have the problem. This was particularly true for feeding and sleeping problems as a baby, as well as at age 5. It was apparent for children who had cried frequently as a baby, those described as irritable, tearful or having one of the hyperactive symptoms at 5, and children with a history of stomach aches, sore throats and mouth breathing.

Children who had *never* visited a dentist presented with a quite different set of problems. They were more likely to have many of the behaviour attributes associated with the difficult or hyperactive child. They also included more children than expected who were described as fussy, over-particular, or solitary. They were less likely than expected to have a history of eczema, hay fever or to suck their thumbs.

Children who never attended a child health clinic or a dentist were less likely to be suspected of having hearing difficulty. Whether this means that fewer children with hearing loss were included in these groups, or alternatively that the index of suspicion was lower and the children with hearing loss were less likely to have been identified, is one which we shall examine when analysing data from the audiograms in the 10-year follow-up.

Conclusions

1. Health visitor home visits in the first 6 months of life were significantly less likely to occur: (a) if both parents were Asian; (b) if the child had an unsupported single parent, or neither natural parent; (c) if the child had moved house; and (d) if the child was resident in London and the South East of England.
2. Children were less likely to have ever attended a child health clinic if their mother smoked heavily, they were residents in a rural area or in Scotland, the East Midlands or East Anglia.
3. Children never seen at a child health clinic were significantly less likely to to have behaviour, sleeping or feeding problems, intermittent stomach aches, sore throats or mouth breathing.
4. Low birthweight children were more likely to be seen at a birth follow-up clinic.
5. Children seen at birth follow-up clinics were more likely to have a variety of sensory, respiratory and behaviour problems.
6. Failure to visit a dentist was more likely if: (a) the child was in the manual social classes; (b) the mother was a single parent; (c) the child had three or more siblings; (d) the household had moved three or more times; (e) the child lived in a poor urban area; or (f) the child resided in East Anglia or the Midlands.

CHAPTER 20

Immunisations

by JEAN GOLDING ~

Introduction

Even with the advanced technology of the 1980s there is still no known cure for many of the major infections of childhood, although treatment may ameliorate the diseases. As has been recognised since the eighteenth century, the most effective method of preventing major epidemics of infection is by means of inoculation or vaccination. This process results in antibodies to the particular disease being created in the patient without their having to undergo the disease itself. It is true that in some cases a very mild form of the illness will result from the vaccination, but until recently this has been considered a very small price to pay for immunity from the disease.

Information on immunisations was not collected on the children involved in the 1946 cohort. The 1958 study, however, enquired as to whether the children had been immunised against diphtheria, polio and smallpox. Analysis of the data collected when the children were 7 (Davie, Butler and Goldstein, 1972) showed that three-quarters of the children had been vaccinated against smallpox, 95% had had at least one immunisation against polio and 94% had been given some protection against diptheria. For each type, children in the upper social classes were more likely, and those in social classes IV and V were least likely, to be immunised. There were regional differences, with Scotland having higher than average immunisation rates and the North of England having the lowest rates.

The Present Study

Health visitors asked the mothers for details of all immunisations given to the study child up to the time of interview. As shown in Table 20.1, over half the children had had at least some of their immunisations at a child health clinic, and 40% were immunised only at a general practitioner surgery.

Table 20.2 shows that the proportion of children immunised against

TABLE 20.1 Places where the children had received
their immunisation

Place* where immunisation(s) given	Number of children	
GP surgery	4446	(39.8%)
Child health clinic	5279	(47.2%)
GP surgery and child health clinic	1355	(12.2%)
Elsewhere only	87	(0.8%)
All known	11,167	(100.0%)

*Categories mutually exclusive.

TABLE 20.2 Immunisations received by the
12,692 children for whom immunisation
histories were recorded

Immunisation		Number of children	
Diphtheria	1 or more	12,239	(96.4%)
	2 or more	11,793	(92.9%)
	3 or more	11,373	(89.6%)
	4 or more	5322	(41.9%)
Tetanus	1 or more	12,253	(96.5%)
	2 or more	11,797	(92.9%)
	3 or more	11,377	(89.7%)
	4 or more	5345	(42.1%)
Pertussis	1 or more	11,851	(93.4%)
	2 or more	11,364	(89.5%)
	3 or more	10,878	(85.7%)
	4 or more	1339	(10.5%)
Polio	1 or more	12,100	(95.3%)
	2 or more	11,646	(91.8%)
	3 or more	11,195	(88.2%)
	4 or more	5101	(40.2%)
Measles immunisation		7440	(58.6%)
Smallpox immunisation		2747	(21.6%)
BCG		868	(6.8%)
No immunisations at all		317	(2.5%)

diphtheria and polio was almost identical to that found in the 1958 cohort. Altogether 88% of the study children had had at least three immunisations against each of diphtheria, tetanus, pertussis (whooping cough) and polio. The proportion vaccinated against smallpox had dropped from three-quarters to one-fifth, but this was still higher than expected, since in the early 1970s smallpox had been almost eliminated from the world population.

The epidemiological features of diphtheria, tetanus, pertussis and polio immunisation were, at this time, almost identical to one another. We shall, therefore, describe the associations of only one, and have chosen pertussis because of its topicality. In addition, we shall discuss the features associated with measles immunisation and BCG.

Pertussis Immunisation

Pertussis vaccine is normally given in combination with diphtheria and tetanus vaccines, but any adverse reactions appear to be associated with the pertussis part of this combination. That relatively minor reactions are common was clearly demonstrated in a study by Barkin and Pichichero (1979). They studied all children receiving a combined vaccine for diphtheria, tetanus and pertussis (DTP) in their practice, during an 8-month period in 1977–8. Questionnaires were filled in 48 hours after the immunisation of 1232 children. During the 2 days, 49% had had a temperature between 100°–102°F and a further 4% had had a temperature of over 102°F. Only 18% of the sample had reported no behaviour change after the immunisation, 34% had been reported as irritable, 35% as crying more than normally, and 13% as screaming. Other problems which were reported by the parents included listlessness, decreased appetite and vomiting. There were no reports of convulsions.

Several studies have now taken place in an attempt to assess whether pertussis vaccination does result in an increased incidence of convulsions with an encephalopathy. Stephenson (1980) studied the EEG results of twelve children who had had febrile convulsions after receiving pertussis vaccine, and compared these with three children who had had convulsions during an episode of whooping cough itself. He contrasted his results with those from 630 children who had had febrile convulsions, not associated with pertussis or its vaccine. He found that children with febrile convulsions after the vaccine had EEGs that were similar to the children whose convulsions were classified as 'anoxic' (i.e. 'more like fainting fits'); the three children who had had convulsions with their episode of whooping cough had EEGs that were more consistent with a diagnosis of encephalopathy.

In a publication from the Department of Health and Social Security

(1981) three studies were reported. Dudgeon and his colleagues examined fifty apparently well-documented cases of adverse reactions to pertussis vaccine, and showed that thirty-four could possibly be related to the immunisation itself: thirteen of these children had chronic epilepsy; thirteen had an acute encephalopathy; and eight had infantile spasms. This study is difficult to interpret, as the authors recognise, because of lack of comparison with a control population.

The second study was made by Meade and his colleagues who examined records of 229 infants identified either from the archives of the Association of Parents of Vaccine Damaged Children or from notifications to the Committee on Safety of Medicines. They commented that the data were largely unsatisfactory for epidemiological analysis, but nevertheless concluded that the evidence as a whole left little doubt that pertussis vaccine was associated with an increased incidence of convulsions, but that evidence for brain damage was inconclusive.

A different approach again was involved in the National Childhood Encephalopathy Study. This involved 1000 children admitted to hospital with an acute neurological illness in the age group 2–36 months. Two controls were chosen for each case, matched for age and area of residence. Immunisation histories were compared between cases and controls. Significantly more of the index cases (3.5%) had had pertussis vaccine within 7 days of the onset of the illness compared with 1.7% of controls. This gave a relative risk of encephalopathy associated with vaccination of 2.4, significant at the 0.001 level. Of the thirty-five pertussis vaccine associated cases, thirty-two were regarded as neurologically normal before the illness; twenty-one of these recovered completely.

The conclusions of the report were that a link might well exist between pertussis immunisation and neurological illness. The authors emphasise that in many instances where adverse reactions had been noted the immunisation had been given in the presence of contraindications. But this assumes that we know which factors to avoid. Illingworth (1980) reported a strange conglomeration of factors which mothers had stated were the reason for their child not having been immunised against whooping cough. These included: the child had been given oxygen at birth; was pre-term; had had jaundice; was a breech; was a twin; had had nappy rash. In America the OCIP recommendations are largely concerned with any severe side effect noted after a preceding dose. They state that the presence of an evolving neurologic disorder contraindicates the use of pertussis vaccine, but that a static neurologic condition, like cerebral palsy, or a family history of neurologic disease is not a contraindication (MMWR, 1981). Valman (1980b) stated that family or personal history of allergy is not a contraindication to pertussis immunisation, but Anand (1980) reported that, according to the drug firm Wellcome, a history of severe allergy should be a contraindication to the use of the vaccine.

It is salutary to compare the adverse effects of the vaccine with those of the disease. McKendrick, Gully and Geddes (1980) studied abnormalities in children with pertussis admitted to hospital 1978–9. As many as 40% of these children had pneumonia, 13% had cyanotic and apnoeic attacks and 7% had convulsions. They found no difference in the rate of complications among children who were under 6 months of age compared with those who were older. A further interesting study on whooping cough was carried out in Cardiff by Vesselinova-Jenkins and her colleagues (1978). She, too, found that 7% of the children had convulsions, but was also able to analyse the data according to whether the child had had any vaccinations prior to the whooping cough episode. She found that among 101 children who had had whooping cough subsequent to a completed course of immunisations, only one had a convulsion; among twelve children who had inadequate vaccination one child had convulsions with the episode of whooping cough; but among 116 children who had no pertussis immunisation at all, as many as fourteen had convulsions.

An attempt has been made by Koplan and his colleagues (1979) to contrast the benefits and costs of programmes of pertussis vaccination in America. On the basis of information available to them at that time, they predicted that if immunisation were to cease, there would be a 71-fold increase in cases of whooping cough with an almost four-fold increase in deaths from whooping cough, as well as 3.2 cases of encephalitis associated with the disease. With a vaccination programme they predicted 0.1 cases of encephalitis associated with whooping cough and five cases of post-vaccination encephalitis per 1,000,000 children. They concluded that a vaccination programme would reduce by 61% the costs related to pertussis. Such an analysis is still awaited in the British scene.

In this section we shall examine those factors associated with children who either had never been immunised, or who had been immunised, but not for pertussis. As we have already noted, there is considerable anxiety concerning possible adverse effects of pertussis immunisation. It is, therefore, pertinent to examine the data relating to the children who were not immunised at a point in time prior to the adverse propaganda with the consequent drop in uptake.

There were no differences between the sexes in the uptake of pertussis immunisation, nor were low birthweight infants more, or less, likely to receive such an immunisation. There were differences, however, with the type of feed the child had had as a baby (Fig. 20.1). Children who had never been breast fed were twice as likely never to have been immunised at all.

Uptake of immunisations varies with various characteristics of the families. As shown in Fig. 20.1b, the older mothers were those who were less likely to have their children immunised at all—and less likely to have the child immunised against pertussis. This is closely linked to the fact that the children least likely to be immunised were those from the larger families.

As in the 1958 cohort, children in the non-manual social classes were the most likely to be immunised, and children in social class V were

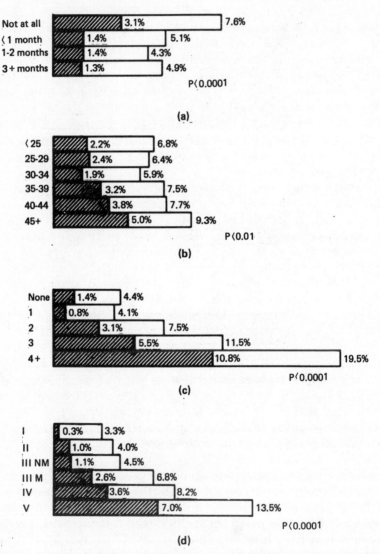

Fig. 20.1 Proportion of children *not* immunised against pertussis by (a) duration of breast feeding, (b) maternal age, (c) number of other children in the household, (d) social class

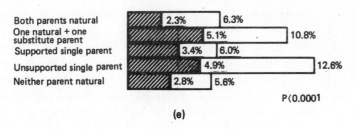

Both parents natural   2.3%   6.3%
One natural + one substitute parent   5.1%   10.8%
Supported single parent   3.4%   6.0%
Unsupported single parent   4.9%   12.6%
Neither parent natural   2.8%   5.6%

P<0.0001

(e)

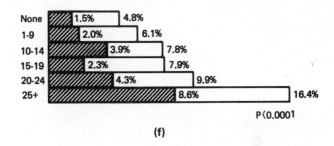

None   1.5%   4.8%
1-9   2.0%   6.1%
10-14   3.9%   7.8%
15-19   2.3%   7.9%
20-24   4.3%   9.9%
25+   8.6%   16.4%

P<0.0001

(f)

All urban   2.8%   7.3%
Rural   1.3%   4.1%

P<0.0001

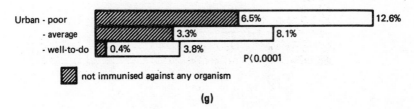

Urban - poor   6.5%   12.6%
- average   3.3%   8.1%
- well-to-do   0.4%   3.8%

P<0.0001

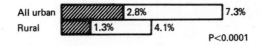 not immunised against any organism

(g)

FIG. 20.1 *continued* (e) parental situation, (f) maternal smoking habit, (g) type of neighbourhood

most likely to be unprotected against pertussis (Fig. 20.1), or any of the other infections against which immunisations are available. A similar pattern was shown with parental situation. Children living with an unsupported single parent, and those with a step-parent, were more likely not to have been immunised.

As with so many of the factors we have examined, there was a strong association with the smoking habit of the mother (Fig. 20.1); the more cigarettes she smoked, the less likely was the child to have been immunised.

Again, as shown for the 1958 cohort, there were significant regional differences (Fig. 20.2). Children living in Scotland were among the most likely to receive immunisations. Children who never received any form of immunisation were found proportionately more often in the northern counties of England and in Wales.

As we have shown in Chapter 19, children from rural areas are less likely to visit a child health clinic. Nevertheless, Fig. 20.1 demonstrates that residents of urban areas are more likely to fail to receive immunisations of any sort. In view of the distribution with social class, it is not surprising that there was a strong trend among the urban areas—compared with those in well-to-do areas, children in poor urban areas were at thirteen times the risk of never being immunised.

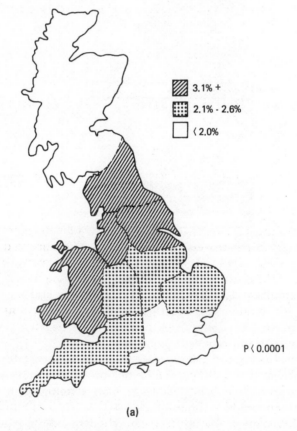

3.1% +

2.1% - 2.6%

< 2.0%

P < 0.0001

(a)

FIG. 20.2 Proportion of children in each region (a) not immunised at all

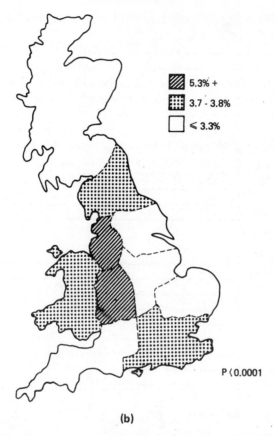

5.3% +

3.7 - 3.8%

⩽ 3.3%

P ⟨ 0.0001

(b)

Fig. 20.2 *continued* (b) immunised but not against pertussis

Analysis of the inter-relationships of the eight factors described above demonstrated that four were of paramount importance in determining the failure of the child to receive pertussis immunisation. These were: the region of the country and type of neighbourhood in which the child lived; the number of other children in the family; and the number of cigarettes the mother smoked (Fig. 20.3). These accounted for the associations we had found with maternal age, social class, parental situation and the duration of breast feeding.

The characteristics of the children who were *never* immunised are shown in the left-hand columns of Table 20.3. As with children who had never been to a child health clinic, in many respects they had fewer problems than would have been expected from the population as a whole. There were, however, more children than expected with bronchitis and pneumonia, and more with hospital admissions. A third

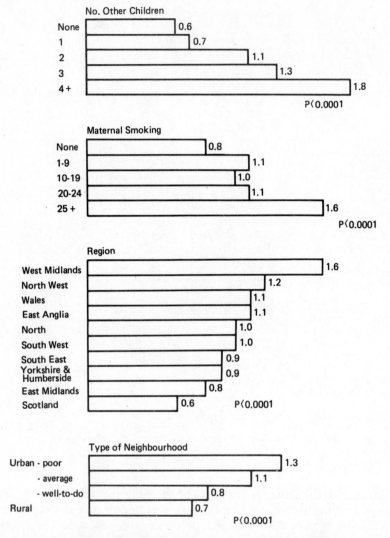

FIG. 20.3 Factors independently associated with failure to receive a pertussis immunisation (Relative Risk of *not* having the immunisation)

of the children who received no immunisations at all had never attended a child health clinic. This group were also less likely to have been taken to a dentist.

Among children who had been immunised, but not against pertussis, there were, again, more than expected who had been admitted to hospital. In addition, more children in this group had attended a birth follow-up clinic but were less likely to have been seen at home by a health visitor in the first months. The group contained an excess of accident

TABLE 20.3   The health and behaviour of children who either (a) were never immunised at all, or (b) were immunised but not against pertussis

Child's history	Never immunised		Not pertussis	
	Observed	R. Risk	Observed	R. Risk
Wets bed (1+ per week)	41	1.1	78	1.3*
Wets by day	34	1.0	48	0.9
Soils	16	1.2	16	0.7
Sleeping problems as a baby	29	0.7*	69	1.0
Sleeping problems at 5	65	0.8	120	0.9
Feeding problems as a baby	31	0.7	71	1.0
Feeding problems at 5	101	0.9	189	1.0
Temper tantrums (1+ per week)	69	1.5***	82	1.2
Destroys belongings	21	1.3	30	1.3
Fights other children	31	1.9***	25	1.0
Is irritable	66	1.5***	52	0.8
Takes things	13	1.7*	11	1.0
Is disobedient	53	1.5**	60	1.1
Tells lies	12	1.3	16	1.2
Bullies	20	3.2****	13	1.5
Is often worried	18	1.0	33	1.1
Is rather solitary	56	1.7****	56	1.1
Is miserable or tearful	18	1.8**	18	1.3
Is fearful or afraid	22	1.0	51	1.5**
Is fussy or over-particular	46	1.4*	48	1.0
Is very restless	110	1.1	173	1.1
Is squirmy or fidgety	47	1.2	65	1.1
Cannot settle	37	1.4*	45	1.2
Crying problem as a baby	31	0.7*	79	1.1
Not much liked	9	1.6	16	2.0**
Twitches/mannerisms	4	0.7	6	1.5
Bites nails	38	1.0	64	1.1
Sucks thumb	21	0.4***	82	1.0
Dysfluency	13	0.6	41	1.3
Other speech problem	45	1.3	76	1.4**
Headaches (1+ per month)	23	1.2	27	0.9
Stomach aches (1+ per month)	30	1.0	45	0.8
2+ Accidents	33	0.8	94	1.5***
Wheezing	81	1.2	149	1.4****
Eczema	20	0.6*	96	1.6****
Hay fever	8	0.6	23	1.1
Vision problem	7	0.6	22	1.2
Squint	24	1.0	47	1.2
Bronchitis	84	1.5***	112	1.3*
Pneumonia	11	1.9*	12	1.4
Repeated sore throats	42	0.7**	101	1.0

Continued

Table 20.3 continued

Child's history	Never immunised Observed	R. Risk	Not pertussis Observed	R. Risk
Ear discharge	35	1.0	61	1.2
Mouth breathing	66	1.0	102	1.0
Suspected hearing disorder	15	0.7	38	0.9
One hospital admission	76	1.3	114	1.2
2+ hospital admissions	36	1.5*	56	1.5**
Tonsillectomy	6	0.9	5	0.5
Adenoidectomy	1	0.4	5	0.9
Circumcision	4	0.5	16	1.1
Hernia repair	4	0.8	8	0.9
Attended birth follow-up clinic	37	0.8	100	1.4**
Not seen at home by HV < 6 months	24	1.1	52	1.5**
Never been to child health clinic	110	3.8****	61	1.3
Never been to dentist	169	1.9****	163	1.2*

(Relative Risks computed after standardisation for social class.)
*$P < 0.05$; **$P < 0.01$; ***$P < 0.001$; ****$P < 0.0001$.

repeaters, and more than expected had a history of wheezing or of eczema. These latter two associations could be interpreted in two ways: the lack of pertussis immunisation resulted in allergic diseases; or the presence of the allergic disorders was the reason for witholding the pertussis immunisation. The latter explanation seems the more likely.

Study of these two groups in more detail (Golding, in preparation) has shown that, in both, there was a comparatively high rate of hospital admissions for pertussis (whooping cough) itself. These episodes were frequently associated with bronchitis and pneumonia. Further analysis has shown that the children who had not been immunised against pertussis were more likely to be intellectually retarded by the age of 5. In many cases the retardation occurred in the children who had had the disease itself. As for convulsions associated with pertussis immunisation, we were able to identify four cases where this had occurred within 72 hours. This was twice as many as expected, but none of the four subsequently suffered from retardation or any other disability.

Measles Immunisation

The association of measles vaccine with severe adverse effects has received comparatively little attention in the literature. In America 1114 students were studied, a third having been given measles vaccine. Analysis of symptoms in the subsequent 21 days showed that the frequency of pyrexia was over twice as great in those who had been given the measles vaccine, compared with controls who had not been immunised (MMWR, 1981). In Hamburg Allerdist (1979) analysed eighteen cases where neurological complications had been reported after measles vaccine. Of these, four had had the immunisation less than 6 days prior to the convulsion and were assumed not to be associated with the vaccine; fourteen had had a convulsion between the 7th and 11th day from the immunisation date, and these he assumed to be causally related (this included two with an encephalopathy). He concluded from this data that the risk of febrile convulsions was 1 per 2500 immunisations, and the risk of slight encephalopathy was 1 per 17,650. Analysis of the National Childhood Encephalopathy Study also demonstrated an increased risk of encephalopathy between 7 and 14 days after measles immunisation; the risk was estimated at 1 in 87,000.

It is generally recognised that any harm that might result from the use of the vaccine is more than compensated for by the adverse associations of the disease itself. In the present study there were seven children with a fit 7–14 days after immunisation, but there was no evidence to suggest that this was associated with any long-term adverse effect. Balanced against this should be a least five children who had had convulsions in association with measles itself, one of whom was subsequently found to be severely retarded.

As already noted, over half the study children had been immunised against measles. The majority of these (5822 children) received the immunisation when they were 1 year of age. In this section we shall be describing the ways in which children who received the jab differed from the rest of the cohort.

As found with other health behaviour, there were no differences between the sexes. Children of low birthweight were no more, or less, likely to be immunised than the rest of the study group. There was again, however, an association with breast feeding—children who had been breast fed were more likely to have been immunised (Fig. 20.4).

There was a strong regional variation with South-west among those areas most likely to immunise against measles (Fig. 20.5). Children from Wales were significantly less likely to be immunised than those in England.

As with pertussis immunisation, children in rural areas were more likely to be immunised than those in urban areas (Fig. 20.4). In urban areas it was residents in the well-to-do suburbs that were most likely to have been protected in this way.

There was some evidence that the chance of the child being immunised against measles fell with the number of times the child had

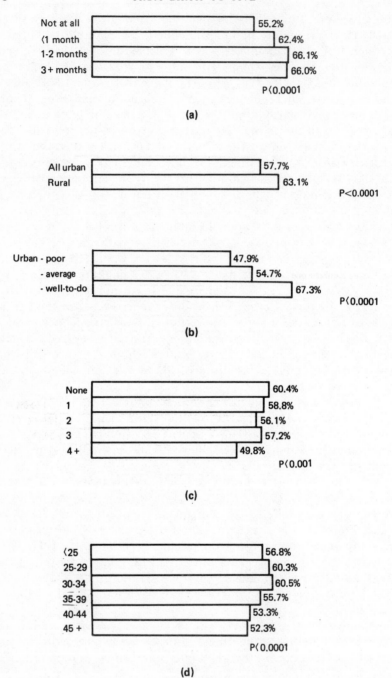

Fig. 20.4 Proportion of children immunised against measles by (a) duration of breast feeding, (b) type of neighbourhood, (c) number of household moves, (d) maternal age

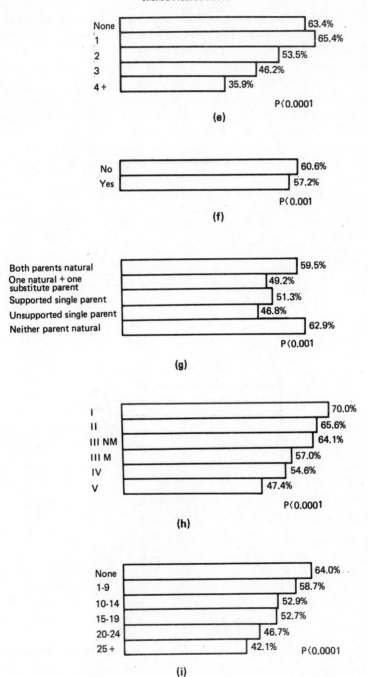

Fig. 20.4 *continued* (e) number of other children in the household, (f) whether mother employed during the child's life, (g) parental situation, (h) social class, (i) maternal smoking habit

moved house. Figure 20.4c shows, however, that the association is mainly among the frequent movers (at least four moves by the time the child was 5).

Other patterns are similar to those found with dental care. Mothers who were in their 40s, those with large families, those who had been employed, and those who were not living with the natural father of the child, were less likely to have had their child immunised against measles.

In addition, there were strong linear trends with social class (Fig. 20.4) and the number of cigarettes smoked by the mother. Thus, the more cigarettes she smoked, or the lower the social class, the less likely the child was to have been immunised against measles.

Indirect standardisation (Fig. 20.6) has shown that the uptake of measles immunisation is independently associated with: the region of

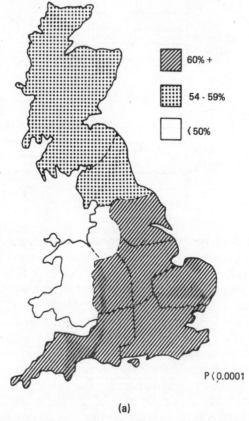

FIG. 20.5 Proportion of children in each region receiving (a) measles immunisation

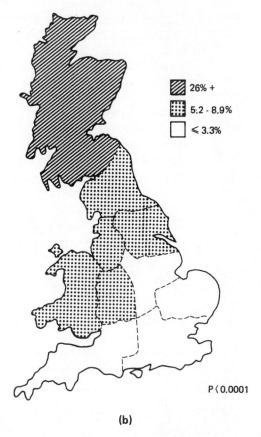

26% +

5.2 - 8.9%

≤ 3.3%

P ⟨ 0.0001

(b)

FIG. 20.5 *continued* (b) BCG

the country and the type of neighbourhood in which the child resides; the number of other children in the household; whether the household has moved frequently; and the maternal smoking habit. The other factors were no longer statistically significant once these five had been taken into account.

Children who had been immunised against measles showed no signs of adverse outcome (Table 20.4). Indeed, they were significantly less likely than expected to have been admitted to hospital on two or more occasions, and less likely to have had bronchitis or pneumonia. Part of these differences may be explained by the contraindications to the vaccine, which include chronic diseases of the heart or lungs (Valman, 1980b). Other explanations include the increase in hospital admissions associated with measles in unimmunised children (nineteen cases) and

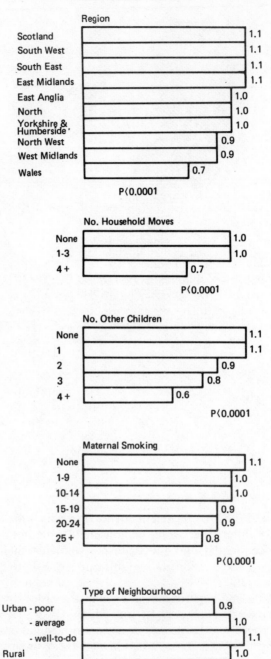

Fig. 20.6 Factors independently associated with uptake of measles immunisation (Relative Risks)

TABLE 20.4   The health and behaviour of children who were immunised against measles or given BCG

Child's history	Immunised against measles		BCG given	
	Observed	R. Risk	Observed	R. Risk
Wets bed (1+ per week)	709	0.9**	94	1.0
Wets by day	746	1.0	76	0.9
Soils	305	1.0	29	0.8
Sleeping problems as a baby	1029	1.0	119	1.0
Sleeping problems at 5	1850	1.0	200	0.9
Feeding problems as a baby	1002	1.0	120	1.1
Feeding problems at 5	2759	1.0	299	1.0
Temper tantrums (1+ per week)	782	0.9**	120	1.1
Destroys belongings	244	0.8**	33	0.9
Fights other children	236	0.8***	48	1.3
Is irritable	787	1.0	99	1.0
Takes things	108	0.8	17	1.0
Is disobedient	626	0.9*	83	1.0
Tells lies	123	0.8*	28	1.4
Bullies	86	0.8	18	1.4
Is often worried	415	1.0	43	0.9
Is rather solitary	624	1.0	91	1.1
Is miserable or tearful	179	1.0	11	0.5*
Is fearful or afraid	465	1.0	59	1.0
Is fussy or over-particular	647	1.0	82	1.0
Is very restless	2059	1.0	265	1.1
Is squirmy or fidgety	810	1.0	100	1.0
Cannot settle	465	1.0	65	1.1
Crying problem as a baby	1076	1.0	118	1.0
Not much liked	80	0.8	12	1.0
Twitches/mannerisms	54	1.0	8	1.2
Bites nails	840	1.0	105	1.1
Sucks thumb	1414	1.1***	119	0.8
Dysfluency	458	1.0	55	1.0
Other speech problem	755	1.0	74	0.8
Headaches (1+ per month)	414	1.0	54	1.1
Stomach aches (1+ per month)	729	1.1	77	1.0
2+ Accidents	863	1.0	125	1.2
Wheezing	1439	1.0	175	1.0
Eczema	868	1.0	102	1.0
Hay fever	327	1.0	36	1.0
Vision problem	242	1.0	24	0.8
Squint	515	0.9	57	0.9
Bronchitis	1112	0.9**	127	0.9
Pneumonia	83	0.7**	11	0.8
Repeated sore throats	1469	1.0	195	1.1
Ear discharge	803	1.0	73	0.8*

Continued

Table 20.4 continued

Child's history	Immunised against measles		BCG given	
	Observed	R. Risk	Observed	R. Risk
Mouth breathing	1396	1.0	167	1.0
Suspected hearing disorder	622	1.0	60	0.9
One hospital admission	1286	0.9*	183	1.1
2+ hospital admissions	437	0.9***	69	1.1
Tonsillectomy	162	1.0	34	1.9***
Adenoidectomy	94	1.1	15	1.6
Circumcision	243	1.1	28	1.1
Hernia repair	123	1.0	16	1.1
Attended birth follow-up clinic	1046	1.0	141	1.2
Not seen at home by HV < 6 months	464	0.9	53	0.9
Never been to child health clinic	492	0.7****	85	1.1
Never been to dentist	1475	0.9****	245	1.1*
Immunised against pertussis	7280	1.1****	805	1.0
Immunised against measles	—	—	450	0.9
BCG	450	0.9	—	—

*P < 0.05; **P < 0.01; ***P < 0.001; ****P < 0.0001.

bronchitis and pneumonia developing in association with the infection. There was no evidence (Golding *et al.*, 1984) for an increase in mental subnormality after immunisation against measles.

BCG Immunisation

Extensive experience has apparently shown that BCG is one of the safest vaccines (*British Medical Journal*, 1980). Currently, in Britain, BCG vaccination is offered to 10–13-year-old school children. A small number of children are immunised as neonates if one member of the family has a history of tuberculosis, or when the child is thought to be at risk of contact with tuberculosis (e.g. Asian immigrant family). BCG should not be given to infants who have shown signs of eczema (Valman, 1980b).

Only 868 study children had received a BCG vaccination by the time they were 5. Epidemiologically, these children differed from those who had had the other immunisations considered above. Presumably this was because the decision is largely made by health professionals in response to a risk, rather than by the mother herself. Approximately half (473) the children involved had had the vaccination during the first week of life.

The most dramatic association was with region (Fig. 20.5b). A quarter of all Scottish children had had a BCG by the age of 5. No other region had given BCGs to even as many as 10% of their children, and in areas in southern Britain less than 3% of children were involved.

Obviously, the regional pattern reflects, to a certain extent, areas in which tuberculosis has a higher prevalence. The same is true of the type of neighbourhood. Though rare, pulmonary TB is more common in urban, as opposed to rural, areas, and is relatively common in poor urban areas. Some 14% of children from poor urban areas had had a BCG compared with 4.3% from rural areas (Fig. 20.7).

There were no differences in BCG rates with the number of

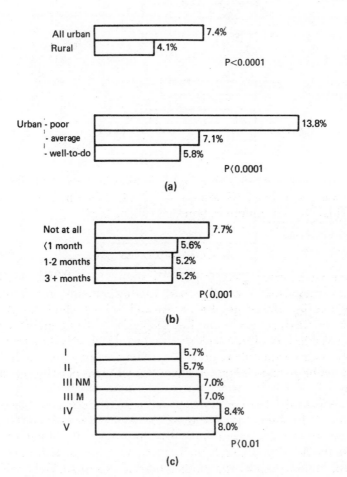

Fig. 20.7 Proportion of children receiving BCG by (a) type of neighbourhood, (b) duration of breast feeding, (c) social class (*continued on next page*)

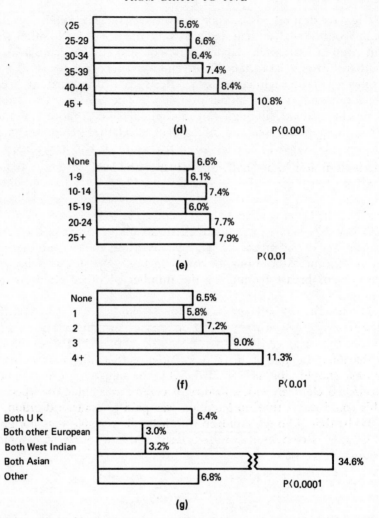

FIG. 20.7 *continued* (d) maternal age, (e) maternal smoking habit, (f) number of other
children in the household, (g) ethnic group of parents

household moves. Boys were as likely as girls to receive the vaccine, and
birthweight did not appear to affect the uptake. Children given BCG
were, however, less likely to have been breast fed (Fig. 20.7). This
finding was due to the predominance of Scottish children among those
who had received BCG— the Scots being unlikely to breast feed their
children (Chapter 4).

Children from social classes IV and V were more likely to receive
BCG, as were children of mothers who were in their 40s, and those who
smoked heavily (Fig. 20.7). All these associations were slight, however, in

comparison with the regional and neighbourhood differences we have shown above.

In addition, there was an association between the likelihood of a child receiving a BCG and the number of siblings in the household (Fig. 20.7). The children who had three or more siblings were more likely to have received a BCG.

The other dramatic variation was shown with ethnic group (Fig. 20.7). Over a third of children of Asian parents had had a BCG. In comparison, children of other immigrant parents had a rate of vaccination less than half that of the children of the indigenous population.

Standardisation showed that the major factors independently associated with BCG being given to a child in the pre-school years are: the area of Britain; the type of neighbourhood; the ethnic group of the parents; and the age of the mother (Fig. 20.8). Over and above these there were no significant associations with social class, parental smoking habit, duration of breast feeding or the number of other children in the household.

The health and behaviour of children who had had a BCG differed little from the rest of the population, apart from the fact that the BCG children were more likely than expected to have had a tonsillectomy (Table 20.4). In spite of the recommendation that children with infantile eczema should not be vaccinated, by the age of 5 the number of vaccinated children with a history of eczema was equal to expectation. This could mean that no attention was paid to contraindication, or it could be that although children with infantile eczema were not given a BCG, the vaccine itself was associated with the onset of eczematous lesions.

Discussion

Finally, it is important to point out the obvious. In assessing the health and behaviour of children who have, or have not been immunised, we have ignored the diseases for which the immunisations were carried out. There was considerable morbidity, and even mortality, attached to each.

One child had died suddenly at 11 weeks during an attack of whooping cough, a boy with Down's Syndrome died at 9 months during an attack of measles, and the 5-year-old daughter of Asian parents died of diphtheria.

Four children had had tuberculosis. Three of these had pulmonary TB and were kept in hospital for up to 9 months. The fourth child was born to an Asian mother. At the time of his delivery, the mother was found to have TB. The child was kept in hospital and treated for 4 months, and returned the following year with a TB cyst in his neck.

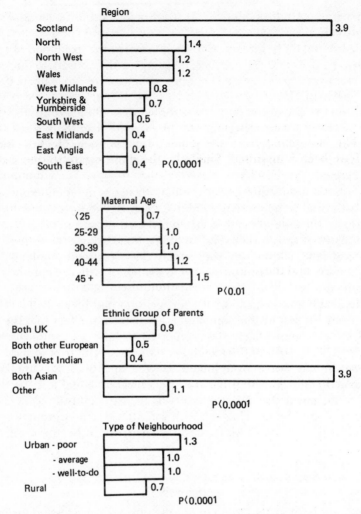

FIG. 20.8 Factors independently associated with the children receiving BCG vaccination
(Relative Risks)

There were twenty children admitted to hospital with measles, and
forty with pertussis. As already mentioned, these children had a high
incidence of convulsions and many of those with pertussis were
subsequently found to be intellectually backward. Whether this association was causal must await further study. It is, however, obvious from the
data presented here that the costs and benefits of the immunisation
programme are weighted heavily in favour of immunisation. It is,
therefore, worth noting that the children who are least likely to be given
most types of immunisation are generally those who would probably

benefit most from it. They tend to come from large families and poor urban areas where infection is passed around more easily.

Conclusions

1. Children who were never immunised against pertussis differed from the rest of the population in that they were more likely to live in urban areas—especially the 'poor' and 'average' urban areas. The more children in the family, the less likely was the child to have been immunised. Similarly, the more cigarettes the mother smoked, the less likely was the child to have been immunised. There were strong regional differences.

2. Uptake of measles immunisation also varied with region and with type of neighbourhood: children resident in poor urban areas were less likely, and those in well-to-do urban areas were more likely, to have been immunised. Again, the more cigarettes the mother smoked, and the more children in the household, the less likely was the study child to have been immunised against measles.

3. BCG was received by a quarter of all Scottish children, but less than 6% of the rest of the country. Rural residents were least likely to receive BCG and those from poor urban neighbourhoods were most likely to do so. The older the mother, the more likely the child was to have had the vaccination. A third of the children of Asian parents had had a BCG by the age of 5.

CHAPTER 21

The end of the beginning

by JEAN GOLDING and N. R. BUTLER

'The child is one, and when the child is taken to pieces for study somebody must remember to put the pieces together again' (Apley, 1982). In this volume we have gazed with some intensity at certain aspects of the child and his background, but we are well aware of the gaps in our knowledge. It is a great pity that no one has yet devised a method of measuring objectively the health of a child. We spend our time detecting symptoms of ill-health in the assumption that lack of symptoms implies a positive healthiness. In spite of its drawbacks, such an approach does have advantages. The aim of any study with data collected in this way would be to increase knowledge of factors associated with aspects of illness. Inherent in such information is the possibility of primary prevention in the future. Thus by endeavouring to eliminate illness we may promote health.

In this chapter we will discuss the ways in which geographical, biological and social factors are associated with various symptoms and conditions in the child. We shall also look at the way in which the attributes of the child himself influence the probability of his developing such conditions.

Influence of Sex

Differentiation between males and females begins very early in gestation. It is manifest in growth *in utero* (the male being heavier but the female physically more mature), and in behaviour patterns immediately after birth—the males being more active (Hutt, 1972), the females spending more time sleeping (Moss, 1967), and males in the early months being considerably more irritable than females. These latter findings were substantiated in our study. More mothers of male infants reported that their children had had sleeping and crying problems in the first 6 months of life (Table 21.1).

The most striking findings were, however, in the contrast in behaviour patterns between the sexes at 5. Germaine Greer, loquacious exponent of feminist views, has described women's special form of pathology. The symptoms she suggests are 'self-censorship, hypocritical modesty, insecurity, girlishness, self-deception, hostility towards her fellow strivers, timidity, poverty and ignorance' (Greer, 1979). Although the present study was not specifically designed to test Germaine Greer's hypotheses as to the nature of the female, the picture that emerges is hardly flattering to the sex. The nail-biting, thumb sucking, miserable creatures demonstrated in Table 21.1 can only be surpassed (in terms of horror) by the typical male behaviour patterns shown. Can this be a true picture of the differences between our children in their early formative years—or is it merely that the study was designed to look at the negative, rather than the positive, aspects of behaviour?

TABLE 21.1 Sex differences in behaviour problems significant at the 1% level

Behaviour problem*	Male/female rate
Destroys belongings	2.5
Fights other children	2.1
Soils	1.8
Takes things	1.7
Is disobedient	1.6
Temper tantrums (1+ per week)	1.5
Tells lies	1.4
Is restless	1.4
Is irritable	1.3
Unable to settle	1.3
Wets bed (1+ per week)	1.3
Sleeping difficulties as a baby	1.2
Crying problems	1.1
Fussy/over-particular	0.8
Wets during day	0.7
Sucks thumb	0.7
Bites nails	0.7

*Only behaviours said to 'certainly apply'.

The sex differences in behaviour have been described by many studies. Susan Isaacs (1932) first documented the fact that boys were more likely to have more 'acting-out', aggressive and delinquent behaviour disorders and girls were more often inhibited and fearful. In the Isle of Wight study it was found that among children with conduct and mixed disorders there were four times as many boys as girls (Rutter, Tizard and Whitmore, 1970).

At the age of 5 the health differences between the sexes were also marked: the boys in general had a medical history considerably more detailed than that of the girls (Table 21.2). There were no conditions where girls were at increased risk. This could be associated partly with the fact that females generally appear to be able to produce higher levels of antibodies to common viruses (Michaels and Rogers, 1971) and associated partly with the male ability to have accidents of all types (see Chapter 10). It is unclear whether the finding that male infants have significantly higher red cell counts, haemoglobin concentration and haematocrit (Lind *et al.*, 1977) has any effect on their morbidity pattern.

TABLE 21.2   Sex differences in medical
history significant at 1% level

Medical or sensory problem	Male/female rate
Circumcision	∞
Hernia repair	4.7
3+ Accidents	2.0
Dysfluency	1.8
Adenoidectomy	1.8
2 Accidents	1.6
Speech problem	1.6
2+ hospital admissions	1.6
Hay fever	1.4
1 hospital admission	1.3
Wheezing	1.3
Bronchitis	1.3
Mouth breathing	1.2
Suspected hearing difficulty	1.2
Frequent sore throats	1.1

That boys are more likely to have hearing and speech problems has long been noted. The latter association was also marked in the 7-year follow-up of the 1958 cohort (Davie, Butler and Goldstein, 1972) when girls were found to make fewer errors in the speech test, and to have only half the risk of being referred to a speech therapist. We have found the boys to be almost twice as likely to have a history of dysfluency and 60% more at risk of speech problems. Although boys were significantly more likely than girls to have been suspected of having hearing difficulty, the increase in rate was only of the order of 20%.

Throughout this volume we are anticipating the analyses of the subsequent development of the study children. Will the behaviour and health differential between boys and girls widen or decrease? Will the more detailed and objective tests of hearing, vision and speech and the results of medical examinations modify our present assessment? Initial analyses certainly suggest that, in spite of equal educational opportunities and health behaviour, there were still major differences in physical ability, behaviour and health.

Low Birthweight

There have now been a number of studies that have demonstrated that delivery of a low birthweight infant is not primarily associated with socio-economic factors. In Kansas, Miller, Hassanein and Hensleigh (1978) showed that if, in the analysis, allowance was made for behavioural indicators such as smoking there was no evidence for an increase in the incidence of low birthweight among the lower socio-economic groups. Similar findings have been reported for all three British cohort studies. For legitimate births in 1946, Douglas (1950) found the incidence to be 6.5%, with major associations of youthful or elderly mothers and first births. There had been a social class trend, but this was largely associated with the fact that mothers at the two extremes of age tended to have come from the lower social classes.

In 1958 the incidence of low birthweight among all singleton births was 6.7%, and the major associations with birthweight were found to be maternal height, primiparity, the presence of pre-eclampsia and whether the mother smoked or not. Once these had been taken into account, there were no significant associations with either maternal age or social class (Goldstein, 1969). The method of analysis was repeated on the 1970 data—and the results were almost identical (Peters et al., 1983).

In the present study we are looking at social factors pertaining at 5 rather than those apparent at birth. We showed, in Chapter 4, that although the proportion of children who were of low birthweight was twice as high in social class V as in social class I, this was due to the fact that more women in the lower social classes either smoked heavily or came from an Asian or West Indian background.

By the age of 5 we are, of course, only looking at the survivors. The death rate was high in the low birthweight group: of the singleton low birthweight infants, 20% were either stillborn or had died before the 28th day. Of the survivors, a further 2.0% had died by the age of 5. These figures should be compared with 1.0% and 0.7% of the remainder.

There has been repeated discussion concerning the quality of life of the surviving very low birthweight infant; most studies have involved the small group of infants weighing 2000 g or even less. For example, Drillien (1964) found that children of 2000 g or less were more backward and more disturbed than controls matched for social factors. Most other studies have involved selected hospital populations and rarely compared results with a control sample. The majority of publications have been concerned with intellectual and sensory outcomes.

An important series of studies were published on the 464 low birthweight (< 5 lb 8 oz) survivors who were included in the 1946 cohort. Douglas and Mogford (1953b) showed that the risk of hospital admission was raised in this group, especially for bronchitis and pneumonia. They showed that this group of children had a higher incidence, too, of all upper and lower respiratory tract infections. In general, however, after the age of 2, they stated that the children appeared to be as healthy as the controls.

Twenty-four years later it is difficult to feel as sanguine about the health of this group. We studied low birthweight infants at the age of 5 and found increased rates of reported vision problems, squint, speech problems, wheezing, pneumonia and operation for hernia. Only the associations with wheezing and speech problems could be explained in terms of other factors. The independent relative risks associated with low birthweight are shown in Table 21.3. In addition to the factors already mentioned, these children were more likely to be admitted to hospital, and they were especially likely to have had crying and feeding problems as a baby—the latter finding has previously been reported to be especially true of growth-retarded infants (Brook, 1983). The children were also much more likely than expected to soil and wet by day, and were also at increased risk of bed-wetting. They were significantly less likely to have had eczema.

TABLE 21.3 Relative Risks of various conditions being present in children who had been of low birthweight when compared with the whole population (listed in order of magnitude of risk)

Problem	Relative Risk
Hernia repair	2.1
Feeding problem as a baby	1.7
Pneumonia	1.7
Soiling at 5	1.6
Wetting by day	1.5
Squint	1.5
Vision problem	1.5
Hospital admission	1.5
Crying problem as a baby	1.3
Eczema	0.7

(Findings statistically significant at 1% level after indirect standardisation for other factors.)

It will be of interest in the future to determine whether these results are true of each of the sub-populations included: do the children of very low birthweight (< 2000 g or even < 1500 g) have progressively more problems than those of between 2250 g and 2500 g? Do children who were of low birthweight, because they were delivered at an early gestation, differ in outcome from growth-retarded infants delivered at term? Do low birthweight infants, born into stable upper social class homes, differ in the degree of adverse medical and behavioural associations from those born later? We hope to address these questions in the near future.

Breast Feeding

Theoretically, breast feeding can be extremely hazardous to the infant: drugs, including salicylates, administered to the nursing mother are increasingly being detected in her milk (Giacoia and Catz, 1979). In addition, certain environmental pollutants such as polychlorinated biphenyls are concentrated in breast milk (Savage et al., 1981). These particular chemicals are used in paints, in the printing industry and in electrical transformers, and are found as contaminants of certain foods. They are very stable, and not excreted in the urine, but stored in the fat for a long period of time. Nine children in Japan ingested them from breast milk, after the mothers had eaten contaminated rice oil. The children subsequently had severe neurological abnormalities (Harada, 1976). Other chemicals found in breast milk still include high levels of the insecticide DDT, in spite of the fact that this has been banned from use in many countries. Indeed, recent reports from the U.S.A. indicate that in some areas the breast fed babies were exceeding by a factor of 10 the maximum level of DDT suggested by the World Health Organisation (Woodard et al., 1976). In another study, in Finland, a significant positive correlation was found between levels of DDT in breast milk and the number of cigarettes smoked daily (Vuori et al, 1977). It was suggested that this could have been due to the tobacco plants having been sprayed with DDT. Further potential hazards to the infant of the smoking mother concern the level of nicotine in the milk, which is said to vary widely (Ferguson et al., 1976). The effects on the infant have not yet been assessed.

In addition to these known pollutants, there are other potential hazards from the diet of the mother, her alcohol, coffee or tea consumption, and the chemicals she may work with (including those used in the house or garden). In an interesting study from New Zealand, Evans et al. (1981) showed that the more diverse the diet of the breast feeding mother, the more attacks of colic displayed by the infant.

In contrast with these adverse effects, diverse claims have been made for the beneficial associations with breast feeding. These have varied from higher I.Q. (Rodgers, 1978), less psychological problems (Taylor, 1977) and clearer speech in the child (Broad, 1972), to protection from subsequent obesity (Taitz, 1971), otitis media (Hooper, 1965), ulcerative colitis (Acheson and Truelove, 1961), coronary heart disease (Osborn, 1968) or cot death (Carpenter and Shaddick, 1965).

To substantiate these claims there is a certain amount of biochemical evidence to suggest that breast fed infants differ from those who are bottle fed. Lucas *et al.* (1980) have, for example, shown that artificially fed infants have higher levels of plasma insulin and other pancreatic and gut hormones. Breast milk certainly contains large amounts of Immuno-globulin A and antibodies specific to various bacteria and viruses. Gunther (1975) has suggested that breast feeding provides part of the infant's immunological defence, between the period of total protection *in utero* and the time when the baby becomes immunologically depen-dent. Nevertheless, a leading article in the *Lancet* in 1981 stated that although breast milk 'has antibacterial properties, there is no conclusive evidence that the infant is protected against infection'. Certainly, in poor conditions with defective hygiene, bottle fed babies are more likely to develop severe gastro-enteritis. This is more likely to be a function of the lack of sterilisation accompanying the use of artificial feeds in such circumstances rather than reflecting a protective effect for breast milk.

Within Britain in the 1970s there are very marked differences in the prevalence of breast feeding with social class. Analysis of outcomes which also vary with social class must, therefore, take this into account. The need for such an approach was ably demonstrated by Silva *et al.* (1976) in New Zealand. They showed that once breast fed children were matched with non-breast fed children from similar social backgrounds, there were no differences in motor coordination, intelligence or behaviour at the age of 3. Also in New Zealand, Fergusson *et al.* (1978) looked at the medical histories of children during the first 16 weeks of life. Those who had been bottle fed throughout had a higher incidence of respiratory illness, but this was due to social factors. They did find an independent association with mild gastro-intestinal disorders—the bottle fed infants were four times more likely to be taken to a medical practitioner for such reasons, though no more likely to be admitted to hospital.

In the present study we found that the prevalence of breast feeding was highest in the non-manual social classes, if the mother did not smoke, if she resided in the South-East or South-West of England and if she originated from the West Indies. These factors were all independent of one another.

Initial tabulation of the information on breast feeding against various aspects of the child's health have been described in Chapters 4 to 20. There were many significant results. There was evidence for a roughly decreasing rate with increasing duration of breast feeding for temper tantrums, wheezing, bronchitis and hospital admissions—but standardisation showed that all these effects were the result of social factors, including the mother's smoking history.

There were three outcome measures where the rates actually

increased with the duration of breast feeding (eczema, hay fever and suspected hearing disorder), though, once again, these associations were explained in terms of geographical and social variables. Other outcome measures that demonstrated significant variation, but which could not be described as a downward or upward trend, included intermittent stomach aches, frequent sore throats, squint, sleeping difficulties at 5 and the crying, feeding and sleeping difficulties as a baby. Of these, the associations with stomach aches, sore throats and squint became statistically insignificant after standardisation for other factors. The only measures that were still related to feeding history after standardisation are shown in Table 21.4.

TABLE 21.4   Relative Risks of various outcome measures after standardisation according to duration of breast feeding

| Outcome/problem | Never | Duration of breast feeding | | |
		< 1 month	1–2 months	3+ months
Crying as a baby	1.0	1.2	1.1	0.8
Sleeping as a baby	1.0	1.2	1.0	0.9
Feeding as a baby	1.0	1.1	1.1	0.5
Sleeping at 5	1.0	1.1	1.1	1.0

It can be seen that, in all instances, it is the children of mothers who ceased to breast feed by the 3rd month who were at increased risk. In no instances were the larger group of children whose mothers had *started* breast feeding at increased risk compared with those who had never been breast fed. It appears likely, therefore, that those mothers who stopped did so because of the problems in the child. There is little evidence to suggest that these problems really were connected with the breast feeding itself. It is probable that, with a fractious or difficult baby, the mother will try another form of feed to see whether that is the problem. The difficulty is that once she has stopped breast feeding, even if she finds that artificial feeding does not help, she is unlikely to be able to return to breast feeding.

The leading article in the *Lancet* (1981) stated: 'We must avoid being prematurely confident that breast is best.' After analysing our data we must confess that once account is taken of the many diverse social and geographic variables that determine whether a child is breast fed, there is little evidence of a beneficial effect. On the other hand, there is no evidence of a deleterious effect either. It could be that any beneficial effects of breast milk are exactly counterbalanced by the deleterious effects of the substances that can be expected in human milk.

Alternatively, it is possible that breast milk has beneficial effects in areas which we have either failed to measure or have not yet analysed.

Age of the Mother

The reasons why a woman decides to become pregnant, or to remain pregnant, are complex and vary with her age. It has been suggested that teenagers are more likely to marry because they are unhappy at home (Wolff, 1981). Those who do marry at an early age are more likely to separate or divorce. The younger mother is said to have unrealistic expectations of her children, and to be impatient and irritable when these are not met (Wolff, 1981).

Perinatal mortality is increased at both ends of the age range (G. Chamberlain *et al.*, 1978), the perinatal deaths in young mothers being mainly due to obstetric reasons, although there is also an increase in the incidence of malformations of the central nervous system such as anencephalus and spina bifida (Golding, 1979). Women over 35 at delivery are, *inter alia*, at increased risk of severe pre-eclampsia, severe antepartum haemorrhage, especially that associated with placenta praevia, with consequent increase in perinatal mortality. In addition, they are more likely to bear malformed infants, especially congenital heart disease and Down's Syndrome (Beard, 1981).

In most studies of morbidity it has been unusual to find the age of the mother separated from the size of her family. This is, of course, of crucial importance—the child of the young mother is likely to be the first born, whereas that of the older mother is likely to be a member of a relatively large family. The epidemiological studies of the sudden infant death syndrome have shown that both maternal youth and the number of siblings are associated independently with the condition (Golding, Limerick and Macfarlane, 1985).

In the present study, as we noted in Chapter 1, the children of very young mothers were under-represented in the follow-up at age 5. The results in relation to this must therefore be considered with less certainty than for the majority of the variables. It is impossible to assess ways in which the results may be biased until the information collected at 10 on the missing children has been analysed.

From the data that were collected when the study child was 5, it was obvious that the youngest mothers (i.e. those who were teenagers at their child's birth and thus under 25 at the time of the follow-up) were not only more likely to be unmarried at the time of study child's birth, they were still likely to be single parents. In addition, they were twice as likely to have moved house frequently, and were more likely to be of low social class and to live in a poor urban area. The young mothers were more likely to have been employed during the child's life, and the children were more likely to be 'only' children.

Mothers who were older at the time of the child's birth, and who were 40 or over when the child was followed up, differed from the rest of the population in that they were more likely to have adopted or fostered the child. They were twice as likely as the rest of the population to have at least three other children, but they were also more likely to have no children other than the study child.

These factors accounted for most of the original relationships between maternal age and health and behaviour. The children of both young and older mothers were more likely to have been of low birthweight, to have had crying and feeding problems as a baby, to wet their beds and have temper tantrums at 5. They had an increased incidence of mouth breathing and hospital admissions, but all these associations were secondary to the coexisting associations.

The only health associations which could not be explained in terms of other variables, which we have examined in this volume, concerned the increased risks of both repeated accidents and speech dysfluency among children of young mothers (Table 21.5).

TABLE 21.5 Relative Risks of various conditions according to the age of the mother when the child was 5

	Maternal age		
Problem	< 25	25–34	35+
Dysfluency	1.5	1.0	0.8
2+ Accidents	1.2	1.0	0.7

(Findings statistically significant at 1% level after indirect standardisation for other factors.)

From the health behaviour point of view, mother's age appeared not to be an important factor in itself, except for the uptake of BCG. There was a strong trend: the older the mother, the more likely the child was to be immunised. This is probably due to the fact that the older the mother, the more likely was she either to have had tuberculosis herself or to have a first degree relative who had had the disease.

In conclusion, there are relatively few of the disorders in the child considered here that are associated with maternal age. It must be pointed out, however, that the lack of association we have shown has related to broad age groups. The important group of very young mothers, who were no more than 17 at the birth of the child, may well not conform to the pattern we have shown.

The crucial factor about maternal youth concerns the adverse social circumstances that such mothers are more likely to live in. Not only is their income lower, they tend to live in areas where problems are more likely to exist. Over and above this there is little to implicate maternal age other than increased risk of accidents and dysfluent speech. We look forward to analysing the information on the 10-year-olds to see whether these associations still persist and, in particular, whether other factors related to accidents, such as clumsiness in the child, might be related to the age of the mother.

Size of Family

The larger the family, the greater are the difficulties that may result. The mechanism by which this may happen has been described vividly by Sula Wolff (1981):

> 'When several pre-school children are being brought up together, the demands for care, protection and kindly control may be more than one mother can fulfil. Unless actively helped in their relationships with each other, a group of under-5s inevitably become belligerent and noisy, stimulating each other to ever more aggressive and destructive conduct (Patterson, Littmann and Bricker, 1967). Their mothers frequently develop depressive illnesses, especially when they are socially isolated and poor (Brown, Bhrolchain and Harris, 1975). When the mothers are depressed they become irritable . . . this increases the children's anxiety level and their impulsive aggression.'

Other factors also contribute to certain of the disadvantages inherent in being a member of a large family. A study by Pringle (1965) of 4-year-old children in a residential home showed their language skills to be significantly less than socially similar children living at home. She concluded that the differences arose because the children in the residential home spent practically all their time with one another and relatively little with adults. In large families similar phenomena are at work—the children spend most of their time interacting with one another and relatively little with their parents.

Study children from large families were more likely than the rest of the population to be from the lower social classes, to have immigrant parents or to live in poor urban areas. Regions with a higher than average proportion of study children from large families included Scotland and the West Midlands. Even after taking account of such associations, in the present study we have shown that a large number of different outcomes appear to be significantly associated with the number of children. The results are summarised in Table 21.6. It can be seen that a third of the factors appeared to be positively related to the number of children in the family. Only one of these (pneumonia) was related to the health of the child, the others were all related to symptoms that could be described as the result of the difficulties described above—with reduced communication between mother and child and resultant speech difficulties and signs of frustration (temper tantrums and enuresis).

TABLE 21.6 Relative Risks associated with various conditions according to number of other children in the household

Problem	Number of other children				
	0	1	2	3	4+
Positive associations					
Wets by day	0.7	0.8	1.2	1.3	1.3
Wets bed (1+ per week)	0.7	0.9	1.1	1.2	1.3
Temper tantrums (1+ per week)	0.8	0.9	1.1	1.2	1.2
Speech dysfluency	0.4	1.0	1.2	1.2	1.5
Speech problem	0.6	0.9	1.2	1.2	1.1
Pneumonia	0.6	0.9	1.0	1.5	1.7
Negative associations					
Crying problem as a baby	1.2	1.1	0.9	0.8	0.7
Sleeping problem as a baby	1.3	1.1	0.9	0.8	0.6
Feeding problem as a baby	1.3	1.1	0.8	0.7	0.6
Sleeping problem at 5	1.3	1.0	1.0	0.9	0.8
Feeding problem at 5	1.2	1.1	0.9	0.8	0.7
Stomach aches (1+ per month)	1.1	1.0	0.9	0.8	0.7
Hay fever	1.6	1.1	0.8	0.8	0.4
Repeated sore throats	1.1	1.1	1.0	0.9	0.7
Other significant associations					
Eczema	0.9	1.1	1.0	0.8	0.6
Squint	1.1	1.0	1.0	1.2	0.6
Suspected hearing loss	0.9	1.0	1.0	1.1	0.5
Hospital admission	0.9	1.0	1.1	1.1	1.0

(Statistically significant at 1% level after standardisation for other factors.)

Many other problems are negatively associated with the number of children. The bulk of these are related to either perceived difficulties when the child was a baby or feeding and sleeping problems present at 5. For all these we have shown that it is the number of *older* rather than *younger* siblings that are crucial in this respect. This implies that the more experienced the mother is the less likely the problem is to be reported. There are at least two interpretations: (i) the problems are less likely to occur, or (ii) the problems are less likely to be perceived as such in an experienced mother. One might suggest that the more children present, the less likely the mother to even notice problems in her children—but if this were so one would expect identical associations with both the number of older and the number of younger children. We showed in Chapter 6 that this was not found.

The pattern for stomach aches was similar to that found for sleeping and feeding difficulties, the number of older children being the crucial factor. For hay fever and sore throats, however, a similar pattern was found for both younger and older siblings. Thus, either the mother with many children is unlikely to notice that the child is frequently sneezing or has sore throats, or there is a genuine reduction in the incidence of the conditions in large families. Only close observational studies are likely to distinguish between the two possibilities.

Finally, there were four factors which, although showing a significant association with the number of children in the household, failed to demonstrate a clear positive or negative trend. The relative risks are shown in the lower section of Table 21.6, and are not easy to interpret. As with all epidemiological findings, they may be a clue to other more important associations, or they may reveal the presence of two separate trends, or they might have arisen by chance. Thus, suppose the genuine incidence of a condition rose with the number of children in the family, but that the mother's memory of, or perception of, the condition fell as the number of children increased, one might obtain the sort of pattern shown for eczema, squint, suspected hearing loss and hospital admission. Alternatively, the results may be due to random fluctuation or the interplay of other factors not considered in this presentation.

The health behaviour of mothers with a large family differed from the rest of the population: they were less likely to attend a child health clinic, less likely to let the child be immunised, and less likely to take the child to a dentist. All this, in spite of the fact that these mothers were less likely to be employed and presumably would have the time to attend.

So far we have not looked at the effects of the sexes of the siblings on the behaviour and problems of the child. Jones, Offord and Abrams (1980) studied the siblings of a group of delinquent boys. They found that the more brothers there were, the more likely it was that those brothers would also be delinquent, but the more sisters there were, the less likely the brothers were to be delinquent. It is possible that equally complex patterns are to be found within our data.

As well as variation with sex, we intend to examine the data to assess whether the effects of large families are similar in manual and non-manual social classes. Poole and Kuhn (1973) analysed information pertaining to university graduates in 1960. They found that although large families did not impede the achievements of those from non-manual groups, a small family was essential for success for a child from the manual classes.

Social Class

As we have quoted previously (Golding and Butler, 1984b), analysis of social class differences provokes the statement of Levenstein: 'Statistics are like a bikini. What they reveal is suggestive but what they conceal is vital.' British social class classification is based on the occupation of the male head of the household. Differences in incidence of various conditions between the social classes provides a challenge, especially in the field of child health. The differences show that various social or environmental factors may be at work. The social class variation provides a clue as to possible aetiologies. The challenge is to identify the factors involved.

The classification is an easy way of splitting the population into six groups which are, in many respects, ranks. Very few people believe that in analysing data with respect to social class one is directly measuring the effects of different occupations. Rather one is identifying groups of people who are likely to take such jobs. The association is not purely a financial one—many of social class III M earn more money than those in III NM or II. There are, however, a large number of attitudes and habits that differ radically across the social classes.

Differences in diet are measured annually by the National Food Survey, but probably more important to the pre-school child are the differences in expectation from the mother. In their detailed study of 4-year-olds in Nottingham, Newson and Newson (1970) found that the 'lower' social classes were more likely to encourage their children to hit other children back; if the mother accidentally breaks one of her child's toys she is far more likely to apologise if from the upper social classes. They found that the upper social class parents tend to put their children to bed earlier and are more likely to tell them stories at bedtime. The mother from the lower classes is more likely to threaten the child with a figure of authority or to say that she 'won't love him any more.'

From our own survey we have already shown the marked differences in health behaviour with social class. The lower the social class, the more likely the mother was to have started her reproductive life at an early age, and the more likely she was to have a large family (Chapter 2). The lower the social class, the more likely is the mother to smoke, and to smoke heavily, and the less likely to breast feed, to take her child to the dentist, or to have him immunised.

The 'difficult', 'troubled' and hyperactive behaviour symptoms of the child varied markedly with social class (Fig. 7.6): in all aspects except thumb sucking the children from the lower social classes had a much higher rate than those from the upper classes. Further analyses have yet to be done on these signs to see whether they can be 'explained' by other facets of social class. An attempt to analyse the social class associations with bed-wetting and frequent temper tantrums was unable to remove social class effects (Table 21.7). In spite of differences between the classes in family behaviour and expectations at bedtimes and mealtimes, there were no differences in the prevalence of sleeping problems. There was a significant association with feeding problems at 5 (with low rate in social class V), but this was shown to be due to the fact that there are more large families in social class V; the more children there are, the less likely the study child is to have feeding problems.

TABLE 21.7 Relative Risks of various conditions by social class

Problem	I	II	Social class III NM	III M	IV	V
Positive associations						
Bed wetting (1+ per week)	0.7	0.8	0.9	1.0	1.1	1.3
Temper tantrums (1+ per week)	0.7	0.8	0.9	1.0	1.0	1.3
Headaches (1+ per month)	0.8	0.6	0.8	1.4	1.3	1.2
Bronchitis	0.8	0.8	1.0	1.0	1.2	1.2
Negative associations						
Eczema	1.2	1.1	1.0	0.9	0.9	0.8
Suspected hearing loss	1.5	1.1	0.9	0.9	0.9	0.8
Adenoidectomy	2.4	1.2	1.0	0.8	0.6	0.8

(Findings statistically significant at 1% level after indirect standardisation for other factors.)

Of the causes of morbidity in our population, there was increased prevalence in the manual social classes of headaches, wheezing, bronchitis, pneumonia, mouth breathing and repeated accidents. Of these, the association with wheezing was shown to be due to the stronger association with maternal smoking; that with pneumonia was no longer significant after standardising for maternal smoking and the number of children in the household; the associations with accidents and mouth breathing disappeared after standardisation for the type of neighbourhood. Only the associations with headaches and bronchitis remained (Table 21.7).

There were three negative associations with social class which remained after standardisation, using the variables described in this volume. Eczema, adenoidectomy and suspected hearing loss were found far more often in social class I than in social class V. Further analyses, however, have shown that the association between eczema and social class disappeared once parental education had been taken into account (Peters, 1985). This is an analysis we have yet to carry out for hearing difficulties or adenoid removal.

It is generally supposed that children from the lower social classes are more likely to be admitted to hospital, and this was indeed true in our study. Nevertheless, the association was not strong, and indirect standardisation showed that it was due to different rates of hospitalisation in the various regions, as well as associations with maternal smoking habit and low birthweight. Once these had been taken into account there was no remaining residual association.

Thus, the major social class differences which we have not been able to 'explain' in terms of other factors concern behaviour more than morbidity. Childhood behaviour problems may be closely associated with emotional and psychiatric disturbance in their parents. Brown, Bhrolchain and Harris (1975) have shown that there is a large social class difference in the prevalence of psychiatric disturbance in the population. They stress that part of the difference may be due to an increase in the numbers of life events that occur in the lower social classes.

Parental Situation

It has been found that among children presenting for psychiatric care, those with neurotic symptoms tended to come from united two-parent families, those with delinquent or aggressive behaviour were more likely to come from broken homes (Wolff, 1981).

In 1965 Gregory reported that boys were more likely to be delinquent if they either lived with their mother alone, or with neither natural parent. Girls, on the other hand, were most likely to behave delinquently if they were living with their father alone, with a step-parent or, again, with neither natural parent.

There are two factors that are likely to influence these findings. Firstly, as Wolff (1981) put it: 'Children model themselves on their parents and learn from them how to manage their own personal relationships . . .. When a parent is absent or when parents are deviant in their behaviour, children are at risk of being disturbed themselves and of developing personality difficulties in later life.' Secondly, personality disorders in the mother contribute towards marital disharmony (Pond, Ryle and Hamilton, 1963) as well as behaviour difficulties in the children (Wolff and Acton, 1968). In order to have the same effects on both the marriage and the child, the father's personality disorder generally has to be much more extreme (Wolff and Acton, 1968).

Previous cohort studies have examined data concerning children from 'broken' homes. The 1946 cohort was concerned only with children born in wedlock. Nevertheless, by the time the children were 4 almost 4% were in single parent situations: in two-fifths a parent had died; in one-fifth divorce had taken place; and in two-fifths the parents had separated. Among this 4% of the population the mother was more likely to have a paid job outside the home, and less likely to take the child to a child health clinic. The children from these families were more likely to wet their beds.

The 1958 cohort study included children born illegitimate. By the age of 7 approximately a quarter of these had been adopted and a quarter were living with both their biological parents. The remainder tended to be living in over-crowded accommodation with frequent household moves (Crellin, Pringle and West, 1971). Those who had been adopted tended to be living in small families of the upper social classes.

On examination of the children at the age of 7 it was shown that the children who had not been adopted did worse on both the educational tests and the behavioural assessments. Nevertheless, other studies have shown that those children who have been adopted are more likely to be emotionally disturbed, especially if they have been adopted late in life (Bohman, 1970).

In the present section we shall consider four groups of children according to the situation in which they were at the age of 5. Ninety percent of children were with both their natural parents, 2.7% had a step- or substitute parent, 5.8% were with a single parent, and only 1.2% had neither natural parent.

Children living with a substitute parent were significantly more likely to have a young mother, to live in a poor urban area, and to have moved house frequently. Their mothers tended to smoke heavily. They were also more likely to be of low social class. Many of these factors are also associated with adverse outcomes in the children. It was not surprising, therefore, that study children living with a substitute parent were more likely to have multiple accidents, to wet their beds or to have hospital admissions. The association with multiple accidents was not significant at the 1% level once standardisation for type of neighbourhood and maternal employment had taken place, but the association with hospital admissions (R. Risk 1.3) and bed-wetting (R. Risk 1.3) remained.

Though there were fifty-two children living with a single father, the majority of children who were living with a single parent tended to be those without a father. This group was more likely to soil (R. Risk 1.5), to wet their beds at least once a week (R. Risk 1.3), to have temper tantrums (R. Risk 1.2) and to be admitted to hospital, especially if the single parent was unsupported by another adult (R. Risk 1.3). These factors continued to be significantly associated with single parent condition even after taking account of the fact that the children were more likely to move house frequently, to live in poor urban areas, to have a young mother or a mother who smokes heavily.

The children living in a single parent situation were less likely to have been immunised against measles or pertussis, and they were less likely to have been taken to a child health clinic, but the extent of such failures was no more than would have been expected from the type of area in which they lived and the other health behaviour of their mothers, as typified by the number of cigarettes they smoked. Children living with a single mother, however, were substantially less likely than expected from other social and regional differences ever to have been taken to a dentist.

The group of children who had been adopted or fostered was small, and thus only very striking differences between them and the rest of the population would be likely to be statistically significant. As a group, these children were more likely to be of low birthweight, but their adoptive/foster parents were likely to be older than the rest of the population (over half the mother figures were 40 or over when the child was 5), the child was more likely to be an 'only' child and to have a stable background with relatively few household moves. These children did have an increased risk of speech dysfluency in the past, but there were no significant differences with current problems. The children were as likely as the rest of the population to have been taken to child health clinics, to visit the dentist and have the appropriate immunisations.

In conclusion, considering the difficulties and stress inherent in belonging to a single parent family, the children show relatively few adverse outcomes in comparison with other children living in similar social circumstances but with two parents. We have not yet analysed our data to see whether the boys and girls differ at 5 in ways that Gregory found among adolescents. Whatever the outcome of that analysis may show, we feel that, in comparison with whether the child comes from a 'broken' home, there are far more pertinent markers of whether the child is likely to have behaviour and health problems. The most obvious of these is the smoking habit of the mother.

Ethnic Group of Parents

To be a member of a minority group, whether defined by culture, religion, diet or race, brings with it tensions and difficulties. Recently immigrated groups are especially at risk. Increased mental disorder among adults and higher mortality rates have been noted in many countries. Within Britain there are two major groups which, although numerically fairly small, form distinct entities. These comprise the West Indians who are of negroid background, and the Asians from the sub-continent of India/Bangladesh/Pakistan. The two groups have little in common, apart from the fact that the colour of their skins is non-white.

Within the present study we examined the differences between the 257 children of Asian parents and the 174 study children whose parents came from the West Indies, and the rest of the population. There were profound social differences when each group was compared with the whole cohort.

Half the children of West Indian parents were living in a large family with three or more siblings (16% overall), only 1% were from social classes I and II (27% overall), and a quarter of the children were living with either a single parent or a substitute parent (10% overall). Hardly any West Indians were living in rural areas, and more than would have been expected, even on social grounds, were living in poor urban areas (R. Risk 2.6).

The West Indian study children were more likely to have been of low birthweight (R. Risk 1.7), but the mothers were considerably more likely to breast feed (R. Risk 2.1). Once social and demographic factors had been taken into account, there was little difference between this group and the rest of the population in the use of the child health services. The only difference lay in the uptake of BCG—fewer than expected of the children had had this vaccination (R. Risk 0.4).

From the health and behaviour point of view, there were several ways in which the West Indian children differed from the rest of the population even after standardisation for other factors. West Indian children were more likely to wet their beds (R. Risk 1.7) and be reported as having feeding problems at 5 (R. Risk 1.4). The children were more likely to have had temper tantrums, speech problems and headaches, but these findings were largely the consequence of other factors such as the size of the family and type of neighbourhood. West Indian children were markedly less likely to be suspected of hearing difficulty (R. Risk 0.3) and less likely to be accident repeaters (R. Risk 0.3). All immigrant groups were more likely to be reported as breathing through their mouths.

Unlike the West Indian children, those children whose parents came from the Indian sub-continent were almost all living with both their natural parents. Although there were more in the unskilled and semi-skilled social classes (40% of Asians, 18% of study population), a considerable proportion were in social classes I and II (15% of Asians, 27% of the study population). Like the West Indians, though, half the study children from this background were from a large family (3+ siblings). The Asian families were nearly four times more likely to live in a poor urban area compared with other families of the same social background. No Asian families lived in rural areas.

From the health behaviour point of view, the Asian mothers were unlikely to smoke. They were slightly more likely than the rest of the population to breast feed (R. Risk 1.2), but a health visitor was less likely to have visited at home in the first 6 months of the child's life.

The Asian children were over twice as likely to have been of low birthweight (R. Risk 2.4). They were four times as likely to have had a

BCG and the boys were three times as likely to be circumcised as the rest of the population.

The only ways in which Asian children had greater health and behaviour problems than the rest of the study children lay in an increased prevalence of temper tantrums and headaches. Neither of these associations were statistically significant after standardisation. Ways in which Asian children had a reduced prevalence remained after standardisation. These included sleeping problems at 5 (0.5), repeated accidents (0.3), wheezing (0.6) and suspected hearing problems (0.6).

Although the Asian and West Indian families probably suffer as much from the stigma that may be associated with their colour, many studies have shown that the two groups have totally different intellectual, behavioural and health problems. As we have shown, both groups are more likely than the indigenous population to have large families, to be of lower social class and live in poor urban areas. The mothers are less likely to smoke and more likely to breast feed.

In considering health outcomes it is always possible that differences are due to the different perceptions of the parents. Both groups of children, for example, were considerably less likely to have repeated accidents. It is possible that this may be a reporting bias, but it is equally likely that these children do have less accidents at this age. Studies of childhood attendance at casualty departments have, indeed, shown fewer than expected from these two groups (Oppe, 1964; Rawlinson, 1983).

Children from West Indian backgrounds have long been noted to have an increased prevalence of behaviour problems. It has been suggested that this may be due to the fact that Caribbean parents exercise considerable control over their children, play is not considered important and there is a lack of appreciation of conditions necessary for intellectual development (Rutter et al., 1975a). Others have suggested that the structure of family relationships is different in the two groups, and that this might contribute towards the findings. Asian families are more tightly knit and strongly patriarchal. West Indian families are more matriarchal and subject to disruption. Lobo (1978) records that a 'curiously cold and unmotherly relationship between many West Indian mothers and their children has been already noticed by observers in Jamaica and London'. We have already noted that the West Indian study children were at risk of bed-wetting. This would fit in with one of the current beliefs about this condition noted in Chapter 5—i.e. that it may be associated with a lack of warm mothering.

Asian children in this country have a relatively high incidence of rickets—compared both with other children in Britain from similar social backgrounds and with Asian children in Asia. This is due to a marked vitamin D deficiency which develops after migration to Britain (Rashid et al., 1983). There is, in addition, a high perinatal mortality rate

(Terry, Condie and Settatree, 1980). Although we have no increases in prevalence of various reported symptoms or disorders among this group at 5, it must be remembered that the size of the group is small and that we have not yet looked at specific rarer signs of morbidity.

Maternal Employment

A mother may work for a variety of reasons, from economic necessity to the need for contacts outside the home. She may work part-time or full-time, for the whole of the child's life or for short periods of time only. In this volume we have considered together all these possibilities. It would be unwise to extrapolate the results to specific points concerning the advantages or disadvantages of a mother working at different times in the child's life.

That having been said, mothers who had not taken any type of job during the child's life differed from the rest of the population in that they were less likely to smoke, more likely to be living with the child's father, older, with a large number of other children.

There were few differences in health behaviour between mothers who had worked and those that had never done so. Children of working mothers were less likely to have been immunised against measles and more likely to be admitted to hospital, but these differences disappear after standardisation. There remain only two significant findings: children of mothers who worked were more likely to have had bronchitis (R. Risk 1.1) and to have repeated accidents (R. Risk 1.1). Osborn, Butler and Morris (1984) have looked in considerably more detail at the children of the mothers who had been employed. They found only slight differences in intellectual ability and certain behaviour characteristics.

Type of Neighbourhood

Hippocrates placed particular emphasis on weather and climate, quality of water, and topographical features of the landscape, not only as determining the patterns of illnesses of people inhabiting different places, but also as being responsible for their physical, behavioural and cultural characteristics (Sargent, 1982).

It has for long been assumed that rural areas are the healthiest for children, but there are relatively few data available on which such conclusions can be based. None of the previous cohort studies have looked at the differences between urban and rural areas, but Rutter and his colleagues (1975b) found striking differences between children living in an inner London area and those in the mainly rural Isle of Wight. There were increases in emotional and conduct disorders in the urban area and the authors felt that this was probably due to the relatively poor social circumstances, an increase in the prevalence of marital discord, marital disruption and parental mental disorder in the London area. It is, however, unlikely that the particular area chosen could be taken as generally representative of urban areas.

In the present study children in rural areas differed in many respects from those in urban areas. They were more likely to be of social classes I and II and less likely to have immigrant parents. Their mothers were more likely to breast feed and less likely to be heavy smokers than residents of urban areas.

Children in rural areas differed significantly in their health behaviour. After standardisation for other factors, the relative risks associated with residence in a rural area were as follows: failure to attend a child health clinic (1.5); failure to attend a dentist (0.9); failure to have the child immunised against pertussis (0.7). In addition, fewer children in rural areas were given a BCG (0.7).

On initial analysis there were significant differences in health and behaviour between urban and rural areas in that children in rural areas were less likely to have repeated accidents, temper tantrums, bronchitis, mouth breathing or to be admitted to hospital. Most of these findings could be 'explained' in terms of the other social and geographical factors considered in this volume. There remained a significant decrease in the proportion of children who were accident repeaters (R. Risk 0.8), mouth breathing (R. Risk 0.8) and in the prevalence of temper tantrums (R. Risk 0.9).

Within urban areas there were major differences in health behaviour. Mothers living in poor urban areas were more likely to be Asian or West Indian, to be single parents or step-parents, to be young, to have moved house frequently and/or to have a large number of children. They were more likely to be heavy smokers. In contrast, mothers from well-to-do urban areas were more likely to be from the non-manual social classes, to be in their 30s (when the child was 5) and to have just two children.

Even when these differences had been taken into account, there were strong differences in health behaviour between the different areas. Children in the well-to-do areas were more likely to be immunised against pertussis and measles and to have visited a dentist. Children in the poor urban areas were more likely to have been given a BCG.

Initial analyses had shown strong trends in the prevalence of many health and behaviour outcomes with increased rates in the poor urban areas and low rates in the well-to-do urban areas. Conditions showing such a pattern were bed-wetting, temper tantrums, speech dysfluency, headaches, wheezing, bronchitis, pneumonia, mouth breathing and risk of hospital admission. Most of these associations were due to the fact that the areas differed in their distribution of social class, smoking habit and ethnic group. After standardisation there only remained significant relationships between type of urban area and speech dysfluency, temper tantrums and mouth breathing (Table 21.8).

TABLE 21.8   Relative Risks of various conditions by type of neighbourhood

Problem	Type of urban neighbourhood		
	Poor	Average	Well-to-do
Temper tantrums (1+ per week)	1.2	1.0	1.0
Dysfluency	1.6	1.1	0.9
Mouth breathing	1.2	1.1	0.9

Region

As we have already noted, Hippocrates was convinced that the environment greatly influenced the prevalence of different diseases. In his work *Airs, Waters and Places*, he described infants living in cities that have a southern exposure as having convulsions, asthma and epilepsy, whereas, he said, children in cities with a northerly exposure mature slowly.

Within the British Isles, differences in mortality patterns have long been noted in the vital statistics. Less obvious, but equally strong, are the relationships with various disorders. Significant differences were found for temper tantrums, headaches, sore throats, suspected hearing loss and repeated accidents. Only the relationship with one of these (repeated accidents) ceased to be significant after standardisation for other factors.

As we showed in Chapters 3, 4, 18, 19 and 20, there are strong differences in the habits and attitudes of the mothers—especially in relation to their health behaviour. There were also major associations with health outcome. Differences which are statistically significant after standardisation are described below only where they are at least 15% greater or less than the overall mean.

North of England

Children from this region were more likely to have mothers who smoked heavily, but less likely to have immigrant parents, to have a large number of siblings or live in a rural area. Once these factors had been taken into account, the differences between the health of these children and those in the rest of Britain revealed significantly low rates of eczema (R. Risk 0.7), and hay fever (R. Risk 0.8), and high rates of bronchitis (R. Risk 1.2). As expected in an area with a high maternal smoking rate, the children were less likely to have been breast fed. Health visitors were more likely to have visited the home and the child was 40% more likely to have had a BCG.

Yorkshire and Humberside

Children in this region were similar to those in the rest of the country in almost all respects. They were slightly more likely to be one of a large family and to live in a rural area. The children in this region were less likely than those in the rest of Britain to be given a BCG (R. Risk 0.7), to have had hay fever (0.7) or be suspected of having a hearing problem (0.8). Only rarely had the health visitor failed to make a home visit.

North-West

In the North-West the mothers were 30% more likely to be heavy smokers and to be of social classes IV and V. Nevertheless, the children were less likely to have made multiple household moves. They were also less likely to have immigrant parents. Children were more likely to have had a BCG (R. Risk 1.2), but also more likely not to have been immunised against pertussis (R. Risk 1.2). They were more likely than the rest of the population to have been taken to a child health clinic.

From the health point of view, the children were less likely to have had eczema (R. Risk 0.8), repeated sore throats (0.8) or temper tantrums at least once a week (0.8). The boys were more likely to have been circumcised (1.3).

East Midlands

Study children from the East Midlands were more likely to live in rural areas, and less likely to have mothers who smoked heavily. The children were significantly less likely to have received a BCG (R. Risk 0.4), and the mothers were at risk of neither attending a child health clinic (R. Risk 1.3), nor a dentist (1.2).

The children in this region were less likely to have had repeated sore throats (0.8) or be suspected of having hearing problems (0.8). They were more at risk, however, of having temper tantrums (1.2) and stomach aches (1.6).

West Midlands

Children in the West Midlands were substantially more likely to have immigrant parents (R. Risk 1.7), and to come from large families. Their mothers, however, were less likely to be heavy smokers. There were differences in the uptake of child health services. In spite of the relatively large proportion of immigrant families, the children were less likely than average to have had a BCG. They were also more likely than expected to have failed to visit a dentist (R. Risk 1.2), or never to have had a pertussis immunisation (1.6). There was, however, only one way in which these children differed in regard to their health—and that concerned the increased prevalence of bronchitis (1.2). In all other respects the children resembled the overall population.

East Anglia

As we showed in Table 3.1, children from East Anglia were over twice as likely to live in rural areas and only rarely were the study children residing in poor urban areas. Relatively few of the parents were immigrants and the mothers were unlikely to smoke heavily. Once these factors had been taken into account, the children were at reduced risk of bronchitis (R. Risk 0.7), repeated sore throats (0.8) or admission to hospital (0.7).

In spite of the positive aspects of the background, the health behaviour of the mothers was not wholly exemplary. The children were at increased risk of *neither* going to a child health clinic (1.2) *nor* to a dentist (1.2). Very few of the study children in this region had had a BCG by the age of 5.

South-East

Follow-up of the children in London and the South-East showed that, as a whole, there were more immigrant parents, more of social classes I and II, fewer very young mothers and fewer large families. The mothers were less likely to be heavy smokers. Independently of all these factors, mothers in the South-East were more likely to breast feed (R. Risk 1.2), they were more likely to take the child to a child health clinic and to a dentist (Chapter 19), but they were at greater risk of not having a home visit by a health visitor (R. Risk 1.4). They only rarely received a BCG (R. Risk 0.4).

The study children in this region differed little from the rest of the country once the social and demographic factors had been taken into account. The boys were more likely to be circumcised (R. Risk 1.2), all the children were both at increased risk of hay fever (1.2) and more likely to be suspected of hearing problems (1.2).

South-West

Study children in the South-West were nearly twice as likely as the rest of the population to live in a rural area. They were also more likely to move house frequently and be of social classes I and II. Immigrant parents were unlikely to live here, there were few poor urban areas, large families or mothers who smoked heavily.

In many respects the ways in which the health and health behaviour of these children differed from the rest of the population was similar to those found for the South-East. Mothers were more likely to have breast fed their children (R. Risk 1.2), and they were more likely to take the child to a dentist. The children were unlikely to have had a BCG (0.5), but had a greater risk of hay fever (1.2) and of suspected hearing difficulty (1.2). Again, the boys were more likely to have been circumcised (1.2).

Wales

The study children from Wales formed a relatively small group of children (numerically). They were more likely to live in rural areas and unlikely to have immigrant parents. The children were more likely than the rest of the population to be visited by a health visitor, to visit a child health clinic and be immunised against measles. Nevertheless, they were significantly less likely to be breast fed (0.7).

As found elsewhere (Colley and Reid, 1970), children in this region were more likely to have respiratory disorders—particularly bronchitis (1.3), repeated sore throats (1.2) and wheezing (1.2). In addition, they had a higher incidence of reported headaches (1.3) and stomach aches (1.2). In contrast, they were less likely than expected to be reported as having had eczema (0.7) or hay fever (0.8).

Scotland

In Chapter 4 we noted the ways in which the study children in Scotland differed from the rest of the population. Although there were fewer with immigrant parents, there were more children with mothers who smoked heavily, more from social classes IV and V, and more from large families. They were more likely to live in poor urban areas.

The children in Scotland were much more likely than the rest of the population to be given a BCG vaccination (R. Risk 3.9), and they were more likely to be immunised against pertussis. Nevertheless, the children were less likely to have attended a child health clinic (Chapter 19). Like the Welsh, the Scottish mothers were less likely to breast feed, even after the analysis had taken account of the other social and environmental factors (0.7).

The children were more likely to be admitted to hospital (1.2) and twice as likely to have a tonsillectomy (with or without an adenoidec- tomy) and also more likely to have an adenoidectomy (without simultaneous tonsillectomy). The boys, however, were substantially less likely to have been circumcised (0.5).

In spite of the increased rate of hospital admission, the Scottish children were reported as having a substantial reduction in the risk of many outcomes including: temper tantrums (0.7), headaches (0.4), stomach aches (0.6), eczema (0.7), hay fever (0.6), wheezing (0.8), bronchitis (0.6) and suspected hearing difficulty (0.4).

Many of these findings had also been apparent in the 1958 cohort (Davie, Butler and Goldstein, 1972). The findings are strong and highly significant. One wonders whether they can be real objective reductions in the prevalence of these disorders or whether it is the mother's perception of problems that is different in Scotland.

Some support for the latter view can be found in data collected on the 1958 cohort. The children were examined by a medical officer and his responses were recorded separately from the questions asked of the mother. Concerning eczema, 3.82% of Scottish mothers stated that their child had had the condition since their 1st birthday compared with 5.20% of the whole cohort. On examination, medical officers in Scotland found signs of eczema in 2.47% of the children, an identical proportion to that found in the whole cohort. The other questions that are relevant concern otitis media. The mother was asked whether the child had ever had 'running ears' (i.e. pus not wax). Of the Scottish mothers, 6.21% replied positively compared with 8.58% overall. The medical officers were asked whether there were signs of past or present otitis media. The prevalence in Scotland was 6.62% compared with 7.17% for the whole nation. It would be dangerous to extrapolate from this slim evidence. Nevertheless, it does support the hypothesis that Scottish mothers are less likely to recognise the fact that their children have specific problems.

Household Moves

Moving from one home to another is considered to be a so-called life event, with disturbance to adults rated as slightly greater than giving up a job (Newton et al., 1979). The reasons for moving vary—they may be associated with change in employment of the head of the household or the splitting up of a family. They may be moving into better accommodation or it may be part of a downward spiral of deprivation.

More than half the study children had moved house at least once in the first 5 years of their lives, and 22% had moved at least twice. Among the 11% who had moved frequently (3+ times), there were significantly more very young mothers, more single parents or those living in a step-parent situation. The mothers who moved frequently were more likely to live in poor urban areas and be members of the immigrant population.

There were trends in the use of health services in that the more often the family had moved, the less likely was the health visitor to have made a home visit, and the less likely the child was to have been taken to a dentist. There were no significant differences in the proportion who had ever attended a child health clinic or who had been immunised against pertussis, but the children who had moved on four or more occasions were substantially less likely to have been immunised.

The proportion of children who had been of low birthweight was positively associated with the number of household moves—but this was due to the fact that the mobile mothers were the heavier smokers and were also weighted with Asian and West Indian parents.

The more often the household moved, the more likely was the mother to have reported that when a baby the study child had cried excessively, had frequent feeding difficulties and sleeping problems. At the age of 5 there was still an increase in prevalence in that the more often the household had moved, the more children were said to have current sleeping difficulties, to wet by day and to wet by night. The children were also more likely to have had dysfluent speech, vision problems, squints and be suspected of hearing difficulty. The children were more likely to be admitted to hospital, to be accident repeaters, to have a history of bronchitis, pneumonia, repeated sore throats and mouth breathing.

Many of these associations ceased to be statistically significant once other factors had been taken into account. Nevertheless, six of these measures were still apparently associated (Table 21.9). Only one is directly related to health: the strong association with pneumonia. It is conceivable that this could be a direct effect—the changing environment associated with moving house, the possible lack of adequate heating or dampness in the days immediately following the move, or the preoccupation of the parents could all be put forward as plausible

TABLE 21.9 Relative Risks of various conditions by number of household moves

| Problem | None | Number of household moves | | | |
		1	2	3	4+
Crying problem as a baby	0.9	1.0	1.1	1.2	1.3
Sleeping problem at 5	0.9	1.0	1.1	1.0	1.2
Dysfluency	0.9	0.9	1.2	1.2	1.6
Vision problem	0.9	0.9	0.9	1.3	1.7
Pneumonia	0.8	1.0	1.3	1.7	1.7
Suspected hearing difficulty	0.9	1.0	1.1	1.2	1.4

(Findings statistically significant at 1% level after indirect standardisation for other factors.)

hypotheses. Alternatively, it could be an association between some psychological or social factor, present in the population who move frequently, that may be responsible for the pneumonia rather than the moving *per se*.

Similar arguments may be put forward for the three problems that may be considered behavioural rather than associated with health or development (i.e. crying as a baby, sleeping problems at 5 and dysfluency). For the first, it is conceivable that the family actually moved because neighbours (or landlords) complained about the crying infant. Sleeping difficulty and dysfluency might well arise because of the psychological and emotional disruption caused by a move.

In contrast, it is difficult to conceive of direct associations between hearing or vision problems and household moves. It seems possible, however, that the more often the child moves, the more health personnel he may come in contact with, and hence the more likely it is for problems to be identified. Analysis of the objective hearing and vision tests on these children when they were 10 should help us to evaluate this hypothesis.

Parental Smoking

Various health consequences of smoking have been well documented for the smoker, and attention is gradually being turned to assessing health consequences for the passive smoker. Most important among the passive smokers must be the young child at a vulnerable stage of growth and development. The first site of passive smoking occurs *in utero* with well-documented consequences of growth retardation. This association has been found in many studies all over the world. One of the largest studies to confirm the initial finding of Simpson (1957) used the birth data of the 1958 cohort (Butler and Alberman, 1969). Subsequent analysis of the 1970 birth survey found a similar association (Peters *et al.*, 1983). Thus, any follow-up study of children of mothers who smoke heavily will include proportionately more low birthweight infants. This was indeed true of the present study, even though we were looking at the amount the mother was smoking when her child was age 5. Among children of non-smokers only 5.4% had been of low birthweight, whereas among heavy smokers (20+ cigarettes per day) the proportion was 10.4%.

There has been considerable interest concerning reasons for the reduction in breast feeding among smoking mothers. There is evidence that the antenatal behaviour of smoking mothers differs in that they are more likely to book late in pregnancy, more at risk of failing to keep their antenatal appointments, less likely to be sure of their dates (Cardozo *et al.*, 1982). These mothers are less likely to wish to breast feed

(Lyon, 1982). Of those who do attempt breast feeding, mothers who smoke are liable to give up breast feeding within a few weeks. There are reasons for thinking that such failures may have a physical, rather than psychological, aetiology. Smoking releases adrenalin which in turn inhibits the milk–ejection reflex and reduces the milk yield (Cross, 1955). Andersen *et al.* (1982) have found that among smoking mothers there were lower levels of plasma prolactin in smoking lactating mothers (prolactin levels being positively associated with milk yield). These findings are of interest but probably of little relevance to our present study since we have shown no associations between breast feeding and any of the health or behaviour problems studied.

Of greater importance is likely to be the personality of the smoking mother. The 1946 cohort study provided valuable information. When aged 16, the members of this cohort were given a personality inventory to complete. The results were related to the proportions who subsequently started smoking. For both sexes there was a relationship with both neuroticism score and extrovert score (Cherry and Kiernan, 1976), implying that these characteristics typified the persons who would start to smoke, rather than developed as the result of smoking. Nevertheless, the scores for the 16-year-olds who were already smoking were much higher on both scales than those who subsequently started.

Other population studies have looked at detailed personality inventories in relation to current smoking. Haines, Imeson and Meade (1980) found that smokers had significantly higher levels of phobic anxiety, of somatic concomitants of anxiety and of hysterical personality traits (all significant at the 0.001 level). They found that for each of the three measures, the mean scores increased with the number of cigarettes smoked.

Within our own study we found that mothers who smoked were likely to come from the lower social classes, to be a single parent or a step-parent. They were more likely to live in poor or average urban areas and to have moved house frequently. Smokers were less likely to reside in the southern half of England and more likely to live in Scotland, the North and North-West of the country.

Of the behaviour problems that we looked at, smoking did not appear to be associated with the crying, feeding and sleeping problems of early infancy, or with feeding and sleeping difficulties at 5. There were strong associations, however, with both bed-wetting and temper tantrums; the more cigarettes the mother smoked, the greater the prevalence of the problem. Neither effect was removed by standardisation (Table 21.10).

Analysis of the factors associated with morbidity measures showed positive associations between the number of cigarettes smoked and the prevalence of wheezing, bronchitis, pneumonia, purulent ear discharge, mouth breathing, speech problems, squint, vision problems, repeated

TABLE 21.10   Relative Risks of various conditions according to the number
of cigarettes smoked by the mother

Problem	None	Cigarettes per day				
		1–9	10–14	15–19	20–24	25+
Bed wetting (1+ per week)	0.8	1.0	1.1	1.2	1.2	1.4
Temper tantrums (1+ per week)	0.9	1.0	1.1	1.1	1.1	1.3
Speech problems	1.0	0.8	1.0	1.0	1.1	1.4
Stomach aches (1+ per week)	1.1	1.1	0.8	0.7	0.9	1.3
2+ Accidents	0.9	0.9	1.0	1.0	1.2	1.4
Wheezing	0.9	1.0	1.1	1.1	1.2	1.3
Bronchitis	0.9	1.0	1.1	1.2	1.3	1.3
Pneumonia	0.8	0.8	1.2	1.3	1.3	1.6
Ear discharge	0.9	1.0	1.0	1.1	1.3	1.3
Mouth breathing	0.9	1.1	1.1	1.1	1.1	1.1
Squint	0.9	1.0	1.0	1.2	1.4	1.7
Hospital admission	0.9	1.0	1.1	1.1	1.2	1.3

(Findings statistically significant at 1% level after indirect standardisation for other factors.)

accidents and hospital admissions. All the effects remained statistically significant after standardisation for the other related associations, with the exception of vision problems (Table 21.10).

In addition, there were strong negative associations between the prevalence of both eczema and hearing disorder with the number of cigarettes smoked, but these disappeared once social class and region had been allowed for. Other significant variations, that did not conform to linear trends, were found for sore throats, headache and stomach aches. The association with sore throats was secondary to that with the number of siblings in the household; that with headaches was due to the variation in the prevalence of headaches with social class, but that with stomach aches remained.

The crucial question in all the significant associations with smoking concerns the question of whether we are looking at an association with passive smoking during the child's early years, whether the association is with passive smoking *in utero*, or whether the association is with the personality of the smoker.

It is interesting in this context that there was no evidence that paternal smoking was associated with any of the outcome measures once we allowed for the fact that smoking fathers were more likely to have wives who smoked. Lack of any paternal smoking association suggests that passive smoking during the child's life could, at most, have only a minor part to play in the genesis of these disorders.

It is conceivable that pregnancy smoking may have played a rôle in some, if not all, of the disorders listed above. The evidence that smoking during pregnancy results in a retardation in fetal growth is now unequivocal. It is certainly feasible to suggest that other disorders may have their genesis in this way—these might include factors indicative of a mild lesion in areas such as the cerebral cortex, with consequences such as increased risk of squint, speech problems, clumsiness resulting in an increase in the accident rate and bed-wetting. Some support for such a possibility can be found in a study by Krous and colleagues (1981). They found that after giving nicotine to pregnant rats, the foetuses showed signs of brain stem injury.

Alternative explanations are equally plausible though: mothers who smoke are more likely to exhibit various neurotic and anxiety-related symptoms. We are not aware of any studies that have looked at the relationship between the smoking mother and child. It is possible that the mothers who smoke heavily are less likely to talk to their children or to respond to their overtures. Mothers who smoke have been reported to be more likely to 'batter' their children (Murphy *et al.*, 1981). It is conceivable that the relationship between the smoking mother and her child is more likely to be tense and stressful. Observational studies to test this hypothesis are urgently needed.

CHAPTER 22

The Way Ahead

BY THE EDITORS

When planning this volume, we had intended that it should end with a series of policy recommendations. In retrospect, that was very arrogant. As we have stressed throughout, the analyses we have presented here have, perforce, been descriptive rather than aetiological. We can present the facts and suggest some of the ways in which they may be interpreted. What we feel unable to do is to say with confidence that altering a particular aspect of a child's environment will result in specific benefits to that child. We are only too aware of the validity of Mencken's statement: 'There's always an easy solution to every human problem— neat, plausible and wrong.'

We are far more confident, however, of ways in which the data should be analysed further. The longitudinal nature of the information we have gathered is not trivial to analyse or interpret. Nevertheless, we have developed statistical methods to take account of the logical sequence of the independent variables and we are looking in some depth at the ways in which different events at birth relate to the subsequent development of the child. For example, we have shown (Peters *et al.*, 1984) that prolonged asphyxia at birth, when measured in terms of delayed onset of regular respiration, is associated with the subsequent health of the child. There was a positive relationship with the prevalence of bronchitis, as well as anticipated associations with cerebral palsy, neonatal and post-natal death.

Linkage to data on these children at the age of 10 will provide an exciting opportunity to test many of the hypotheses raised by the information described in this volume. Analysis of the educational, intellectual and motor abilities of the children will provide a more sensitive basis for the search for associations between antenatal, perinatal or early childhood events and particular abnormalities. The latter may range from behaviour deviance to clumsiness or dyslexia. Preliminary analyses are currently in progress.

Statistical Appendix

Sources of Bias

In interpreting the results of any study it is obviously important to be able to assess the likely biases in the data collected. In 1979 Sackett listed nine potential types of bias in analytic health research. Below we examine each of the potential sources of error that he identified.

(i) *Prevalence—incidence bias.* Also known as the Neyman bias, this relates to the fact that certain conditions are of such short duration, or lead so quickly to demise, that the cases will be omitted.

This bias is unlikely to have existed in this study, since the conditions considered in this volume are only rarely fatal, and where deaths have occurred, such as for accidents, they have been considered in the text; in addition, the information on morbidity was obtained historically, and few episodes are likely to have been omitted.

(ii) *Admission rate bias.* This is also known as the Berkson bias, and relates to the fact that persons who have been admitted to hospital for one condition are more likely to have another condition identified, presumably because examination and history taking are more likely to draw attention to abnormalities that would otherwise have been ignored. There can be little doubt that this type of bias must exist in almost all studies on the relationship between different health disorders, and the present study cannot claim exemption. Nevertheless, the fact that the bulk of the analyses concern the history of symptoms (e.g. wheezing) rather than designated diagnoses (e.g. asthma) probably results in a minimising of the bias.

(iii) *Unmasking bias.* This type of bias results when one finding or association triggers the search for a health factor known to be statistically associated. An example might be the search for evidence of child abuse in an infant known to have been of low birthweight and living with a single mother. Indeed, as a result of this, we are unhappy about our figures for the prevalence of child abuse, which, out of all that we have discussed, are based solely on the suspicions of the health visitor. Other than this, we have not been able to envisage any likely biases of this type.

(iv) *Non-respondent bias.* Here, however, we know that substantial biases exist (see Chapter 1). Although statistically significant, however, the differences are small except for the one major bias—the reduced follow-up of infants born to single mothers. This implies that all information relating to those children in this group must be regarded with caution; it could be that such children of single parents included in the study are under-representing the adverse effects of being born to a single parent, or the converse.

There is little evidence, however, that other substantial biases exist in the group of children excluded, apart from that which must be obvious: these children were different because they could not be traced.

(v) *Membership bias.* This type of bias concerns the definition of the sample. As already stated, this was defined as all children born in a defined week in April 1970, and who were resident in Great Britain at the time of the survey. The major bias, therefore, concerns the fact that the children are not representative of all children born throughout the year. This will create different biases depending on the condition that is being examined; for example, children born in April have less likelihood of dying suddenly and unexpectedly than those born in the autumn, and there has been some suggestion that children born in April have a reduced risk of febrile convulsions, though this has yet to be confirmed.

Nevertheless, the present study, and indeed all three cohort studies, would be extremely boring if they merely considered prevalence as the only *raison d'être*. Rather it is in their ability to relate medical conditions to the social, environmental and medical backgrounds that is responsible for providing the wealth of information that exists, and the potential for further research.

(vi) *Diagnostic-suspicion bias.* This arises when the interviewer is aware of what the researchers may wish to find. In the present case, where the interviews were conducted by over a thousand different health visitors, there is little likelihood of any consistent bias of this type. Indeed, we have been unable to even envisage how such a bias may have affected the associations described in this volume.

(vii) *Exposure–suspicion bias.* This bias is similar to that above: 'a knowledge of a patient's disease status may influence both the intensity and outcome of a search for exposure to the putative cause' (Sackett, 1979). Here it is conceivable that the interviewer who had noted that the child had been admitted to hospital for gastro-enteritis, for example, would fail to elicit the fact that he had been breast fed. Again, such a bias is unlikely; as can be seen from the questionnaires published at the end of this volume, there are few opportunities for any such bias. Almost all questions concern the eliciting of specific answers to specific questions; there was very little need or opportunity for the probing question.

(viii) *Recall bias.* Here there may be a certain amount of bias in the ability of the mother to remember events relating to the early months or years of her 5-year-old. This is especially likely to happen if the mother has several children—it is conceivable that the more she has, the less likely she is to remember which child had had a given condition. Maternal intelligence might also bias the response.

(ix) *Family information bias.* Here we had definite evidence of bias, and were able to allow for it accordingly. Thus, although a mother is aware of her own medical history and that of her children, there is evidence from our study that she often only knew of, or remembered, her husband's history if the condition under consideration actually arose in the immediate family. Thus, she was much more likely to know that the father had had convulsions as a child, if the study child or one of his siblings had had convulsions. We have, therefore, felt that information relating to the father's medical history should be omitted from any analyses.

In conclusion, most of the possible types of bias were not present in this survey, and one (number ix) we were able to take into account. There remains potential bias from differential recall of certain groups of mothers together with that due to differential follow-up.

Statistical Presentation

The data presented in this volume has taken a logical construct. There are thirteen background social and environmental factors; these are introduced, with their inter-relationships, in Chapters 2, 3 and 4. Subsequent chapters examine the relationship between these same factors and various items pertaining to the behaviour, health and hospital admissions of the children. The final three chapters relate the background factors to various measures of the use of services. Chapter 21 then takes each of the background factors in turn, and summarises the associations of that factor with the health and behaviour outcomes.

For each of Chapters 2 to 20, the analysis started with basic two-way tables, with a chi-squared goodness of fit test to assess the level of statistical significance. These tables are all available in microfiche, indexed at the end of this volume. From the tables, those significant at the 1% level were selected for further analysis.

Two factors determined the use of analytical technique: (a) funds were not available for complex logistic regression methods; but, more importantly, (b) the method of indirect standardisation was intuitively more appealing, was easier to use in a step-wise progression, and resulted in observed and expected numbers that were immediately meaningful.

The method uses indirect standardisation as defined by Armitage (1971), but adapts it to standardise for several factors. The method is similar, but not identical, to that described by Mantel and Stark (1968). Comparison of observed and expected values used the fact that for large sample sizes such as we have invariably used, $(O-E)^2/E$ is distributed as a chi-squared statistic (Armitage, 1971).

Where several factors were initially significantly associated with the condition under analysis, the data were first examined by eye to assess which one appeared to be the one most likely to be responsible for the other findings. Simple indirect standardisation using this factor was then carried out. Differences between the observed and expected numbers would then be assessed to see whether the differences were still statistically significant at the 1% level. If not, then the results appear as a table on microfiche, and the text will state that 'the association with j was due to the association with social class', for example.

If the differences were still significant, however, a similar process would be undertaken. All the remaining significant factors would be examined and the next most likely candidate selected. A similar process would then be undertaken; this would produce a new estimate of the expected value—the process would continue until all significant factors had been taken into account. Although relying initially on the decision as to which factor was most likely to be responsible for a given association, errors in this subjective assessment would be thrown up by the results and alternative orders then examined.

This method is simple, though tedious. It does mean that anyone may take our results and, using the tables in the microfiche, test the method for themselves.

Suppose K is the disorder under consideration and that n_k of the N children in the study were reported as having the disorder.

Suppose initial analyses had shown statistical associations in the prevalence of k and variables 1–7, and that the association most likely to remain stable was thought to be that with 7.

Let r/N_7 be the proportion of children with k in each category of variable 7 and n_{17}, n_{27}, ... be the numbers of children in the whole population in each category of 1 and 7, 2 and 7, etc.

Then the expected number to have k in each category of 1 after standardising for 7 will be

$$e_1 = \sum_7 (n_{17} \cdot r_7/N_7).$$

Similar computations will be carried out for variables 2 to 6.

Tests of significance will compare the observed and expected values:
$$\sum_1 \{(r_1 - e_1)^2/e_1\} \text{ with a chi-squared}$$

Suppose as the result of this procedure variables 6 and 5 ceased to be significant, and 4 was now considered to be the strongest association. New standardisation techniques would be carried out on 1–3 and 7, standardising for 4.

Combination of two standardisations on 1 is given by:
$$e_1 = \sum_7 (n_{17} \; r_7/N_7) + \sum_4 (n_{14} \; r_4/N_4) - r_1/N_1$$

and that for standardising for three variables 3, 4 and 7 would be given by:

$$e_1 = \sum_7 (n_{17} \; r_7/N_7) + \sum_4 (n_{14} \; r_4/N_4) +$$
$$+ \sum_3 (n_{13} \; r_3/N_3) - 2 \; r_1/N_1$$

and so on.

In essence, one starts with the basic expected numbers and sums the divergences revealed by each standardisation.

Possible sources of error. The method described above implicitly relies on the assumption that the factors taken into account in the standardisation process are mutually independent of one another. The fact that for many of these there is a degree of dependence means that, using this method, we have tended to over- rather than under-compensate. This means that the results are probably under estimates of the relative risks associated with each particular factor.

During the course of the analyses it became obvious that some significant results might be due entirely to the inclusion of the small 'not known' groups. Although, given the structure of the data, it was not possible to leave these out of the calculations, in retrospect it would have facilitated the analysis if all cases with 'not known' categories were left out of the original tables. In the event we perforce calculated the expected numbers for the 'not known' group, but only summed the contributions to chi-squared from the other expected and observed numbers.

Other difficulties in the analyses entailed the attempts at analysing the separate associations with social class and parental status. The difficulty arises because of overlap between the two: social class is dependent on the father's occupation; parental situation largely distinguishes the single parent from the rest. Thus, wherever the two factors were both found to be significant, the category in the social class variable denoting 'no father figure' took precedence. It was not possible for the single parent to have a separate significant association once this was taken into account, though it was still possible for a significant contribution to be made by, for example, the step-parent group.

Final justification for the method must, however, remain with the intuition. The results 'smell' right. By carrying out analyses in the iterative way described, it is possible to actually assess the way in which the factors influence one another. Final corroborative evidence is provided by alternative methods of analysis. In spite of the defects inherent in each, the results are substantially the same, whether one uses a logistic regression model or the method described above.

Glossary

Breast feeding This concerns whether the baby was breast fed partly or fully, even if only for a few days. The categories used were: no, never; yes, breast fed for less than 1 month; breast fed for between 1–3 months; and breast fed for 3 months or more.

Employment of mother This concerns whether the mother had had a paid job outside the home at any time during the child's life.

Ethnic group of parents The health visitor was asked to state to which broad ethnic category the parents belonged; the options she was given were European (UK); European (other); West Indian; Indian/ Pakistani; Other Asian; African; Other. In the present analyses we were concerned about the association of ethnic origin on the upbringing of the child, rather than with genetic effects. For this purpose, we used the ethnic groups of the parent figures at interview. Where only one parent was present, that ethnic group was taken. For the present volume, the categories used were: children with both parents of European (UK) origin; children with both parent figures of European (other) origin; both parents of West Indian origin; both parents of Indian/Pakistani origin; and all other categories.

Father The male figure living with the child.

Household moves The number of times the child had moved home since birth.

Indirect standardisation See pages 356 to 357.

Low birthweight Less than 5 lb 8 oz (2500 g)

Maternal age Age of the mother figure when the child was 5.

Mother The female figure living with the child and taking responsibility for the day-to-day management of that child.

Parental situation This concerns the parents, or parent figures, with whom the child was living at the time of the survey. Categories used were: both natural parents; one natural plus one substitute parent; single supported parent; single unsupported parent; and neither natural parent. Definitions are provided on page 18.

Prevalence The proportion of children with a history of a condition.

Region At the time of the survey, sixty-four children were abroad with fathers who were in the Armed Services. They have been included in our population since their absence is only temporary and completed questionnaires were filled in on all of them. For obvious reasons, however, they have been omitted from any regional analysis. The regions used in describing the children are defined as follows:

The regional classification is that used by the OPCS and comprises the following Area Health Authorities. Regions are only occasionally identical with Regional Health Authorities.

North: Cleveland, Cumbria, Durham, Gateshead, Newcastle-upon-Tyne, North Tyneside, Northumberland, South Tyneside, Sunderland.

Yorkshire & Humberside: Humberside, North Yorkshire, Bradford, Calderdale, Kirklees, Leeds, Wakefield, Barnsley, Doncaster, Rotherham, Sheffield.

North-West: Bolton, Bury, Cheshire, Lancashire, Liverpool, Manchester, Oldham, Rochdale, St. Helens and Knowsley, Salford, Sefton, Stockport, Tameside, Wigan, Wirral.

East Midlands: Derbyshire, Leicestershire, Lincolnshire, Nottinghamshire, Northamptonshire.

West Midlands: Birmingham, Coventry, Dudley, Hereford and Worcester, Salop, Sandwell, Solihull, Staffordshire, Walsall, Warwickshire, Wolverhampton.

East Anglia: Cambridgeshire, Norfolk, Suffolk.

South-East: Barking and Havering, Barnet, Bedfordshire, Berkshire, Brent and Harrow, Bromley, Camden and Islington, City and East London, Croydon, Ealing, Hammersmith and Hounslow, East Sussex, Enfield and Haringey, Essex, Greenwich and Bexley, Hampshire, Hertfordshire, Hillingdon, Isle of Wight, Kensington, Chelsea and Westminster, Kent, Kingston and Richmond, Lambeth, Southwark and Lewisham, Merton Sutton and Wandsworth, Oxfordshire, Redbridge and Waltham Forest, Surrey, West Sussex.

South-West: Avon, Cornwall, Devon, Dorset, Gloucestershire, Somerset, Wiltshire.

Wales

Scotland

Relative risk The risk of a condition occurring compared with the population at large. The latter is taken as 1.0.

Sample studied Children born during the week 5–11 April 1970 and normally resident in England, Scotland and Wales at the age of 5.

Social class In the present study the classification has been based on the employment status, occupation and industry, of the child's father figure at the time of the 5-year survey, using the published classification (Office of Population Censuses and Surveys, 1970). Where the mother was living with no male support, the classification NFF (no father figure) was used.

The social classes comprise six groups:

Social class I Professional occupations, including doctors, lawyers, ministers of religion, university teachers, professional engineers, etc.

Social class II Managerial and other professionals, including nurses, school teachers, company directors, etc.

Social class III NM Non-manual skilled occupations, including shop assistants, company representatives, clerical workers, draughtsmen, etc.

Social class III M Skilled manual workers, including mechanics, craftsmen of all types, skilled engineers, etc.

Social class IV Semi-skilled workers, including machine operators, postmen, storekeepers, porters, caretakers, etc.

Social class V Unskilled workers, including labourers, cleaners, dustmen, etc.

Although the classification does not provide codes for the Armed Services, we have coded on rank, based on a modification of the Hall-Jones Scale (Oppenheim, 1966). The details are shown below:

Social class	Army	Navy	RAF
I	Major and above	Lieutenant-Commander and above	Squadron-leader and above
II	All other commissioned officers	All other commissioned officers	All other commissioned officers
III NM	Staff-Sergeant Sergeant Warrant Officer	Chief Petty Officer Petty Officer Warrant Officer	Flight-Sergeant Sergeant Warrant Officer
III M	Lance Corporal Corporal	Leading Seaman	Leading Aircraftsman Corporal
IV	Private	Able-bodied Seaman	Aircraftsman 1 Aircraftsman 2

BTF-M*

Type of neighbourhood The health visitor, after the interview was over, was asked to rate the area in which the family resided. She was given four descriptions and an optional 'other' in which she was to describe the characteristics of the neighbourhood. The four descriptions were classified as: *Urban-poor* (houses were closely packed together and many were in a poor state of repair, multi-accommodation was common and most families were in the low-income bracket). *Urban-average* (this district consisted largely of council houses. Multi-accommodation was unusual and most families had average incomes. New towns were included here). *Urban-well-to-do* (these areas consisted of houses that were well spaced and the majority well maintained. Multi-occupation was rare and most families had higher than average incomes). *Rural* (this included small market towns, rural communities and villages. Some families lacked basic amenities, but others may have been fairly well-to-do. It is mainly characterised by the fact that well-to-do and poorer families lived fairly close together in the community). For 11% of the children the health visitor had written a description, rather than choose one of these options. From descriptions, coders decided which of the criteria were most appropriate.

References

Abramovich, S. J., Gregory, S., Slemick, M., Stewart, A. (1979) 'Hearing loss in very low birthweight infants treated with neonatal intensive care.' *Archives of Disease in Childhood*, **54**, 421–426.

Acheson, E. D., Truelove, S. C. (1961) 'Early weaning in the aetiology of ulcerative colitis: a study of feeding in infancy in cases and controls.' *British Medical Journal*, **2**, 929–933.

Adelstein, A. M. (1952) 'Accident proneness: a criticism of the concept based upon analysis of shunters accidents.' *Journal of the Royal Statistical Society*, **115**, 354–400.

Adelstein, A., White, G. C. (1976) 'Causes of children's deaths analysed by social class 1959–63.' *OPCS Studies on Medical and Population Subjects*, No. 31, Study No. 3. London: HMSO.

Alberman, E., Benson, J., Evans, S. (1982) 'Visual defects in children of low birthweight.' *Archives of Disease in Childhood* **57**, 818–822.

Alberman, E. D., Butler, N. R., Gardiner, P. A. (1971) 'Children with squints; a handicapped group?' *The Practitioner*, **206**, 501–506.

Allerdist, H. (1979) 'Über zentralnervose Komplikationen nach Masernschutzimpfung.' *Monatsschrift und Kinderheilkunde* **127**, 23–28.

Alphey, R. S. (1974) 'Accidental death in the home.' *Royal Society of Health Journal*, **3**, 97–101.

Anand, J. K. (1980) 'Contraindications to immunisation. *British Medical Journal*, **2**, 1533–1534.

Anders, T. F., Weinstein, P. (1972) 'Sleep and its disorders in infants and children: a review.' *Pediatrics*, **50**, 312–324.

Andersen, N. A., Andersen, L. C., Larsen, F. J., Cristensen, J. N., Legros, J. J., Louis, F., Angelo, H., Molin, J. (1982) 'Suppressed prolactin but normal neurophysin levels in cigarette smoking, breast-feeding women.' *Clinical Endocrinology*, **17**, 363–368.

Anthony, E. J. (1957) 'An experimental approach to the psychopathology of childhood encopresis.' *British Journal of Medical Psychology*, **30**, 146–175.

Apley, J. (1982) 'One Child.' In: Apley, J., Ounstead, C. (eds.), *One Child*. London: William Heinemann Medical Books, pp. 23–47.

Apley, J., MacKeith, R., Meadow, R. (1978) *The Child and His Symptoms: a Comprehensive Approach*, 3rd edition. Oxford: Blackwell.

Arbous, A. G., Kerrich, J. E. (1951) 'Accident statistics and the concept of accident proneness: Part I: A critical evaluation. Part II; The mathematical background.' *Biometrics*, **7**, 340–432.

Armitage, P. (1971) 'Statistical Methods in Medical Research.' Oxford: Blackwell Scientific Publications.

Atkins, E., Cherry, N., Douglas, J. W. B., Kiernan, K. E., Wadsworth, M. E. J. (1981) 'The 1946 British Birth Cohort: an account of the origins, progress and results of the National Survey of Health and Development.' In: Mednick, S. A., Baert, A. E., Backman, B. P. (eds.), *Prospective Longitudinal Research: an Empirical Basis for the Primary Prevention of Psychosocial Disorders*. London: Oxford University Press, pp. 25–30.

Backett, E. M., Johnston, A. M. (1959) 'Social pattern of road accidents to children: some characteristics of vulnerable families.' *British Medical Journal*, **1**, 409–413.

Backett, T. T., Sumner, G., Kilpatrick, J., Dingwall-Fordyce (1966) 'Hospitals in the N.E. Scotland region.' In: McLachan, G. (ed.), *Problems and Progress in Medical Care*. Nuffield Provincial Hospitals Trust. London: Oxford University Press.

Baldwin, J. A. (1980) 'Deaths from non-accidental injury in children.' *British Medical Journal*, **2**, 1533.

Baldwin, J. A., Oliver, J. E. (1975) 'Epidemiology and family characteristics of severely abused children.' *British Journal of Preventive and Social Medicine*, **29**, 205–221.

Baltimore, C. L., Meyer, R. J. (1968) 'A study of storage, child behavioural traits and mother's knowledge of toxicology in 52 poisoned families and 52 comparison families.' *Pediatrics*, **42**, 312–317.

Barkin, R. M., Pichichero, M. E. (1979) 'Diptheria-pertussis-tetanus vaccine: reactogenicity of commerical products.' *Pediatrics*, **63**, 256–260.

Barnes, F. (1975) 'Accidents in the first three years of life.' *Child: Care, Health and Development*, **1**, 421–433.

Bax, M. C. O. (1980) 'Sleep disturbance in the young child.' *British Medical Journal*, **2**, 1177–1179.

Beal, J. F., Dickson, S. (1974) 'Social differences in dental attitudes and behaviour in West Midland mothers.' *Public Health*, **89**, 19–30.

Beal, J. F., Dickson, S. (1975) 'Differences in dental attitudes and behaviour between West Midlands mothers of various ethnic origins.' *Public Health*, **89**, 65–70.

Beard, R. J. (1981) 'Risks and problems for the older parent.' In: Roberts, D. F., Chester, R. (eds.), *Changing Patterns of Conception and Fertility*. London: Academic Press.

Bellman, M. (1966) 'Studies on encopresis.' *Acta Paediatrica Scandinavica*, Suppl. 170.

Bemporad, J. R., Kresch, R. A., Asnes, R., Wilson, A. (1978) 'Chronic, neurotic encopresis as a pardigm of multifactorial psychiatric disorder.' *Journal of Nervous and Mental Disorders*, **166**, 472–479.

Bennett, A. N., Pethybridge, R. (1979) 'A study of abused children on the Gosport (Hampshire) Peninsular.' *Journal of the Royal Society of Medicine*, **72**, 743–747.

Berg, I., Fielding, D., Meadow, R. (1977) 'Psychiatric disturbance, urgency and bacteriuria in children with day and night wetting.' *Archives of Disease in Childhood*, **52**, 651–657.

Bernal, J. F. (1972) 'Crying during the first ten days of life and maternal responses.' *Developmental Medicine and Child Neurology*, **14**, 362–372.

Bernal, J. F. (1973) 'Night waking in infants during the first fourteen months.' *Developmental Medicine and Child Neurology*, **15**, 760–769.

Black, J. A., Hughes, F. (1979) 'Legal aspects of child injury or neglect.' *British Medical Journal*, **2**, 910–912.

Blair, H. (1969) 'Aspects of asthma.' *Proceedings of the Royal Society of Medicine*, **62**, 1008–1010.

Blomfield, J. M., Douglas, J. W. B. (1956) 'Bedwetting prevalence among children aged 4–7 years.' *Lancet*, **1**, 850–852.

Blurton Jones, N., Rossetti Ferreira, M. C., Farquar Brown, M., Macdonald, L. 'The association between perinatal factors and later night waking.' *Developmental Medicine and Child Neurology*, **20**, 427–434.

Bohman, M. (1970) *Adopted Children and Their Families*. Stockholm: Proprius.

Brimblecombe, F. S. W. (1975) 'Congenital malformations in Devon: their incidence, age, and primary source of detection.' In: McCachlan, G. (ed.), *Bridging in Health: Reports of Studies on Health Service for Children*. London: Oxford University Press, pp. 201–215.

Brimblecombe, F. S. W., Cruickshank, R., Masters, P. L., Reid, D. D., Stewart G. T. (1958) 'Family studies of respiratory infections.' *British Medical Journal*, **1**, 119–128.

British Medical Journal, Leading Article (1974) 'Squint.' *British Medical Journal*, **3**, 430.

British Medical Journal, Leading Article (1976) 'Breast feeding: the immunological argument.' *British Medical Journal*, **2**, 1167–1168.

British Medical Journal, Leading Article (1976) 'Safety for children.' *British Medical Journal*, **4** 833–834.

British Medical Journal, Leading Article (1976) 'Children who die through social disadvantage.' *British Medical Journal*, **4**, 962–963.

British Medical Journal, Leading Article (1979) 'Epidemiology: unnecessary smallpox vaccinations.' *British Medical Journal*, **4**, 1155.

British Medical Journal, Leading Article (1980) 'Recognising child abuse.' *British Medical Journal*, **1**, 881.

British Medical Journal, Leading Article (1980) 'B.C.G. in Britain.' *British Medical Journal*, **3**, 825.

Broad, F. E. (1972) 'The effects of infant feeding on speech quality.' *New Zealand Medical Journal*, **76**, 28–31.

Broder, I., Barlow, P. P., Horton, R. J. M. (1962) 'The epidemiology of asthma and hay fever in a total community, Tecumsch, Michigan. 1: Description of study and general findings.' *Journal of Allergy*, **33**, 513–523.

Brook, C. G. D. (1983) 'Consequences of intrauterine growth retardation.' *British Medical Journal*, **1**, 164–165.

Brown, G. W., Bhrolchain, M. M., Harris, T. (1975) 'Social class and psychiatric disturbance among women in an urban population.' *Sociology*, **9**, 225–254.

Brown, G. W., Davidson, S. (1978) 'Social class, psychiatric disorder of mother and accidents to children.' *Lancet*, **1**, 378–380.

Bryant, G. M. (1982) 'How effective are our child health clinics?' *British Medical Journal*, **1**, 820.

Buchanan, A., Oliver, J. E. (1977) 'Abuse and neglect as a cause of mental retardation: a study of 140 children admitted to subnormality hospitals in Wiltshire.' *British Journal of Psychiatry*, **131**, 458–467.

Burghes, L. (1980) 'Living from hand to mouth: a study of 65 families living on supplementary benefit.' *Poverty Pamphlet* 50. Family Services Unit, Child Poverty Action Group.

Burns, C. (1958) 'Childhood encopresis.' *Medical World (London)*, **89**, 529–532.

Butler, N. R., Bonham, D. G. (1963) *Perinatal Mortality: The First Reports of the 1958 British Perinatal Mortality Survey*. Edinburgh: E. & S. Livingstone.

Butler, N. R., Alberman, E. D. (1969) *Perinatal Problems: The Second Report of the 1958 British Perinatal Mortality Survey*. Edinburgh: E. & S. Livingstone.

Butler, N. R., Goldstein, H., Ross, E. M. (1972) 'Cigarette smoking in pregnancy: its influence on birthweight and perinatal mortality.' *British Medical Journal*, **2**, 127–130.

Butler, N. R., Peckham, C., Sheridan, M. (1973) 'Speech defects in children aged 7 years: a national study.' *British Medical Journal*, **1**, 253–257.

Butler, N. R., Goldstein, H. (1973) 'Smoking in pregnancy and subsequent child development.' *British Medical Journal*, **4**, 573–575.

Butler, N. R., Golding, J., Haslum, M. Stewart-Brown, S. (1982) 'Recent findings of the 1970 Child Health and Education Study: preliminary communication.' *Journal of the Royal Society of Medicine*, **75**, 781–784.

Calnan, M. (1974) 'Accidental child poisoning and health education.' *British Journal of Preventive and Social Medicine*, **28**, 67.

Calnan, M., Douglas, J. W. B., Goldstein, H. (1978) 'Tonsillectomy and circumcision: comparisons of two cohorts.' *International Journal of Epidemiology*, **7**, 79–85.

Calnan, M., Peckham, C. S. (1977) 'Incidence of insulin dependent diabetics in the first 16 years of life.' *Lancet*, **1**, 589–590.

Calnan, M., Wadsworth, M. (1977) 'Accounting for accidental injury in childhood.' In: Burman, S., Glenn, H. (eds.), *Accidents in the Home*. London: Croom Helm, pp. 27–37.

Cardozo, L. D., Gibb, D. M. F., Studd, J. W. W., Cooper, D. J. (1982) 'Social and obstetric features associated with smoking in pregnancy.' *British Journal of Obstetrics and Gynaecology*, **89**, 622–627.

Carpenter, R. G., Shaddick, C. W. (1965) 'Role of infection, suffocation and bottle-feeding in cot death. An analysis of some factors in the histories of 110 cases and their controls.' *British Journal of Preventive and Social Medicine*, **19**, 1–7.

Carter, C. O. (1963) *Human Heredity*. Harmondsworth, Middlesex: Penguin Books, pp. 239–240.

Cater, J. I., Easton, P. M. (1980) 'Separation and other stress in child abuse.' *Lancet*, **1**, 972–973.

Chakravartti, R., Roy, A. K., Rao, K. U. M., Chakravartti, M. R. (1979) 'Hereditary factors in stammering.' *Journal de Genetique Humane*, **27**, 319–328.

Chamberlain, G., Philipp, E., Howlett, B., Masters, K. (1978) *British Births 1970*. Volume 2: *Obstetric Care*. London: Heinemann Medical Books.

Chamberlain, R., Chamberlain, G., Howlett, B., Claireaux, A. (1975) *British Births 1970*. Volume 1: *The First Week of Life*. London: Heinemann Medical Books.

Chamberlain, R., Davey, A. (1975) 'Physical growth in twins, postmature and small-for-dates children.' *Archives of Disease in Childhood*, **5**, 437–442.

Chamberlain, R., Davey, A. (1976) 'Cross-section study of development test items in children aged 94–97 weeks: report of the British Birth Child Study.' *Developmental Medicine and Child Neurology,* **18**, 54–70.

Chamberlain, R., Simpson, N. (1979) *The Prevalence of Disease in Childhood.* London: Pitman Medical Publishers.

Chandra, R. K. (1979) 'Prospective studies on the effect of breast feeding on incidence of infection and allergy.' *Acta Paediatrica Scandinavica,* **68**, 691–694.

Cherry, N., Kiernan, N. (1976) 'Personality scores and smoking behaviour.' *British Journal of Preventive and Social Medicine,* **30**, 123–131.

Chester, R. (1977) 'Divorce in England and Wales.' In: Chester, R. (ed.), *Divorce in Europe.* Leiden: Nijhoff.

Chin, K. C., Beattie, T. J. (1980) 'Household product poisoning in children.' *Lancet,* **2**, 206.

Clements, F. W. (1955) 'Accidental injuries in pre school children 1: A general survey. 2: Traffic accidents. 3: Burns and scalds.' *The Medical Journal of Australia,* **1**, 348–352, 388–391, 421–424.

Coles, E. C., Cotter, S., Valman, H. B. (1978) 'Increased prevalence of breast feeding.' *British Medical Journal,* **2**, 1122.

Colley, J. R. T. (1976) 'The epidemiology of respiratory disease in childhood.' In: Hull, D. (ed.), *Recent Advances In Paediatrics* No. 5. London: Churchill Livingstone.

Colley, J. R. T., Douglas, J. W. B., Reid, D. D. (1973) 'Respiratory disease in young adults: influence of early childhood lower respiratory tract illness, social class, air pollution and smoking.' *British Medical Journal,* **3**, 195–198.

Colley, J. R. T., Holland, W. W., Corkhill, R. T. (1974) 'Influence of passive smoking and parental phlegm on pneumonia and bronchitis in early childhood.' *Lancet,* **2**, 1031–1035.

Colley, J. R. T., Reid, D. D. (1970) 'Urban and social origins of childhood bronchitis in England and Wales.' *British Medical Journal,* **2**, 213–217.

Collins, E. M., Klein, R. (1980) 'Equity and the NHS: self-reported morbidity, access and primary care.' *British Medical Journal,* **4**, 1111–1115.

Comfort, A. (1975) 'Ill health and child abuse.' *Lancet,* **2**, 876.

Correa, P., Pickle, L. W., Fontham, E., Lin, Y., Haenszell, W. (1983) 'Passive smoking and lung cancer.' *Lancet,* **2**, 595–597.

Court Report, The (1978) Health Services Department: *The Court Report on Child Health Services.* London: H.M.S.O.

Crabtree, N., Gerrard, J. (1950) 'Perceptive deafness as associated with severe neonatal jaundice: a report of 16 cases.' *Journal of Laryngology,* **64**, 482–506.

Creighton, S. (1980) 'Deaths from non-accidental injury in children.' *British Medical Journal,* **3**, 147.

Crellin, E., Pringle, M. L. K., West, P. (1971) *Born Illegitimate: Social and Educational Implications.* A Report by the National Children's Bureau for the National Foundation for Educational Research in Enlgand and Wales, Slough.

Cross, B. A. (1955) 'The hypothalamus and the mechanism of sympathetico-adrenal inhibition of milk ejection.' *Journal of Endocrinology,* **12**, 15-18.

Cullinan, T. R. (1971) 'Children at risk of accident.' *Community Health,* **2**, 175–178.

Dalton, K. (1970) 'Children's hospital admissions and mother's menstruation.' *British Medical Journal,* **2**, 27–28.

Dalton, K. (1975) 'Paramenstrual baby battering.' *British Medical Journal,* **2**, 279.

Davenport, H. T., Werry, J. S. (1970) 'The effects of general anesthesia, surgery and hospitalization upon the behaviour of children.' *American Journal of Orthopsychiatry,* **40**, 806.

Davie, R., Butler, N., Goldstein, H. (1972) *From Birth to Seven: a Report of the National Child Development Study.* London: Longman.

Dawson, B., Horobin, G., Illsley, R., Mitchell, R. (1969) 'A survey of childhood asthma in Aberdeen.' *Lancet,* **1**, 827–830.

Department of Health and Social Security (1981) *Whooping Cough Reports.* The Committee on Safety of Medicines and The Joint Committee on Vaccination and Immunisation. London: H.M.S.O.

Department of Prices and Consumer Protection (1979) *The Home Accident Surveillance System: Analysis of Domestic Accidents to Children.* London: Consumer Safety Unit.

Donnally, H. H. (1930) 'The question of elimination of foreign protein (egg-white) in women's milk.' *Journal of Immunology*, **19**, 15–40.

Douek, E., Bannister, L. H., Dodson, H. C., Ashcroft, P., Humphries, K. N. (1976) 'Effects of incubator noise on the cochlea of the new born.' *Lancet*, **2**, 1110–1113.

Douglas, A. A. (1963) In: Smith, V. H. (ed.), *Visual Disorders and Cerebral Palsy. Little Club Clinics in Developmental Medicine*, No. 9. London: Heinemann Medical Books.

Douglas, J. W. B. (1950) 'The extent of breast feeding in Great Britain in 1946, with special reference to the health and survival of children.' *British Journal of Obstetrics and Gynaecology of the British Empire*, **57**, 335–361.

Douglas, J. W. B. (1951) 'Social class differences in health and survival during the first two years of life.' *Population Studies*, **5**, 35–58.

Douglas, J. W. B. (1951) 'Health and survival of infants in different social classes: a national survey.' *Lancet*, **2**, 440–446.

Douglas, J. W. B. (1954) 'Birthweight and history of breast feeding.' *Lancet*, **2**, 685–688.

Douglas, J. W. B. (1956) 'The age at which premature children walk.' *The Medical Officer*, **95**, 33–35.

Douglas, J. W. B. (1960) 'Premature children at primary schools.' *British Medical Journal*, **1**, 1008–1013.

Douglas, J. W. B. (1964) 'The environmental challenge in early childhood.' *Public Health*, **78**, 195–203.

Douglas, J. W. B. (1970) 'Broken families and child behaviour.' *Journal of the Royal College of Physicians*, **4**, 203–210.

Douglas, J. W. B. (1973) 'Early disturbing events and later enuresis.' 'Bladder control and Enuresis'. Kolvin, I., MacKeith, R. C., Meadow, S. R., (eds.) *Clinics in Developmental Medicine* 48–49, London: Spastics International Medical Publishers, pp. 109–117.

Douglas, J. W. B. (1975) 'Early hospital admissions and later disturbances of behaviour and learning.' *Developmental Medicine and Child Neurology*, **17**, 456–480.

Douglas, J. W. B., Blomfield, J. M. (1956) 'The reliability of longitudinal surveys.' *The Millbank Memorial Fund Quarterly*, **34**, 227–252.

Douglas, J. W. B., Blomfield, J. M. (1958) *Children Under Five.* London: Allen & Unwin.

Douglas, J. W. B., Gear, R. (1976) 'Children of low birthweight in the 1946 National Cohort: behaviour and educational achievement in adolescence.' *Archives of Disease in Childhood*, **51**, 820–827.

Douglas, J. W. B., Mogford, C. (1953a) 'The results of a national enquiry into the growth of premature children from birth to four years.' *Archives of Disease in Childhood*, **28**, 436–445.

Douglas, J. W. B., Mogford, C. (1953b) 'Health of premature children from birth to four years.' *British Medical Journal*, **1**, 748–754.

Douglas, J. W. B., Ross, J. M. (1968) 'Adjustment and educational progress.' *British Journal of EducationalPsychology*, **38**, 2–4.

Douglas, J. W. B., Waller, R. E. (1966) 'Air pollution and respiratory infection in children.' *British Journal of Preventive and Social Medicine*, **20**, 1–8.

Drillien, C. M. (1964) *The Growth and Development of the Prematurely Born Infant.'* Edinburgh: Livingstone.

D'Souza, S. W., McCartney, E., Nolan, M., Taylor, I. G. (1981) 'Hearing, speech and language in survivors of severe perinatal asphyxia.' *Archives of Disease in Childhood*, **56**, 245–252.

D'Souza, S. W., Richards, B. (1978) 'Neurological sequelae in new born babies after perinatal asphyxia.' *Archives of Disease in Childhood*, **53**, 564–569.

Duke, R. F. (1976) 'Attitudes to children's accidents.' *Lancet*, **1**, 257.

Dutau, G., Corberand, J., Leophonte, P., Rochiccioli, P. (1979) 'Manifestations respiratoires liees a l'inhalation passive de fumee de tabac chez l'enfant d'age pre-scholaire.' *Le Poumon et le Coeur*, **35**, 63–69.

Edfors-Lubs, M. L. (1971) 'Allergy in 7,000 twin pairs.' *Acta Allergologica*, **26**, 249–285.

Essen, J., Fogelman, K., Head, J. (1978a) 'Children's housing and their health and physical development.' *Child: Care, Health and Development*, **4**, 357–69.

Essen, J., Fogelman, K., Head, J. (1978b) 'Childhood housing experience and school attainment.' *Child: Care, Health and Development*, **4**, No. 1, 41–58.

Essen, J., Lambert, L. (1977) 'Living in one parent families: relationships and attitudes of

16 year olds.' *Child: Care, Health and Development*, **3**, 301–318.

Essen, J., Peckham, C. (1976) 'Nocturnal enuresis in childhood.' *Developmental Medicine and child Neurology*, **18**, 577–589.

Evans, R. W., Fergusson, D. M., Allardyce, R. A., Taylor, B. (1981) 'Maternal diet and infantile colic in breast fed infants.' *Lancet*, **1**, 1340–1342.

Eyler, J. M. (1979) *Victorian Social Medicine: the Ideas and Methods of William Farr*. Baltimore and London: Johns Hopkins University Press.

Fallon, S. J. J. S., Watson, G. S. (1982) 'Survey of dental caries experience in 5 and 15-year-old Humberside school children.' *Public Health*, 15–19.

Farn, K. T., Valman, H. B. (1980) 'Deaths from non-accidental injury in children.' *British Medical Journal*, **2**, 1145.

Fedrick, J., Adelstein, P. (1973) 'Influence of pregnancy spacing on outcome of pregnancy.' *British Medical Journal*, **4**, 753–756.

Fedrick, J., Alberman, E. D. (1972) 'Reported influenza in pregnancy and subsequent cancer in the child.' *British Medical Journal*, **2**, 485–488.

Ferguson, B. B., Wilson, D. J., Schaffner, W. (1976) 'Determination of nicotine concentrations in human milk.' *American Journal of Disease of Children*, **130**, 837–839.

Fergusson, D. M., Horwood, L. J., Shannon, F. T., Taylor, B. (1978) 'Infant health and breast feeding during the first 16 weeks of life.' *Australian Paediatric Journal*, **14**, 254–258.

Fergusson, D. M., Horwood, L. J., Shannon, F. T. (1980) 'Parental smoking and respiratory illness in infancy.' *Archives of Disease in Childhood*, **55**, 358–361.

Fogelman, K. (1980) 'Smoking in pregnancy and subsequent development of the child.' *Child: Care, Health and Development*, **6**, 233–249.

Fogelman, K., Wedge, P. (1981) 'The National Child Development Study (1958 British Cohort).' In: Mednick, S. A., Baert, A. E., Backman, B. P. (eds.), *Prospective Longitudinal Research: an Empirical Basis for the Primary Prevention of Psychosocial Disorders*. Oxford: Oxford University Press.

Fomufod, A. K., Sinkford, S. M., Louy, V. E. (1975) 'Mother-child separation at birth: a contributing factor in child abuse.' *Lancet*, **2**, 549.

Fraser, G. R. (1964) 'Profound childhood deafness.' *Journal of Medical Genetics*, **1**, 118–151.

Friedreich, W. N., Boriskin, J. A. (1976) 'Ill health and child abuse.' *Lancet*, **1**, 649.

Fry, J., Dillane, J. B., McNab-Jones, R. F., Kalton, G., Andrew, E. (1969) 'The outcome of acute otitis media (a report to the Medical Research Council).' *British Journal of Preventative and Social Medicine*, **23**, 205–209.

Gairdner, D. (1949) 'The fate of the foreskin.' *British Medical Journal*, **2**, 1433–1437.

General Household Survey (1981) Office of Population Census and Surveys. London: H.M.S.O.

Giacoia, G. P., Catz, C. S. (1979) 'Drugs and pollutants in breast milk.' *Clinics in Perinatology*, **6**, 181–196.

Goel, K. M., House, F., Shanks, R. A. (1978) 'Infant feeding practices among immigrants in Glasgow.' *British Medical Journal*, **2**, 1181–1183.

Golding, J. (1979) 'The epidemiology of malformations of the central nervous system.' *The Journal of Maternal and Child Health*, **4**, 328.

Golding, J., Butler, N. R. (1984a) Wheezing and Stress? *Stress and Disability in Childhood: the long-term problems.*' Butler, N. R., Corner, B. D. (eds.). Bristol: Wright, 87–93.

Golding, J., Butler, N. R. (1984b) 'The Socioeconomic Factor. In 'Prevention of Perinatal Mortality and Morbidity' Faulkner, F. (ed.) *Child Health and Development* **3**, 31–46. Karger: Basel.

Golding, J., Limerick, S., Macfarlane, J. A., (1985) 'Sudden Infant Death Syndrome: Patterns, Puzzles and Problems.' Shepton Mallet: Open Books Ltd.

Golding, J., Butler N. R., Taylor, B., (1982) 'Breast feeding and eczema/asthma.' *Lancet*, **1**, 623.

Goldman, A. S., Smith, C. W. (1973) 'Host resistance factors in human milk.' *Journal of Paediatrics*, **82**, 1082–1090.

Goldstein, H. (1969) 'The effect of maternal age, parity, social class, height, degree of pre-eclampsia and smoking in pregnancy on birthweight.' Butler, N. R., Alberman, E. (eds.), pp. 65–67.

Gordon, A. G. (1981) 'Breast is best but bottle is worst.' *Lancet*, **2**, 151.

Gordon, R. R. (1977) 'Predicting child abuse.' *British Medical Journal*, **1**, 841.

Graham, P. J., Rutter, M. L., Yule, W., Pless, I. B. (1967) 'Childhood asthma: a psychosomatic disorder? Some epidemiological considerations.' *British Journal of Preventative and Social Medicine*, **21**, 78–85.

Greer, G. (1979) *The Obstacle Race*. London: Secker.

Gregory, I. (1965) 'Anterospective data following childhood loss of a parent. 1: Delinquency and high school drop out.' *Archives of General Psychiatry*, **13**, 99–109.

Griffiths, E. (1979) 'Incidence of E.N.T. problems in general practice.' *Journal of the Royal Society of Medicine*, **72**, 740–742.

Gunther, M. (1975) 'The neonate's immunity gap, breast feeding and cot death.' *Lancet*, **1**, 441–442.

Gustafsson, L. H. (1977) 'Childhood accidents.' *Scandinavian Journal of Social Medicine*, **5**, 5–13.

Haines, A. P., Imeson, J. D., Meade, T. W. (1980) Psychoneurotic profiles of smokers and non-smokers. *British Medical Journal* **280**, 1422–

Hall, J. G. (1964) 'The cochlea and the cochlear nuclei in neonatal asphyxia.' *Acta Oto-laryngologica* (suppl.), **194**, 1–93.

Hall, M. H. (1974) 'Hazards to children in the home environment.' *Community Health*, **5**, 238–245.

Hallgren, B. (1957) 'Enuresis: a clinical and genetic study.' *Acta Psychiatrica et Neurologica Scandinavica Suplementum*, **114**, 32.

Hamman R. F., Halil, T., Holland, W. W. (1975) 'Asthma in school children.' *British Journal of Preventative and Social Medicine*, **29**, 228–238.

Harada, M. (1976) 'Intrauterine poisoning: clinical and epidemiological studies and significance of the problem.' *Bulletin of the Institute of Constitutional Medicine, Kumamoto University*, supplement 25.

Harker, P. (1977) 'Primary immunisation and febrile convulsions in Oxford (1972–1975).' *British Medical Journal*, **2**, 490–493.

Hart, H., Bax, M., Jenkins, S. (1981) 'Use of child health clinics.' *Archives of Disease in Childhood*, **56**, 440–445.

Hart, J. T. (1971) 'The inverse care law.' *Lancet*, **1**, 405–412.

Haslum, M., Morris, A. C., Golding, J. (1983) 'What do Britain's five year olds eat? *Health Visitor*, 57: 178–9.

Havard, J. D. J. (1974) 'Child pedestrian casualties as a public health problem.' *Medicine, Science and the Law*, **14**, 168–179.

Helfer, R. E., Slovis, T. L., Black, M. (1977) 'Injuries resulting when very small children fall out of bed.' *Pediatrics*. **60**, 533–535.

Helfer, R. E. (1973) 'The etiology of child abuse.' *Pediatrics*, **51**, 777–779,

Henderson, F. W., Clyde, W. A., Collier, W. A., Denny, F. W. In collaboration with Senior, R. J., Sheaffer, C. I., Conley, W. G., Christian, R. M. (1979) 'The etiologic and epidemiologic spectrum of bronchitis in pediatric practices.' *Journal of Pediatrics*, **95**, 183–190.

Hendrickse, W. A. (1982) 'How effective are our child health clinics?' *British Medical Journal*, **1**, 575–577.

Herbst, A. L., Ulfelder, H., Poskanzer, D. C. (1971) 'Adenocarcinoma of the vagina: association of maternal stiboestrol with tumour appearance in young women.' *New England Journal of Medicine*, **284**, 878–881.

Hersher, L. (1978) 'Minimal brain dysfunction and otitis media.' *Perception and Motor Skills*, **47**, 723.

Hippocrates (460–377 B.C.) *Airs, Water and Places*.

Holland, W. W., Bailey, P., Bland, J. M. (1978) 'Long term consequences of respiratory disease in infancy.' *Journal of Epidemiology and Community Health*, **32**, 256–259.

Hooper, P. D. (1965) 'Infant feeding and its relationship to weight gain and illness.' *The Practitioner*, **194**, 391–395.

Howie, V. M. (1980) 'Developmental sequalae of chronic otitis media: a review.' *Journal of Developmental and Behavioural Pediatrics*. **1**, 34.

Hunter, R. S., Kilstrom, N., Kraybill, E. N., Loda, F. (1978) 'Antecedants of child abuse and neglect in premature infants: a prospective study in a newborn intensive care unit.' *Pediatrics*, **61**, 629–635.

Husband, P. (1973) 'The accident prone child.' *The Practitioner*, **211**, 336–344.
Husband, P. (1975) 'The child with repeated injuries: a family problem.' *Journal of the Royal College of General Practitioners*, **25**, 419–423.
Hutt. C. (1972) 'Neuroendocrinological, behavioural and intellectual aspects of sexual differentiation in human development.' In: Ounstead, C., Taylor, D. C. (eds), *Gender Differences: Their Ontogeny and Significance*. Edinburgh and London: Churchill Livingstone, pp. 73–121.
Hutt, C. (1972) *Males and Females*. Harmondsworth: Penguin Books.
Illingworth, C. M. (1974) 'Childhood poisonings: who is to blame?' *The Practitioner*, **213**, 73–78.
Illingworth, R. (1980) 'Whooping cough immunisation.' *British Medical Journal*, **1**, 179.
Isaacs, S. (1932) 'Some notes on the incidence of neurotic difficulties in young children.' *British Journal of Educational Psychology*, **2**, 71.
Izon, R. J., Pullen, R. C., Scivier, G. A. (1978) 'The prevalence of dental caries in 5 and 15 year old Hereford children.' *Public Health*, **92**, 125–130.
Jackson, R. H. (ed.) (1977) *Children, the Environment and Accidents*. Tunbridge Wells: Pitman Medical Publishing Co.
Jackson, R. H. (1979) 'Accidents in childhood.' *Developmental Medicine and Child Neurology*, **21**, 534–536.
Jenkins, S., Bax, M., Hart, H. (1980) 'Behaviour problems in pre school children.' *Journal of Child Psychology and Psychiatry*, **21**, 5–17.
Johnstone, D. E., Roghmann, K. J., Pless, I. B. (1975) 'Factors associated with the development of asthma and hay fever in children: the possible risks of hospitalisation, surgery and anaesthesia.' *Pediatrics*, **56**, 398–403.
Jones, B. N., Ferreira, R. M. C., Brown, F. M., Macdonald, L. (1978) 'The association between perinatal factors and later night waking.' *Developmental Medicine and Child Neurology*, **20**, 427–434.
Jones, M. B., Offord, D. R., Abrams, N. (1980) 'Brothers, sisters and anti-social behaviour.' *British Journal of Psychiatry*, **136**, 139–145.
Jones, R. S. (1976) *Asthma in Children*. London: Edward Arnold.
Justice, B., Duncan, D. F. (1976) 'Life crisis as a precursor to child abuse.' *Public Health Reports, Washington*, **91**, 110–115.
Kastrup, M. (1976) 'Psychic disorders among pre school children in a geographically delimited area of Aarhus county, Denmark.' *Acta Psychiatrica Scandinavica*, **54**, 35–50.
Keen, J. H., Lendrum, J., Wolman, B. (1975) 'Inflicted burns and scalds in children.' *British Medical Journal*, **4**, 268–269.
Kierkegaard, S. (1813–1855) Quoted by Peter., L. (1977) *Quotations of Our Time*. Magnum Books. London: Methuen Paperbacks Ltd.
Kiernan, K. E., Colley, J. R. T., Douglas, J. W. B., Reid, D. D. (1976) 'Chronic cough in young adults in relation to smoking habits, childhood environment and chest illness.' *Respiration*, **33**, 236–244.
Kiernan, K. E. (1980) 'Teenage motherhood—associated factors and consequences: the experiences of a British birth cohort.' *Journal of Biosocial Science*, **12**, 393–405.
Kjellman, N. I. M., Harder, H., Hansson, L. O., Lindwall, L. (1978) 'Allergy, otitis media and serum immunoglobulins after adenoidectomy.' *Acta Paediatrica Scandinavica*, **67**, 717–723.
Kohler, L., Stigmar, G. (1978) 'Visual disorders in 7 year old children with and without previous vision screening.' *Acta Paediatrica Scandinavica*, **67**, 373–377.
Kolvin, I., Fundidus, T. (1982) Chapter 10 'Speech and language disorders in childhood.' In: Apley, J., Ounstead, C. (eds.), *One Child*. London: Heinemann Medical Books Ltd., pp. 147–163.
Koplan, J. P., Schoenbaum, S. C., Weinstein, M. C., Fraser, D. W. (1979) 'Pertussis vaccine—an analysis of benefits, risk and costs.' *The New England Journal of Medicine*, **301**, 906–911.
Krous, H. F., Cambell, G. A., Fowler, M., Catron, A. C., Farber, J. P. (1981) 'Maternal nicotine administration and fetel brain stem damage: a rat model with implications for sudden death syndrome.' *American Journal of Obstetrics and Gynaecology*, **140**, 743–746.
Kuzemko, J. A. (1978) *Allergy in Children: a Guide to Practical Management* Tunbridge Wells: Pitman Medical Books.

Lancet, Leading Article (1979) 'Accident prevention in childhood.' *Lancet*, **2**, 564–565.

Lancet, Leading Article (1981) 'The how of breast milk and infection.' *Lancet*, **1**, 1192–1193.

Learmonth, A. (1979) 'Factors in child burn and scald accidents in Bradford, 1969–1973.' *Journal of Epidemiology and Community Health*, **33**, 270–273.

Leeder, S. R., Corkhill, R. T., 'Irwig, L. M., *et al.* (1976a) Influence of family factors on the incidence of lower respiratory illness during the first year of life. *British Journal of Preventive and Social Medicine*, **30**, 203–212.

Leeder, S. R., Corkhill, R. T., Irwig, L. M., Holland, W. W., Colley, J. R. T. (1976b) 'Influence of family factors on asthma and wheezing during the first 5 years of life.' *British Journal of Preventive and Social Medicine*, **30**, 213–218.

Leeder, S. R., Corkhill, R. T., Wysocki, M. J. *et al.*, (1976c) 'Influence of personal and family factors on ventilatory function of children.' *British Journal of Preventive and Social Medicine* **30**, 219–224.

Leeson, J. (1980) 'Separation stress and child abuse.' *Lancet*, **1**, 1300.

Leete, R. (1977) 'Changing patterns of marriage and remarriage.' In: Chester, R., Peel, J. (eds.) *Equalities and Inequalities in Family Life*. London: Academic Press, p. 8.

Leete, R. (1978) 'One parent families: numbers and characteristics.' *Population Trends*, **13**, 4–9.

Leete, R. (1979) 'New directions in family life.' *Population Trends*, **15**, 4–9.

Leete, R., Fox, J. (1977) 'Registrar General's social classes: origins and uses.' *Population Trends*, **8**, 1–7.

Lehmann, M. D., Charron, K., Kummer, A. (1979) 'The effect of chronic middle ear effusion on speech and language development: a descriptive study.' *International Journal of Paediatrical Otorhinolaryngology*, **1**, 137.

Lennox, W. G. (1946) *Science and Seizures*. London and New York: Harper Brothers, p. 46.

Levine, M. D. (1975) 'Children with encopresis: a descriptive analysis.' *Pediatrics*, **56**, 412–416.

Lind, T., Gerrard, J., Sheridan, T. S., Walker, W. (1977) 'Effect of maternal parity and infant sex upon the haematological values of cord blood.' *Acta Paediatrica Scandinavica*, **66**, 333–337.

Lobo, E. de H. (1978) *Children of Immigrants to Britain: Their Health and Social Problems*. London: Hodder & Stoughton.

Lucas, A., Blackburn, A. M., Aynsley-Green, A., Sarson, D. L., Adrian, T. E., Bloom, S. R. (1980) 'Breast and bottle: endocrine responses are different with formula feeding.' *Lancet*, **1**, 1267–1269.

Lynch, M. A. (1975) 'Ill health and child abuse.' *Lancet*, **2**, 317–319.

Lynch, M. A., Roberts, J. (1977) 'Predicting child abuse: signs of bonding failure in the maternity hospital.' *British Medical Journal*, **1**, 624–626.

Lyon, A. J. (1982) 'Effects of smoking on breast feeding.' *Archives of Disease in Childhood*, **58**, 378–380.

MacCarthy, D., Douglas, J. W. B., Mogford, C. (1952) 'Circumcision in a national sample of 4 year old children.' *British Medical Journal*, **4**, 755–756.

MacFarlane, J. W. (1954) *A Developmental Study of the Behaviour Problems of Normal Children Between 21 months and 14 Years*. Berkeley: University of California Press.

MacMillan, B. G. (1974) 'Burns in children.' *Clinics in Plastic Surgery*, **1**, 633–644.

Maitland-Jones, A. G. (1947) In: Paterson, D., Moncrieff, A. (eds.) *Garrod's Disease of Children*, 4th edition. London: Arnold.

Madge, N. (1983) 'Families at risk.' *SSRC/DHSS studies in deprivation and disadvantage*, No. 8. London: Heinemann Educational Books.

Manheimer, D. I., Mellinger, G. D. (1967) 'Personality characteristics of the child accident repeater.' *Child Development*, **38**, 491–513.

Mantel, N., Stark, C. R. (1968) 'Computations of indirect-adjusted rates in the presence of confounding.' *Biometrics* **24**, 997–1005.

Marcus, I. M., Wilson, W., Kraft, I., Swader, D., Southerland, F., Schulhofer, E. (1960) 'An interdisciplinary approach to accident patterns in children.' Society for research in child development. The family study unit, Tulane University. 25, serial no. 76, 3–77.

Margolis, J. A. (1971) 'Psychosocial study of child poisoning: a 5 year follow up.' *Pediatrics*, **47**, 439–444.

Marmot, M. G., Page, C. M., Atkins, E. (1980) 'Effect of breast feeding on plasma cholesterol and weight in young adults.' *Journal of Epidemiology and Community Health*, **34**, 164–167.

Martin, H. L. (1970) 'Antecedants of burns and scalds in children.' *British Journal of Medical Psychology*, **43**, 39–47.

Martin, J. (1978) *Infant Feeding 1975: Attitudes and Practices in England and Wales.*' London: Her Majesty's Stationery Office.

Maternity in Great Britain. (1948) Joint report from: Royal College of Obstetricians and Gynaecologists and Population Investigation Committee. London: Oxford Unversity Press.

Matheny, A. P. (Jr.), Brown, A. M., Wilson, R. S. (1971) 'Behavioural antecedants of accidental injuries in early childhood: a study of twins.' *Journal of Pediatrics*, **79**, 122–125.

Mawson, S. R., Adlington, P., Evans, M. (1967) 'A controlled study evaluation of adeno-tonsillectomy in children. Part 1' *Journal of Laryngology*, **81**, 777–790.

Mawson, S. R., Adlington, P., Evans, M. (1968) 'A controlled study evaluation of adeno-tonsillectomy in children.' Part 2. *Journal of Laryngology* **82**, 963–979.

McCall, M. G., Acheson, E. D. (1968) 'Respiratory disease in infants.' *Journal of Chronic Diseases*, **21**, 349–359.

McKee, W. J. E. (1963) '1. A controlled study of the effects of tonsillectomy and adenoidectomy in children. 2. The part played by adenoidectomy in the combined operation of tonsillectomy with adenoidectomy (a 2nd part of a controlled study in children).' *British Journal of Preventive and Social Medicine*, **17**, 49–69, 133–140.

McKendrick, M. W., Gully, P. R., Geddes, A. M. (1980) 'Protection against pertussis by immunisation.' *British Medical Journal*, **4**, 1390–1391.

McKeown, T. (1979) *'The Role of Medicine; Dream, Mirage or Nemesis.'* Oxford: Blackwell.

McNicol, K. N., Williams, H. E. (1973) 'Spectrum of asthma in children 1. clinical and physiological components.' *British Medical Journal*, **4**, 7–11.

McNicol, K. N., Williams, H. E., Allan, J., McAndrews, I. (1973) 'Spectrum of asthma in children. no. 3 physchological and social components.' *British Medical Journal*, **4**, 16–20.

McRae, K. N., Fergusson, C. A., Lederman, R. S. (1973) 'The battered child syndrome.' *C.M.A. Journal*, **108**, 859–866.

Melia, R. J. W., Florey, C. du V., Altman, D. G., Swan, A. V. (1977) 'Association between gas cooking and respiratory disease in children.' *British Medical Journal*, **2**, 149–152.

Mellinger, G. D., Manheimer, D. I. (1967) 'An exposure coping model of accident liability among children.' *Journal of Health and Social Behaviour*, **8**, 96–107.

Menninger, W. C. (1947) 'Psychosomatic medicine, somatic reactions.' *Psychosomatic Medicine*, **9**, 92–7.

Michaels, R. H., Rogers, K. D. (1971) 'A sex difference in immunologic responsiveness.' *Pediatrics*, **47**, 120.

Miller, D. L., Ross, E. M., Alderslade, R., Bellman, M. H., Rawson, N. S. B. (1981) 'Pertussis immunisation and serious acute neurological illness in children.' *British Medical Journal*, **2**, 1595–1599.

Miller, F. J. W., Court, S. D. M., Walton, W. S., Knox, E. G. (1960) *Growing up in Newcastle upon Tyne.* London: Oxford University Press for the Nuffield Foundation.

Miller, H. C., Hassanein, K., Hensleigh, P. A. (1978) 'Maternal factors in the incidence of low birthweight infants among black and white mothers.' *Pediatric Research*, **12**, 1016–1019.

Mitchell, R. G., Dawson, B. (1973) 'Educational and social characteristics of children with asthma.' *Archives of Disease in Childhood*, **48**, 467–471.

MMWR. (1981) Recommendations of the Immunization Practices Advisory Committee. 'Diptheria, tetanus and pertussis: guidelines for vaccine prophylaxis and other preventive measures.' *MMWR*, **30**, 392–408.

Montgomery-Smith, J. (1974) 'Incidence of atopic disease.' *Medical Clinics of North America*, **58**, 3–24.

Moore, B., O'Donnell, B. (1979) 'Fatal road traffic accidents in Dublin children.' *Journal of the Irish Medical Association*, **72**, 58–61.

Morrison-Smith, J. (1961) 'Prevalence and natural history of asthma in school children.'

British Medical Journal, **1**, 711–713.

Mortimer, J. G. (1980) 'Acute water intoxication as another unusual manifestation of child abuse.' *Archives of Disease in Childhood*, **55**, 401–403.

Moss, H. (1967) 'Sex, age and status as determinants of mother infant interaction.' *Merril-Palmer Quarterly*, **13**, 19–36.

Murdock, R., Eva, J. (1974) 'Home accidents to children under 15 years: survey of 910 cases.' *British Medical Journal*, **3**, 103–106.

Murphy, J. F., Jenkins, J., Newcombe, R. G., Sibert, J. R. (1981) 'Objective birth data and the prediction of child abuse.' *Archives of Disease in Childhood*, **56**, 295–297.

National Council For One Parent Families (1982) 'Training Course Worksheet.'

Needleman, H. (1977) 'Effects of hearing loss from early recurrent otitis media on speech and language development.' In: Jaffe, B. (ed.), *Hearing Loss in Children*. Baltimore: University Park Press, pp. 640–649.

Nelson, K. B., Ellenberg, J. H. (1976) 'Predictors of epilepsy in children who have experienced febrile seizures.' *New England Journal of Medicine*, **295**, 1029–1033.

Nelson, K. B., Ellenberg, J. H. (1980) 'Seizures in early childhood.' *Developmental Medicine and Child Neurology*, **22**, 261–262.

Newson, J., Newson, E. (1968) *Four-Year-Olds in an Urban Community*. London: George Allen & Unwin.

Newson, J., Newson, E. (1970) *Four-Year-Olds in an Urban Community*. Harmondsworth: Penguin.

Newton, R. W., Webster, P. A. C., Binu, P. S., Maskrey, N., Phillips, A. B. (1979) 'Psychosocial stress in pregnancy and its relation to the onset of premature labour.' *British Medical Journal*, **2**, 411–413.

Nixon, H. H., Court, S. D. M. (1973) 'Non accidental injury in children.' *British Medical Journal*, **4**, 656–660.

Nowotny, M. (1976) 'Some aspects of community child health in an inner urban area.' *Child: Care, Health and Development*, **2**, 283–294.

Nyboe-Anderson, A., Lund-Anderson, C., Falk-Larsen, J., Juel-Christensen, N., Legros, J. J., Louis, H., Angelo, H., Molin, J. (1982) 'Suppressed prolactin but normal neurophysin levels in cigarette smoking, breast feeding women.' *Clinical Endocrinology*, **17**, 363–368.

Office of Population Censuses and Surveys (1970). *Classification of Occupations*. London: H.M.S.O.

Ogra, P. L. (1971) 'The effect of tonsillectomy and adenoidectomy on nasopharyngeal antibody responses to polio virus.' *New England Journal of Medicine*, **284**, 59–64.

Olatawura, M. O. (1973) 'Encopresis: a review of 32 cases.' *Acta Paediatrica Scandinavica*, **62**, 358–364.

Oppe, T. E. (1964) 'Medical problems of coloured immigrant children in Britain.' *Proceedings of The Royal Society of Medicine*, **57**, 321–323.

Oppel, W. C., Harper, P. A., Rider, R. V. (1968) a. 'The age of obtaining bladder control.' b. 'Social, psychological and neurological factors associated with nocturnal enuresis.' *Pediatrics*, **42**, 614–641.

Oppenheim, A. N. (1966) 'Questionnaire Design and Attitude Measurement.' London: Heinemann.

Osborn, G. R. (1968) Colloques Internationaux du Centre National de la Recherche Scientifique. Paris: Editions du Centre National de la Recherche Scientifique.

Osborn, A. F., Butler, N. R., Morris, A. C. (1984) *The Social Life of Britain's 5-Year-Olds*. London: Routledge & Kegan Paul.

Osborn, A. F., Carpenter, A. P. (1980) 'A rating of neighbourhood types.' *Clearing house for local authority social services research*. University of Birmingham, No. 3, 1–37.

Padilla, E. R., Rohsenow, D. J., Bergman, A. B. (1976) 'Predicting accident frequency in children.' *Pediatrics*, **58**, 223–226.

Palmer, S. R., Avery, A., Taylor, R. (1979) 'The influence of obstetric procedures and social and cultural factors on breast feeding rates at discharge from hospitals.' *Journal of Epidemiology and Community Health*, **33**, 248–252.

Pape, K. E., Buncie, R. J., Ashby, S., Fitzhardinge, P. M. (1978) 'The status at 2 years of low birthweight infants born in 1974 with birthweights of less than 1001g.' *Journal of Pediatrics*, **92**, 253–260.

Paradise, J. L. (1981) 'Otitis media during early life: how hazardous to development? A critical view of evidence.' *Pediatrics,* **68,** 869–873.

Partington, M. W. (1960) 'The importance of accident proneness in the aetiology of head injuries in childhood.' *Archives of Disease in Childhood,* **35,** 215–223.

Pasamanick, B. (1975) 'Ill health and child abuse.' *Lancet,* **2,** 550.

Patterson, G. R., Littman, R. A., Bricker, W. (1967) 'Assertive behaviour in children: a step towards a theory of aggression.' *Monographs of The Society for Research in Child Development,* **32,** No. 5.

Paulett, J. D., Tuckman, E. (1958) 'Onset enuresis.' *British Medical Journal,* **2,** 1266–1268.

Pearn, J. H., Wong, R. Y. K., Brown, J., Ching, Y. C., Bart, R., Hammar, S. (1979) 'Drowning and near drowning involving children : a 5 year total population study from the city and county of Honolulu. *American Journal of Public Health,* **69,** 450–454.

Pearson, R. C. M., Peckham, C. (1972) 'Preliminary findings at the age of 11 years on children in The National Child Development Study (1958 Cohort).' *Community Medicine,* **127,** 113–116.

Peckham, C., Butler, N. (1978) 'A national study of asthma in childhood.' *Journal of epidemiology and Community Health,* **32,** 79–85.

Peckham, C., Essen, J. (1976) 'Nocturnal enuresis in childhood.' *Developmental Medicine and Child Neurology,* **18,** 577–589.

Peckham, C. S., Sheridan, M. D., Butler, N. R. (1972) 'School attainment of 7-year-olds with hearing difficulties.' *Developmental Medicine and Child Neurology,* **14,** 592–302.

Peel, Sir J. (1969) Foreword. In: Butler, N. R., Alberman, E. D. (eds.) *Perinatal Problems.* Edinburgh: Livingstone E. & S.

Peltonen, M. L., Kasanen, A., Peltonen, T. E. (1955) 'Occurrence of allergic reactions in school children.' *Annals Paediatriae Fenniae,* **1,** 119–129.

Peters, T. (1985) 'A statistical investigation of risk indicators for perinatal outcome and early child development.' Ph.D. Thesis: University of Exeter.

Peters, T., Golding, J., Fryer, J., Lawrence, C., Butler, N. R., Chamberlain G. (1983) 'Plus ca change: a comparative analysis of predictors of birthweight.' *British Journal of Obstetrics and Gynaecology,* **90,** 1040–1045.

Peters, T. J., Golding, J., Lawrence, C. J., Fryer, J. G., Chamberlain, G. V. P., Butler, N. R. (1984) 'Delayed onset of regular respiration and subsequent development.' *Early Human Development,* **9,** 225–239.

Pionis, E. M. (1971) 'Family functioning and childhood accident occurrence.' *American Journal of Orthopsychiatry,* **47,** 250–263.

Pollard, J. A., Troy, V. G., Shanahan, T. A., Hobday, J. B. (1971) 'The prevalence of wheezing and other respiratory symptoms in school children aged 6 to 11 years from Perth, Western Australia.' *Medical Journal of Australia,* **2,** 521–523.

Pond, D. A., Ryle, A., Hamilton, M. (1963) 'Marriage and neurosis in a working class population.' *British Journal of Psychiatry,* **109,** 592–598.

Popay, J., Rimmer, L., Rossiter, C. (1983) *One Parent Families. Parents, Children and Public Policy.* London: Study Commission on the Family.

Pringle, M. L. K. (1965) *Deprivation and Education.* London: Longman.

Quinton, D., Rutter, M. (1976) 'Early hospital admissions and later disturbances of behaviour. An attempted replication of Douglas' findings.' *Developmental Medicine and Child Neurology,* **18,** 447–459.

Rantakallio, P. (1978) 'The effect of maternal smoking on birthweight and subsequent health of the child.' *Early Human Development,* **2,** 371–382.

Rashid, A., Mohammed, T., Stephens, W. P., Warrington, S., Berry, J. L., Maner, E. B. (1983) 'Vitamin D state of Asians living in Pakistan. *British Medical Journal,* **1,** 182–184.

Rawlinson (1983) M.D. Thesis.

Richardson, K., Hutchison, D., Peckham, C. S., Tibbenham, A. (1977) 'Audiometric thresholds of a national sample of British 16 year olds: a longitudinal study.' *Developmental Medicine and Child Neurology,* **19,** 797–802.

Richman, N. (1974) 'The effects of housing on preschool children and their mothers.' *Developmental Medicine and Child Neurology,* **16,** 53–58.

Richman, N. (1981) 'A community survey of characteristics of 1 to 2 year olds with sleep disruptions.' *Journal of the American Academy of Child Psychiatry,* **20,** 281–291.

Richman, N., Stevenson, J., Graham, P. (1975) 'Prevalence and patterns of psychological disturbance in children in primary age.' *Journal of Child Psychology and Psychiatry*, **6**, 101–113.

Roberts, J. C., Hawton, K. (1980) 'Child abuse and attempted suicide.' *Lancet*, **1**, 882.

Robinson, D. (1971) 'Becoming a patient: mothers' ideas about tonsillectomy.' *Medical Officer*, **125**, 37–41.

Rodgers, B. (1978) 'Feeding in infancy and later ability and attainment: a longitudinal study.' *Developmental Medicine and Child Neurology*, **20**, 421–426.

Rodgers, D., Tripp. J., Bentovim, A., Robinson, A., Berry, D., Goulding, R. (1976) 'Non accidental poisoning: an extended syndrome of child abuse.' *British Medical Journal*, **1**, 793–796.

Rowntree, G. (1950) 'Accidents among children under 2 years of age in Great Britain.' *Journal of Hygiene*, **48**, 323–337.

Rowntree, G. (1955) 'Early childhood in broken families.' *Population Studies*, **8**, 247–263.

Rush, D. (1983) Personal communication.

Rutter, M., Madge, N. (1976) *Cycles of Disadvantage: a Review of Research*. London: Heinemann.

Rutter, M., Tizzard, J., Whitmore, K. (1970) *Education, Health and Behaviour*. London: Longman.

Rutter, M., Yule, B., Morton, J., Bagley, C. (1975a) 'Children of West Indian immigrants. 3. Home circumstance and family patterns. *Journal of Child Psychology and Psychiatry*, **16**, 105–123.

Rutter, M., Yule, B., Quinton, D., Rowlands, O., Yule, W., Berger, M. (1975b) 'Attainment and adjustment in two geographical areas: 3. Some factors accounting for area differences.' *British Journal of Psychiatry*, **126**, 520-533.

Saarinen, U. M., Kajosaari, M., Backman, A., Siimes, M. A. (1979) 'Prolonged breast feeding as prophylaxis for atopic disease.' *Lancet*, **2**, 163–166.

Sackett, D. L. (1979) Bias in analytic research. *Journal of Chronic Diseases*, **32**, 51–63.

Said, G., Zalokar, J., Lellouch, J., Patois, E. (1978) 'Parental smoking related to adenoidectomy and tonsillectomy in children.' *Journal of Epidemiology and Community Health*, **32**, 97–101.

Salk, L., Grellong, B. A. (1974) 'Perinatal problems in the history of asthmatic children.' *American Journal of Diseases in Children*, **127**, 30–33.

Sargent, F. (1982) 'A history of ideas about weather and human health. Part IV. *Hippocrates Confirmed*. Hippocratic Heritage. Oxford: Pergamon Press.

Savage, D. C. L., Wilson, M. I., Ross, E. M., Fee, W. M. (1969) 'Asymptomatic bacteriura in girl entrants to Dundee primary schools.' *British Medical Journal*, **3**, 75–80.

Savage, E. P., Keefe, T. J., Tessari, J. D., Wheeler, H. W., Appelhans, F. M., Goes, E. A., Ford, S. A. (1981) 'A national study of chlorinated hydrocarbon insecticide residues in human milk.' *American Journal of Epidemiology*, **113**, 413–422.

Schulte, F. J., Stennert, E. (1978) 'Hearing defects in pre-term infants.' *Archives of Disease in Childhood*, **53**, 269–270.

Schulte, F. J., Stennert, E., Lenard, H. G. (1977) 'The ontogeny of sensory perception in pre-term infants.' *Pediatric Research*, **11**, 1027.

Sears, R. R., Maccoby, E. E., Levin, H. (1957) *Patterns of Childhood Rearing*. Evanston, Illinois: Row.

Segal, L. (1983) 'No turning back—Thatcherism, the family and the future.' In: Segal, L. (ed.), *What Is to be Done About the Family?* Harmondsworth: Penguin, pp. 215–231.

Shaffer, D. (1973) 'The association between enuresis and emotional disorder: a review of the literature.' In 'bladder control and enuresis' Kolvin, I., MacKeith, R. C., Meadow, S. R. (eds.), *Clinics in Developmental Medicine* 48–49. London: Spastics International Medical Publishers, pp. 118–136.

Shannon, R. S., Mann, J. N. O. V., Harper, E., Harnden, D. G., Morten, J. E. N., Herbert, A. (1982) 'Wilm's tumour and aniridia: clinical and cytogenetic features.' *Archives of Disease in Childhood*, **57**, 685–690.

Shaw, C. (1977) 'A comparison of the patterns of mother–baby interaction for a group of crying, irritable babies and a group of more amenable babies.' *Child: Care, Health and Development*, **3**, 1–12.

Shaw, G. B. (1944) 'Everbody's Political What's What? Chapter IX, p. 74.

Sheridan, M. D. (1972) 'Reported incidence of hearing loss in children of 7 years.'

Developmental Medicine and Child Neurology, **14**, 296–303.

Sheridan, M. D., Peckham, C. S. (1978) 'Follow up to 16 years, of school children who had marked speech defects at 7 years.' *Child: Care, Health and Development*, **4**, 145–157.

Sibert, J. R. (1975) 'Stress in families of children who have ingested poisons.' *British Medical Journal*, **3**, 87–89.

Sibert, J. R., Minchom, P. E., Craft, A. W., Jackson, R. H., George, A. M. (1979) 'Child resistant containers really are effective.' *Lancet*, **2**, 522.

Sibert, J. R., Newcombe, R. G. (1977) 'Accidental ingestion of poisons.' *Postgraduate Medical Journal*, **53**, 254–256.

Sibinga, M. S., Friedman, C. J. (1971) 'Restraint and speech.' *Pediatrics*, **48**, 116–122.

Silva, P. A., Buckfield, P., Spears, G. F. (1978) 'Some maternal and child development characteristics associated with breast feeding: a report from The Dunedin Multidisciplinary Child Development Study.' *Australian Paediatric Journal*, **14**, 265–268.

Simpson, R. (1982) 'How effective are our child health clinics?' *British Medical Journal*, **1**, 284, 820.

Simpson, W. J. (1957) 'A preliminary report on cigarette smoking and the incidence of prematurity.' *American Journal of Obstetrics and Gynecology*, **73**, 808–815.

Smialek, J. E., Smialek, P. Z., Spitz, W. U. (1977) 'Accidental bed deaths in infants due to unsafe sleeping situations.' *Clinical Pediatrics*, **16**, 1031–1036.

Smith, D. J. (1977) *Racial Disadvantage in Britain*. Harmondsworth: Penguin.

Smith, S. M., Hanson, R. (1974) '134 battered children: a medical and psychological study.' *British Medical Journal*, **3**, 666–671.

Smith, S. M., Hanson, R., Noble, S. (1973) 'Parents of battered babies: a controlled study.' *British Medical Journal*, **4**, 388–391.

Smith, S., Honigsberger, L., Smith, C. A. (1973) 'E.E.G. and personality factors in baby batterers.' *British Medical Journal*, **3**, 20–22.

Snook, H. (1977) 'The use of Glasgow hospital beds by children under the age of 1 year.' *Child: Care, Health and Development*, **3**, 165–173.

Sobel, R. (1970) 'The psychiatric implications of accidental poisoning in childhood.' *Pediatric Clinics of North America*, **17**, 653–685.

Spence, J., Walton, W. S., Miller, F. J. W., Court, S. D. M. (1954) *A Thousand Families in Newcastle-upon-tyne*. London: Oxford University Press.

Stacey, M., Dearden, R., Pill, R., Robinson, D. (1970) '*Hospital Children and Their Families: the Report of a Pilot Study.*' London: Routledge & Kegan Paul.

Stein, Z. A., Susser, M. W. (1967) 'The social dimensions of a symptom: a socio-medical study of enuresis.' *Social Science Medicine*, **1**, 183–201.

Stein, Z. A., Susser, M. W., Wilson, A. E. (1965) 'Families of enuretic children. 1. Family type and age. 2. Family culture, structure and organization. *Developmental Medicine and Child Neurology*, **7**, 658–676.

Stephenson, J. B. P. (1980) 'Convulsions after pertussis immunisation are not evidence of encephalopathy.' *Developmental Medicine and Child Neurology*, **22**, 266–267.

Stewart-Brown, S., Haslum, M., Butler, N. R. (1983) 'Evidence for an increasing prevalence of diabetes mellitus in childhood.' *British Medical Journal*, **286**, 1855–1857.

Sundell, C. (1922) 'Sleeplessness in infants.' *Practitioner*, **109**, 89–92.

Sweetnam, W. P. (1974) 'Accidental poisoning in children.' *British Medical Journal*, **2**, 331.

Taitz, L. S. (1971) 'Infantile over nutrition among artificially fed infants in the Sheffield region.' *British Medical Journal*, **1**, 315–316.

Taylor, B. (1977) 'Breast versus bottle feeding.' *New Zealand Medical Journal*, **85**, 235–238.

Taylor, B., Golding, J., Wadsworth, J., Butler, N. R. (1982) 'Breast feeding, bronchitis and admissions for lower-respiratory illness and gastroenteritis during the first five years.' *Lancet*, **1**, 1227–1229.

Taylor, B., Wadsworth, J., (1984) Breast feeding and child development at five years. *Developmental Medicine and Child Neurology*, **26**, 73–80.

Terry, P. B., Condie, R. G., Settatree, R. S. (1980) 'Analysis of ethnic differences in perinatal statistics.' *British Medical Journal*, **4**, 1307–1308.

Thompson, R. J., Cappelman, M. W., Zeitschel, K. A. (1979) 'Neonatal behaviour of infants of adolescent mothers.' *Developmental Medicine and Child Neurology*, **21**, 474–482.

Tissier, J., Golding, J. (1984) 'Bedwetting at 5 years of age.' *Health Visitor*, **56**, 333–335.

Titterington, D. M., Murray, G. D., Murray, L. S., Spiegelhalter, D. J., Skene, A. M., Habbema, J. D. F., Gelpke, G. J. (1981) 'Comparison of discrimination techniques applied to a complex data set of head injured patients.' *Journal of the Royal Statistics Society A*, **144** part 2.

Tokuhata, G. K., Colflesh, V. G., Digon, E., Ramaswamy, K., Mann, L. A., Hartman, T. (1974) 'Childhood injuries associated with consumer products.' *Preventative Medicine*, **3**, 245–267.

Truby-King, Sir F. (1937) *Feeding and Care of Baby*. London: Oxford Unversity Press.

Valman, H. B. (1980a) 'Respiratory infection in the older infant.' *British Medical Journal*, **2**, 1438–1442.

Valman, H. B. (1980b) 'Contraindications to immunisation.' *British Medical Journal*, **2**, 1138–1139.

Van Den Berg, B. J., Yerushalmy, J. (1969) 'Studies on convulsive disorders in young children.' *Pediatric Research*, **3**, 298–304.

Veltri, R. W., Sprinkle, P. M., Keller, S. A., Chicklo, J. M. (1972) 'Immunoglobulin changes in pediatric otolaryngic patient sample subsequent to tonsillectomy and adenoidectomy.' *Journal of Laryngology and Otology*, **86**, 905–916.

Venters, G. A., Bloor, M. J. (1974) 'A review of investigations into adenotonsillectomy.' *British Journal of Preventative and Social Medicine*, **28**, 1–9.

Vesselinova-Jenkins, C. K., Newcombe, R. G., Gray, O. P., Skone, J. F., Howell, H. L., Lennox, M., Hine, D. J., Jenkins, P. M., Munro, J. A. (1978) 'The effects of immunisation upon the natural history of pertussis: a family study in the Cardiff area.' *Journal of Epidemiology and Community Health*, **32**, 194–199.

Vianna, N. J., Lawrence, C. E., Davies, J. N. P., Arbuckle, J., Harris, S., Marani, W., Wilkinson, J. (1980) 'Tonsillectomy and childhood Hodgkin's Disease.' *Lancet*, **2**, 338–339.

Vuori, E., Tyllinen, K., Paganus, A. (1977) 'The occurrence and origin of DDT in human milk.' *Acta Paediatrica Scandinavica*, **66**, 761–765.

Wadsworth, J. (1983) Personal communications to M. Haslum.

Wadsworth, M. E. J. (1979) *Roots of Delinquency: Infancy, Adolescence and Crime*. Oxford: Robertson, M.

Walker, W. A. (1975) 'Antigen absorption from the small intestine and gastrointestinal disease.' *Pediatric Clinics in North America*, **22**, 731–746.

Watkins, C. J., Burton, P., Leeder, S., Sittampalam, Y., Wever, A. M., Wiggins, R. (1982) 'Doctor diagnosis and maternal recall of lower respiratory illness.' *International Journal of Epidemiology*, **11**, 62–66.

Watkins, C. J., Leeder, S. R., Corkhill, R. T. (1979) 'The relationship between breast and bottle feeding and respiratory illness in the first year of life.' *Journal of Epidemiology and Community Health*, **33**, 180–182.

Wilson, J. M. G. (1978) 'Adeno-tonsillectomy: a study of Scottish hospitals in-patient data.' *Health Bulletin (Edinburgh)*, **36**, 5–13.

Winter, S. T., Lilos, P. (1974) 'Prediction of hospitalization during infancy. Scoring the risk of admission.' *Pediatrics*, **53**, 716–720.

Wolff, S. (1981) *Children under Stress*. Harmondsworth: Penguin Books.

Wolff, S., Acton, W. P. (1968) 'Characteristics of parents of disturbed children.' *British Journal of Psychiatry*, **114**, 593–601.

Wood, C. B. S. (1973) 'Immunological factors and tonsillectomy.' *Proceedings of the Royal Society of Medicine*, **66**, 411–413.

Woodard, B. T., Ferguson, B. B., Wilson, D. J. (1976) 'DDT levels in milk or rural indigent blacks.' *American Journal of Diseases of Children*, **130** No. 4, 400–403.

Woolcock. A. J., Leeder, S. R., Peat, J. K., Blackburn, C. R. B. (1979) 'The influence of lower respiratory illness in infancy and childhood and subsequent cigarette smoking on lung function in Sydney school children.' *American Review of Respiratory Diseases*, **120**, 5–15.

Wright, I. (1978) 'Tonsils and adenoids: what do we find?' *Journal of the Royal Society of Medicine*, **71**, 112–116.

Wynn, A. (1976) 'Health care systems for pre-school children.' *Proceedings of the Royal Society of Medicine*, **69**, 340–343.

Yarnell, J. W. G., St. Leger, A. S. (1981) 'Respiratory morbidity and lung function in school children aged 7–11 years in South Wales and the West of England.' *Thorax*, **36**, 842–846.
Zaleski, A., Gerrard, J. W., Shokeir, M. H. K. (1973) 'Nocturnal enuresis: the importance of a small bladder capacity.' In: Kolvin, I., MacKeith, R. C., Meadow, S. R. (eds.) *Bladder Control and Enuresis. Clinics in Developmental Medicine*, Nos. 48/49. S.I.M.P., London: Heinemann.
Zinkin, P. M., Cox, C. A. (1976) 'Child health clinics and inverse care laws: evidence from a longitudinal study of 1878 pre-school children. *British Medical Journal*, **3**, 411–413.

Child Health and Education in the Seventies

A national study in England, Wales and Scotland of all children born 5th—11th April 1970

Under the auspices of the University of Bristol
and the National Birthday Trust Fund

Director: Professor Neville R. Butler, MD, FRCP, DCH

Research team:
 N. R. Butler
 A. F. Osborn, BA
 B. C. Howlett, BSc, FSS, MBCS
 S. F. O. Dowling, BSc, MB, BS
 M. C. Fraser, SRN, SCM, HV Tutor Cert.

Department of Child Health Research Unit
University of Bristol
Bristol   BS2 8BH

Tel. Bristol 27745/22041

In association with:
 Area Health Authorities in England and Wales
 Health Boards in Scotland

Co-sponsors:
 Health Visitors' Association

CONFIDENTIAL

HOME INTERVIEW QUESTIONNAIRE

Health District Code   Child's Local Serial Number   Child's Central Survey Number

`1—5`
`6`
`0 4`
`7,8`
`9—11`
`12,13`
`14—17`
`18`
`19,20`
`21—24`

Details of child born 5th—11th April 1970
If twins use separate questionnaire for each.   Please use block capitals.

Full name of the Child .... **Sex** ....

Singleton or twin, specify .... **Date of birth** .... **April 1970**

Present home address in full ....

....

Address of child's present placement if living away from home. *Please specify if hospital, residential home, etc.*

....

....

Child's National Health Service Number ....

N.H.S. Doctor with whom child is registered. *If not registered, put NONE.*

 Name ....

 Full address of practice ....

 ....

Full home address of mother at time she gave birth to child.
If not known, put NOT KNOWN. If same home address as above, put AS ABOVE.

....

....

If born abroad, give approximate date child came to live in this country ....

Mother's maiden name ....
(These details are needed for matching purposes only)

Address of place of birth. *Please specify whether maternity hospital, G.P. unit, home, etc.*

....

....

NOTES

1. Please read "Survey Notes and Information" in conjunction with this questionnaire.

2. Throughout the questionnaire the study child is designated by the letter N.

3. It is important that no question should remain unanswered without explanation.

SECTION A FAMILY COMPOSITION

A.1 (a) People in the household

A household consists of a group of people who all live at the same address and who are all catered for by the same person.

List below **all** the members of this household. Include the study child, N, the present parents and others, e.g. relatives or lodgers, who are members of this household. Exclude any who are only at home for short periods; enter these in table **(b)** below.

Relationship to N (e.g. father, step-brother) or status in the household (e.g. lodger)	Surname	First name(s)	Sex	Date of birth
1. Study child—N				/ 4 / 70
2.				/ /
3.				/ /
4.				/ /
5.				/ /
6.				/ /
7.				/ /
8.				/ /
9.				/ /
10.				/ /

(b) List below any members of the family not included in the above table, for example, those who are only home for holidays or leave, and enquire or state from your own knowledge the reason for absence, for example at residential school, or working away.

Relationship to N	Surname	First name(s)	Sex	Date of birth	Reason for absence from home

A.2 (a) What is the relationship to N of the person now acting as his/her mother?

Relationship to N

Natural mother 1
Mother by legal adoption 2
Stepmother 3
Foster mother 4
Grandmother .5
Elder sister 6
Cohabitee of father 7
Other mother figure, specify 8
. . . .
No mother figure 9

(b) please give reason(s) for any past changes in N's situation, e.g. family changes, mother died, etc.

. . . .
. . . .
. . . .

(c) If N is not now living with natural mother, i.e. 2—9 ringed, please ask when this situation began.

             Month   Year

Situation began . . . .

A.3 (a) What is the relationship to N of the person now acting as his/her father?

Relationship to N

Natural father 1
Father by legal adoption 2
Stepfather 3
Foster father .4
Grandfather 5
Elder brother .6
Cohabitee of mother 7
Other father figure, specify 8
. . . .
No father figure 9

(b) please give reason(s) for any past changes in N's situation, e.g. family changes, father died, etc.

. . . .
. . . .
. . . .

(c) If N is not now living with natural father, i.e. 2—9 ringed, please ask when this situation began.

             Month   Year

Situation began . . . .

25—29

30—34

Except in Q's B.1 to B.4 and B.23 where information is specifically required about N's natural mother or father, the terms "father" or "present father" are used to denote the present father figure identified in Q. A.3(a). The terms "mother" or "present mother" are used to denote the present mother figure identified in Q. A.2(a).

SECTION B MEDICAL HISTORY AND PRESENT HEALTH

B.1 Enter obstetric details on the study child, N, and on all liveborn and stillborn children born **subsequently** to N's natural mother. Include also children no longer living with their natural mother. Record each member of twin pair separately. Exclude miscarriages. (Some children in this table will be included also in table A.1 on page opposite).

Name	Sex	Date of birth	Birthweight—lbs.—ozs.	Gestation — Over 3 weeks early	At term (37–41 weeks)	Over 2 weeks late	Not known	Method of delivery — Vertex	Breech	Forceps	Caesarean	Other	Not known	Survival — Alive now	Died 7 days and over	Died under 7 days	Stillborn	Not known	If died, cause of death
N................	....	/4/70	/	1	2	3	0	1	2	3	4	5	0	1	2	3	4	0	....
....	....	/ /	/	1	2	3	0	1	2	3	4	5	0	1	2	3	4	0	....
....	....	/ /	/	1	2	3	0	1	2	3	4	5	0	1	2	3	4	0	....
....	....	/ /	/	1	2	3	0	1	2	3	4	5	0	1	2	3	4	0	....
....	....	/ /	/	1	2	3	0	1	2	3	4	5	0	1	2	3	4	0	....
....	....	/ /	/	1	2	3	0	1	2	3	4	5	0	1	2	3	4	0	....

B.2 How soon after N's birth did the mother first start to have regular contact with N, to hold and/or feed, not just look at?

Within 24 hours of birth 1

Between 25 and 48 hours after birth 2

On the third day or later, i.e. more than 48 hrs. after birth.............. 3 **(35)**

Not known 0

If **on third day or later**, how many days after N's birth did regular contact start? ➔ .... ☐☐ **(36,37)**

e.g. for third day enter **0 3** *, if number of days not known enter* **9 9**

Please give reason(s) for delay in regular contact ....

....

B.3 After regular contact was established, was there any period of 24 hours or more during the first month of N's life when mother was not in normal contact with N, e.g. to hold and/or feed?

No separation(s) of 24 hours or more 1

Mother and N out of contact for 24 hours or more .... 2 **(38)**

Cannot remember 3

Not known 0

If **separated**, give total duration of separation in completed days ➔ .... ☐☐ **(39,40)**

e.g. for 2¾ days enter **0 2** *, if number of days not known enter* **9 9**

Give reason(s) for separation(s) ....

....

B.4 Was N breast fed partly or wholly, even for a few days?

Yes —

for less than 1 month 1

for 1 month or more but less than 3 months 2

for 3 months or more 3

Yes but cannot remember for how long .... 4 **(41)**

No, was not breast fed at all 5

Not known 0

B.5 At what ages did N receive immunisation, against what diseases and where?

Enter everything given for each attendance, e.g. if on first attendance given triple and polio, ring 1, 2, 3, 4. If more than six attendances for immunisation please continue on back page.

Attendance	N's age in months	Diseases immunised against — Diphtheria	Tetanus	Whooping-cough	Poliomyelitis	Smallpox*	Measles	B.C.G.	Other	Not known	Where given — G.P.'s Surgery	Child Health Clinic	Other place	Not known
First att.	....	1	2	3	4	5	6	7	8	0	1	2	3	0
Second att.	....	1	2	3	4	5	6	7	8	0	1	2	3	0
Third att.	....	1	2	3	4	5	6	7	8	0	1	2	3	0
Fourth att.	....	1	2	3	4	5	6	7	8	0	1	2	3	0
Fifth att.	....	1	2	3	4	5	6	7	8	0	1	2	3	0
Sixth att.	....	1	2	3	4	5	6	7	8	0	1	2	3	0

*Please include smallpox vaccination, although now not recommended nationally.

B.6 Has N ever been seen at any of the following places for reasons specified, and if so at what ages, if known.

Ring all that apply in each row	Never seen	Seen at age:							Not known if ever seen
At—		48m+	36–47m	24–35m	12–23m	6–11m	under 6 mth	not known	
(a) Home by H.V. for any reason	1	2	3	4	5	6	7	8	0
(b) Child Health Clinic for any reason	1	2	3	4	5	6	7	8	0
(c) G.P. surgery or health centre for devel. screening	1	2	3	4	5	6	7	8	0
(d) Hospital birth follow-up clinic	1	2	3	4	5	6	7	8	0
(e) Assessment Centre or clinic for handicap	1	2	3	4	5	6	7	8	0

42—45

46—49

50,51

B.7 Has N ever been separated from his/her mother or mother substitute for one month or more? Exclude N's hospital admissions and check these are detailed in B.9.

Yes 1
No 2   **(52)**
Not known 0

If yes, give total number of separations of one month or more, excluding N's hospital admission(s) ➡ ....   **(53,5**

e.g. if 2 separations enter | 0 | 2 | *if number of separations not known enter* | 9 | 9 |

Please give details below for all separations of **one month or over**. Exclude all N's hospital admissions. *If more than three separations, continue on back page.*

	First	Second	Third
Age (years and months)			
Reason for separation			
Number of months (and weeks) separated			
Place of care of N?*			
Was the person looking after N known to him/her?			
Was N separated also from father?			

55—59

60—62

*Place of care: State if in child's own home, other's home, institutional placement, or specify if elsewhere.

B.8 Did the mother herself, as far as she can remember, ever spend more than a short time away from her parents as a child?   *Ring all that apply*

Yes —
  fostered/in care 1
  other reason(s), specify 2
  ....   **(63)**
No, never spent more than a short time away from parents 3
Not known 0

B.9 Has N ever been in hospital overnight or longer for any reason whatsoever? Exclude initial stay in maternity home/hospital.

Yes 1
No 2   **(64)**
Not known 0

If yes, give total number of hospital admissions overnight or longer ➡ ....   **(65,66**

Please give details below for every hospital admission.

If more than three admissions, continue on back page.

	First	Second	Third
Age (years and months)			
Diagnosis and nature of all special procedures, including operations			
Number of nights in hospital			
Name and address of hospital in full			
Type of ward and specify if children only admitted			

67—70

71—73

1—5

6

| 0 | 5 |
7,8

B.10 Has N ever attended a hospital outpatient department or any other specialist clinic?

Yes 1

No 2 (9)

Not known 0

If **yes**, please give details below for each condition or illness resulting in attendance(s) at out-patients or specialist clinic.

If more than three conditions or illnesses, continue on back page.

	First	Second	Third
Age at first attendance (years and months)			
Total number of attendances			
Diagnosis and treatment			
Name and address of department, hospital or clinic, **in full.**			

10—13

14—16

B.11 Please enquire or state from your own knowledge whether N has been seen by any of the following since the fourth birthday and/or previous to fourth birthday.

Ring all that apply in each row.	Yes, after 4th b'day	Yes, before 4th b'day	No never	Not known	
Seen by a general practitioner*—					
at surgery/health centre	1	2	3	0	(17)
at home visit	1	2	3	0	(18)
Seen by dentist—					
for inspection, not therapy	1	2	3	0	(19)
for filling(s), extraction(s), etc.	1	2	3	0	(20)
Seen by doctor for routine medical exam.					
in nursery or school situation, specify	1	2	3	0	(21)
Seen by speech therapist—	1	2	3	0	(22)
age first seen.............yrs............mths					
Seen by child guidance clinic	1	2	3	0	(23)
age first seen.............yrs............mths					
Problem/diagnosis............................					

*For medical reasons, not for development screening or immunisation.

B.12 Has N had any of the following in the past year and/or previous to past year?

Ring all that apply in each row.	Yes, after 4th b'day	Yes, before 4th b'day	No never	Not known	
Operations					
(a) Tonsillectomy or T's & A's	1	2	3	0	(24)
(b) Adenoidectomy alone	1	2	3	0	(25)
(c) Circumcision	1	2	3	0	(26)
(d) Hernia operation	1	2	3	0	(27)
(e) Appendicectomy	1	2	3	0	(28)
(f) Any other operation, namely	1	2	3	0	(29)
....					
Medical Conditions					
(g) Eczema	1	2	3	0	(30)
(h) Hay fever or sneezing attacks	1	2	3	0	(31)
(i) Ear discharge (pus not wax)	1	2	3	0	(32)
(j) Repeated sore throats requiring medical attention	1	2	3	0	(33)
(k) Habitual snoring or mouth breathing	1	2	3	0	(34)
(l) Bronchitis	1	2	3	0	(35)
(m) Pneumonia	1	2	3	0	(36)
(n) Meningitis or encephalitis	1	2	3	0	(37)
(o) Hearing difficulty (suspected or confirmed)*	1	2	3	0	(38)
(p) Any vision problem (except squint) (suspected or confirmed)*	1	2	3	0	(39)

*If any suspected or confirmed hearing or eyesight problem, please give details below.

....

....

B.13 Were there any of the following difficulties with N when he/she was a baby (i.e. under 6 months of age)?

		Yes	No	Not known	
(a)	Excessive crying	1	2	0	(40)
(b)	Frequent feeding problems	1	2	0	(41)
(c)	Frequent sleeping difficulty at night	1	2	0	(42)

B.14 Has N ever had an accident requiring medical advice or treatment?
Please include accidents in the road, home and elsewhere, accidental ingestion of medicines/poisons, burns/scalds, fractures, eye injuries, near-drowning, bad cuts and other injuries, with or without unconsciousness, and non-accidental injuries.

Ring all that apply.

Yes —

accidental swallowing of medicines or poisons	1
burn(s), scald(s)	2
road traffic accident(s)	3
Accident resulting in unconsciousness	4
other accidents	5
No accident	6
Not known	0

43,44

If yes, please state total number of accidents specified above ⟶ ...... (45,46)

e.g if 3 accidents enter | 0 | 3 |

Please give details of every "accident"
Check that all "accidents" resulting in hospital admission or outpatient/casualty attendance are also included in B.9 and B.10 respectively. If more than four "accidents", continue on back page.

	First	Second	Third	Fourth
Age (years and months)				
Where did it happen? (Road, home, school, etc.)				
What happened?*				
Description of "injuries" (e.g. burn/scald, fracture, head injury with unconsciousness, etc.)				
Part(s) of body involved (head eyes, limbs, etc.)				
Where treated? (G.P., Casualty, Inpatient)				
Treatment, including stitches, operation(s), plaster cast(s), traction, etc.				
Name and address of hospital **in full**, if attended or admitted				

47–49

50–53

*If ingestion of medicines/poisons, give name of substance.

B.15 Has N ever had one or more attacks or bouts in which he/she had wheezing on the chest, regardless of the cause?

Yes	1
No	2 (54)
Not known	0

If **yes**, please complete the following details.

(a) Age at first or only attack in which he/she wheezed on the chest: ....years .... mths

55–57

(b) How many attacks occurred:

(a) in first 12 months of life? ⟶ .... (58,59)

(b) between first and fourth birthdays? ⟶ .... (60,61)

(c) since fourth birthday? ⟶ .... (62,63)

(c) Number of times ever admitted to hospital with any wheezing in the chest, whatever the cause ⟶ ..... (64,65)

(d) Please describe what the mother was told about the diagnosis in her own words ....

....

66

Check whether there have been any hospital admission(s) or out-patient attendance(s) for the above, if so, make sure they are included in B.9 and B.10 respectively.

B.16 Has N ever had any form of convulsion, fit, seizure or other turn in which consciousness was lost, or any part of the body made abnormal movements?

Yes 1
No, never 2   **(67)**
Not known 0

If yes,

(a) from health visitor's and mother's knowledge, and from records if possible, please give the most accurate diagnosis of the attack(s).

Ring all that apply

Epilepsy 1
Febrile convulsion(s) 2
Fainting, blackout(s) 3
Other diagnosis, namely 4   **68,69**

....
Not known 0

(b) please ask mother to describe the **first attack**

   (i) form it took ....

   ....

   (ii) how soon seen by G.P., or admitted, if at all ....

   ....

(c) please ask mother to describe **subsequent attack(s)**, if any.

   (i) form they took if different from above ....

   ....

   (ii) investigations, if any ....

   (iii) medication and dates ....

   ....

(d) give number of convulsions, fits or seizures in each agegroup specified below.

	First four weeks	1–12 months	Over 1 yr under 2	Over 2 under 3	Over 3 under 4	Over 4 years
Number of attacks						

70–72

73–75

Check whether there have been any hospital admission(s) or out-patient attendance(s) for the above, if so, make sure they are included in B.9 and B.10 respectively.

B.17 Has N ever worn or been prescribed glasses?

Yes —
  still has to wear them 1
  but does not have to wear them now 2   **(76)**
No 3
Not known 0

B.18 Has N ever had a squint?

Yes —
  now 1
  in past but not now 2
No, never 3   **(77)**
Not known 0

If **yes**, what treatment was given?

Ring all that apply

Medical advice — "No treatment needed" 1
Patch over one eye 2
Glasses 3
Eye exercises 4   **1—10**
Operation 5
Treatment advised, but not known what 6
Never attended for advice or treatment 7
Not known 0

B.19 Has N ever had a stammer or stutter or any other difficulty with speech?

	Stammer or stutter	Other speech difficulty
Yes, at present—		
mild	1	1
severe	2	2
Yes, in past but not now	3	3
No	4	4
Not known	0	0

1—5

6

0 6
7,8

9,10

If ever difficulty in speech, other than stammer or stutter, give details

....

....

BTF-N

B.20 Do people outside N's household easily understand what he/she says?
If N's main language not English, ring 1.

N's main language not English 1
All or nearly all of N's speech is understood outside immediate family 2
Some of N's speech understood outside immediate family 3
Hardly any of N's speech understood outside immediate family 4 (11)
N's speech understood only by immediate family 5
Even immediate family have difficulty in understanding N's speech 6
Other answer, namely 7
Not known if others understand N 0

B.21 From the health visitor's knowledge, observation and from records, has N ever been diagnosed as having any congenital abnormality or suspected congenital abnormality?

Ring all that apply

Yes –

Mongol 1
Spina bifida (meningomyelocele) 2
Hydrocephalus 3
Hare-lip 4
Cleft palate 5
Congenital heart condition (diagnosed) 6
Suspected congenital heart condition (murmur, etc.) .... 7 | 12-14 |
Skin naevus (portwine, strawberry, etc.) 8
Any other congenital abnormality, specify 9
....
No, none of the above 0

If **yes**, please describe abnormalities ....
....

B.22 From the health visitor's knowledge and observations, and where necessary from available records, does N have any physical or mental disability or handicap, or any other condition interfering with normal everyday life or which might be a problem at school?

Yes –

but no real handicap 1
mild handicap 2
severe handicap .... 3 | 15 |
No disability or handicap 4
Not known 0

If **yes**, (a) please give following details

Actual diagnosis ....
....

Effect on home or school life, if any .... | 16 |
....

(b) indicate into which of the following categories the condition, handicap or disability falls

Ring all that apply

Visual defect 1
Hearing defect 2
Speech defect 3
Mental handicap or disability 4
Emotional problem 5
Motor/locomotor problem .... 6 | 17-19 |
Respiratory problem 7
Severe congenital condition 8
Severe acquired condition (e.g. malignancy) 9
Other condition, specify 0
....

B.23 Has N's natural mother or natural father or any brothers or sisters of N's ever had any of the following?

Ring all that apply in each column	Natural mother	Natural father	Sibling(s)
Asthma	1	1	1
Hayfever	2	2	2
Eczema	3	3	3
Late reader, i.e. not reading by 7 years	4	4	4
Poor reader or non-reader at present	5	5	5
Convulsion(s) or fit(s)	6	6	6
Bedwetting, after 5 years of age	7	7	7
Late in learning to speak	8	8	8
None of above	9	9	9
No siblings	—	—	10

| 20-22 |
| 23-25 |
| 26-28 |

SECTION C TELEVISION VIEWING AND READING

C.1 Does N ever watch television at home?

Yes —
almost every day 1
occasionally .... 2 **(29)**
No, never 3
Not known 0

If N never watches TV proceed to C.6

C.2 Complete the following details of N's television viewing at home in the past seven days, by ringing all appropriate numbers for each day. Start with yesterday and go back day by day through the week.

Ring all that apply for each day.	Mon	Tue	Wed	Thur	Fri	Sat	Sun
Morning (e.g. before 1 pm)	1	1	1	1	1	1	1
Early afternoon (e.g. 1 pm—4 pm)	2	2	2	2	2	2	2
Late afternoon (e.g. 4 pm—6 pm)	3	3	3	3	3	3	3
Early evening (e.g. 6 pm—9 pm)	4	4	4	4	4	4	4
Late evening (e.g. after 9 pm)	5	5	5	5	5	5	5
Did not watch TV that day	6	6	6	6	6	6	6
Not known	0	0	0	0	0	0	0

30—33
34—37
38—41
42,43
44—47

C.3 Give total number of hours N watched each day in the past seven days

	Mon	Tue	Wed	Thur	Fri	Sat	Sun
Enter hours watched							

48—50

Enter 0 for any day on which N watched TV under 1 hour or not at all. If not known on any day, enter NK

Is this the usual amount of TV N watches?

Yes 1
No .... 2 **(51)**
Not known 0

If **no**, how many hours a day on average does he/she usually watch TV? ⟶ .... ☐ **(52)**

If less than 1 hour a day enter ☐0☐

C.4 What **types** of TV programmes does N watch at home?
Ring all that apply.

Children's programmes (e.g. Playschool, Sesame Street, etc.) 1
Cartoons 2
Thriller/dramatic programmes (e.g. cowboy, gangster, science fiction, war films, etc.) 3
Comedy programmes/series 4
Competition/quiz programmes (e.g. Double Your Money, Golden Shot, etc.) 5
Sport .... 6 *53—55*
News programmes 7
Documentary programmes (e.g. animal, travel films, etc.) 8
Other types of programmes, please give details 9
....

C.5 Which is N's favourite TV programme?

Specify title or series N likes best ....

56,57

C.6 Ring in column A all who have read to N at home at least once in the past 7 days.
Ring in column B the one person who reads to N most often

	A	B
Mother	1	1
Father	2	2
Other adults, specify	3	3
Child(ren) 11 and over	4	4
Child(ren) under 11....................................	5	5
Nobody read to child	6	6
Not known	0	0

58—60

C.7 On how many days has N been read to at home in the past 7 days? ⟶ .... ☐ **(61)**

If not read to in past 7 days enter ☐0☐ *, if not known enter* ☐9☐

Is this the usual amount N is read to at home?

Yes 1
No .... 2 **(62)**
Not known 0

If **no**, how many days a week is he/she usually read to? ⟶ .... ☐ **(63)**

SECTION D   NURSERY, PLAYGROUP AND SCHOOL EXPERIENCE

D.1   A.   Ring in the **first** column **A** any school, playgroup, or nursery placements N attends at the **present** (or attended last term if at present on holiday).
If **currently** attending more than one, ring all he/she attends in column A.

B.   Ring in the **second** column, **B all** other placements attended **previously for three months or longer**, that he/she has since stopped attending.   *Ring all that apply in both columns*

	A Present placement(s)	B Previous placement(s)
Nursery school—		
Local Education Authority (free)	1	1
Private (fee charged)	2	2
Nursery class attached to infant/primary school—		
Local Education Authority (free)	3	3
Private (fee charged)	4	4
Normal school, full or part-time—		
Infant/primary school (L.E.A.)	5	5
Independent/private	6	6
Playgroup	7	7
Special day school, nursery or unit for physically or mentally handicapped children	8	8
Day nursery—		
Local Authority	9	9
Private	10	10
Creche, kindergarten	11	11
Mother and toddler club	12	12
Sunday school	13	13
Other placement, please specify	14	14
....		
Attends/attended none of these	15	15
Not known	0	0

If child has attended none of the above in the past or at the present proceed to D.10.

If child is attending, or has attended any of the above, *please complete D.2 onwards.*
Do not give further details of "mother and toddler club" or Sunday school.

D.2   Present placement — **A**

Name and address in full of the place N attends **at present** or, if on holiday, attended last term. (If child currently attends more than one place, please give details of the main one).

Designation of main place N attends now, i.e. as specified in D.1 A. ....

Name of place N attends now ....

Full postal address ....

....

Name of head teacher, supervisor, etc. ....

D.3   Previous placement — **B**

Name and address in full of place N has attended **previously** that he/she has since stopped attending.
(If the child has attended more than one place previously for three months or longer give details of **the one he/she left most recently**).

Designation of previous place N attended, i.e. as specified in D.1 B ....

Name of **previous** place N attended ....

Full postal address ....

....

Name of head teacher, supervisor, etc. ....

The following questions D.4 to D.8 refer to: **A**– *the present placement and* **B**– *the previous placement as identified above.*

D.4   Type of premises N attended for present and previous placements

	A Present placement	B Previous placement
Normal school or nursery premises	1	1
Village or community hall	2	2
Church hall	3	3
Private house	4	4
Nursery in factory/industrial premises	5	5
Other kind of premises, please specify	6	6
....		
Not known	0	0

D.5 (a) At what age did N start attending:

	years	months
A – present placement?		
B – previous placement?		

(b) At what age did N stop attending the previous placement?

(c) What was the main reason he/she stopped attending the previous placement? ....
....
....

D.6 Days and periods of N's attendance

Ring the appropriate numbers under each day of the week to show whether N attended in the morning, afternoon or both. Enter in the last column the average length of a morning or afternoon session in hours.

		Mon	Tue	Wed	Thu	Fri	Sat	Sun	Hours attended per session
A – Present placement	Morning	1	2	3	4	5	6	7	.... hrs
	Afternoon	1	2	3	4	5	6	7	.... hrs
B – Previous placement	Morning	1	2	3	4	5	6	7	.... hrs
	Afternoon	1	2	3	4	5	6	7	.... hrs

D.7 Has the mother noticed any changes in N felt to be due to his/her attendance at present or previous placements?

	A Present placement	B Previous placement
Yes, change noticed	1	1
No, no change	2	2
Not attended long enough to say	3	3
Cannot say	4	4
Not known	0	0

If yes, what kind of changes have you noticed? If only one or two are mentioned, ask, 'are there any other changes in him/her you have noticed?'

A – Present placement ....
....

B – Previous placement ....
....

D.8 Has mother regularly taken part or helped in any way in the place(s) N attended? (e.g. looking after the children, helping with the administrative side or in other ways)

	A Present placement	B Previous placement
Yes—		
at least once a week	1	1
1–3 times a month	2	2
once or twice a term....................................	3	3
less than once a term	4	4
No—		
Mother's help was not required	5	5
mother was busy doing other things	6	6
mother preferred not to take part	7	7
Child not attended long enough to say	8	8
Other reply, please give details	9	9
....		
Not known	0	0

If mother has taken part, please describe what it was she did.

If only one or two things mentioned, ask 'were there any other things you did?'

A – Present placement ....
....

B – Previous placement ....
....

D.9 Have N's mother and/or father met the head teacher, supervisor or other staff from the **present placement** either **before or since** N started? (e.g. to discuss his/her settling down, N's school entry or anything else concerning N)

Ring all that apply in each column

	Before N started		Since N started	
	Mother	Father	Mother	Father
Yes, met staff to discuss N—				
at school, playgroup, etc.	1	1	1	1
at parents' home	2	2	2	2
elsewhere	3	3	3	3
No, never met staff	4	4	4	4
No mother figure/no father figure	5	5	5	5
N has no present placement	6	6	6	6
Not known	0	0	0	0

46—49

If **yes**, who initiated the meeting(s)?

Ring all that apply

Parents 1

Staff 2

Other reply, give details 3

....

Cannot say 0

(50)

D.10 If N is **not at present attending infant/primary school** (LEA or private) please give name and address of the school mother expects him/her to attend later.
If mother does not know which infant/primary school N is to attend, put NOT KNOWN.

(a) Name of infant/primary school ....

Full postal address ....

....

Name of head teacher ....

51

(b) When does the mother expect N to start attending this infant/primary school?

Summer term 1975 1

Autumn term (September) 1975 2

Other date, please specify 3

....

Cannot say 0

(52)

D.11 Irrespective of whether or not N attended, did the mother ever have his/her name down on a waiting list to go to a playgroup, nursery school or class, or day nursery?

Yes— *Ring all that apply*

had name down on at least one waiting list for nursery school/class or playgroup 1

had name down on waiting list for day nursery 2

No, name has never been on a waiting list............................. 3

Cannot remember 0

(53)

D.12 Has N ever been regularly looked after during the day in **someone else's house,** for three months or longer? (For this purpose "regularly" is taken as two or more hours weekly)

Ring all that apply

Yes—

by a friend or neighbour 1

by paid child minder 2

by relative 3

by other person, please specify... 4

....

No, never 5

Not known... 0

54,55

If **yes**, give age in completed years N was first regularly looked after in someone else's house ....➤.............. (56)

If under one, enter $\boxed{0}$ *, if 3¾ years enter* $\boxed{3}$ *, if age not known enter* $\boxed{9}$

SECTION E   EDUCATION AND OCCUPATION OF PARENTS

E.1   Educational or occupational qualifications of present parents   *Ring all that apply in both columns*

	Mother	Father
Qualifications in shorthand and/or typing, trade apprenticeships, or other vocational training, e.g. State Enrolled Nurse (SEN) or Enrolled Nurse (Scotland), hairdressing diploma, etc.	1	1
G.C.E. 'O' level, S.C.E. 'O' grade, Certificate of Secondary Education (CSE), City and Guilds Intermediate Technical Certificate, City and Guilds Final Craft Certificate	2	2
G.C.E. 'A' level, High School Certificate (HSC), Higher Grade of Scottish Leaving Certificate (SLC), Ordinary National Diploma/Certificate (OND, ONC), City and Guilds Final Technical Certificate, Higher Grade of Scottish Certificate of Education (SCE)	3	3
State Registered Nurse (SRN) or Registered Nurse (Scotland)	4	4
Certificate of Education (Teachers), Teaching Qualification (Primary/ Secondary Education in Scotland)..	5	5
Degree (e.g. BSc, BA, PhD), Higher National Diploma/Certificate (HND, HNC), Membership of Professional Institution (e.g. FCA, FRICS, MIMechE, MIEE, etc.) City and Guilds Full Technical Certificate	6	6
Other qualifications, please specify	7	7
....		
No qualifications	8	8
Not applicable, no mother or no father figure	9	9
Qualifications not known	0	0

57—59

60—62

E.2   At what age did the present parents leave school?

(a)   Age mother left school .... years

(b)   Age father left school .... years

63,64

65,66

E.3   How many completed years of **full-time** education did the present parents have **after** leaving school? (e.g. at college of education, at polytechnic, at university, etc.)   *If none, put NONE*

(a)   Mother, number of years .... years

(b)   Father, number of years ....years

67

68

E.4   Occupation of present father

E.4 to E.6 refer to the father or father substitute, including foster father, adoptive father, stepfather or any other father substitute.

If N has no father or substitute father now, please ring 8 in E.4 and proceed to E.8.

(a)   What is the father's actual job, occupation, trade or profession, or the last occupation if unemployed or retired?   *Full and precise details of occupation are required. See "Survey Notes and Information".*

Actual job ....

69

(b)   What is the industry or business in which the father is engaged? *Give details of goods, materials or services. See "Survey Notes and Information".*

Type of industry ....

70

(c)   Father's employment status

1—5

Self-Employed

With 25 or more employees .... | 1

With less than 25 employees .... | 2

Without employees other than family workers .... | 3

6

Employed

In managerial position .... | 4

As foreman, supervisor, chargehand, etc. .... | 5

Not in supervisory role .... | 6

0 8

7,8

Other

Unemployed, sick, etc.

Please describe situation .... | 7

....

No father figure .... | 8

Not known, please explain situation .... | 0

....

E.5 Do any of the following apply?

	Never or hardly ever	Sometimes	Often	Not known	
(a) Father away evenings until after N has gone to bed	1	2	3	0	(9)
(b) Father away most of Saturday and/or Sunday	1	2	3	0	(10)
(c) Father works away for long periods (i.e. a month or more at a time)	1	2	3	0	(11)
(d) Father works overnight	1	2	3	0	(12)
(e) Father works shifts	1	2	3	0	(13)

E.6 For how many weeks has the father been off work in the past 12 months, through illness or unemployment or for other reasons?

e.g. If off work 9½ weeks enter ⬚0⬚9   If never off work enter ⬚0⬚0   if not known enter ⬚9⬚9

Number of weeks off work through: (a) Illness or accident ⟶ .... ⬚⬚ (14,15)

(b) Unemployment ⟶ .... ⬚⬚ (16,17)

(c) Other reasons, give details ⟶ .... ⬚⬚ (18,19)

....

E.7 When the present father left school, what was his own father's job?
See "Survey Notes and Information". If occupation not known put NOT KNOWN.

(a) Actual job ....

(b) Type of industry ....

⬚ (20)

E.8 When the present mother left school, what was her own father's job?
See "Survey Notes and Information". If occupation not known put NOT KNOWN.

(a) Actual job ....

(b) Type of industry ....

⬚ (21)

E.9 Does present mother have a job, either out of the home or at home, or is she a full-time housewife?

Mother works out of the home –

regularly: full-time or part-time employment, including evenings, overnight or weekends 1

occasionally: casual or freelance worker obtaining work on a day-to-day basis or seasonally, e.g. fruit picking, etc. 2

Mother works at home –

regularly: family business, e.g. shop, farm, boarding house, clerical work for a self-employed husband; home industry i.e. working for a firm of manufacturers at home, etc. 3

occasionally: seasonal work done at home, e.g. holiday bed and breakfast business 4   (22)

Full-time housewife, no other kind of work 5

Other work situation, please give details 6

....

Not known.. 0

If mother works regularly at home or out of the home (i.e. ringed 1 or 3 in E.9) at the present time, please complete E.10 onwards.

If mother is now a full-time housewife or only works occasionally, (i.e. ringed 2, 4 or 5 in E.9) please proceed to E.17 on next page.

E.10 Describe mother's present job. *See "Survey Notes and Information".*

What is her actual job? (e.g. shop assistant, teacher, assembly line worker, typist, stitcher, etc.)

....

⬚ (23)

(b) What type of industry or business does she work in? (e.g. greengrocery, infant school, tobacco, insurance, glovemaking, etc.)

....

(c) What kind of position does mother occupy at work?

Managerial 1

As forewoman or supervisor, etc 2

Non-supervisory position 3

Works at home.. 4   (24)

Other, please specify 5

....

Cannot say/not known.. 0

(d) How many years has mother been doing this job? (Ignore short breaks for pregnancies or illness)

If 4½ years enter ⬚0⬚4 .   If under one year enter ⬚0⬚0 ,   if not known enter ⬚9⬚9

Number of years ⟶ ⬚⬚ (25,26)

E.11 Please show in the table below the times (giving a.m. or p.m.) the mother started and finished work and the total hours worked each day last week. If not working last week, give details of the last week worked.

	Mon	Tues	Wed	Thurs	Fri	Sat	Sun
Time started							
Time finished							
Total hours worked*							

27—31

32—36

*Include meal breaks as part of the working period. Enter **0** for any day not worked.

37—40

E.12 Does mother work these hours regularly every week?

Yes, every week the same 1

No, mother works a shift system 2

No set pattern of work, hours or days worked vary .... 3 **(41)**

Other reply, please give details 4

....

Cannot say 0

E.13 Please give average travelling time to and from work

(a) travelling to work .... hours .... mins

(b) returning home .... hours .... mins

If works at home put AT HOME

42,43

E.14 When mother is at work, is N usually looked after at home or away from home? (If N is sometimes looked after at home and sometimes away from home ring where he/she is **mainly** looked after).

Looked after at home 1

Looked after away from home .... 2 **(44)**

Varies 3

Cannot say 0

E.15 Who looks after N during mother's working hours? *Ring all that apply*

N's father 1

Mother at home 2

Accompanies mother to work 3

Adult relative e.g. grandparents, aunt, etc. 4

Older sibling 5

Paid childminder .... 6 **45—48**

Friend or neighbour (not paid) 7

Local authority day nursery 8

Day nursery run by an employer or private individual(s) 9

School, nursery school or class, or playgroup 10

Some other person or place, namely 11

....

Not known 0

If **more than one**, who mainly looks after N during mother's working hours?

....

49,50

E.16 Please ask the mother if she could say what are the main reasons she works. (If "for money" ask, "what is money mainly spent on?") *Ring all that apply*

Financial necessity (e.g. contribution to housekeeping or rent, clothes, etc.) 1

Financial advantage (e.g. savings, holidays, household appliances, luxuries, car, to gain independence, etc.) 2

Social reasons (e.g. for company, making friends, relief of boredom, keep you young, etc.) 3 **51,52**

Career/enjoys the work 4

Other reasons, describe... 5

....

If more than one reason given, ask, "which of these is the most important reason", and write in

....

53

E.17 Has mother had a **regular** full-time or part-time job **out of the home** since the time of N's birth **which she subsequently gave up?**

Ring all that apply

Yes —

full-time job(s)... 1

part-time job(s)... 2

No, never had a job out of the home since N's birth 3

Other reply, give details.. 4 **54**

....

Not known.. 0

If **yes**, give total time worked since N's birth in completed years (exclude present job if any) **(55)**

If worked under one year enter **0**

BTF-N*

SECTION F THE HOME AND SOCIAL ENVIRONMENT

F.1 What accommodation is occupied by this household?

Whole detached house or bungalow 1
Whole semi-detached house or bungalow 2
Whole terrace house (including end of terrace) 3
Flat/maisonette (self-contained) .... 4 **(56)**
Rooms (non self-contained flat) 5
Other, please give details.. 6

....

If Flat or Rooms, give the lowest floor on which rooms are situated

If on ground floor or basement, enter $\boxed{0\,|\,0}$

Floor .... $\longrightarrow$ **(57,58)**

F.2 Is the accommodation owned or rented by the household?

Owned outright 1
Being bought.. 2
Rented from Council 3
Privately rented — unfurnished .... 4 **(59)**
Privately rented — furnished or partly furnished 5
Tied to occupation of father 6
Other situation, please give details 7

....

F.3 Does the household have sole use of, share with another household, or lack any of the following amenities?

		Sole use	Shared use	None available	
(a)	Bathroom	1	2	3	(60)
(b)	Indoor lavatory	1	2	3	(61)
(c)	Outdoor lavatory....	1	2	3	(62)
(d)	Hot water supply........	1	2	3	(63)
(e)	Garden or yard..........	1	2	3	(64)
(f)	Kitchen	1	2	3	(65)

F.4 How large is the kitchen and is it used for living in (e.g. for having meals in)?

Less than 6 feet wide —
    Not used for living in 1
    Used for living in 2
6 feet or more wide —
    Not used for living in .... 3 **(66)**
    Used for living in 4
No kitchen 5
Not known 0

F.5 How many rooms are there within the accommodation? (Include all rooms except kitchen, bathroom, toilet, and any rooms used solely for business purposes. For complete definition see "Survey Notes and Information")

Number of rooms $\longrightarrow$ .... **(67,68)**

F.6 Does N share a bedroom with others?

Yes 1
No .... 2 **(69)**
Not known 0

If yes, how many sleep in the same room $\longrightarrow$ .... **(70)**

F.7 Does N share a bed with others?

No 1
Yes —
    with one other 2
    with two others.. 3 **(71)**
    with more than two others 4
Not known 0

72—74

F.8 Which of the following does the family have?

Ring all that apply

Refrigerator 1
Washing machine 2   **1—5**
Spin dryer 3
Colour T.V. 4
Black and White T.V. 5   **6**
Van or car 6
Telephone 7   **09**
None of the above 8   **7,8**

F.9 In the past seven days has anyone helped mother at all with any of the following? (Include father, members of the household, friends, neighbours, relatives and paid help).

Ring all that apply in each row	Yes father	Yes others	No	Not known	
(a) Housework/shopping	1	2	3	0	(9)
(b) Looking after N for part of the day while mother shops, attends appointments, does housework, etc.	1	2	3	0	(10)
(c) Babysitting in the evening	1	2	3	0	(11)
(d) Putting N to bed	1	2	3	0	(12)
(e) Taking N to school/nursery/playgroup, etc.	1	2	3	0	(13)

F.10 In the past 7 days has N done any of the following with others or by him/herself:

Ring all that apply in each row.	Yes with adult(s)	Yes with child(ren)	Yes by self	No	Not known	
(a) been to a friend's or relative's house	1	2	3	4	0	(14)
(b) been to a park, recreation ground, adventure playground	1	2	3	4	0	(15)
(c) been on a bus or train	1	2	3	4	0	(16)
(d) been to the shops, launderette, etc.	1	2	3	4	0	(17)

F.11 Indicate to which of the following broad ethnic categories N and the present parents belong.

	N	Mother	Father
European (U.K.)	1	1	1
European (other)	2	2	2
West Indian	3	3	3
Indian/Pakistani	4	4	4
Other Asian	5	5	5
African	6	6	6
Other, specify	7	7	7
....			
Not known	0	0	0

(18—20)

F.12 What language is mainly used with N in the home?

English 1
Other language, namely 2   (21)
....
Not known 0

F.13 How many times has N moved since birth?
If no moves enter [0][0] . *If not known enter* [9][9]

Number of moves .... ☐☐ (22,23)

F.14 Has N ever been in any of the following situations?

Ring all that apply in both columns	Now	In the past but not now
"In care"* (voluntary or statutory) in —		
fosterparents' home	1	1
assessment centre	2	2
family group home	3	3
children's home	4	4
In "Part III" accommodation	5	5
In homeless family unit	6	6
None of the above	7	7
Not known if any of above	0	0

(24—27)

*For each "in care" situation please give the following details:

Name & address of home, centre, etc., if known	Local Authority or Voluntary Society	Age when first entered this situation	Length of stay	Reason N in care

F.15 From your knowledge and anything you have learned from the interview, has anyone in the household since N's birth had contact with any statutory or voluntary social work or welfare organisations? (For example, Social Services or Social Security Departments, Probation Service, etc.)

Yes 1
No 2   (28)
Not known 0

If yes, give details ....
....

SECTION G   FAMILY HEALTH AND SMOKING

G.1   Has anyone in N's household since N's birth had any severe or prolonged illness (medical, surgical or psychiatric) or any handicap or disability?

Ring all that apply

Yes—

mother 1

father 2

other adult in household.. 3

child in household (excluding N).. 4

No, none.. 5

Not known.. 0

☐ **29,30**

If **yes**, please give the following details for each member of the household concerned.

Relationship to N	
Diagnosis or nature of condition	
Date of onset	
Duration of condition (years and months)	
Outcome (i.e. recovered, died, condition still present)	
In what way, if any, has condition caused any interference with N's everyday care?	

G.2   (a) Do either N's mother or father smoke at all at present?
(Cigarette smoking is defined as smoking an average of one or more cigarettes a day)

Ring all that apply in both columns	Mother	Father
No, is non-smoker	1	1
Yes —		
smokes cigarettes..........	2	2
smokes pipe or cigars....	3	3
Not known if smokes.............	0	0

31,32

If **smokes cigarettes**, how many are smoked per day on average?

If not known how many, enter ☐9☐9 Average number smoked: Mother ⟶ .... **(33,34)**

Father ⟶ .... **(35,36)**

(b) Irrespective of whether or not N's mother or father smoke at present, for how many years since N's birth have they smoked cigarettes, if at all?

During the period since N's birth —	Mother	Father
Smoked all the time	1	1
Smoked for more than 3 years................	2	2
Smoked for between 1 and 3 years	3	3
Smoked for less than 1 year.....................	4	4
Smoked but not know for how long........	5	5
Non-smoker all the time	6	6
Not known if smoked at all.....................	0	0

37,38

From interviewer's and mother's knowledge or any other source, has N ever previously had any special test(s) of progress in connection with a follow-up of the British Births Survey or any other study of child development?

No 1

Yes 2

Not known 0

☐ **39**

If **yes**, please complete details below.

Age(s) of N	Name of study, if known	Where tested and by whom

Relationship of informant to N

Mother 1

Father .... 2 **(40)**

Other, specify 3

....

END OF INTERVIEW

Please thank the mother for her help in this confidential enquiry. When doing so, please mention that the study will be continued in the nurseries, playgroups, hospitals and other places already attended by the children taking part. We will also record the results of screening tests and medical examinations undergone by the children to complement the information that the mother has so kindly given.

If there are any further points the mother would care to add concerning N or the survey, we would be grateful if these could be noted on the back page.

SECTION H TO BE COMPLETED AFTER THE INTERVIEW IS OVER

Please complete H.1 to H.5 from your knowledge and any impression you have gained during the interview.

H.1 Please ring the descriptions which you feel best characterise the home and relationship of family with neighbours.

(a) Furniture/equipment in home	(b) Tidiness of home	(c) Relationship of family with neighbours
Luxurious 1	Over-tidy 1	Very good terms 1
Well equipped 2	Very tidy 2	Good terms.................2
Adequate 3	Average.......................3	Satisfactory.................3
Low standard 4	Untidy.........................4	Don't mix....................4
Very low standard 5	Chaotic 5	Bad terms...................5
Can't assess 0	Can't assess.................0	Can't assess.................0

41–43

H.2 In order to get some impression of the kind of district N lives in, please ring which one of the following descriptions best characterises the district.

In this district, houses are closely packed together and many are in poor state of repair. Multi-occupation is a common feature, and most families have low incomes 1

This district consists largely of council houses and flats or less expensive privately owned houses, for example, older terrace houses. Multi-occupation is unusual and families have average incomes. Include 'new towns' here 2

In this district houses are well spaced and the majority are well maintained. Multi-occupation is rare and most families have higher than average incomes... 3 **(44)**

This district is part of a small market town, rural community or village. Some families may lack basic amenities but others may be fairly well-to-do. It is mainly characterised by the fact that well-to-do and poorer families live fairly close together in the community 4

If none of these descriptions seem to characterise the district N lives in, please describe in your own words what it is like: 5

....

....

H.3 From the health visitor's knowledge and observations of the child, and where necessary from available records, what is N's intellectual development considered to be?

Normal or above average 1

Slightly backward 2

Definitely backward .... 3 **(45)**

Other situation, please describe 4

....

Insufficient information 0

If at all backward in intellectual development, give any relevant diagnosis and details of assessment procedure(s) or investigations, if any.

....

....

H.4 How well do you know this family?

Very well... 1

Fairly well... 2

Slightly .... 3 **(46)**

Never in contact before this interview 4

Other situation, please describe................................ 5

....

H.5 Were there any interruptions, distractions or other problems which made interviewing difficult?

No, no difficulty 1

Yes, slight difficulty .... 2 **(47)**

Yes, considerable difficulty.. 3

If yes, please describe any difficulty

....

H.6 What procedure was adopted for the completion of the Maternal Self-completion Questionnaire?

Questionnaire left with mother and collected after completion 1

Mother completed it without help during the home interview 2

Mother completed it with some help from the interviewer.......................... 3 **(48)**

Interviewer read out all the questions for mother to respond 4

Other procedure, ... 5

If 3, 4 or 5 ringed, please give reason(s), e.g. mother couldn't read, etc. ....

....

Date of interview .... | 49–51 |

Name of Health Visitor conducting the interview: ....

Employing Area Health Authority/Health Board ....

Health District, if applicable .... | 52–55 |

Please note below:
(i)   any other relevant information which you feel has not already been brought out in the interview form,
(ii)   any comments or observations by the General Practitioner, if he so wishes,
(iii) any further details about questions if insufficient space earlier in questionnaire.

H.7   **Please indicate degree of completeness of the documents.**

	Fully completed	Partly completed	Not completed	If not fully completed, give reason(s)
Home Interview Questionnaire	1	2	3	
Maternal Self-completion Questionnaire	1	2	3	
Test Booklet	1	2	3	

We are most grateful for the time you have given. Thank you for your help.

Child Health and Education in the Seventies

A national study in England, Wales and Scotland of all children born 5th—11th April 1970

Under the auspices of the University of Bristol
and the National Birthday Trust Fund

Department of Child Health Research Unit
University of Bristol
Bristol   BS2 8BH

Health District Code   Child's Local Serial Number

Child's Central Survey Number

CONFIDENTIAL

MATERNAL SELF-COMPLETION QUESTIONNAIRE

Full Name of the Child .... Sex ....

Address .... Date of birth.............. April 1970

....

To the Mother:

This questionnaire is part of a survey into the health and education of 5 year old children. In this form we are asking about the behaviour of your child, your own health and your opinions on a number of subjects. We hope that you will be able to find time to complete the form and that you will find it of interest. We would be grateful to have any remarks you may care to make about the questions in this form and you will find space for this on the last page. All information will be treated in the strictest confidence.

If you should have any difficulty in filling in any part of the form, the Health Visitor will be pleased to advise you.

SECTION 1   Child's Behaviour

Please leave blank

Please put a cross in the box by the answer which best describes which is true about your child's behaviour.

The following examples will help you to see what is required.

Example 1

PLEASE SAY IF:

	Never in the last 12 months	Less than once a month	At least once a month	At least once a week
Child has dizzy spells	☐	☒	☐	☐
Child complains of aching back or limbs	☐	☐	☐	☒

The crosses in these boxes mean that this child has dizzy spells less than once a month, and complains of aching back or limbs at least once a week.

Example 2

DOES CHILD HAVE ANY DIFFICULTY DRESSING?

NO   ☐

YES   ☒————— IF YES, is this with:

Shoes .... ☐

Socks .... ☒

Pants .... ☐

Shirts/dresses etc.. ☐

Buttons .... ☒

Zips .... ☐

The crosses in these boxes mean that this child has difficulty in dressing, and socks and buttons are the main problems.

PLEASE TURN OVER THE PAGE AND ANSWER THE QUESTIONS

1. Below is a list of minor health problems which most children have at some time. Please tell us how often each of these happens with your child by putting a cross in the box which best describes this.

	Never in the last 12 months	Less than once a month	At least once a month	At least once a week
Complains of headaches	☐	☐	☐	☐
Complains of stomach-ache or has vomited	☐	☐	☐	☐
Complains of biliousness	☐	☐	☐	☐
Has temper tantrums (that is, complete loss of temper with shouting, angry movements, etc.)	☐	☐	☐	☐

9—12

Most children go through "difficult" stages. Please show by putting a cross in the correct boxes whether or not your child has any of the following difficulties **at the present time.**
Please answer every question.

2. **DOES YOUR CHILD HAVE ANY SLEEPING DIFFICULTY?**

NO ☐

YES – MILD ☐
YES – SEVERE ☐ ——— IF YES, which of the following difficulties does he/she have?

getting off to sleep .... ☐

waking during the night .... ☐

waking early in the morning .... ☐

nightmares or night terrors .... ☐

sleepwalking... ☐

Please describe any sleeping difficulties, including those above:
....

13

14, 15

3. **DOES CHILD EVER WET THE BED AT NIGHTS?**

NO ☐ ——— IF NO, at what age did he/she .... become dry at night?

YES ☐ ——— IF YES, is it:

very occasionally (less than once a week)........ ☐

occasionally (at least once a week) .... ☐

most nights .... ☐

every night .... ☐

16

4. **DOES CHILD EVER WET HIS/HER PANTS IN THE DAYTIME?**

NO ☐

YES ☐ ——— IF YES, is it:

very occasionally (less than once a week)........ ☐

occasionally (at least once a week)................... ☐

most days... ☐

every day .... ☐

17

5. **DOES CHILD EVER SOIL OR MAKE A MESS IN HIS/HER PANTS?**

NO ☐

YES ☐ ——— IF YES, is it:

very occasionally (less than once a week)........ ☐

occasionally (at least once a week) .... ☐

most days... ☐

every day .... ☐

18

6. DOES CHILD HAVE ANY EATING OR APPETITE PROBLEMS?

NO ☐

YES – MILD ☐
YES – SEVERE ☐ ──── IF YES, is it:

    not eating enough .... ☐

    over-eating for more than the occasional meal. ☐

    faddiness .... ☐

Please describe any other eating problem:

....

`19,20`

7. DOES CHILD ATTEND SCHOOL, NURSERY SCHOOL, PLAYGROUP OR ANYTHING LIKE THAT?

NO ☐

YES ☐ ──────── IF YES, has he/she had tears on arrival

    NO .... ☐

    YES, once or twice a week .... ☐

    YES, every day .... ☐

`21`

8. Below is a series of descriptions of behaviour often shown by children. After each statement are three columns – "Doesn't apply", "Applies somewhat", and "Certainly applies". If your child definitely shows the behaviour described by the statement put a cross in the box under "Certainly applies". If he/she shows the behaviour described by the statement but to a lesser degree or less often, place a cross under "Applies somewhat". If, **as far as you are aware,** your child does not show the behaviour, place a cross under "Doesn't apply".

Please put **one** cross against **each** statement.

	Doesn't apply	Applies somewhat	Certainly applies
Very restless. Often running about or jumping up and down. Hardly ever still	☐	☐	☐
Is squirmy or fidgety	☐	☐	☐
Often destroys own or others' belongings	☐	☐	☐
Frequently fights with other children	☐	☐	☐
Not much liked by other children	☐	☐	☐
Often worried, worries about many things	☐	☐	☐
Tends to do things on his own – rather solitary	☐	☐	☐
Irritable. Is quick to "fly off the handle".	☐	☐	☐
Often appears miserable, unhappy, tearful or distressed	☐	☐	☐
Sometimes takes things belonging to others	☐	☐	☐
Has twitches, mannerisms or tics of the face or body	☐	☐	☐
Frequently sucks thumb or finger	☐	☐	☐
Frequently bites nails or fingers	☐	☐	☐
Is often disobedient	☐	☐	☐
Cannot settle to anything for more than a few moments	☐	☐	☐
Tends to be fearful or afraid of new things or new situations	☐	☐	☐
Is fussy or over particular	☐	☐	☐
Often tells lies	☐	☐	☐
Bullies other children	☐	☐	☐

`22-25`

`26-29`

`30-33`

`34-37`

`38-40`

SECTION 2 Mother's Health

Many mothers find caring for their children difficult if their own health is not very good. Listed below are a number of common symptoms that mothers often describe to doctors. We would like you to say if these happen to you by putting a ring round Yes or No as in the examples given.

Here are two EXAMPLES:

Do your hands often tremble? .... Yes **(No)**

Are you worried about travelling long distances?................................. **(Yes)** No

This means my hands do not tremble but I am worried about travelling long distances.

PLEASE RING THE CORRECT ANSWER TO EACH OF THE FOLLOWING:

Do you often have back-ache?	Yes	No
Do you feel tired most of the time?	Yes	No
Do you often feel miserable or depressed?.............................	Yes	No
Do you often have bad headaches?	Yes	No
Do you often get worried about things?	Yes	No
Do you usually have great difficulty in falling asleep or staying asleep?	Yes	No
Do you usually wake unnecessarily early in the morning?........	Yes	No
Do you wear yourself out worrying about your health?...........	Yes	No
Do you often get into a violent rage?	Yes	No
Do people often annoy and irritate you?...............................	Yes	No
Have you at times had a twitching of the face, head or shoulders?	Yes	No
Do you often suddenly become scared for no good reason?	Yes	No
Are you scared to be alone when there are no friends near you?	Yes	No
Are you easily upset or irritated?	Yes	No
Are you frightened of going out alone or of meeting people?........	Yes	No
Are you constantly keyed up and jittery?...............................	Yes	No
Do you suffer from indigestion?	Yes	No
Do you often suffer from an upset stomach?.........................	Yes	No
Is your appetite poor?	Yes	No
Does every little thing get on your nerves and wear you out?	Yes	No
Does your heart often race like mad?....................................	Yes	No
Do you often have bad pains in your eyes?............................	Yes	No
Are you troubled with rheumatism or fibrositis?...................	Yes	No
Have you ever had a nervous breakdown?	Yes	No
Do you have any other health problems worrying you?..........	Yes	No

IF YES, please describe in your own words:

....

....

....

....

....

....

41-44

45-48

49-52

53-56

57-60

61-64

65-68

SECTION 3 Opinions

This section asks for your opinion about a wide range of subjects. Please give your own opinions and do not worry about what others may think. There are no "correct" answers to the questions. We expect you will agree with some statements and disagree with others.

If you strongly agree, ring the 'A'

If you mildly agree, ring the 'a'

If you mildly disagree, ring the 'd'

If you strongly disagree, ring the 'D'

If you cannot say whether you agree or disagree with a statement, for instance when it "depends on circumstances", ring the 'X'

Please try to answer every one, but if you do not understand a statement leave it out.

These three examples should help you to see how to answer the questions.

Example 1

	Strongly agree	Mildly agree	Cannot say	Mildly disagree	Strongly disagree
People are not very co-operative these days	A	a	X	d	(D)
This means I strongly disagree with this statement					

Example 2

If people were not so selfish the world would be a happier place	A	(a)	X	d	D
This means I mildly agree with this statement					

Example 3

No marriage is complete without children	(A)	a	X	d	D
This means I strongly agree with this statement					

PLEASE ANSWER EVERY QUESTION

		Strongly agree	Mildly agree	Cannot say	Mildly disagree	Strongly disagree
1.	Women need something more from life than they can get by just looking after the home and children	A	a	X	d	D
2.	Such activities as painting and playing should take second place to teaching reading and arithmetic in infant schools	A	a	X	d	D
3.	Girls should accept the fact that they will marry and have children and not think about starting a career	A	a	X	d	D
4.	Strictly disciplined children rarely grow up to be the best adults	A	a	X	d	D
5.	Young children who never see children's T.V. miss a lot which is of value	A	a	X	d	D
6.	It's best not to visit children under five in hospital because it is too upsetting for the child	A	a	X	d	D
7.	Women should have the same work opportunities as men	A	a	X	d	D
8.	If a child is often allowed to have his own way while he is young he will be uncontrollable later	A	a	X	d	D

		Strongly agree	Mildly agree	Cannot say	Mildly disagree	Strongly disagree		Please leave blank

9. A person that does not let others stand in his way is to be admired

A   a   X   d   D

10. Things should be made easier for unmarried mothers

A   a   X   d   D

11. Increases in vandalism and delinquency are largely due to the fact that children nowadays lack strict discipline

A   a   X   d   D

12. Children should not be allowed to talk at the meal table

A   a   X   d   D

13. Children under five should always accept what their parents say as being true

A   a   X   d   D

14. Mothers need a break from their children from time to time during the day

A   a   X   d   D

15. T.V. is a useful way of keeping the children amused

A   a   X   d   D

16. It is unreasonable to expect hospitals to upset their routine by allowing unlimited visiting in children's wards

A   a   X   d   D

17. Parents should treat young children as equals

A   a   X   d   D

18. Young children pick up a lot of bad habits from T.V.

A   a   X   d   D

19. One of the things parents must do is sort out their children's quarrels for them and decide who is right and wrong

A   a   X   d   D

20. Some equality in marriage is a good thing, but by and large the husband ought to have the main say-so in family matters

A   a   X   d   D

21. Nothing is worse than a person who does not feel a great love, gratitude, and respect for his parents

A   a   X   d   D

22. Unquestioning obedience is not a good thing in a young child

A   a   X   d   D

23. The State should open more day nurseries so as to make it easier for mothers of young children to go out to work

A   a   X   d   D

24. The trouble with hospital specialists is that they never have time to explain all their patients would like to know

A   a   X   d   D

25. People should be satisfied with their lot in this world and not struggle to get more

A   a   X   d   D

26. A mother who always gives in to her young child's demands for attention will spoil him

A   a   X   d   D

		Strongly agree	Mildly agree	Cannot say	Mildly disagree	Strongly disagree

27. There is nothing wrong with a mother going out to work if her children can be properly cared for by someone else

    A   a   X   d   D

28. Teaching 5 year old children obedience and respect for authority is not as important as all that

    A   a   X   d   D

33-36

29. If pre-school children would pay more attention to what they are told instead of just having their own ideas they would learn more quickly

    A   a   X   d   D

30. A mother who leaves her children with someone else in order to go out to work is not fit to be a mother unless she needs the money for food and clothes

    A   a   X   d   D

31. A child should not be allowed to talk back to his parents

    A   a   X   d   D

32. There are many things a 5 year old child must do with no explanation from his parents

    A   a   X   d   D

37-40

33. A young child must be allowed to be himself even if this means going against his parents' wishes

    A   a   X   d   D

34. Parents must face the fact that teenagers have different morals to their own when they were that age and must put up with it

    A   a   X   d   D

35. It is not surprising if educational standards are falling when children have so much freedom in school nowadays

    A   a   X   d   D

36. A wife must sacrifice her right to go out to work once she has children

    A   a   X   d   D

41-44

37. A mother should accept that her children are sometimes too busy to do as she asks

    A   a   X   d   D

38. You cannot expect a child under five to understand how another person feels

    A   a   X   d   D

39. A well brought up child is one who does not have to be told twice to do something

    A   a   X   d   D

40. A mother's proper place is at home with her children

    A   a   X   d   D

45-48

41. Children under five should never be allowed to watch adult T.V.

    A   a   X   d   D

42. Children who get upset whilst in hospital soon get over it afterwards

    A   a   X   d   D

43. Girls are just as capable as boys of learning to be engineers

    A   a   X   d   D

49-51

The last few questions on this page are to give us some idea about how you got on with the form.

1. Did you have any difficulty in understanding any of the questions?

NO, no difficulties .... ☐

YES, some questions were difficult.. ☐

YES, many questions were difficult .... ☐

IF YES, please say which questions were difficult and why

....

....

....

2. Did you have any difficulty in making up your mind about any questions?

NO, no difficulty.. ☐

YES, some difficulty .... ☐

YES, a lot of difficulty .... ☐

IF YES, please say which questions and why

....

....

....

3. Who answered this form?

Mother alone .... ☐

Father alone .... ☐

Mother and father together .... ☐

4. How long did it take to complete?

.... minutes

5. Any other comments about the form:

....

....

....

....

....

....

....

THANK YOU VERY MUCH FOR ALL YOUR HELP

Index

Numbers in italics refer to the text, all other numbers refer to Figures or Tables; those preceded with A comprise tables in the second volume (see page 9); those A numbers in brackets give the results of standardisation.